DATE DUE

N

TH

JE 2 5 '08			

Demco, Inc. 38-293

Creativity Research

Marc A. Runco, Series Editor

NURTURING AND DEVELOPING CREATIVITY:
THE EMERGENCE OF A DISCIPLINE

edited by
Scott G. Isaksen
Mary C. Murdock
Roger L. Firestien
Donald J. Treffinger

Center for Studies in Creativity
State University College at Buffalo

ABLEX PUBLISHING CORPORATION
NORWOOD, NEW JERSEY

Printed in the United States of America

Library of Congress Cataloging-in-Publication Data

The Emergence of a discipline / edited by Scott G. Isaksen . . . [et al.].
     p. cm. — (Creativity research)
  Proceedings of the Fourth International Networking Conference on Creativity and Innovation, and of the Conference on Creativity Research, held in 1990 at the State University College at Buffalo.
  Includes bibliographical references and indexes.
  Contents: v. 1. Understanding and recognizing creativity — v. 2. Nurturing and developing creativity.
  ISBN 0-89391-982-9 (v. 1 : cl.). — ISBN 1-56750-006-4 (v. 1 : pbk.). — ISBN 1-56750-008-0 (v. 2 : cl.). — ISBN 1-56750-007-2 (v. 2 : pbk.)
  1. Creative ability—Congresses. 2. Creative thinking—Congresses. I. Isaksen, Scott G. II. International Networking Conference on Creativity and Innovation (4th : 1990 : State University College at Buffalo) III. Conference on Creativity Research (1990 : State University College at Buffalo) IV. Series.
BF408.E44 1993
153.3′5—dc20   93-29992
                                               CIP

Ablex Publishing Corporation
355 Chestnut St.
Norwood, NJ 07648

Contents

II. Stimulating Creativity: Organizational Perspectives

III. Stimulating Creativity: Outcomes

Dedication

This publication is dedicated to those professionals in the field of creativity—past, present, and future—who regard its deliberate study as important and useful. We hope that theorists and practitioners will find the contents valuable in meeting the challenging task of assisting individuals, groups, or organizations to make productive contributions in their diverse societies and cultures. All royalties derived from the sale of this book will be utilized for continuing work to fund further collaborative research and activity among scholars at the Center for Studies in Creativity.

Foreword

As an academic administrator in higher education, I am keenly aware of the challenges involved in achieving excellence. Buffalo State College has been noted for its positive response to these challenges and for its dedication to preparing professionals to meet them.

The process of achieving excellence is a demanding one, not accomplished without extended effort on the part of many people who are willing to work together toward a common goal. It is also not a static process that operates within the confines of any academic institution. To be effective in education, there must be a commitment to action, and a willingness to persist.

Seldom does an academic administrator in higher education have the opportunity to encounter these challenges as closely as I have since I assumed academic responsibility for the Center for Studies in Creativity. Its beginning on our campus was unique, and its path has been full of discovery, change, and growth.

The Center's progress has led to a unique academic program whose purpose is to instruct, conduct research and inquiry, and facilitate the development of creative individuals, teams, and organizations. The Center's faculty has built on this sound educational program base, and by doing so they have taken a role in shaping an emerging discipline.

The 1990 International Creativity Conferences and this collection of work representing the outcomes are an indication of the disciplinary vitality and strength found in this area of academic pursuit. The work of the scholars represented in this volume is an example of how with persistence, commitment, collaboration, and action, educators in the field of creativity are demonstrating how to achieve excellence. I applaud and support these and future efforts.

Dr. Gerald F. Accurso, Associate Vice President
Dean, Graduate Studies and Research
State University of New York College at Buffalo

Preface

These volumes represent an achievement for creativity research and for the university. They represent the efforts of the faculty, staff, and students of our Center for Studies in Creativity to initiate and actualize the concept of the Conference on Creativity Research as part of the Fourth International Networking Conference on Creativity and Innovation.

A university must stand for the growth of knowledge and recognize the debt to those members of the community that have made this growth possible. The Conference on Creativity Research and its proceedings are consistent with these two themes. The study of creativity is a worthy and important subject of inquiry. It represents the searching of one of the last great frontiers of human kind, the inner self. It seeks to improve our understanding of the processes of the human mind and spirit for benefit of all. I can envision no greater goal for the research community represented at the conference, in these volumes, and for this university than the realization of growth in this area.

This conference and these proceedings, I believe, are measures of the stature and maturity of a new academic discipline. Many colleagues, both current and from former times, have contributed greatly to the corpus of this work. We must recognize that by their efforts, these scholars have allowed us to stand on their shoulders.

It is within this context that the university rises to its challenge—here is the forum for the expansion of the frontiers of knowledge. Here flourishes the exchange of ideas, the critical analyses of these, the insights, reflections, and comradeship in a community of scholars.

Bringing together this community of scholars made possible real progress in breaching the frontiers of creativity research and represents the achievement of the three dozen or more individuals whose ideas and papers we are about to read and remember.

Richard A. Wiesen
Past Provost and Vice President for Academic Affairs
State University of New York College at Buffalo

Acknowledgments

Things don't just happen; they are made to happen
—John F. Kennedy

Two conferences and proceedings of this scope could not have happened without the vision, effort, and diverse contributions of many individuals and organizations. For purposes of brevity we would like to specifically acknowledge key areas of contribution and key people within them. All who were involved, however, were needed and appreciated.

Two areas of contribution were central to the conferences and this volume: participating scholars and sponsors who provided support for their participation. During the conferences, the enthusiasm and dedication of the scholars and practitioners toward the field and their work provided a rich atmosphere for learning, developing, and connecting. During the publication process, authors in these two collections were helpful and patient. They took long-distance communication, timelines, and creative tension in stride.

Equal enthusiasm and dedication were provided by individuals and groups who believed enough in the importance of the conference to contribute financial support. The following organizations generously helped advance research and practice in the field of creativity by contributing financial support for scholar attendance and participation and networking activities: Office of Graduate Studies, Buffalo State College; The Research Foundation of the State of New York Buffalo State College Foundation; Center for Studies in Creativity (CSC); Creative Education Foundation (CEF); The Procter and Gamble Company (P&G); Homemakers Upstate Group (HUG); the Center for Creative Leadership (CCL); and the Norwegian Center for Leadership Development.

The Buffalo State College faculty and staff and the Center for Studies in Creativity Conference staff dedicated for some, a summer; for others, two to three years of planning and finding resources, space, time, and energy for this event. We would like to especially recognize Dr. F. C. Richardson, President, Buffalo State College; Dr. Richard Wiesen, Past Provost and Vice President for Academic Affairs; and Dr. Gerald Accurso, Associate Vice President and Dean of Graduate Studies and Research for their support and enthusiasm. From the Center staff we would particularly note the contributions of Barbara Piwko as administrative assistant to the conferences and our secretary Debi Johnson and her team who worked diligently on the details of all aspects of the conferences.

Volunteers gave their time and energy in a variety of areas; as a group they represent a huge assembly of skills. Generous time and resource contributions were made by a variety of campus personnel and off-campus individuals. From providing copying services to flags to audio and videotapes, they responded to our problem-solving efforts with advice and action.

We would like to thank our former and current Master's degree students who provided various kinds of professional support central to the conference and outcomes in this publication. The professionalism and expertise demonstrated in the process support provided by the facilitators was central to the conference and the outcomes in this publication. The computer, photography, and logistical knowledge and skills provided by others enabled many activities to happen simultaneously within the conference agenda.

Countless conference volunteers provided additional support in the following ways: administrative assistance prior to the conference, graphic support, audiovisual assistance, hosting, public relations, CBIR support, registration, and trouble shooting. Jon Rachko's design work on the conference brochure and Lee Takats's photography were greatly appreciated. Without such support we would not have been able to accomplish so complex a task.

In the direct publication of this volume, we once again recognize both the undergraduate and graduate students, who for the sake of learning and scholarship, assisted with editing and graphics in this volume. Specifically, we note the students in CRS 625, "Current Issues in Creativity," who devoted many extra hours to reading and proofing the initial manuscripts, and especially to Mary Mallon, who provided editing and indexing support.

In particular we thank our editorial assistant, Suzanne Vosburg, who provided both inspiration and perspiration for us and for her fellow students. Her own love of learning and commitment in helping us make this publication a reality exemplify a positive future image of scholars in the field of creativity.

To all, thank you for making it happen.

Scott G. Isaksen
Mary C. Murdock
Roger L. Firestien
Donald J. Treffinger

Contributors

Min Basadur is a professor of organizational behavior in the Michael G. DeGroote School of Business at McMaster University in Hamilton, Ontario and founder of the Center for Research in Applied Creativity, a worldwide network of research and consulting associates. He was awarded three U.S. patents during early in his career at Procter & Gamble, where his research and development of creative problem solving applications to business and industry won him the American Psychological Association's Best Doctoral Dissertation Award in 1980. A lifetime colleague of the Creative Education Foundation, he is a member of the Association of Professional Engineers of Ontario, the Academy of Management, the American Psychological Association, the American Psychological Society, and the Association of Japanese Business Studies. He consults internationally and has published in leading research journals.

Susan P. Besemer is Director of Reed Library at the SUNY College at Fredonia. She has written many reviews and articles for library and education journals, and is the author of a book: *From Museums, Galleries, and Studios: A Guide to Artists on Film and Tape,* published by the Greenwood Press. Her publications in creative product analysis include several empirical studies and articles written for the parents of gifted and talented children.

Jan Buijs is a Professor in Management and Innovation at the School of Industrial Design Engineering at the Delft University of Technology. His teaching covers strategic management, organizational behavior, creative problem solving, management of innovation, product development and consulting skills. He has published a number of papers and articles and his book Innovation and Intervention was chosen as 1985 Book of the Year by the Netherlands Association of Management Consultants. He is editor-and-chief of the Netherlands management journal *Mens & Organisatie.*

John F. Feldhusen is the Robert B. Kane Distinguished Professor of Education and Director of Purdue Gifted Education Resource Institute at Purdue University. He is licensed for private practice in psychology in the State of Indiana and is a member of several professional organizations including The American Psychological Association, American Educational Research Association, the National Council on Measurement in Education and Phi Delta Kappa. He has developed instructional materials for teachers and students of education as well as a series of radio programs teaching creative thinking to fourth graders. He has published extensively, frequently delivers workshops and lectures, and regularly reviews new books in the field of education.

Roger L. Firestien is Associate Professor at the Center For Studies in Creativity at Buffalo State College where he teaches graduate and undergraduate courses in creativity and innovation. His research focuses on how creativity training influences problem-solving behavior in individuals, teams, and organizations. Additionally, his work in guided imagery and mental rehearsal is being used by individuals in business, education, the arts, and athletics to help them achieve "peak performance." He has written for many magazines and newspapers, and he is the author of the creativity fable *Why Didn't I Think of That.* He conducts seminars on creativity and speaks on the topic throughout the world.

Horst Geschka is a Professor at the Technical University at Darmstadt, Germany and president of a consulting firm that specializes in innovation management. In the early 1970s he headed a fundamental study on creativity techniques at Battelle-Frankfurt and has continued to work in the field since that time, initiating new creativity techniques and authoring a number of publications. He has applied these methodologies in numerous projects for companies and government agencies mainly in Germany but also in other European countries and in the United States.

Les Jones is a Visiting Fellow at the Manchester Business School. His current research program is an outgrowth of his work on Psychological Barriers for which he received a Master's Degree, and from which the development of the "Jones Inventory of Barriers to Effective Problem Solving" emerged. He is presently looking at the differences in creativity within organizations resulting from age, grade, and occupation differences. He is also involved in a cross-cultural study that is looking at the effects of organizational culture on creativity. In 1984 he set up his management consultancy and has since worked with a wide range of industrial, commercial, and government organizations in the U.K. He is an associate fellow of the British Psychological Society.

Roberta M. Milgram is an Associate Professor at the School of Education, at Tel-Aviv University, Israel. Prior to that she worked as a teacher, supervisor, and principal of elementary and secondary-level Jewish religious schools. She has been studying creativity in children and adolescents for more than 20 years, has published many scientific papers and chapters, and has edited three books.

Michael Moore is an Associate Professor of Reading and Director of Advisement, Assessment, and Retention at Georgia Southern University. He teaches a wide variety of graduate and undergraduate courses in reading theory and composition theory. The focus of his work is the problem finding process a result from studying his creative process. He is presently working on how experienced and novice teachers plan and whether these planning processes are communicable or transferable.

Karen O'Quin is an Associate Professor of Psychology at Buffalo State College where she teaches a range of courses from Introductory Psychology to senior seminars. She has developed, with Sue Besemer, the Creative Products Analysis Matrix which is currently under revision. They have published several articles on their research. She has also published many articles and technical reports in the field of psychology.

Sally M. Reis is an associate professor of Educational Psychology at the University of Connecticut where she also serves as Principal Investigator of The National Research Center on the Gifted and Talented. She was a teacher for 15 years, 11 of which were spent working with gifted students on the elementary, junior high, and high school levels. She has authored more than 40 articles, five books, seven book chapters, and numerous monographs and technical reports. She has traveled extensively across the country conducting workshops and providing inservice for school districts designing gifted programs based on The Enrichment Triad Model and The Revolving Door Identification Model. She is co-author of *The Revolving Door Identification Model, The Schoolwide Enrichment Model, The Secondary Triad,* and *The Triad Reader.* Sally has written and co-authored many articles on gifted education, serves on the Editorial Board of the *Journal for Education of the Gifted*, and *Gifted Child Quarterly*, and is on the Board of the National Association for Gifted Children.

Joseph S. Renzulli is a Professor of Educational Psychology and Director of The National Research Center on the Gifted and Talented at the University of Connecticut School of Education. He has authored books and been published extensively in the field of creativity and gifted education. He is active in professional organizations, including the National Association for Gifted Children. He is an Associate Editor of the *Gifted Child Quarterly*, and is on the editorial boards of the *Journal of Law and Education*, *Learning Magazine*, and *Exceptionality*.

Tudor Rickards is a Senior Lecturer in creativity at the Manchester Business School. His areas of interest include the management of innovation and creative problem solving and he has written extensively on these topics. He lectures and consults regularly in 16 different countries; is the UK representative on the European Network for Innovation and Creativity; and is co-editor of both the *Creativity and Innovation Yearbook* published by the Manchester Business School, and of *Leadership and Organizational Development Journal* published by MCB University Press. He is also co-editor, with Susan Moger, of *Creativity & Innovation Management,* a new journal published by Blackwell

Publishers, Oxford, U.K. His latest book, *Creativity & Problem Solving at Work,* is published by Gower Press, Aldershot, U.K.

Reginald J. Talbot is a lecturer in psychology at the School of Management, UMIST. He teaches organizational psychology to engineering manufacture and management undergraduates. He also teaches creative problem solving, management development, organizational change, and research methods to postgraduate students in a master's course in organizational psychology. He also supervises master's and doctoral level research. Currently he is actively researching the area of the creative individual. He is a member of many learned societies, including the Ergonomics Society, the Society for General Systems Research, and the Design Research Society, of which he is a founding member. He is founding co-editor of *Design Studies,* the journal of the Design Research Society.

Donald J. Treffinger is currently Director of the Center for Creative Learning in Sarasota, Florida, and Professor of Creative Studies at the State University College at Buffalo, New York. He has worked extensively in educational psychology, particularly in the area of gifted children. He has contributed much literature to the field, including more than 90 articles, 14 books, and over 120 professional presentations. He is a Fellow of the American Psychological Association and has served as chair of the Educational Psychology department at the University of Kansas.

Solange Wechsler is a Professor at Pontificial Catholic University of Campinas, Sao Paulo, Brazil, and is a member of the Graduate Psychology Department. She has been concerned with the problems of dropouts in the Brazilian schools, and in 1988 she founded the first Brazilian Association for School and Educational Psychology, with intentions of training, research, and communicating the importance of creativity for school success. She has investigated the specificity of Brazilians' creative characteristics as well as their preferred learning and thinking styles. Her current interests involve developing creativity in Brazilian children and adults, considering their learning styles, and comparing the results with data from cross-cultural studies.

Introduction

THE 1990 INTERNATIONAL WORKING CONFERENCE: AN OVERVIEW

In August 1990, the Center for Studies in Creativity hosted an International Working Creativity Research Conference for 30 invited scholars in the field of creativity. Unique features of the conference related to the purpose, design, and potential outcomes of the event. The purpose of the conference was to clarify and develop the disciplinary potential of the field and to collegially present our best thinking about the past, present, and future state of the field. Given this unique disciplinary focus, the overall charge to the scholars contained a philosophical and curricular focus. They were asked to synthesize what they knew about the field of creativity, how they knew it, and what this knowledge might mean for future directions in the field.

The conference design, in turn, reflected process decisions to achieve these goals and a content focus on disciplinary issues. Unique features of the design involved a deliberate attempt to (a) balance divergent and convergent processes in discussion and interaction, (b) provide opportunities for collaboration and sharing of information, and (c) connect theory to practice. The research conference involved four days of participation in working sessions with large- and small-group interaction between and among functional task teams of five to seven people. The opening session focused on conceptions of creativity and identification of key definitions and assumptions underlying the field. Two full days were devoted to discussion and synthesis on recognizing creativity and nurturing and developing it. The final day's activities focused on an examination of beliefs and values that might serve as guidelines for future inquiry.

Participating scholars were asked to use their content expertise around these issues within an organizing framework of the creative person, process, product, and press or environment. The purpose of this structure was to maximize the variety of divergent experience and knowledge of the scholars while focusing on

1

synthesis, commonality, and convergence of content. Collegial interaction, opportunities for dialogue, and discussion were provided. An additional opportunity for connecting theory and practice occurred through the scholars' participation in an overlapping International Creativity Networking Conference for the remainder of the week to increase dialogue among theorists and practitioners.

Potential conference outcomes were directly related to its disciplinary focus. Intended outcomes presented to the scholars prior to the conference were (a) identification of key questions and assumptions relevant to the field; (b) identification of current limitations of existing knowledge about creativity; (c) identification of common themes, current issues, and recommendations for future action; (d) increased clarity of language, methods, and procedures; (e) decreased likelihood of repetitive and nonproductive inquiry; (f) planned future directions for further inquiry; (g) better utilization of human resources; and (h) improved use of creative problem solving.

Using the conference design and outcomes as a framework, all invited scholars were asked to prepare a working paper to share at the conference. Papers were to contain a synthesis of research in the field of creativity from each scholar's unique perspective and area of expertise. Scholars were asked to include basic definitions of creativity and a summary of safe assumptions related to their areas of interest and experience. Papers were exchanged before the conference to maximize working time in task forces. Scholars were encouraged to further discuss, test, and refine their initial thoughts before synthesizing and revising their papers in light of the conference experience.

The papers resulting from the research conference experience were subsequently compiled into two volumes. *Understanding and Recognizing Creativity: The Emergence of a Discipline* contains an analysis and report of the conference proceedings and an additional 13 chapters that address key issues and assumptions about creativity as a potential discipline. *Nurturing and Developing Creativity: The Emergence of a Discipline,* represented here in 14 chapters, focuses on issues surrounding the stimulation of creativity.

NURTURING AND DEVELOPING CREATIVITY: COMMENTS AND VOLUME OVERVIEW

The necessity to respond to complexity and rapid change in modern society has resulted in a general awareness of the need to stimulate, nurture, and develop creativity. In responding to the need to nurture and develop creativity, serious and persistent creativity scholars have functioned as change agents in the scientific community. This role, although challenging, has not necessarily been generally accepted nor well understood; yet in the greater than 40-year span of deliberate, scientific research on creativity, scholars in the field have continued to focus their research on the application and usefulness of creativity in many contexts. Their responsiveness to the need to develop creative ways to respond to change and complexity and their efforts to stimulate useful applications of creativity in education and organizations have been considerable.

The belief that creativity is important to society at large and the assumption that it could be stimulated and nurtured has been a strong and driving force in our field. This perspective is exemplified in a comment by Paul Torrance in a 1959 paper presented at the Summer Guidance Institute Lecture Series at the University of Minnesota: "It is tremendously important to our society that our creative talent be identified, developed, and utilized. The future of our civilizationour very survivaldepends on the quality of the creative imagination of our next generation." Scholars in the field of creativity have accepted these values and assumptions acted upon them. For over 40 years they have addressed the challenges of defining initial parameters for creativity and of validating its usefulness and teachability in both research and application.

In spite of these efforts, widespread attention to and acceptance of the study of creativity as a legitimate area of inquiry have been limited in the scientific community. External factors such as novelty of content and relative youth of the field have contributed to this situation. Additionally, an internal, action-oriented response to the belief that creativity could be nurtured, combined with a simultaneous demand for its application, have created an unusual situation in the development of the field. Research focusing on stimulation and practice has lead—and often outstripped—research on conceptual development. This situation, although the reverse of what observers or critics might expect, need not be regarded as a deficiency. It is instead a positive foundation on which to establish future directions.

The early Roman writer Epictetus proposed that, "Whatever you would make habitual, practice it, and if you would not make a thing habitual, accustom yourself to something else." The desire of creativity professionals to nurture and develop creativity until it becomes a habitual part of their actions, and their unwillingness to accustom themselves to something less, has been and continues to be a strength in our field.

The 14 chapters in this volume exemplify this strength and represent continued current efforts to examine how creativity might be nurtured and developed. The contributors are leaders in the field with a variety of linkages to practice as well as research. Their work in this volume is organized by educational, organizational, and product/outcome categories. Cross-cultural perspectives are included in both areas. The lead chapters at the beginning of each section (Treffinger, Jones, Firestien) function as bridging pieces between the topic subdivisions. Works within the subdivisions focus on the authors' individual perspectives and research.

NURTURING AND DEVELOPING CREATIVITY: EDUCATIONAL VIEWPOINTS

Donald Treffinger's opening chapter, "Stimulating Creativity: Issues and Future Directions," sets the framework and tone for the volume. He discusses the current status of research and practice on stimulating creativity and challenges creativity professionals to move beyond the question of the possibility of stimulating creativity toward a focus on how best to accomplish this task.

John Feldhusen's chapter, "A Conception of Creative Thinking and Creativity Training," has two frameworks. The first framework describes concepts in creative cognition resulting from internal and external predisposing conditions in childhood and youth; the second is a five-factor conception of giftedness used as a parallel explanatory support system for creative cognition. The five factors are used to define the mechanisms involved in creative conception.

Michael Moore's chapter, "Implications of Problem Finding on Learning and Teaching," explores nurturing and developing creativity in educational settings to better understand and replicate the cognitive processes developed there. He uses three groups of subjects: experienced teachers, student teachers, and pre-student-teaching subjects. The broad focus of his research is to examine (a) when teachers become teachers, (b) when and how teachers are able to use their problem-defining skills most effectively, (c) the possiblity of helping students structure knowledge about teaching, and (d) where the transfer of knowledge occurs among different disciplines.

Joseph Renzulli's chapter, "Developing Creative Productivity Through the Enrichment Triad Model," describes the current version of the Enrichment Triad Model. The model's purpose is to capture and replicate the technology used in stimulating creative productivity in students. Via an overview and case studies, the author presents both research and theory underlying the model, and concludes with a presentation of research related to product evaluation.

Solange Wechsler's cross-cultural perspective is derived from her interest in developing creativity in Brazilian educational settings. Her chapter, "Issues on Stimulating Creativity in the Schools: A South American Perspective," presents her work, framed around the observation that creativity is entering a higher scientific developmental stage and emerging as a discipline. She stresses the importance of creativity research in finding solutions to Brazil's educational, economic, and social problems. The chapter identifies current gaps and suggests directions in which further investigation is needed for the country's benefit.

NURTURING AND DEVELOPING CREATIVITY: ORGANIZATIONAL PERSPECTIVES

Les Jones's chapter, "Barriers to Creativity and Their Relationship to Individual Group and Organizational Behavior," provides a bridge between organizations and group perspectives. Jones supports the perspective that the interactive model of creativity is essential to understanding both the nature of creativity and the barriers that inhibit it. He approaches nurturing and developing creativity by systematically looking at blocks and barriers. Building on the belief that previous blocks and barriers research has not represented the topic's importance, he describes the development of and the research on the Jones Inventory to Blocks and Barriers and describes how different blocks come from different information-processing deficiencies.

Tudor Rickards's chapter, "Creativity From a Business School Perspective: Past, Present, and Future," suggests that the area of industrial creativity is fragmented and identifies a need to unify it for creativity to be considered more legitimate. He discusses his work at the Manchester Business School Creativity Research Unit by defining five different products: literature surveys, training experiences, action research work, laboratory experiments, and networking activities. In so doing he suggests a research agenda for the future work of the unit.

Reg Talbot is interested in the organizational context in which people are or are not creative. In his chapter "Creativity in the Organizational Context: Implications for Training," he describes his experiences as a trainer and poses questions for creativity researchers to consider. He differentiates between characteristics of four kinds of organizational settings as well as individual motives, means, and opportunities in order to describe challenges participants might face in attempting to implement their training.

Horst Geschka focuses on the development and use of creativity techniques in business and industry in "The Development and Assessment of Creative Thinking Techniques: A German Perspective." Techniques discussed include brainwriting, confrontation techniques, basic synectics, quickstorming, morphology, morphological tableau, and morphological matrix. He blends theory with practical observations taken from a cross-cultural survey about creative behavior among German, Swiss, and Austrian managers, and compares those results with a survey taken with Japanese subjects.

Jan Buijs's chapter, "Creativity and Innovation in The Netherlands: Project Industrial Innovation and its Implications," focuses on creativity in industry. His contribution describes his work with Project Industrial Innovation (PII)a project initiated by The Netherlands Organization for Applied Scientific Research (TNO) and the Dutch government. Information about business applications and future recommendations are integrated with a detailed discussion about TNO and PII's formation and purpose.

NURTURING AND DEVELOPING CREATIVITY: PRODUCT AND OUTCOMES

Roger Firestien's chapter, "The Power of Product," is the bridging piece for the product and outcome section. He presents conceptual development, conclusions, and shifts in belief from the 1990 International Working Creativity Research and Conference Product group. Basic assumptions underlying the chapter are that (a) the study of the creative product is essential for nurturing and developing creativity, and (b) by studying actual creative products or outcomes of individual or group creative behavior, we can begin to concretize the multifaceted concept of creativity.

In "Impacts and Outcomes of Creativity in Organizational

Settings," Min Basadur presents an approach to nurturing and developing creativity in organizations as a process of continuous improvement: continuous finding and solving of problems and continuous implementation of new solutions for the betterment of organizations. He distinguishes between economic outcomes and people outcomes and describes how to increase both. Using Japanese organizational experiences and systems as models, he presents situations in which creativity has been successfully implemented and describes how it was managed.

Roberta Milgram's chapter, "Predicting Outcomes of Giftedness Through Intrinsically Motivated Behavior in Adolescence," presents her hypothesis that certain unconventional predictors like original or creative thinking and creative leisure activities might be a more effective means of identifying significant adult achievement than the more conventional ones, such as IQ and school grades. She includes results from an 18-year follow-up study comparing the predictive validity of conventional versus unconventional predictors, using a 4 x 4 model of giftedness.

In "Assessing Creative Products: Progress and Potentials," Susan Besemer and Karen O'Quin present a theoretical framework for stimulating creativity using assessment as a focus. They describe the development of a multipurpose judging instrument and elaborate on problems of defining a creative product, deliberate analyzation, analyzation as an afterthought, bridging unique and sometimes isolated environments, and the need for a multipurpose judgment instrument which includes product developer and creator. They suggest future prospects for research and development in this area.

1

Stimulating Creativity:
Issues and Future Directions

Donald J. Treffinger

For many years, stimulating creativity has been a topic of considerable interest to researchers in education and the behavioral
sciences, as well as to many practitioners in schools, corporations,
and other human services organizations. Several recent volumes
have surveyed theories and research on various aspects of creativity (e.g., Glover, Ronning, & Reynolds, 1989; Isaksen, 1987;
Runco & Albert, 1990). For at least the past three decades, many
workshops, conferences, courses, and institutes have been offered, and a variety of instructional programs and resources have
been published, purporting to stimulate creativity, creative behavior, or creative productivity among individuals or groups of all
ages. A recent survey of published thinking skills resources
(Treffinger, Feldhusen, Isaksen, & Tallman, 1992), for example,
reviewed 100 publications, and located and catalogued more than
200 additional published materials.

Drawing on the current literature in the field, as well as the
presentations and extended discussions during and following the
1990 International Creativity Conferences in Buffalo, two major
purposes will be addressed in this chapter. These are to identify
some of the principal contemporary research issues related to
efforts to stimulate creativity, and to explore and forecast some of
the significant directions for research in this area. Many of these
issues are, in fact, persistent concerns which have been areas of
concern for several years (e.g., Isaksen, 1987; Treffinger, 1986),
while others are more recently emerging trends and directions.

ISSUES

The topic of stimulating creativity provides fertile soil for the
cultivation of many complex and controversial issues, even

among those who are avid proponents of the importance and plausibility of such efforts. A comprehensive analysis of these issues, or even a complete catalog, is beyond the scope of a single chapter. This chapter seeks to identify several issues which might be considered particularly significant because, if resolved, there would be substantial progress for both theoretical perspectives and practical consequences.

Need for Conceptual and Operational Clarity

Stimulating creativity certainly does not mean the same thing to everyone interested in creativity. Neither the word stimulating, nor the word creativity is used by professionals, or by the public, with any consensus definition or uniformity of meaning. Does stimulate mean to create new potential where previously little or none existed? Or does it mean to free or release potential to whatever extent or degree it was previously present but unrealized or unexpressed? Or does it suggest an intervention that is more proactive and deliberate than merely releasing or activating? By creativity, do we mean productivity in an artistic, scientific, or inventive context? Is creativity a kind of thinking, a way of solving problems, or a way of feeling, growing, or behaving? Might it take the form of attaining a higher degree of consciousness, or an expression of a certain lifestyle or a degree of personal self-fulfillment? Or none, or all, or any of these? How certain are we, really, about what we want to discuss when we consider stimulating creativity?

The issue is not that we lack a definition of creativity, for in fact, there are many definitions of creativity throughout the social and behavioral sciences, literature, and philosophy. The major issue is that there has been no widely accepted structural framework or synthesis among the models and definitions before us; as Kaufmann (1993) also argues, there is little or no conceptual clarity in the field.

During the International Research Conference in Buffalo, the diversity of approaches, models, and definitions was readily apparent as four different working groups (organized around the classical 4 Ps of Creativity) struggled with the challenges of understanding, assessing, and nurturing creativity. There were many areas of agreement, but these tended to emerge from very specific research results or syntheses, and hence tended to be more concerned with specific hypotheses or propositions than with more global definitions or models (see also Murdock, Isaksen, Vosburg, & Lugo, 1993). For example, in the process working group, it was relatively easy for group members to analyze and discuss matters relating to the effectiveness of, limitations in, or constraints upon specific techniques or strategies (e.g., brainstorming, forced relationships, or other diverging techniques). It was easy to share, compare, and discuss the results of specific research efforts, to examine various methodological questions, and to explore intriguing new questions. Perhaps not unpredictably within a group rather extensively comprised of empirically oriented researchers, we were much more diverse, and often much more animated, when, as four working groups reconvened, the diversity of viewpoints expanded as the discussion turned to more global issues.

As the dialogue expanded, for example, from very clearly operational or quantitative perspectives to more qualitative and philosophical levels, the prospects for an overall or consensual synthesis diminished rapidly. Magyari-Beck's proposal for a new discipline, organized around his creatology matrix drew interest, for example, as a potentially useful generative tool for researchable hypothesesagreement, once again, at the level of narrower questions and perspectivesbut considerably less concurrence as a macro-organizer for the construct of creativity (see also Murdock, Isaksen, & Coleman, 1993). At a follow-up research meeting in Buffalo, in October, 1991, there was no significant indication of any further progress toward synthesis at the broadest levels of analysis (see, for example, Csikszentmihalyi, 1990; Magyari-Beck, 1991; Treffinger, 1991).

Many other frameworks have been proposed, in continuing efforts to clarify and synthesize the varied dimensions of creativity (e.g., Gardner, 1983; Rhodes, 1961; Sternberg, 1988; Torrance & Safter, 1990; Treffinger, 1988, 1992; Treffinger, Feldhusen, Isaksen, & Tallman, 1992; Treffinger, Sortore, & Tallman, 1992), but the quest for consensus remains substantially unattained. Papers prepared for the Buffalo Research Conference by Runco and Feldhusen, for example, both provided valuable insights into the variety of frameworks for understanding creativity and their implications for nurture or instruction.

Research, theory, and practice on stimulating creativity will be enhanced by research that undertakes more extensive comparisons, reviews, and discussion of many of these frameworks. Greater conceptual clarity about the nature and components of creativity, as a construct, would pave the way for greater operational clarity. By attaining greater clarity in operationalizing important variables in creativity, we would have a substantially better foundation for efforts to assess and stimulate creativity among individuals or groups.

Some specific research issues which might be addressed include:

- Which criteria might be widely accepted across disciplines and used most effectively to analyze, compare, or synthesize definitions or conceptions of creativity?
- What are the essential components of an effective definition of creativity?
- What are the strengths, limitations, and most promising potentials of various existing definitions of creativity?

Distinguishing Among Problem Finding, Problem Solving, and Creativity

This issue is closely related to the concern for conceptual and operational clarity, but it is a problem which also involves issues beyond definition. Does problem finding differ from, or involve different structures or strategies than, problem solving? Does creativity subsume problem solving, or vice versa, or should these terms be viewed as entirely independent of one another? Efforts to make the kinds of distinctions suggested by these questions are both meaningful and important in research on creativity, and especially in relation to efforts to stimulate creativity.

While some researchers have advocated differentiation between problem finding and problem solving, for example, it is certainly not universally accepted that it is necessary to do so. In the tradition of the Creative Problem Solving (CPS) model, for example, it has generally been the case that problem finding is viewed as one dimension or stage within the more comprehensive problem solving process. This view certainly does not imply that efforts to understand, construct, or structure the problem are in any way less important than the efforts to generate possible solutions, responses, or action plans, nor that problem finding can or should be disregarded. In fact, in considering the evolutionary development of CPS (from Parnes, 1967, for example, through Treffinger & Isaksen, 1992), it is readily apparent that the component of understanding or structuring the problem, which we often describe as the front end of CPS work, has increased in its salience and contribution to the overall CPS process.

There are similar challenges in efforts to define and interrelate (or separate) creativity and problem solving. From one perspective, it might be contended that some forms of creative expression can hardly be adequately described as problem solving. Unexpected, momentous, or boundary-breaking strides, especially in any of the fine or performing arts or inspired creative expressions arising from a sudden flash of insight appear to extend beyond our conventional definitions of problem solving, for example. In addition, many kinds of problems, especially those calling for a single solution based primarily on technical knowledge, data, or rigorous deductive reasoning, are seldom described as incorporating creativity to any significant degree. On the other hand, we do routinely link creativity and problem solving together into a single phrase. To understand these issues more fully, and to be able to move toward a productive resolution, there is a definite need for much greater definitional analysis, synthesis, and clarity.

Some specific questions which seem to warrant continuing inquiry include:

- What are the essential steps in problem finding?
- What are the differences among problem finding, problem structuring, problem constructing, or other related terms?
- To what extent does the first component of CPS (including Mess-Finding, Data-Finding, and Problem-Finding; Treffinger & Isaksen, 1992) incorporate the essential elements of problem finding or problem construction?
- What are the effects, if any, of separating problem finding from problem solving, as opposed to incorporating both dimensions into a single process framework?
- How are concerns for problem finding addressed in other creativity or problem-solving process models, such as deBonos CoRT VI (deBono, 1976) or the SES Synectics model (Gordon & Poze, 1981)?

Getting Beyond, "Can we stimulate creativity?"
Toward "How best to . . . "

Journalists and freelance writers for the mass media never seem to lose their fascination with the question, "Can we stimulate creativity?" For them, the question always seems to stir deeply fascinating images. Is really possible to deliberately nurture a new Mozart, Rembrandt, Einstein, or Edison? Could psychologists possibly know enough about the complex inner workings of the brain, the mind, or the soul to probe and manipulate the most complex and mysterious of all stirrings withinthe urge to bring forward something new to the world? From a researcher's viewpoint, however, the challenge is hardly so mysterious or consuming; rather clearly, given any reasonable operational representation of creativity, the evidence is unambiguous and affirmative.

Neither educational nor organizational psychology really needs any more master's theses or doctoral dissertations on the simple question, "Can we, through some deliberate instructional or training program, enhance peoples performance on some specified measure of creativity?" The answer, unequivocally, is, "If you devise and carry out a reasonable treatment, and choose variables carefully to represent a realistic operational definition of creativity, yes, you can enhance subjects' performance significantly" (see also Talbot, this volume). Research supporting this assertion has accumulated very extensively (e.g., Parnes, 1987; Torrance, 1972, 1987; VanGundy, 1987).

The more intriguing questions confronting researchers today are much more complex. Some approaches, under the broad descriptive category of generative learning models (e.g., Wittrock, 1990), emphasize that algorithms or process structures created by the learners themselves are more effective or powerful for many purposes than algorithms or strategies presented by others. This suggests, for example, many hypotheses relating to helping individuals discover or create their own heuristics for creativity and problem solving. To what extent do such self-generated frameworks enhance creative performance? Are the frameworks that individuals generate similar to, or different from, existing process models? What are the comparative effects of process models taught to participants versus self-generated models on their performance on various outcome criteria?

The issue of how creative productivity might best be stimulated also highlights the need for continuing research on the impact of organizational, environmental, or ecological variables on individuals creative efforts and accomplishments (e.g., Amabile, 1990; Harrington, 1990; Puccio, 1990), as well as further clarification of the complex relationships of intrinsic or extrinsic motivation and cooperative or competitive goals on creativity (e.g., Amabile, 1990; Dunn, Dunn, & Treffinger, 1992).

We also need a better and more thorough understanding of the factors influencing long-term retention and transfer of the effects of training or instruction. We need systematic longitudinal studies. We need to understand better the developmental issues surrounding efforts to stimulate creativity, such as the appropriateness of particular strategies at certain age levels. We need to understand much more about ways to make creativity instructional efforts more responsive to the learning styles or other unique characteristics of learners. In short, rather than asking whether it can be done, we need to ask how to do it as effectively as possible.

Are We Confident Yet That There is a Generalizable Set of Tools or Strategies to Nurture Creativity?

Much practical interest in creativity, among educators, business people, and practitioners in other applied settings, has focused on specific methods and techniques for stimulating new ideas, such as brainstorming, forced relationships, idea checklists, or morphological techniques; these concerns are reflected for example, in Geschka's chapter, and in many discussions among the researchers throughout the conference. These discussions often involved (a) a description of various techniques, and (b) anecdotal and experimental evidence regarding the effects of various techniques on ideational productivity or originality. As popular as the development and use of creativity techniques has been, however, a number of important questions must still be resolved. Too often, for example, the discussions reflected little or no distinction between the development and application of a specific strategy or tool (such as brainstorming, for example) and a more complex and extensive process or system for solving problems creatively (such as CPS, in which brainstorming certainly plays an important role, but which includes many other strategies and stages). Deliberate efforts need to be made to describe and distinguish among several possible levels of complexity, from simple techniques for generating ideas to much more extensive and sophisticated frameworks for productive thinking.

A number of more specific questions might also be very fruitful to investigate in this area of inquiry. These include:

- Are certain strategies most productively used for particular purposes or for very specifically targeted outcomes? For example, are some strategies more effective for stimulating flexibility, while others produce higher levels of originality, or yet others lead to greater elaboration? We have just begun to identify promising hypotheses for linking objectives and strategies (e.g., Gryskiewicz, 1987).

- Might some tools or strategies for diverging, or generating ideas, be more effectively applied in harmony with certain tools for converging? If so, what combinations work best, and under what circumstances?
- Can the proposition that effective problem solving relies on a balance of both divergent and convergent strategies be supported by direct evidence?
- Will the preference for, and the effectiveness of, various strategies for diverging or converging be related in any predictable ways to style dimensions of individuals? That is, do individuals of one learning style prefer, and use more successfully, different strategies than are employed by individuals of different styles?
- Are there limits to the applicability or generalizability of certain strategies, related either to the stages in a problem-solving session in which they can be used effectively, or in relation to certain types of problems or problem-solving contexts in which they will be more or less effective?
- Are some strategies more readily learned or more successfully applied by individuals at particular age levels?
- Do expert problem solvers differ from novices in their selection and use of various diverging or converging tools during a CPS session?
- What role do metacognitive skills play in learning, using, and transferring specific productive thinking strategies?
- Are some strategies more amenable than others to application as individual or group strategies? Do certain strategies operate or function differently when applied by individuals or by groups?

Dealing With the Technological Gap and the Consequences of its Becoming Wider

The potential power of the computer and related modern technology for stimulating creativity is an important emerging issue. It can be expected to become an increasingly vital issue with continuing technological progress and increasing computer sophistication throughout the population. We already have software to guide individuals or groups in brainstorming or idea generation tasks, as well as in using a variety of evaluation matrix or decision-making strategies. Software has been created to emulate basic facilitation strategies for guiding or prompting the user for greater flexibility or ideation. Current developments in information storage, retrieval, and display technologies, such as compact discs, CD/ROM resources, and interactive video programs will soon extend our ability to introduce more complex techniques (such as visual connections or forced relationship strategies, for example) to an individual or groups at an individual computer or workstation.

Telecommunications and networking have developed to the extent that virtually unlimited informational resources are accessible to the public, and consultation or mentoring through telecommunication are already being implemented in some areas. Complex computer design and modeling or CAD/CAM systems, and continuing advances in interactive technology and artificial intelligence will certainly open a variety of new opportunities to larger groups of computer users in the near future.

At the same time, the relentless forward movement of technology also creates a very significant problem: There is a very wide gap between those who are comfortable and involved with modern technology and those who are not. This gap is, by some reports, steadily growing wider, and perhaps nearing the point of creating a gulf so wide that it may be difficult, if not virtually impossible, to span. Children today who are not competent and comfortable with technology face increasingly great obstacles in competing successfully in tomorrows world, while those who are already involved may soon reach levels of involvement and sophistication in their work that are unimaginable and incomprehensible to those who lack the training and experience. Thus, those who are involved move faster and farther ahead, and those who have not been involved fall further and further behind.

Increasing Recognition of the Vitality of Creativity in the Basics of Life, School, and the Workplace

Almost one-half century after the early pioneering efforts of Guilford, Torrance, Parnes, Taylor, MacKinnon, and others, the field of creativity has continued to struggle for recognition and legitimacy. For many, the very mention of the term conjures up images of silliness and trivialityof people who do not deserve to be taken seriously and their efforts. The challenge has been exacerbated by the prominence of "quick and easy" creativity formulas and their peddlers ("Unleash your hidden creative potency by listening to these ten audiotapes. Use your car's tape player to turn the traffic jam into a steady flow of creative genius."). Creativity has always been, and still remains, a favorite topic of many gurus and marketeers.

There are indications, however, that today's leaders in government, education, and the business world have become better able to separate the sales pitches from the serious efforts, and that there is growing recognition of the power and importance of creativity in schools, corporations, and other organizations. In education alone, for example, many recent reports offering proposals for defining essential dimensions of educational and curricular reform have given specific attention to the importance of creativity and problem solving (e.g., Carnevale, Gainer, & Meltzer, 1991; Dow Chemical, 1991; Motorola, 1991; U. S. Department of Labor, 1991).

Scope and Sequence Issues in Nurturing Creativity Remain Unresolved

While there may be increasing agreement that deliberate efforts should be made to nurture creativity, there is still little clear evidence concerning the necessary or optimum instructional sequences for accomplishing that goal. Treffinger (1980, 1987), Treffinger, Isaksen, and Firestien (1983), and Treffinger, Sortore, and Tallman (1992) have proposed and applied a model for guiding instructional delivery of creativity and CPS; for example, proposing three sequential stages: teaching and applying basic tools for creative and critical thinking, learning and practicing a systematic creative problem-solving process, and dealing with real problems and challenges. While this model has been applied with apparent success in both schools and other organizational contexts, many research questions remain unanswered. These include:

- Do students or trainees who have initially learned and applied a variety of Level One tools or strategies function more successfully in subsequent CPS applications than individuals who first learned those strategies in a CPS context?
- Does it make any difference, in relation to performance in Level Two or Level Three, which tools were learned in Level One?

Are some basic tools more important, or more readily transferred to subsequent levels, than others?

- Is there a particular sequence in which Level One tools should be learned for optimum effectiveness?
- What is the role of metacognitive skills in learning and applying a systematic CPS process at Level Two?
- Are there specific collaborative or teamwork skills which are essential to be learned at any stage of the model?
- What differences can be observed among subjects who learn a CPS process through immediate applications to real problems (Level Three), as opposed to those who have first had process instruction and practice with contrived problems (Level Two)? Is the importance or need for Level Two instruction related to age, personality, style, or ability?
- What effects do varying levels of content expertise have on subjects ability to learn and apply methods at each level or on the appropriateness of each level in the instructional process? More generally, what is the role of knowledge and information in creativity and its stimulation?
- What task or contextual characteristics influence the appropriateness or effectiveness of various practice problems in an instructional setting? How, and for whom, do such influences occur?
- What are the most significant task, personal, or interpersonal dimensions that distinguish real (Level Three) problems from contrived or practice (Level Two) problems?

FUTURE DIRECTIONS

The seven major issues described above certainly provide creativity researchers with an extensive and varied array of opportunities over an extended period of time. From these, however, it may be useful to summarize by identifying several broader issues around which many of the more specific issues and questions seem to focus or gather. Four major future directions appear to offer particular opportunities and challenges for our field.

Understanding What Works Best, for Whom, and Under What Conditions?

The question of aptitudetreatment interactions (ATI) has been tantalizing but elusive (and controversial) in many areas of instructional research (Cronbach & Snow, 1977; Snow, 1989, 1992). For creativity researchers, it remains a major challenge. Snow (1992), for example, reviewed ATI research that leads to the hypothesis that thinking skills reside in the person-situation interaction, not solely in the mind of the person (pp. 19–20). Creativity researchers are challenged by the ATI literature, then, to explore new conceptions of thinking skills, new process variables, and most importantly, to investigate the complex and varied interactions among learner characteristics, process variables, and situational or contextual variables. Indeed, many of the issues addressed in this chapter involve questions that relate directly or indirectly to this problem. This should certainly be a concern to which considerable energy and attention are devoted in the future.

Encouraging Different Kinds of Research on Creativity

The many and varied challenges of nurturing creativity will not all be addressed successfully through one mode or method of research (see also Novelli, 1993; Raina, 1993). Indeed, it is certainly true that creativity can and should be a valid and important topic for researchers from a variety of disciplines, employing methods, designs, or analytical procedures of many kinds. Each of these methods deals with its unique way of posing questions or hypotheses, and, in turn leads to different kinds of procedures or search strategies.

Figure 1.1 briefly summarizes nine different methods of research which might be considered basic approaches to studying creativity or other dimensions of human behavior. These nine basic methods are listed in the first column of the figure and are explained very briefly in the second column. More extensive explanations and discussions of these models can be found in many textbooks on research methods. The chart is intended only to offer concise definitions and examples, not comprehensive explanations. The third column of the figure presents a simple illustration of each of the nine methods, based on an informal, light-hearted, everyday sample area of inquiry, which may help illustrate more clearly the uniqueness of each method and the differences among them. Perhaps this example will also serve as a reminder that research does not have to refer only to a stodgy, technical, burdensome inquiry. The example begins with a familiar notion: Chicken soup is a good cure for the common cold. If we were to examine this notion as a potential topic for research, how might each of the nine basic research methods deal with it? How might they lead to different kinds of questions and inquiry, and to different procedures? Finally, the fourth column presents illustrations of each of the nine methods related specifically to the area of creativity and creative learning. These examples may help to expand our awareness and appreciation of the ways in which various research methods can contribute to our understanding of the complex phenomenon of creativity.

Improving Stimulation of Creativity by Linking Appropriate Assessment with Carefully Designed Instruction

It will be increasingly important in the future to recognize that creativity assessment and the nurture of creativity are not unrelated topics, but are highly interdependent. In part, this emerges from the need to work on aptitude-treatment interactions and the questions of how best to nurture creativity. For both research and practice, advances in creativity assessment open the door for new investigations and insights into nurturing creativity. As we increase our understanding of the many and varied ways creativity can be manifested in individual behavior, we also enhance our ability to formulate and test new hypotheses about diagnosis for instruction or training.

The linkage of assessment and nurturance is also important as researchers and practitioners become increasingly cognizant of diversity. The more effectively we are able to discern differences among individuals characteristics, skills, and styles, the more effectively we can address creative operations or strategies and outcomes that are uniquely appropriate for them. Thus, we become increasingly aware that stimulating creativity is not a process of homogenization. It is not teaching everyone a fixed set of strategies, to be applied in a linear, prescribed manner, to a particular set of tasks. Rather, the power of efforts to nurture creativity arises from our ability to help individuals recognize, develop, and realize their unique strengths and talents, to learn, and to be creatively productive in their own way, not just in our way.

Continuing research exploring the linkages between assessment and instruction is also important if we are to gain greater

Historical	To reconstruct the past objectively and accurately, often in relation to the tenability of an hypothesis	When did people first begin to pose the idea of chicken soup as a cure for the common cold? Where/when/with whom did this idea originate?	What are the origins of the myth that "there is a fine line separating creative genius from insanity? How did this myth develop? When and how was it debunked?
Descriptive	To describe systematically a situation or area of interest factually and accurately	Thorough description of the chicken soup cure and its use; describe the cure, and the step-by-step procedures for its preparation and implementation	Thorough description of the nature of "divergent thinking," including its components, in-struments used to measure it, and the rationale for its relationship to creativity
Developmental	To investigate patterns and sequences of growth and/or change as a function of age or time	How has the chicken soup cure changed during time? Or, what variations in the cure are prescribed at various age or developmental levels?	Do creative characteristics change with age? Or, are efforts to enhance creativity at various age levels differentially effective?
Case/Field	Intensive study of the background, current status, and environmental interactions of a given individual or group	In-depth study of the use of chicken soup as a cure for the common cold by New York City mothers	In-depth study of the ways that architects express and apply creativity in their personal and professional life
Correlational	To investigate the extent to which variations in one or more other factors, using correlation coefficients to describe the relationship	What is the relationship between amount of chicken soup consumed (or rate of consumption) and selected measures (e.g., sneezing) of common cold symptoms?	What is the relationship between measures of various creative thinking components (e.g., fluency) and other cognitive variables (e.g., memory, or IQ scores)?

Figure 1.1. Nine Basic Methods of Research

Causal-Comparative or "Ex Post Facto"	To explore possible cause-and-effect relationships by observing some existing consequences and searching back through the data for plausible causal factors	In-depth analysis of many reported cases of the chicken soup cure, in order to try to understand what happened and to pose possible explanations	Observing that personal criticism inhibits the creativity of children and searching through data from parents and teachers to examine interaction patterns that encouraged or discouraged creativity
True Experimental	Investigating possible cause-and-effect relationships by exposing experimental group(s) to treatment condition(s) and comparing results to control group(s) not receiving the treatment (random assignment being essential)	Experimental (chicken soup cure) versus control (no treatment or placebo) comparisons, with common cold sufferers randomly assigned to conditions; specific outcome measures	Experimental (training in Creative Problem Solving) versus control (no CPS training) comparisons, with subjects randomly assigned to conditions; assessing creative thinking and problem-solving skills and attitudes as outcomes
Quasi-Experimental	Approximation of true experiment, in which not all relevant variables may not be controlled or manipulated (but in which experimenters take these limitations into account)	Studying a group receiving the chicken soup "treatment," compared to a control group (no soup), within a nonresidential setting, so you cannot control the outside factors to which the subjects are also exposed	Conducting a training program in which intact groups must be assigned to treatments, or in which you have little or no control over subjects' other activities or experiences
Action	To develop new skills or new approaches with emphasis on direct application within an applied setting (e.g., classroom or organization)	Creating a "new and improved" chicken soup cure (e.g., fortified with extra Vitamin C)	Creating a new program to help parents stimulate creativity among infants and pre-school children

Figure 1.1. (Continued)

insight into the nature of, effectiveness of, and procedures for authentic assessment and tasks. Authentic tasks are those in which instructional activities closely approximate important situations or experiences learners will encounter in real life. Authentic assessment refers to the design and use of procedures to assess such tasks in a more realistic performance setting than can be attained from traditional paper-and-pencil testing procedures (e.g., performance demonstrations or realistic individual or small-group simulation experiences). These challenges, which are attracting increasing interest in general education (with respect to assessment of valued educational or academic outcomes) may be particularly relevant for development and use in relation to complex outcomes such as creativity and problem solving. Progress in creating, using, and evaluating such tasks and assessments relies on our ability to define clearly what behaviors and tasks are authentic in relation to creativity, and then on our ability to devise appropriate and consistent assessment procedures.

Research on innovative directions in creativity assessment and its linkage to creativity instruction or stimulation activities should also involve new and expanded efforts to define and differentiate profiles and portfolios. A creativity profile, for example, might be viewed as a structured analysis of an individuals characteristics, strengths, talents, interests, skills, and needs, assembled primarily as a diagnostic tool (i.e., intended to guide the person and his or her instructor or mentor in designing an appropriate learning or growth plan). In contrast, a portfolio might be viewed as an individuals collected and organized documentation of accomplishments and progress in relation to valued goals and objectives. While both the profile and the portfolio might contain some common components, such as product samples, it is also likely that each might contain some elements that are unique. Test data, for example, might be incorporated in a meaningful way into a profile, but might be much less likely to be found in a portfolio. Both assessment and instruction will be enhanced by research that clarifies the appropriate structure, components, and uses of both profiles and portfolios.

Recognizing that Different Levels of Stimulation Involve Different Intervention Behaviors

In the future, we must also extend our ability to distinguish among direct instruction, effective leadership, and facilitation, and to recognize the most appropriate ways to use each. Through experience with many groups, it has become apparent that the terms teach (or instruct), lead, and facilitate are often used ambiguously or even interchangeably. Many educators and trainers, even with considerable experience with a variety of creativity techniques or methods, have never been challenged to consider explicitly the similarities and differences among the terms. In relation to nurturing creativity, however, it may be very important for us to define and distinguish among them, and to seek a better understanding of the circumstances or situations under which each represents the most appropriate choice. One might hypothesize, for example, that teach or instruct refers most appropriately to the goal of helping students learn and use basic tools or strategies for creative and critical thinking (Level One in the creative learning model). Given a contemporary, situational conception of leadership (e.g., Blanchard, 1985), selecting and using an appropriate leadership style on the basis of the participants developmental level and the nature of the task and support parameters involved appears to be most appropriately linked to the tasks of learning and practicing a structured process approach such as CPS (in Level Two of the creative learning model). Facilitation, defined in relation to specific goals and objectives described by Treffinger, Isaksen, and Firestien (1982), Isaksen (1983), or Firestien and Treffinger (1989), for example, may be viewed as most relevant and appropriate in dealing with real problems and challenges (Level Three).

In summary, although nurturing or stimulating creativity is an area within creativity research to which considerable effort and attention has been given for many years, it remains a topic which presents many varied opportunities and challenges for the researchers of today and tomorrow.

REFERENCES

Amabile, T.M. (1990). Within you, without you: The social psychology of creativity, and beyond. In M.A. Runco & R.S. Albert (Eds.), *Theories of creativity* (pp. 61–91). Newbury Park, CA: Sage.

Blanchard, K. (1985). *SL II: A situational approach to managing people.* San Diego, CA: Blanchard Training and Development.

Carnevale, A.P., Gainer, L.J., & Meltzer, A.S. (1991). *Workplace basics: The skills employers want.* San Francisco, CA: Jossey-Bass.

Cronbach, L.J., & Snow, R.E. (1977). *Aptitudes and instructional methods: A handbook for research on interactions.* New York: Irvington.

Csikszentmihalyi, M. (1990). The domain of creativity. In M.A. Runco & R.S. Albert (Eds.), *Theories of creativity* (pp. 190–211). Newbury Park, CA: Sage.

deBono, E. (1976). *Thinking action.* Dorset, UK: Direct Educational Services.

Dow Chemical Company. (1991). *Education: Dows commitment to the partnership.* Midland, MI: Dow Chemical Company.

Dunn, R., Dunn, K., & Treffinger, D.J. (1992). *Bringing out the giftedness in your child.* New York: John Wiley.

Firestien, R.L., & Treffinger, D.J. (1989). Update: Guidelines for effective facilitation of Creative Problem Solving (three-part series). *GCT Magazine* (July-August), pp. 35–39; (September-October), pp. 44–47; and (November-December), pp. 40–44.

Gardner, H. (1983). *Frames of mind.* New York: Basic Books.

Glover, J.A., Ronning, R.R., & Reynolds, C.R. (Eds.). (1989). *Handbook of creativity.* New York: Plenum Press.

Gordon, W.J.J., & Poze, T. (1981). *The basic course in synectics.* Cambridge, MA: Porpoise Books.

Gryskiewicz, S.S. (1987). Predictable creativity. In S.G. Isaksen (Ed.), *Frontiers of creativity research: Beyond the basics* (pp. 305–313). Buffalo, NY: Bearly Limited.

Harrington, D.M. (1990). The ecology of human creativity: A psychological perspective. In M.A. Runco & R.S. Albert (Eds.), *Theories of creativity* (pp. 143–169). Newbury Park, CA: Sage.

Isaksen, S.G. (1983). Toward a model for the facilitation of creative problem solving. *Journal of Creative Behavior, 17*(1), 18–31.

Isaksen, S.G. (Ed.). (1987). *Frontiers of creativity research: Beyond the basics.* Buffalo, NY: Bearly Limited.

Isaksen, S.G., & Treffinger, D.J. (1985). *Creative problem solving: The basic course.* Buffalo, NY: Bearly Limited.

Kaufmann, G. (1993). The logical structure of creativity concepts: A conceptual argument for creativity as a coherent discipline. In S.G. Isaksen, M.C. Murdock, R.L. Firestien, & D.J. Treffinger (Eds.), *Understanding and recognizing creativity: The emergence of a discipline* (pp. 141–157). Norwood, NJ: Ablex.

Magyari-Beck, I. (1991). Dignity of creative studies. *International Creativity Network Newsletter, 1*(3), 1–2.

Motorola, Inc. (1991). *The crisis in American education.* Chicago, IL: Motorola Corporation.

Murdock, M., Isaksen, S.G., & Coleman, S.E. (1993). Moving to a desired future state in the field of creativity: A postscript. In S.G. Isaksen, M.C. Murdock, R.L. Firestien, & D.J. Treffinger (Eds.), *Understanding and recognizing a discipline: The emergence of a discipline* (pp. 499–528). Norwood, NJ: Ablex.

Murdock, M., Isaksen, S.G., Vosburg, S., & Lugo, D. (1993). The progress and potential of an emerging discipline. In S.G. Isaksen, M.C. Murdock, R.L. Firestien, & D.J. Treffinger (Eds.), *Understanding* and recognizing creativity: The emergence of a discipline (pp. 105–140). Norwood, NJ: Ablex.

Novelli, Jr., L. (1993). Using alternative perspectives to build more robust theories of organizational creativity. In S.G. Isaksen, M.C. Murdock, R.L. Firestien, & D.J. Treffinger (Eds.), Understanding and recognizing creativity: The emergence of a discipline (pp. 281–295). Norwood, NJ: Ablex.

Parnes, S.J. (1967). Creative behavior guidebook. New York: Charles Scribner's Sons.

Parnes, S.J. (1987). The creative studies project. In S.G. Isaksen (Ed.), Frontiers of creativity research: Beyond the basics (pp. 156–188). Buffalo, NY: Bearly Limited.

Puccio, G.J. (1990). Person-environment fit: Using Kirton's Adaptor Innovator theory to determine the effect of stylistic fit upon stress, job satisfaction, and creative performance. Unpublished doctoral dissertation, University of Manchester Institute of Science and Technology, Manchester, UK.

Raina, M.K. (1993). Ethnocentric confines in creativity research. In S.G. Isaksen, M.C. Murdock, R.L. Firestien, & D.J. Treffinger (Eds.), Understanding and recognizing creativity: The emergence of a discipline (pp. 235–253). Norwood, NJ: Ablex.

Rhodes, M. (1961). An analysis of creativity. Phi Delta Kappan, 42, 305–310.

Runco, M.A. & Albert, R.S. (Eds.). (1990). Theories of creativity. Newbury Park, CA: Sage.

Snow, R.E. (1989). Aptitude-treatment interaction as a framework for research in individual differences in learning. In P.L. Ackerman, R.J. Sternberg, & R. Glaser (Eds.), Learning and individual differences: Advances in theory and research (pp. 11–34). New York: Freeman.

Snow, R.E. (1992). Aptitude theory: Yesterday, today, and tomorrow. Educational Psychologist, 27 (1), 5–32.

Sternberg, R.J. (1988). The nature of creativity. New York: Cambridge University Press.

Torrance, E.P. (1972). Can we teach children to think creatively? Journal of Creative Behavior, 6, 114–143.

Torrance, E.P. (1987). Recent trends in teaching children and adults to think creatively. In S.G. Isaksen (Ed.), Frontiers of creativity research: Beyond the basics (pp. 204–215). Buffalo, NY: Bearly Limited.

Torrance, E.P., & Safter, H.T. (1990). The incubation model of teaching. Buffalo, NY: Bearly Limited.

Treffinger, D.J. (1980). Encouraging creative learning. Ventura, CA: Ventura County Superintendent of Schools, LTI Publications.

Treffinger, D.J. (1986). Research on creativity. Gifted Child Quarterly, 30(1), 15–19.

Treffinger, D.J. (1987). Research on creativity assessment. In S.G. Isaksen (Ed.), Frontiers of creativity research: Beyond the basics (pp. 103–119). Buffalo, NY: Bearly Limited.

Treffinger, D.J. (1988). Components of creativityAnother look. *Creative Learning Today, 2* (5), 1–4.

Treffinger, D.J. (1991). Dignity without discipline? A response to Magyari-Beck. *International Creativity Network Newsletter, 1*(3), 2–3.

Treffinger, D.J. (in press). Creativity: Understanding its nature and sources. *Gifted Child Quarterly.*

Treffinger, D.J., Feldhusen, J.F., Isaksen, S.G., & Tallman, M.C. (1992). *Thinking Skills Programs Handbook* (Vol. I). Sarasota, FL: Center for Creative Learning.

Treffinger, D.J., & Isaksen, S.G. (1992). *Creative problem solving: An introduction.* Sarasota, FL: Center for Creative Learning.

Treffinger, D.J., Isaksen, S.G., & Firestien, R.L. (Eds.). (1982). *Handbook of creative learning* (Vol. I). Williamsville, NY: Center for Creative Learning.

Treffinger, D.J., Isaksen, S.G., & Firestien, R.L. (1983). Theoretical perspectives on creative learning and its facilitation: An overview. *Journal of Creative Behavior, 17*(1), 9–17.

Treffinger, D.J., Sortore, M.R., & Tallman, M.C. (1992). *Dimensions of creativity.* Sarasota, FL: Center for Creative Learning.

U. S. Department of Labor. (1991). *What work requires of schools: A SCANS report for America 2000.* Washington, DC: U. S. Department of Labor.

VanGundy, A. (1987). Organizational creativity and innovation. In S.G. Isaksen, (Ed.), *Frontiers of creativity research: Beyond the basics* (pp. 358–379). Buffalo, NY: Bearly Limited.

Wittrock, M. (1990). Generative processes of comprehension. *Educational Psychologist, 24*(4), 345–376.

PART I

STIMULATING CREATIVITY: EDUCATIONAL PERSPECTIVES

2

A Conception of Creative Thinking and Creativity Training

John F. Feldhusen

Creative thinking is adaptive thinking or reconceptualization. For the most part, it is not overt behavior; it is covert cognition. Most of our daily cognitions and behaviors are automatic. They satisfy our daily needs. The ways of satisfying our needs become routines, even rigidly so. In all aspects of our daily lives, such as eating and socializing, within occupations and professions, within religions, within the arts, and within scholarly disciplines, we develop standard modes of operational, automatic cognitions and behaviors to meet fundamental needs. We go to McDonald's and eat Big Macs to satisfy hunger needs; our social contacts with relatives are ritualized in family reunions; our physician attends monthly briefings on new drug therapies; and scholars regularly attend conferences to share new research findings. All of these activities are ways we have created of meeting needs. However, all may be creatively adapted, reconceptualized, or changed from time to time to make them more effective in meeting our needs or achieving our goals.

Cognitive conceptions are our ideas about the world around us that evolve through thinking, overt behavior, and the feedback generated by our behavior. Our conceptions are projections of reality. Ideas or conceptions can change and behavior can change as a result of reconception. What mechanisms lead to or produce those changes? How do they occur? Are there skills of adaptation? Are there dispositions or motivational states which facilitate adaptation or change? How does our existing knowledge base (our network of conceptions or schemata) affect the potential for change?

CREATIVE COGNITION

Creative thinking is a cognitive activity that may result in a creative production that is perceived as new and useful. The products may be pieces of writing such as books, essays, poems, or short stories; physical creations such as new robots, works of art, buildings, or miniature representations; new systems, theories, or conceptualizations such as quality circles, management by objectives, the wave theory of light, the self-concept theory in psychology, or the periodic theory of elements in chemistry; performances in drama, music, dance, or speech; or inventions such as the automobile, the airplane, or the automatic can opener. We call the products creative if they represent a transformation or a reconceptualization, have aesthetic coherence and appeal, represent a new configuration or connection of ideas, or serve some functional or explanatory purpose. Problem solutions may have all these criterial elements, plus relevance or resolution to the original problem.

We have found no indirect and reliable way to test creative ability as we have for intelligence, achievement, and aptitudes. At best, creativity tests measure lesser cognitive elements in the creative thinking process. Measures of creativity should be valid in the sense of predicting real-world creativity (Runco, 1993). The true test of creativity is an evaluation of the product, conception, or presentation. Such an evaluation is based on criteria set in the field which one creates in. The creative product is always preceded by a creative cognition or idea.

The creative cognition is variously described as a magic synthesis by Arieti (1976), as synthesis by Bloom (1956), as a "chance configuration" by Simonton (1988, p. 8), as a selective combination of ideas by Sternberg (1986), as an illumination by Wallas (1926), and as design by Perkins (1986). All of these conceptions of creative cognition stress the association of ideas into new, larger, meaningful complexes of ideas. A variety of ability, motivation, stylistic, and environmental conditions within and surrounding the creator facilitate the occurrence of creative or adaptive cognitions. The latter term, adaptive cognition, seems to be most appropriate to refer to early forms of creative cognitions in youth (Cohen, 1989).

From Idea to Reality

But alas, "between the idea and the reality falls the shadow" (Eliot, 1942). Translating the creative cognition—the new conception—to a new written and published statement of the theory, the challenge to an existing paradigm, the new artistic performance of

Beethoven's Eroica, the new system of management, the new car designhere is the challenge calling for production skills. For Torrance (1962) it may be chiefly an elaboration process. For Wallas (1926) it may all have been summed up in "verification." "Synthesis" as described by Bloom (1956) surely includes all of the production activities that lead to product, performance, presentation, or invention. Here, according to Simonton (1988), is where the production skills of the discipline come into play. For the scholar it may mean the library searches, the delineation of the original conception, the written presentation, and persistence in getting published. This is the thinking through and the development of a conception to a reality which involves presentations to the world at large and especially to the world of evaluation within one's discipline or art form.

The Readying Process

A huge amount of research suggests that creative cognition and problem solving results from readying and predisposing conditions in childhood and youth. Among these are superior general intelligence; specific talents; motivating dispositions, attitudes, and productivity styles; specific metacognitive skills and strategies; and a large, fluent knowledge base. In addition to all of these factors, there is a set of external conditions, the culture and the zeitgeist, which set the stage for creative cognition and problem solving. Feldman (1986) suggested that prodigies become productive or successful because of "coincidences" of being born and growing up in a certain era, when a field is at a certain level of development, when historical and cultural trends are supportive (Raina, 1993), and when the general evolutionary context supports or facilitates creative cognitions. The family environment is also a crucial support system. While Feldman (1986) presented this theoretical formulation to explain the manifestation of giftedness and talent in prodigies, it seems reasonable to apply the same framework to explain creative cognition and problem solving.

I also draw upon Tannenbaum's (1983) five-factor conception of giftedness as a parallel explanatory support system for creative cognition, especially for his chance factor which may in part be analogous to Feldman's (1986) coincidences. Tannenbaum (1983) saw five factors which contribute to a psychosocial explanation of giftedness: (a) superior general ability for the field in which one will function, (b) special talent or ability as needed in the field, (c) supportive environmental conditions, (d) nonintellective factors such as curiosity or persistence, and (e) chance. The latter, according to Tannenbaum (1983), is the unpredictable event or malady that arises to block or retard creative pursuits such as ill health or lack of needed resources. Conversely, it is the unexpected opportunity that suddenly presents itself. The individual who is ready seizes the opportunity to produce, to create.

SUPERIOR GENERAL INTELLIGENCE

With these two theoretical frameworks to guide us, we turn first to the necessary base of superior general intelligence. We may agree with Tannenbaum (1983) that the level of "g" or "fluid intelligence" (Cattell, 1971) required is related both to the field in which one wishes to operate creatively and also to the level of creative functioning to which one aspires in that field. Cohen's (1989) taxonomy of creative functioning ranges across the following seven levels:

1. Learning something new
2. Making rare connections in relation to peers
3. Demonstrating talent
4. Developing heuristics
5. Producing information
6. Creating by extending a field
7. Creating by revolutionizing a field

Presumably, creative cognition and problem solving at Levels 6 and 7 require much higher levels of general or fluid intelligence than Levels 1 and 2, and it is possible that high-level creative functioning in theoretical physics and pure mathematics requires higher level general intelligence than functioning in the design of advertising media.

Simonton (1988) noted the threshold-like role of intelligence when he says "High intelligence . . . does not guarantee that a person has a talent for doing innovative science, yet a person whose intellectual ability is average or lower has virtually no chance whatsoever of making the grade" (p.186).

Similarly, after his studies of architects, research scientists, inventors, mathematicians, artists, and writers, MacKinnon (1978) concluded as follows:

Clearly a certain degree of intelligence, in general a rather high degree, is required for creativity, but above that point the degree of intelligence does not seem to determine the level of one's creativeness. In some fields of endeavor, mathematics and theoretical physics for example, the requisite intelligence for highly creative achievement is obviously high. (p. 180)

Beyond the threshold concept of creative functioning, Walberg, Rasher, and Hase (1978) found that those individuals who achieved eminence because of their creative productivity have mean estimated IQs of 158.9.

It seems clear that the higher the level of creative functioning, the higher the level of intelligence. However, that high intelligence in itself is not a sufficient predictor of high-level creative cognition. Again we would stress that the type of intelligence required is probably Cattell's (1971) fluid intelligence which is the more general capacity for thinking, reasoning, induction, and figural activity, as opposed to crystallized intelligence which denotes the intelligence of knowledge and experience. We will recognize the latter as a component of creative cognition later.

THE TALENT FOCUS

Creative cognition must find focus. Within any individual there are facilitating and limiting physical, neurological, and psychological attributes which more or less predispose that individual to success or failure in particular lines of human endeavor such as dance, mathematics, piano, management, nuclear science, or investment analysis (Dacey, 1989). The particular focus may be called "talent." Talent is a combination of facilitating abilities and interests evoked in relation to societally defined areas of human endeavor. To a great extent "talent domains" define the areas, occupations, or professions in which creative cognition and problem solving can occur. Without a talent focus it is unlikely that one can develop and carry on creative activity.

Gagne (1985) presented a model, shown in Figure 2.1, which links the ability domains of giftedness to specific talent fields with the psychological catalytic conditions of motivation and personality mediated by the environmental conditions of home and school. Gagne classified creative ability as one of the ability domains in the model. He also described talent as the ability or

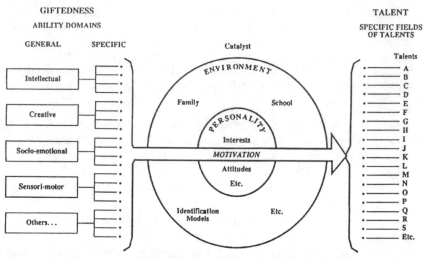

Figure 2.1. Gagne's model

aptitude which links performance or productivity to a field of activity such as painting, mathematics, music, or law.

MacKinnon (1978) also offered a definition of talent as "a complex of traits which qualify one for superior performance in some occupation, or more typically, some profession" (p. 23). MacKinnon recognizes talent as embracing both abilities and other psychological factors such as attitudes, motivations, and emotions. Elsewhere, he wrote that "talent is a veritable complex of aptitudes, developed abilities, special skills, abstract knowledge and technical know-how as well as complicated motivational structures of personality" (p. 26). Through the functions of talent in a specific domain, creative cognition may occur.

Gardner's (1983) seven intelligences may also be thought of as broad talent domains: linguistic, musical, logical-mathematical, spatial, bodily kinesthetic, intrapersonal, and interpersonal. This conception of intelligences contrasts with the more functional view presented in the Talents Unlimited model (Taylor & Ellison, 1983). The five cognitive operations in the Talents Unlimited model are (a) productive thinking, (b) forecasting, (c) communicating, (d) planning, and (e) decision making. However, both models present a conception of human ability as specialized in talent outlets, as opposed to a single overarching "g," or general intelligence factor.

Tannenbaum (1983) defined four kinds of talent. The first he calls scarcity talent, the type that is forever in short supply. This is the high-level, creative talent, possessed by those few who make major discoveries or offer the world major new conceptions— Albert Einstein, Jonas Salk, Martin Luther King Jr., or Alexander Fleming. The second is surplus talent, which represents the creative talent of those who enrich our lives through the arts, such as Pablo Picasso, Sir Lawrence Olivier, or Beethoven. The third type is called quota talent, which is the high-level skill society needs to produce goods and services. The creative role is very limited at this level. They are physicians, teachers, lawyers, engineers, politicians, and business executives. The final type is anomalous talent. This is unique or highly specialized talent— gourmet cooking, speed reading, trapeze artistry, oration, sales-manship, or cabinetry.

In summary, talent is the vehicle through which creative cognition may be expressed. While there are highly capable people who make creative contributions in several fields and different talent domains, it is predominantly the power of general intelligence brought to effectiveness in one talent area which makes it possible to go beyond skilled performance or competence to reveal true creative contribution through inventions, reconceptualization, or the production of a new work of art.

MOTIVATING DISPOSITIONS AND ATTITUDES

What drives the process of creative cognition or adaptation? Why do humans create, change, develop new understandings, and invent? In describing the great creators he studied, MacKinnon (1978) said:

> They are perhaps the prototype of the person of strong ego, the man of will and deed. Confident of themselves and basically self accepting, they are to an unusual degree able to recognize and give expression to most aspects of inner experience and character, and thus are able more fully to be themselves and to realize their own ideals. (p. 150)

Elsewhere he suggested:

> It is . . . his openness to experience, his freedom from crippling restraint and impoverishing inhibitions, his esthetic sensitivity, his cognitive flexibility, his independence in thought and action, his unquestioning commitment to creative endeavor, and his unceasing

striving for solutions to the ever more difficult problems that he constantly sees for himself. (p. 186)

Clearly the drive or motivation to create springs from within as a perception of external circumstances. But the external circumstances involve not only the problem or condition which may be changed, but also potential payoffs or reward. New products, performances, or conceptions evoke the gratitude and admiration of recipients, users, or reviewers. The Nobel Prize, an Oscar, or an Obie award may come to the creator. Do they stimulate further creative activity? "Fame is the spur that the clear spirit doth raise, That last infirmity of noble mind, To scorn delights and live laborious days" (Milton, 1940).

But Hennessey and Amabile (1988) persistently reminded us that "intrinsic motivation is conducive to creativity, and extrinsic motivation is detrimental; as extrinsic constraints increase, intrinsic motivation and creativity must decrease" (p. 31). However, a bit later they offered a sort of compromise when they said, "perhaps, under certain circumstances or with certain individuals, intrinsic and extrinsic force combine in an additive fashion" (p. 31). Amabile (1983) presented a comprehensive review of her own research and theoretical integration of the conception of creativity and intrinsic motivation in her book *The Social Psychology of Creativity*.

Perkins (1988) also gave us a picture of the internal motivating states and traits which evoke real-world creative cognitions:

> Creative individuals tend to be autonomous, independent, and self reliant . . . They value originality, tolerate ambiguity and uncertainty, have an aesthetic appreciation for things rather than just a pragmatic mind set, and reveal strong intrinsic motivation in pursuing their projects. (p. 379)

Feldman (1986) reinforced further the importance of intrinsic motivation when he said:

> Prodigies are characterized by an intense personal desire to pursue a particular field passionately, relentlessly, and for the sheer joy and pleasure of doing it well . . . Motivation to sustain his effort day in and day out must be primarily intrinsic. (p. 164)

Bloom (1985) saw the genesis of this intrinsic motivation in home and school when he said:

These children come to be treated as special by their families, teachers, and immediate acquaintances . . . . The majority of parents were strongly committed to the work ethic. They raised their children to believe in the importance of doing something well, to place work and duties before pleasure, to believe in the importance of hard work, and to strive for future goals. (p. 539)

We conclude that the motivation to create springs from within, but it may come from interactions at home and at school that stimulate deep, intrinsic interest in particular areas of study or art. It may very well develop through the creative leisure-time activities which Milgram (this volume) describes as antecedents of adult creative production. It probably relates to assertions of independence and autonomy, to a sense of self-efficacy, and a willingness to take risks. Capacity for long, sustained, hard work, and delay of gratification are also essential elements. Striving for excellence and the setting of lofty future goals are also characteristic motivations. Perhaps there is a combination of intrinsic interest in the phenomena to be explained, the performance to be created, or the problem to be solved and long-range extrinsic perceptions of payoffs for the creator through hard work, delay of gratification, and striving for the excellent result or goal. Parents, mentors, and teachers can model and teach about such motivational conditions, and youth who are exposed to such influences from early childhood onward may develop the motivational dispositions to create and to solve problems creatively.

SPECIFIC STRATEGIES AND COGNITIVE SKILLS

There are specific strategies and skills by which creative cognition can be facilitated or enhanced, and almost assuredly they can be fostered, developed, and taught. Students who are above average in intelligence, exhibit signs of particular talent, and show signs of intrinsic motivation can develop the higher skills and strategies which facilitate creative cognition. Runco (1993) reviews the strategies, metacognitive skills, and heuristics associated with creative activity and concludes that they can be taught just as knowledge or information can be taught. Students can acquire skill in recognizing problems, clarifying problems, and using certain orienting or metacognitive skills in attempting to solve problems. They can be taught to monitor their own cognitive activity, to purposely seek alternatives, recognize new ideas or solutions when they come to mind, and test the validity of potential solutions or new conceptions. The set of strategies called "creative problem solving" (Treffinger, 1982) is widely promulgated and seemingly taught well in school programs all over the United States.

The basic component skills of creative problem solving have been delineated in nontechnical terminology by Treffinger and others (Feldhusen & Treffinger, 1985; Parnes, 1967; Parnes, Noller, & Biondi, 1977; Treffinger, 1982) as follows:

1. Mess-finding
2. Data-finding
3. Problem-finding
4. Idea-finding
5. Solution-finding
6. Acceptance-finding

Feldhusen (1988) described the six skills of creative problem solving as follows:

> The main purpose of "Mess-finding" is to sort through a problem situation and find direction toward a broad goal or solution. In "Data-finding," participants sort through all available information about the mess and clarify the steps or direction to a solution. In "Problem-finding," a specific problem statement is formulated. "Idea-finding" is a process of finding many ideas for solutions to the problem or parts of the problem. "Solution-finding" is an evaluation or judgmental process of sorting among the ideas produced in the last step and selecting those most likely to produce solutions. Finally, in "Acceptance-finding," a plan is devised for implementing the good solutions. (p. 327)

Speedie, Houtz, Ringenbach, and Feldhusen (1973) analyzed the basic components of the problem-solving process and of related creative thinking skills. Their analyses identified the following factors, all of which probably can be taught or enhanced through explicit instruction (Feldhusen & Guthrie, 1979; Houtz & Feldhusen, 1976; Speedie, Houtz, Ringenbach, & Feldhusen, 1973):

1. Sensing that a problem exists
2. Formulating questions to clarify the problem
3. Determining causes of the problem

4. Identifying relevant aspects of the problem
5. Determining the specific problem
6. Clarifying the goal or desired solution
7. Judging if more information is needed to solve the problem
8. Redefining or creating a new use of a familiar object or concept
9. Seeing implications of a possible action
10. Selecting the best or most unusual solution among several possible solutions
11. Sensing what follows problem solution

Mess-finding and problem-finding in creative problem solving are probably analogous to the factors "sensing that a problem exists," "asking questions about the problem," "identifying a problem specifically," "clarifying the goal," and "identifying relevant aspects of the problem situation." Idea-finding is probably related to the factor "judging if more information is needed to solve the problem." Solution-finding seems parallel to the factor "selecting the best or most unusual solution among several possible solutions," and the factor "seeing implication of some action" may be related to the more assertive acceptance-finding.

Sternberg (1988) identified three major metacomponents which can be used in planning, monitoring, and evaluating problem-solving activity: (a) recognizing the existence of a problem, (b) problem definition, and (c) formulating a strategy and mental representation of the solution.

He also describes three knowledge acquisition activities which relate to the specialized creative process of insight: (a) "selective encoding," which is identifying relevant or critical elements in new information, (b) "selective combination," which is synthesizing information into a new, unique, and productive configuration, and (c) "selective comparison" which is the process of relating new information to information or schemata in long-term memory.

These studies and theoretical conceptions of creative problem solving point the way to specific training activities. Houtz and Feldhusen (1976) found that an explicit program of instruction in the 11 fundamental skill components of creativity and problem solving discussed above could be taught to fourth graders. Other research reviewed by Wechsler (this volume) and Runco (1993) attests to the trainability of creative thinking skills and strategies.

Mansfield, Busse, and Krepelka (1978) were quite pessimistic about the effects of creativity training. They concluded that it is often simply creativity test performance rather than true creative thinking that is taught. However, after reviewing all the major published materials designed to teach creative thinking skills, Feldhusen and Clinkenbeard (1986) concluded that positive effects seemed to predominate. The specific skills and strategies that are basic components of creative cognition and problem solving are probably learned most often from parents, siblings, mentors, and teachers who model the skills as well as teach them explicitly. A host of training programs have also been developed to teach general thinking skills (Beyer, 1987; Halpern, 1984; Nickerson, Perkins, & Smith, 1985; Tiedt, Carlson, Howard, & Watanabe, 1989). A general sense of optimism reigns concerning our potential to teach all kinds of thinking including creative thinking and problem-solving skills and strategies. There is also a great deal of caution concerning the need to link the teaching of thinking skills to subject matter and real-life contexts if appropriate transfer to generalized use is to occur (Feldhusen, 1988). Runco (1993) also suggests that the focus of training be chiefly in the actual discipline or field such as creative writing, piano composition, chemistry, or photography, with the creative thinking skills and strategies being taught in the applied context.

Skills and strategies are closely linked to enabling conditions of intelligence and talent which undoubtedly set limits to training and development of these abilities. However, for the present we can be quite optimistic about the possibility of enhancing the fundamental underlying skills which are needed to carry on effective creative cognition and problem solving. Geschka's review (this volume) of creativity training in Eastern and Western Europe confirms the conclusion that creativity training is widely viewed as effective in business and industry. The set of skills which can be taught is well represented in the creative problem-solving model, in the set of 11 factors presented by Speedie et al. (1973), Feldhusen and Houtz (1975) and Feldhusen and Guthrie (1979), and by the six metacognitive skills delineated by Sternberg (1986).

THE KNOWLEDGE BASE

Creative thinking and problem solving are operations performed on information currently arriving and being processed in the cognitive system, drawing on the knowledge base already in the system (see Runco, 1993, for further discussion of the role of the knowledge base). The knowledge base helps us interpret or understand situations or problems confronting us, and it provides specific information and conceptions which we use in adapting, creating, and solving. The knowledge base is also the storage center for the skills and strategies we use to facilitate creative thinking and problem solving. There is no creative thinking or problem solving apart from a knowledge base, but it is probably possible to learn new cognitive strategies and skills as metacognitive operations abstractly before learning how to use them in real knowledge-base contexts or applying them in academic disciplines, the arts, or business and industry.

Glaser (1984) presented the case well for the importance of the knowledge base when he said:

> Much recent work emphasizes a new dimension of difference between individuals who display more or less ability in thinking and problem solving. This dimension is the possession and utilization of an organized body of conceptual and procedural knowledge, and a major component of thinking is seen to be the possession of accessible and usable knowledge. (p. 97)

He went on to suggest that it is large knowledge bases—which are conceptually well organized and which can be used in an efficient, fluent, and relatively automatic manner—that facilitate high-level creative thinking and problem solving. People think, he argued, in terms of what they know. The acquisition of the knowledge base is not a dead storage process. Instead it is always linked, during learning stages, with purposes such as reasoning, predicting, or extrapolating. Thus, we may infer that the best way to acquire the knowledge base is through a dynamic interaction with information and immediate exploration in creative thinking and problem solving with it. Glaser (1984) also acknowledged the critical role of the metacognitive skills of self-regulation and monitoring in both the learning and using stages of creative operations and problem solving.

Knowledge bases are organized conceptually for retrieval and later use or application into schema or complex systems. Productive creative thinkers are able to retrieve and use such schema or systems in solving new problems or in designing new and still more complex or different solution or product systems.

The critical role of the knowledge base is echoed by a number of key creativity researchers. MacKinnon (1978), for example, observed that "creative persons have an unusual capacity to record, retain, and have readily available the experiences of their life history . . . they have a wide range of information at their command" (p. 180).

Sternberg (1988) also stressed the role of the knowledge base in creative thinking when he said:

> The role of intelligence . . . and knowledge would seem to play a role in creativity as well. In particular, it is impossible to have novel ideas about something if one knows nothing about it. One needs knowledge to extend from in order to see how to apply or extend it creatively. (p. 137)

In discussion of creativity, Schank (1988) also suggested that

> The overall premise . . . is that understanding requires an active memory, full of knowledge based on repeated ossified experiences and also full of novel experiences that are unmerged with other events. In order to understand, one must have a set of knowledge structures and experiences that one can draw on as a kind of reference point. (p. 221)

Using "domain" to refer to a discipline or the knowledge base in a particular field Feldman (1988) wrote, "Creative work requires mastery of a domain, but it does not have mastery as an end point; rather, significant extension and transformation of the domain are its goals" (p. 284).

Walberg (1988) reinforced the same basic concept when he said, "Achieving general knowledge and specialized mastery quickly and efficiently not only enables creativity but also allows additional time for its development" (p. 340).

Langley and Jones (1988) placed major stress on the knowledge base and its organization when they argued that:

> Humans possess no general creativity factor. . . . Instead, humans possess a wealth of knowledge structures indexed by concepts that a person judges important. The level of creativity that one exhibits will depend on one's knowledge, one's indexing scheme, and the particular situation in which one finds oneself. One cannot expect to be creative in any domain until one has achieved knowledge of that domain. (p. 199)

It seems apparent that one must become a relative expert in a domain before one can hope to operate creatively or solve significant problems in the domain. There is now a rich base of research on how experts in a field differ from novices. Hoover (1988) concluded his review of that literature by delineating the following characteristics of experts:

1. Experts tend to structure specific knowledge (more so than novices) around the major principles of the domain. They also tend to possess large amounts of domain-specific knowledge as well as specific strategies for solving problems in the domain.

2. Experts tend to have superior domain specific memory capacity facilitated by perceptions and representable as "chunks" built up from vast experiences with a domain. Furthermore, memory appears to be organized hierarchically as a network structure oriented around abstract concepts and specific principles.

3. Experts are more efficient at searching solution space and applying more coherent solution strategies which are driven by domain-specific knowledge.

4. Experts, when solving a problem, tend to construct a physical representation of the problem, allowing them to generate diagrams as an aid in problem representation.

5. Experts tend to use forward-working strategies in solving problems while novices tend to use a backward strategy in analysis.

6. Through problem representation, experts engage specific and appropriate schemata to solve problems, whereas novices' schemata may be incomplete and too incoherent for appropriate problem solving.

Clearly the creative expert has a functional, working grasp of key concepts and information in a domain of knowledge. The expert's knowledge base is well organized to facilitate fluent accessing. The expert is able to represent problems physically or with appropriate schemata. Experts use their knowledge base creatively in solving problems and in designing new systems, complex conceptions, or products.

CONCLUSIONS

Superior general or fluid intelligence is clearly an asset, but not a sufficient condition, for creative cognition, reconceptualization, and problem solving. Crystallized intelligence is represented in our model by the knowledge base and the experts' effective use of the knowledge base in creating and in solving problems. From creative cognition and problem solving to the creative solution or concept there is elaboration, development, synthesis, and development based on a set of production skills appropriate to the domain in which one is operating. Talent within a particular domain represents the unique abilities one has and develops to operate in it. It is akin and precedent to the concept of the "expert" or "expertise."

There are motivating conditions, attitudes, and dispositions which facilitate, drive, or energize creative cognitions and problem solving, such as openness to change, a drive to excel, risk taking, a questioning posture, capacity to delay gratification in favor of distant goals, and being able to tolerate ambiguity and certainty. There are also specific metacognitive skills and strategies which are fundamental abilities in creative cognition, reconceptualization, and problem solving. They include self-monitoring, problem finding and clarification, self-monitoring during creative problem solving, and evaluation or verification skills.

Finally, there is the knowledge base within which creative cognition and problem solving occur. The creative problem solver has a large, fluent, conceptually well-organized knowledge base on which he or she draws selectively to create a new schema or synthesis which solves the problem. The creative individual is a relative expert in a domain who can analyze problems effectively, perceive deficiencies, and envision the outcomes of potential solutions or designs.

Little can be done to increase intelligence, but talent, while partially determined by intelligence, can be nurtured and developed through specific early experiences in a domain. The motivating conditions and dispositions can probably be cultivated by family and school. The specific strategies and metacognitive skills probably can be taught, both by explicit tutelage and by a process of modeling on the part of parents and teachers. The skills and strategies can be introduced in a relatively abstract mode, but they should be linked to specific domains or disciplines to facilitate transfer or generalized use.

As an example, children who are talented in mathematics can be taught advanced math concepts and skills at an early age; they can be taught a variety of metacognitive skills and strategies for identifying problems, detecting critical elements, planning solution strategies, monitoring steps to solution, verifying a final solution, and deriving schema for the solution. Parents and teachers can model all these processes and induce motivation through their enthusiasm for the activities.

The foundation of the creative process is the knowledge base. Intelligence, talent, motivating conditions, and specific skills and strategies operate on or through the knowledge base. Information in the forms of facts, concepts, principles, or schemata must be retrieved selectively and utilized in determining new concepts, new modes of operating, new paradigms, or new performances. Creative experts use their knowledge base well. They grasp and are open to the new configurations that creative cognition may generate. All new creative adaptations or creations enter and become part of the knowledge base.

We can judge capacity for creative thinking only by evaluating the products of thinking or solutions to problems. I agree with Hocevar's (1981) conclusion that

> Peer nominations, supervisor ratings, teacher nominations, and judgments of products are often inadequate indicators of creativity due to the rater's inability to discriminate creativity from other traits. Divergent thinking, biographical characteristics, attitudes and interests, and personality characteristics are best described only as correlates of real life creative behavior, and they should not be taken as direct measures of creativity. In addition, most approaches generally fail to discriminate creativity in one area from creativity in another area. Thus, despite the voluminous literature on the measurement of creativity, a simple and straightforward inventory of creative achievement and activities appears to be more defensible than the more commonly used methods. (p. 459)

Finally, then, how do we judge creative production? What are the criteria? One obvious answer is to wait and let society decide. Over the long haul, good ideas and good inventions will be used and found useful or wanting. Works of art will stand the test of time. Retrospectively, we can say that Edison was a creative inventor, Shakespeare a great creative dramatist, Jonas Salk a creative scientist, and Mozart a highly creative composer. But we often want the more immediate gratification of knowing early on whether a concept or production is creative. Besemer and Treffinger (1981) suggested three basic criteria: (a) novelty, (b) resolution or the extent to which a problem is solved, and (c) elaboration and synthesis, the degree to which the product represents a good gestalt. All three criteria probably require time and consensus to attain reliability.

Creative cognition and production may be cyclical as Dacey

(1989) argued. He presented evidence for six periods in which high creative work may occur:

0–5 years old
11–14 years old
18–20 years old
29–31 years old
40–45 years old
60–65 years old

He noted that large increases in creative cognition and production are not likely in the later years. Early creative activity is most influential in setting the pattern for later years. Then, early establishment of a pattern of creative protection is the best predictor of later and sustained creative production, but bursts are likely in the time frames delineated. Perhaps it is a combination of sustained energy and motivation to create with continuing strength or growth in the five areas described in this chapter that combine to facilitate creative cognition and production throughout the lifespan of some individuals.

REFERENCES

Amabile, T.M. (1983). *The social psychology of creativity.* New York: Springer-Verlag.

Arieti, S. (1976). *Creativity, the magic synthesis.* New York: Basic Books.

Besemer, S.P., & Treffinger, D.J. (1981). Analysis of creative products: Review and syntheses. *Journal of Creative Behavior, 15,* 158–178.

Beyer, B.K. (1987). *Practical strategies for the teaching of thinking.* Boston, MA: Allyn & Bacon.

Bloom, B.S. (1956). Taxonomy of education objectives, Handbook I. *Cognitive domain.* New York: Longmans, Green & Co.

Bloom, B.S. (Ed.). (1985). *Developing talent in young people.* New York: Ballantine Books.

Cattell, R.B. (1971). *Abilities: Their structure, growth and action.* Boston, MA: Houghton-Mifflin.

Cohen, L.M. (1989). A continuum of adaptive creative behaviors. *Creativity Research Journal, 2*(3), 169–183.

Dacey, J.S. (1989). *Fundamentals of creative thinking.* Lexington, MA: D.C. Heath.

Eliot, T.S. (1942). The hollow men. In L. Untermeyer (Ed.), *Modern American poetry, modern British poetry* (pp. 435–436). New York: Harcourt Brace.

Feldhusen, J.F. (1988). Thinking skills and curriculum development. In

J. vanTassel-Baska, J. Feldhusen, K. Seeley, G. Wheatley, L. Silverman, & W. Foster (Eds.), *Comprehensive curriculum for gifted learners* (pp. 314–344). Boston, MA: Allyn & Bacon.

Feldhusen, J.F., & Clinkenbeard, P.R. (1986). Creativity instructional materials: A review of research. *The Journal of Creative Behavior, 20*(3), 153–182.

Feldhusen, J.F., & Guthrie, V.A. (1979). Models of problem solving processes and abilities. *Journal of Research and Development in Education, 12*(2), 22–32.

Feldhusen, J.F., & Houtz, J.C. (1975). Problem solving and the concrete-abstract dimension. *Gifted Child Quarterly, 19*, 122–129.

Feldhusen, J.F., & Treffinger, D.J. (1985). *Creative thinking and problem solving in gifted education.* Dubuque, IA: Kendall-Hunt.

Feldman, D.H. (1986). *Nature's gambit.* New York: Basic Books.

Feldman, D.H. (1988). Creativity: Dreams, insights, and transformations. In R.J. Sternberg (Ed.), *The nature of creativity* (pp. 271–297). New York: Cambridge University Press.

Gagne, F. (1985). Giftedness and talent: Re-examining a re-examination of the definitions. *Gifted Child Quarterly, 29*(3), 103–112.

Gardner, H. (1983). *Frames of mind: The theory of multiple intelligences.* New York: Basic Books.

Glaser, R. (1984). Education and thinking: The role of knowledge. *American Psychologist, 39*(2), 93–104.

Halpern, D.F. (1984). *Thought and knowledge. An introduction to critical thinking.* Hillsdale, NJ: Erlbaum.

Hennessey, B.A., & Amabile, T.M. (1988). The conditions of creativity. In R.J. Sternberg (Ed.), *The nature of creativity* (pp. 11–38). New York: Cambridge University Press.

Hocevar, D. (1981). Measurement of creativity: Review and critique. *Journal of Personality Assessment, 45*, 450–464.

Hoover, S.M. (1988). *An exploratory study of high ability students' problem finding ability.* Unpublished doctoral dissertation, Purdue University, West Lafayette, IN.

Houtz, J.C., & Feldhusen, J.F. (1976). The modification of fourth graders' problem solving abilities. *Journal of Psychology, 93*, 229–237.

Langley, P., & Jones, R. (1988). A computational model of scientific insight. In R.J. Sternberg (Ed.), *The nature of creativity* (pp.177–201). New York : Cambridge University Press.

MacKinnon, D.W. (1978). *In search of human effectiveness.* Buffalo, NY: Creative Education Foundation.

Mansfield, R.S., Busse, T.V., & Krepelka, E.J. (1978). The effectiveness of creativity training. *Review of Educational Research, 48*(4), 517–536.

Milton, J. (1940). Lycidas. In M.E. Speare (Ed.), *The pocket book of verse* (pp. 51–57). New York: Pocket Books.

Nickerson, R.S., Perkins, D.N., & Smith, E.E. (1985). *The teaching of thinking.* Hillsdale, NJ: Erlbaum.

Parnes, S.J. (1967). *Creative behavior guidebook.* New York: Charles Scribner.

Parnes, S.J., Noller, R.B., & Biondi, A.M. (1977). *Guide to creative action.* New York: Charles Scribner.

Perkins, D.N. (1986). *Knowledge as design.* Hillsdale, NJ: Erlbaum.

Perkins, D.N. (1988). The possibility of invention. In R.J. Sternberg (Ed.), *The nature of creativity* (pp. 362–385). New York: Cambridge University Press.

Raina, M.K. (1993). Ethnocentric confines in creativity research. In S.G. Isaksen, M.C. Murdock, R.L. Firestien, & D.J. Treffinger (Eds.), *Understanding and recognizing creativity: The emergence of a discipline* (pp. 235–253). Norwood, NJ: Ablex.

Runco, M.A. (1993). Cognitive and psychometric issues in creativity research. In S.G. Isaksen, M.C. Murdock, R.L. Firestien, & D.J. Treffinger (Eds.), *Understanding and recognizing creativity: The emergence of a discipline* (pp. 331–368). Norwood, NJ: Ablex.

Schank, R.C. (1988). Creativity as a mechanical process. In R.J. Sternberg (Ed.), *The nature of creativity* (pp. 220–238). New York: Cambridge University Press.

Simonton, D.K. (1988). *Scientific genius, a psychology of science.* New York: Cambridge University Press.

Speedie, S.M., Houtz, J.C., Ringenbach, S., & Feldhusen, J.F. (1973). Abilities measured by the Purdue Elementary Problem Solving Inventory. *Psychological Reports, 33,* 959–963.

Sternberg, R.J. (1986). A triarchic theory of intellectual giftedness. In R.J. Sternberg & J.E. Davidson (Eds.), *Conceptions of giftedness* (pp. 223–243). New York: Cambridge University Press.

Sternberg, R.J. (1988). A three-facet model of creativity. In R.J. Sternberg (Ed.), *The nature of creativity* (pp. 125–147). New York: Cambridge University Press.

Tannenbaum, A.J. (1983). *Gifted children: Psychological and educational perspectives.* New York: Macmillan.

Taylor, C.W., & Ellison, R.L. (1983). Searching for student talent resources relevant to our USDE types of giftedness. *Gifted Child Quarterly, 27*(3), 99–106.

Tiedt, I.M., Carlson, J.E., Howard, B.D., & Watanabe, K.S.O. (1989). *Teaching thinking in K-12 classrooms.* Boston, MA: Allyn & Bacon.

Torrance, E.P. (1962). *Guiding creative talent.* Englewood Cliffs, NJ: Prentice-Hall.

Treffinger, D.J (1982). *Encouraging creative learning for the gifted and talented.* Ventura, CA: Ventura County Superintendent of Schools, LTI Publications.

Walberg, H.J. (1988). Creativity and talent as learning. In R.J. Sternberg (Ed.), *The nature of creativity* (pp. 340–361). New York: Cambridge University Press.

Walberg, H.J., Rasher, S.P., & Hase, K. (1978). IQ correlates with high eminence. *Gifted Child Quarterly, 22,* 196–200.

Wallas, G. (1926). *The art of thought.* New York: Harcourt Brace.

3

Implications of Problem Finding on Teaching and Learning

Michael T. Moore

*"Unconfusion submits
its confusion to proof"*

"The mind is an enchanting thing."
—Marianne Moore

CONFUSION TO PROOF

The problem with problem finding is that no one seems to agree where it begins or ends. Confusion stems from the knowledge that until a problem is posed, a solution is not needed. The solution is proof of the need for the problem. Frederiksen (1984) suggested that the problem solver begin by encoding the problem statement and constructing a representation of the problem. But problem finding need not either begin or end at these stages. Problem finding's birth is at the preconscious confusion where a gap (Henle, 1974) is sensed. Problem finding's recursive nature suggests that it is not completed even with the solution since solutions to creative problems often open the way for more gaps. Smilansky and Halberstadt (1986) report data that support the notion that "creativity is, in part, the ability to pose high-level problems and questions" (p. 199). Their research dispels the idea that the production of a large quantity of original responses does not seem to be a useful indication for the ability to be creative.

Getzels and Csikszentmihalyi (1976), Dillon (1982, 1985), and Subotnik and Moore (1988) in their respective reviews of the literature on problem finding agreed with the many and varied definitions of problem finding. The proof in the studies they reviewed has thus far been descriptive. The most innovative proof, however, is in the transformation of the originally posed problem into an entire new set of transformations leading to a new series of, as yet, unposed problems. When these descriptive studies begin to cross fields of study, when posed problems fuse and blend with other posed problems, when the tip of the iceberg reveals not an iceberg but a continent, only then can we realize that problem finding can no more be broken apart from creativity than creativity can be broken from experience or the synthesis resulting from life experiences. When a teacher sees a student's furrowed brow and senses confusion, as yet a problem is still to be formed, but a gap at a preconscious level exists. Tolstoy (1967) wrote,

> The best teacher will be he who has at his tongue's end the explanation of what it is that is bothering the pupil. These explanations give the teacher the knowledge of the greatest number of methods, the ability of inventing new methods and, above all, not a blind adherence to one method but the conviction that all methods are one-sided, and that the best method would be the one which answers best to all possible difficulties incurred by a pupil, that is, not a method but an art and talent.

When that newly discovered method becomes the basis for the formulation of another problem posed by the grown student for another student, then we understand that these transformations are never complete.

PROBLEM FINDING AND TEACHING

The ways teachers reason knowledge into accessible forms and the ways this knowledge is represented form the heart of teacher education (Borko & Livingstone, 1989; Shulman, 1987). This ability is relatively undeveloped in novice teachers (Feiman-Nemser & Buchmann, 1986). Although teacher-education programs try mightily to bridge this experiential gap, what is useful to a practitioner may not be accessible to or hold much meaning for a novice (deGroot, 1965; Egan & Schwartz, 1979) because experienced teachers appear to represent problems differently. They tend to see problems embedded within several contexts rather than as discrete entities; they appear to make better use of managerial structures and routines; and they tend to be recursive in the ways they form and solve classroom problems (see, for example, Berliner, 1987; Borko & Livingstone, 1989; Clark &

Yinger, 1987; Cochran-Smith & Lytle, 1990; Leinhardt & Greeno, 1986; Moore, 1990; Schoenfeld & Hermann, 1982).

Problem Finding and the Culture of Teaching

Paulo Freire called culture a "form of production" which represents lived experiences and whose processes are bound by the structuring of social formations that helps us to "transform society" through language and other material resources (Freire, 1985).

The culture of teaching is bound by the thinking, planning, and decisions made by teachers as they interpret the structure of curriculum and act on pedagogical formations. Central to the culture of teaching is the notion of problem finding as a subset of Wallas's (1926) preparation stage in his four-part creative problem-solving paradigm (cf. Subotnik & Moore, 1988). In education, for instance, there is a very ill-defined notion of the problems facing teachers as they prepare to teach. Often there are a variety of ways of both problem posing and problem solving. McKay and Marland (1978) noted that teachers make about ten significant decisions per hour for example, when to move from studying fractions to studying decimals or whether a student should be moved from group A to group B. In addition to the significant problems, there are the myriad additional problems, such as when to collect lunch money and who should stand next to whom in the bus line. Donald Schon (1983) in *The Reflective Practitioner* reflected on the artistry of this stage, "If it is true that there is an irreducible element of art in professional practice, it is also true that gifted engineers, teachers, scientists, architects, and managers sometimes display artistry in their day to day practice . . . professional practice has as much to do with finding the problem as with solving the problem found" (p. 18).

Although there is much literature on the types of problems teachers face (Veenman, 1984), there is little on how teachers discover problems to be solved. Teachers possess not only knowledge about a subject area, but also insightful knowledge about teaching (Leinhardt, 1990). The task is not to determine what teachers know about a subject or even to list what they know about teaching, but, rather to determine what teachers have learned through experience in solving a wide variety of problems in multiple contexts and whether this experiential knowledge can be transferred to novices. The nature of the problems teachers face are complex and multistaged. A student's anxious expression may reflect a comprehension problem, or it may reflect a social problem which is affecting comprehension. Thus, by sensing the emerging problem, the teacher can find the real problem and solve it before it develops into a classroom disturbance.

Cognitive Processes and Improvisation in Teaching

Knowledge that experienced teachers bring to bear on problematic contexts falls into two frameworks (Borko & Livingstone, 1989). The first framework characterizes teachers problem solving as the result of complex cognitive processing. Shulman (1987) referred to this as the process of transforming subject matter "into forms that are pedagogically powerful and yet adaptive to the variations in ability and background presented by the students" (p. 15). He referred to this knowledge as a blending of content and pedagogy which is then applied to how problems and issues are organized, represented, and adapted to learners' abilities.

Central to this framework is the concept of "schema" as a complex knowledge structure that summarizes what the teacher has stored from experience allowing adaptable application to new problems (Anderson, 1984; Shavelson, 1986). Leinhardt and Greeno (1986) stated, "a skilled teacher has a complex knowledge structure composed of interrelated sets of organized actions" (p. 75). Brown, Collins, and Duguid (1989) referred to this as "situated cognition." They claimed that "The activity in which knowledge is developed and deployed is not separable from or ancillary to learning and cognition . . . it is an integral part of what is learned. Situations might be said to co-produce knowledge through activity" (p. 32). Thus, the schema of experienced teachers can be said to be more elaborate, more complex, more accessible, and more interconnected than the schema of novices (Borko & Shavelson, in press; Leinhardt, 1986; Moore, 1990).

The second framework draws upon the metaphor of improvisational performance (Borko & Livingstone, 1989). Teachers can be said to begin a "performance" with background knowledge or "scripts." These scripts are composites of previous performances, routines, extensive patterns, and sensitivity to audience. The performer then creates a tailored performance depending on a variety of external variables. For instance, a math teacher who has planned to begin a new unit on decimals and who has created a script allowing for a certain amount of introductory work, may see furrowed brows and worried looks and thus improvise the routine to spend much more time at the introductory stage. This second framework operates in much the same way as the first framework in that it provides an integrated way to understand and explain the effects of teacher experience on problem contexts.

Problem Finding and Teacher Experience

Only a few studies (Allender, 1969; Arlin, 1976; Berliner, 1987; Getzels & Csikszentmihalyi, 1976; Michael, 1977; Moore, 1985, 1990; Shulman, 1964; Subotnik, 1984) have attempted to examine how problems are raised and what the relationship may be between the problems raised and their solutions.

Shulman's (1964) study with 21 teacher trainees who raised potential problems from a teacher's in-basket established that problem sensing can be observed and quantified, and that problem-sensing ability is related to observable cognitive behavior.

Getzels and Csikszentmihalyi (1976) and Moore (1985) studied artists and student writers, respectively. Both studies made use of a table with many common objects that somehow had to be worked into the solution of the drawn or written product. Subjects were encouraged to manipulate or otherwise examine the objects prior to painting or writing, and the relationships between their "problem finding" behaviors and their final products were studied. The Getzels and Csikszentmihalyi (1976) study established a realistic and reasonable method for studying problem finding at two stages, problem formulation and problem solution as a behavior preceding problem solving.

Moore (1985), using the same procedure, found a similar relationship with student writers, who remarkably resembled art students in problem-finding behavior. He suggested that the objects used in both studies and the way subjects were observed examining them may be a manifestation of the way writers and artists synthesize life experiences and analyze feelings, which, in turn, may provide a glimpse at the unobservable ways people analyze and synthesize.

Michael (1977), in his study of the models of the problem-solving process, proposed that previous models were too linear to describe the continuous feedback loops taking place at each step of the process. Michael suggested that problem finding may occur at different evaluation points, such as choosing a solution and in problem reformulation.

Berliner (1987) studied nine experienced teachers, six student teachers, and six postulants who had college degrees and wanted to teach. His subjects role played being assigned an additional math or science class from a teacher who left abruptly. Subjects could examine a short note from the teacher, a grade book with grades and attendance, student information cards, and the textbook. From these, experienced teachers and novices had 40 minutes to prepare for a debriefing session and write a lesson plan for two days of work. A study of the protocols collected during this experiment led Berliner to conclude that experienced teachers differed from postulants in profound ways. He stated that experienced teachers operate from fully developed student schemas. Experienced teachers' memories are organized differently, their perceptions are different, and what they remember appears more functional. Berliner noted that expert/experienced teachers were less interested in learning specific information about students and instead merged information into a group picture. Expert/experienced teachers indicated that they would likely disregard most of what was left by the previous teacher, whereas novices were more likely to hold on to the information left. Expert/experienced teachers appeared to have routines that they employed for beginning instruction while novices attempted to apply incomplete routines. Finally, "Experts generally appeared to attend in greater detail and a substantially deeper level than novices and postulants to content, instructional, and curricular issues that 'surfaced' in the homework and test information that was left for them" (p. 74).

Problem Finding and Teacher Experience: A Study of 30 Novice and Experienced Teachers

The purpose of this article is to discuss a cross-case analysis of the thinking and actions of novice and experienced teachers in order to explore the relationship between cognitive processes and teacher improvisation strategies and the differences between experienced teachers and novices in the way the knowledge structures change (for the analysis of the data from this study, see Moore, 1990). An experimental problem context was developed to simulate a task often encountered by teachers. The 30 teachers, singly, were presented with this scenario: "You have been asked to take over a classroom for a colleague who has been called away unexpectedly. The room is exactly as she left it at the close of school the day before." In fact, the simulated class was based on a real third-grade class, and a room and teacher's desk were recreated exactly as the real class with the same books, materials, plan book, and grade book. The subjects were told that students would be arriving soon and that they should begin making plans to take over the class. When they felt ready, the principal would come in and answer any questions they might have. All subjects were interviewed after the experimental session.

PROBLEM FINDING AS A COMPLEX COGNITIVE PROCESS

Planning

Berliner (1987) reported three observations in his study of experienced/expert teachers, novices, and postulants. Expert/experienced teachers were more critical of the previous teacher. His experienced teachers held a different conception of how to begin planning to take over the class and they seemed to have established routines for beginning class. Finally, his experts had a different conception about the kinds of information students could provide them.

Like Berliner's expert/experienced teachers, experienced teachers in this study, although not openly critical of the previous teacher's lack of clear plans, were certainly not intimidated by the sparse directions. The plan book left by the teacher was on the desktop under the grade book. All of the experienced teachers found it right away. Most of the student teachers also found it immediately. Half of the prestudent-teaching subjects did not find it or did not open it. These subjects expressed concern about going through another teacher's belongings. These novices tended to rely on the interview with the principal to answer planning questions. The plan book itself was cryptic in that it contained only subjects and page numbers. The plans did not reveal dates or days of the week. Experienced teachers were not intimidated by the lack of plans. They opened the plan book to the last page and tended to work backward by days. They did not appear to be very interested in any of the planning before the last few days.

The protocols and videotapes revealed that experienced teachers clearly differed from student teachers and that student teachers differed slightly from pre-student-teaching subjects. Experienced teachers were far less intimidated by their surroundings and another teacher's desk. Experienced teachers were often unconcerned about individual student differences or specific information about students. Instead, they launched complex search procedures through the room and desk, merging information into a sense of the whole class as an entity, whereas both groups of novices were concerned about individual grades, test scores, and anecdotal information. Only the experienced teachers were concerned about school routines, class routines, material to be covered, and availability of materials.

Jackie, an experienced middle-grade teacher, began by initiating a sequenced search of the teacher's desk. Starting from left to right, she examined each book briefly and settled on the plan book and grade/attendance book which she placed open, one on the other. She rifled through the teacher's in-basket, pulling items and stacking these for further examination. She then started with the top-left desk drawer and examined each drawer, pulling folders and items to add to her stack. Once her search was complete, she sat at the desk. Using the contents of a folder from the center desk drawer, Jackie proceeded to make notes on a yellow pad. She would refer from the folder to various textbooks and to activity sheets taken from the in-basket. After making notes and quickly searching through the desk again, she indicated that she had some questions for the principal. Jackie raised seven questions, and as she posed problems, she also offered solutions— a total of 14 solutions to her seven problems. Her questions were about the routines the children followed and about locations like the bus line and the lunch line. She indicated that once she found the teacher's schedule she was able to make appropriate plans for the students' arrival.

The center desk drawer contained a detailed timetable of the typical class day and structure in a folder mislabeled "assertive discipline." None of the pre-student-teaching subjects found the folder, one of the student teachers found it, and five experienced teachers found the folder. Knowing the daily schedule changed the nature of the problems raised. The post hoc interview revealed that of those who found the folder, all were looking for some type of daily structure and felt that one should exist somewhere in the problem context. These teachers then tended to ask more content-loaded questions and felt free to improvise on both the schedule and content. This may be because they knew the schedule. The questions reflecting improvisation of content and schedule resulted in more complex questions as measured by the Guilford

Structure of the Intellect Model Intellectual Products Categories (Guilford, 1956, 1976). Experienced teachers reflected a "situated knowledge" of teachers' routines. These teachers appeared to know where to look, thus reflecting their experience. The differences among the three groups are clearly shown in the interviews.

Experienced Teachers

Jackie: I finally found the schedule and that was a help and I was wondering what daily plans I had to follow . . . Um . . . I didn't know if there were any other reports I needed to turn in like the lunch report at the lunch counter or whatever.

Cheryl (Reading plan book): There appears to be a self-contained classroom and she covers all the subjects. The planning book shows where they left off at a certain point in time and I think I can go from there.

Debbie (Reading plan book): They are all self-contained. It looks like its all here.

Responses from student teachers and pre-student-teaching novices were much different. Serious attention was given to the lack of plans. Comments at the principal's interview indicated that novices did not feel they could go on without adequate plans. Student teachers did not, for the most part, attempt to "second guess" the teacher.

Student Teachers

Susan: I would like to have a complete list of plans with an adequate amount of work for the students, adequate instructions and materials for myself, a list of the class names with seating chart, a time chart knowing when to go to lunch, when buses arrive, time for activities, time for each subject, etc.

Yvette: OK, the first thing is I guess is, did the teacher leave plans with (the) principal like the written plans other than the plans left? That would leave the substitute with not knowing how the teacher wanted to go about teaching whatever the skills were for the day. It doesn't say which day it was so I just kinda look through each book and each day's activities, and you know . . . it didn't say which day or anything.

Pre-student-teaching novices appeared overwhelmed by the problem context. Even the ones who explored the problem context could not formulate a strategy from the plan and materials in and on the desk. Not surprisingly, therefore, these novices tended to signal for the principal very soon after examining the desk's materials. Their interviews with the principal indicated that they were totally relying on the principal to tell them what to do. Only one of the ten had formulated any plans from the materials.

Pre-Student-Teaching Novices

Kim: What are they gonna do? What are they doing while I'm in here?

Theresa: Do I choose the activities that are not specifically in the plan book?

Mary: I don't know if I did what I was supposed to do. Really, in my opinion, there was nothing here that I could follow through with. Um . . . the basic problem would be what I'm supposed to teach or how I'm supposed to guide the children.

PROBLEM FINDING AS AN IMPROVISATIONAL PROCESS

Borko and Livingston (1989), in their study of expert and novice math teachers, developed the metaphor of teaching as improvisational performance, describing it as a means by which teachers use "scripts" or general outlines of lessons that are filled in through interaction and response to student performance.

Teachers' abilities to find and solve problems in a classroom context could also be viewed as an ability to improvise from a variety of possible problems and outcomes. In this problem context, teachers had only what was left them from the previous teacher. Like experienced teachers in previous studies (e.g., Borko & Livingston, 1989; McCutcheon, 1980; Morine-Dershimer, 1978–1979), teachers reported that much of their planning occurred outside of formal planning and was never written down. The teacher whose desk served as the problem context exemplified this. She left only page numbers to serve as script guides. Experienced teachers who encountered this problem context appeared to be able to improvise lesson content from page numbers, whereas student teachers attempted to improvise but generally gave up, and pre-student-teaching subjects could only role play the part of teacher.

Thinking About the Problem Context

During the principal's session, each teacher was asked what questions she had first, and then what she considered the most important problems to be solved before the students arrived (see Appendix B). An analysis of their responses revealed that experienced teachers asked significantly fewer questions than either novice group. This was contrary to what one would expect. Experienced teachers ought to ask more and better questions. Nevertheless, problem finding as an improvisational act might be examined through this unanticipated result of the study. Even though experienced teachers asked fewer questions, they generated significantly more solutions to the questions they raised, even though solutions were never requested. Each problem posed by experienced teachers was often accompanied by several possible solutions. These may be seen as incomplete outlines that would be completed, as Borko and Livingston (1989) suggested, through interaction with first the principal and later the students. When the questions raised by the subjects were examined using the Guilford Structure of the Intellect Product Categories (Guilford, 1956, 1976; see Appendix C), the experienced teachers' questions were complicated, higher order questions, indicating concern for the routines, systems, implications and transformations involved in teaching. Both groups of novices were primarily concerned with units of information and class levels.

Susan, Gwen, and Mary are all experienced teachers who improvised a flexible plan from the problem context. Their protocols indicate concern for solving rather than just presenting problems. All three experienced teachers also are concerned with class routine and the rhythm of the day. All three indicate that their improvised scripts are adapted from other contexts and are open to change.

Susan: OK . . . I can start off my day with my lab . . . I could start off with my math, and I knew if nothing else, I could bring my science up and do my science and surely I would have lunch or something that I could speak with somebody about language arts models support. If need be, I would switch subjects and do whatever best fits the situation.

Gwen: Well, I just . . . as I said, I checked the lesson plans the teacher had left and quickly just ran through my mind the needs for the day and the time schedule that she had and be sure the academic areas had been covered and it looked as though everything was there, so I knew I had covered everything. I might have a problem later but at this time I do not anticipate any.

Mary: I would start with something going by a routine that maybe I would set. You know, even if it wasn't the routine the teacher had set. You start somewhere.

Experienced teachers' readiness to improvise, their flexibility in planning, their embedded solutions in their questions, and their lack of intimidation by the problem context is sharply contrasted with both groups of novices. When asked what they were thinking about during planning, both groups of novices appeared apprehensive about meeting the students.

Student Teachers

Yvette: Just what was missing, like what's missing in this puzzle or something. What do I need to know that I don't know by sitting here?

Danette: Will it tell you in that book how to use it? And you don't know where the tests come from?

Lisa: Yes, the fact that these (plans) weren't detailed. I couldn't teach, you know, if I didn't have detailed plans and this was a little bit confusing, these plans are. It seems like there are a lot of different things going on at different days. This is very confusing.

Gaye: I assume that this is the order (referring to plan book) that these courses are taught. I don't see any time so I couldn't know how long to spend on each one. I would need to find out.

Pre-Student-Teaching Novices

Eleanor: When I started feeling desperate, when I realized that if I didn't even know the sequence that I was teaching or what I was teaching or where in the book that would be and also that the students were expected quickly or soon.

Amy: Can I be creative and use my own style of teaching as long as it meets the curriculum requirements?

Mary: Really, in my opinion, there was nothing here that I could follow through with.

Valerie: It's just pages from the chapters. There's no real, you know, explanation of what I should do with the chapters.

TOWARD A MODEL OF PROBLEM FINDING AND
TEACHER EXPERIENCE

Although models of teachers' instructional activity have been formulated (Bromme, 1987; Peterson & Clark, 1978; Shavelson & Stern, 1981) none of these overtly deal with teachers' ability to find or sense emerging problems. How teachers sense problems in as ill-defined a domain as education is certainly open to speculation. However, studying problem finding in teaching may provide a window into the thought processes of experienced and novice teachers, even though this window is nearly opaque. A model of problem finding and teacher experience must take into consideration not only the recursive nature of problem finding and planning, but also a notion of consensus of appropriate problem generation and solution.

The evidence from this study indicated that among experienced teachers there may be a consensus of what experienced teachers should have in their classrooms. This consensus revealed knowledge of what may be termed "the collective student" (Bromme, 1987). This knowledge reflects both experience in problem finding and experience in planning. A general model of problem finding and teaching could be analogous to extensions in other domains (e.g., diagnosis in medicine, trouble shooting in electronics) to the extent that experience relies on knowledge of expert systems. This knowledge then allows for improvisation and interaction with the problem context. Problems in teaching may be sensitive to knowledge of expert systems and consensus due to the ill-formed notion of the impression of the collective student. The Intellectual Products Categories weighted scores revealed that experienced teachers relied on an experienced/expert knowledge of both classroom systems and knowledge of the collective student. Thus, the data from this study suggest that problem finding in teaching may rely on activation of "consensus" knowledge that experienced teachers share, in addition to a reliance on knowledge of expert/experienced teaching systems allowing experienced teachers a different cognitive approach of which novice teachers were unaware.

IMPLICATIONS FOR FUTURE RESEARCH

This report has dealt with only problem-finding behavior between three groups varying on teacher experience. Moore (1985) wrote:

> If touching objects, manipulating objects or otherwise inspecting objects is a manifestation of the way writers and artists analyze feelings and synthesize life experience, then touching and manipulating (the observables) may provide us a window for studying the unobservable ways students analyze and synthesize. (p. 94)

Experienced teachers and student teachers differ from those subjects who have no teaching experience on the "observables." Future research should focus on whether, indeed, the observables do affect the solution to the problem. However, this study has also raised new research concerns: When do student teachers begin to resemble experienced teachers in their cognitive strategies in the approach to a problem? Is this change gradual or sudden? What role does observation play in this change? When student teachers are actually in front of children, do they shift cognitive strategies and start operating from a situational schema? What are the characteristics of students who possess these different change patterns? Are the behaviors of student teachers a function of experience, or observation or both? Is there a knowledge of the collective student? How is this knowledge assimilated? Is problem finding in teaching analogous to problem finding in art, medicine, or writing?

To what extent is a cognitive apprenticeship appropriate in developing skill in sensing emerging classroom problems? Is such an apprenticeship equally useful to physicians, artists, or physicists? To what extent do other professionals improvise in their work? Why or why not? Do students change faster if they teach sooner? How do student teachers activate behaviors which resemble experienced teachers? Why are student teachers seemingly so different from pre-student-teaching students, especially since the subjects were similar in both educational backgrounds and ages? What aspects of the student teaching experience cause such a cognitive shift?

Further research is necessary to determine whether others can identify the three groups of subjects by their responses to these problem solution variables. If, for instance, administrators and experienced teachers can differentiate between the three groups, then perhaps there are aspects of experience and problem-finding ability that could be further studied. Perhaps a more important question is whether novices can differentiate between experienced teachers and other novices. If novices lack experience, then it would seem reasonable that they could not recognize the situational behaviors in other groups. However, if they are able to distinguish between experienced teachers and novices, this may reflect that this particular type of knowing is not situational, but it is knowledge structured, stored, and retrieved differently.

If it is accepted that experience aids in the ability to successfully formulate ill-structured problems, can these improvisational formulas be taught? Frederiksen (1984) suggested that, "We know little about how to teach students to develop representations of ill-structured problems, to develop plans for solving such problems, or to employ appropriate strategies or heuristic approaches" (p. 396). Perhaps there are processes and heuristics we learn from cognitive apprenticeship that we can teach or simulate, or perhaps these processes and techniques can only be learned in situational manners. If the former is true, then educational situations for our novice teachers could be enhanced so that such processes and heuristics could be discovered more easily.

The real goal, then, is to determine when teachers become teachers. Student teachers differed from pre-student-teaching subjects, although these two groups are similar in chronological age. Thus, it would seem that the student-teaching experience does at least begin to prepare students to find and solve classroom problems. However, they were still significantly different from the experienced teachers.

Such research will eventually help us determine whether we are adequately preparing education students for student teaching. More importantly, it may help us determine whether content and methods courses help students structure knowledge about teaching or whether such knowledge can only exist after several years of teaching.

REFERENCES

Allender, J.S. (1969). A study of inquiry activity in elementary school children. *American Educational Research Journal, 6,* 543–558.

Anderson, R.C. (1984). Some reflection on the acquisition of knowledge. *Educational Researcher, 13*(9), 5–10.

Arlin, P.K. (1976). A cognitive process model of problem finding. *Educational Horizons,* 99–106.

Berliner, D.C. (1987). Ways of thinking about students and classrooms by more and less experienced teachers. In J. Calderhead (Ed.), *Exploring teachers thinking* (pp. 60–83). London: Cassell.

Borko, H., & Livingston, C. (1989). Cognition and improvisation: Differences in mathematics instruction by expert and novice teachers.

American Educational Research Journal, 26, 473–498.

Borko, H., & Shavelson, R.J. (in press). Teachers' decision making. In B. Jones & L. Idols (Eds.), *Dimensions of thinking and cognitive instruction.* Hillsdale, NJ: Erlbaum.

Bromme, R. (1987). Teachers' assessments of student difficulties and progress in understanding in the classroom. In J. Calderhead (Ed.), *Exploring teachers' thinking* (pp. 125–146). London: Cassell.

Brown, J.S., Collins, A., & Duguid, P. (1989). Situated cognition and the culture of learning. *Educational Researcher, 18,* 32–42.

Clark, C.M., & Yinger, R.J. (1987). Teacher planning. In J. Calderhead (Ed.), *Exploring teachers' thinking* (pp. 84–103). London: Cassell.

Cochran-Smith, M., & Lytle, S. (1990). Research on teaching and teacher research: The issues that divide. *Educational Researcher, 19,* 2–11.

deGroot, A.D. (1965). *Thought and choice in chess.* The Hague: Mouton.

Dillon, J.T. (1982). Problem finding and solving. *Journal of Creative Behavior, 16,* 97–111.

Dillon, J.T. (1985). *An exploration into problem finding.* Unpublished manuscript, University of California, Riverside.

Egan, D.E., & Schwartz, B.J. (1979). Chunking in recall of symbolic drawings. *Memory and Cognition, 7,* 149–158.

Feiman-Nemser, S., & Buchmann, M. (1986). The first year of teacher preparation: Transition to pedagogical thinking? *Journal of Curricular Studies, 18,* 239–256.

Frederiksen, N. (1984). Implications of cognitive theory for instruction in problem solving. *Review of Educational Research, 54*(3), 363–407.

Friere, P. (1985). *The politics of education: Culture, power and liberation.* South Hadley, MA: Bergin & Garvey.

Getzels, J.W., & Csikszentmihalyi, M. (1976). *The creative vision: A longitudinal study of problem finding in art.* New York: Wiley.

Guilford, J.P. (1956). The structure of the intellect. *Psychological Bulletin, 53,* 267–293.

Guilford, J.P. (1976). Factor analysis, intellect, and creativity. In A. Rothenberg & C.R. Hausman (Eds.), *The creativity question* (pp. 200–208). Durham, NC: Duke University Press.

Henle, M. (1974). The snail beneath the shell. In S. Rosner & L.E. Alit (Eds.), *Essays in creativity.* New York: North Riner Press.

Leinhardt, G. (1990). Capturing craft knowledge in teaching. *Educational Researcher, 19,* 18–25.

Leinhardt, G. (1986, April). *Math lessons: A contrast of novice and expert competence.* Paper presented at the annual meeting of the American Educational Research Association, San Francisco, CA.

Leinhardt, G., & Greeno, J.G. (1986). The cognitive skill of teaching. *Journal of Educational Psychology, 78,* 75–95.

McCutcheon, G. (1980). How do elementary school teachers plan? The nature of planning and influences on it. *Elementary School Journal, 81,* 4–23.

McKay, D.A., & Marland, P.W. (1978, April). *Thought processes of teachers*. Paper presented at Annual Meeting of the American Education Research Association, Toronto, Canada.

Michael, W.B. (1977). Cognitive and affective components of creativity in mathematics and the physical sciences. In J.C. Stanley, W.C. Solano, & C.H. George (Eds.), *The gifted and creative: A fifty year perspective*. Baltimore, MD: Johns Hopkins University Press.

Moore, M.T. (1985). The relationship between the originality of essays and variables in the problem discovery process: A study of creative and noncreative middle school students. *Research in the Teaching of English, 19*(1), 84–95.

Moore, M.T. (1990). Problem finding and teacher experience. *Journal of Creative Behavior, 24,* 39–58.

Morine-Dershimer, G. (1978–1979). Planning and classroom reality: An in-depth look. *Educational Research Quarterly, 3,* 83–99.

Peterson, P.L., & Clark, C.M. (1978). Teachers' reports of their cognitive processes during teaching. *American Educational Research Journal, 15,* 555–565.

Shavelson, R.J. (1986). *Interactive decision making: Some thoughts on teacher cognition*. Invited address, I Congreso Internacional, "Pensamientos de los Profesores y Toma de Decisiones," Seville, Spain.

Shavelson, R.J., & Stern, P. (1981). Research on teachers' pedagogical thoughts, judgements, decisions, and behavior. *Review of Educational Research, 51*(4), 455–498.

Schon, D. (1983). *The reflective practitioner: How professionals think in action*. New York: Basic Books.

Schoenfeld, A.II., & Hermann, D.J. (1982). Problem perception and knowledge structure in expert and novice mathematical problem solvers. *Journal of Experimental Psychology, 8,* 484–494.

Shulman, L.S. (1987). Knowledge and teaching: Foundations of the new reform. *Harvard Educational Review, 57,* 1–22.

Shulman, L.S. (1964). Seeking styles and individual differences in patterns of inquiry. *School Review, 73,* 258–266.

Smilansky, J., & Halberstadt, N. (1986). Inventors versus problem solvers: An empirical investigation. *Journal of Creative Behavior, 20,* 183–201.

Subotnik, R. (1984). *Scientific Creativity: 1983 Westinghouse Science Talent Winners' problem finding behavior*. Unpublished dissertation, University of Washington, Seattle.

Subotnik, R.F., & Moore, M.T. (1988). Literature on problem finding. *Questioning Exchange, 2*(2), 87–93.

Tolstoy, L. (1967). On teaching the rudiments. In L. Wiener (Ed.), *Tolstoy on education*. Chicago, IL: University of Chicago Press.

Veenman, S. (1984). Perceived problems of beginning teachers. *Review of Educational Research, 54*(2), 143–178.

Wallas, G. (1926). *The art of thought*. London: C.A. Watts.

APPENDIX A

PRINCIPAL'S INTERVIEW

1. Do you have any questions?
2. What are the problems that you feel you will have to solve and how will you solve them?
3. What are the most important problems? Least important?
4. Are you ready for the students to arrive?

APPENDIX B

POST HOC INTERVIEW QUESTIONS

1. Why did you write what you did? Why did you raise the problems that you did?
2. What were you thinking while you were planning? What were your major concerns?
3. How did you begin your planning?
4. As you were going through the desk, did you know what you were going to do?
5. What did you think about before you started planning/writing?
6. What did you choose on the desk to help you formulate the problem?
7. How did subsequent problems arise? Were they from the first ones? Are they connected? How do you think they are connected?
8. How did you get your ideas?
9. Did you change your mind as you planned? How? When?
10. Did you revise any of your plans or writing?
11. Would the responses of others have any effect on your own problems or plans?
12. How did you know when you were done?

APPENDIX C

INTELLECTUAL PRODUCT CATEGORIES
EXAMPLES

1. **Units:** Does she take class roll each period?

2. **Classes:** What level class will I be working with? Are they above average students or lower combination?
3. **Relations:** She's got down here Decoding, Composition, and Research, and right here she's got ATT and language experience, phonics, spelling, are these the same things? Does decoding go with ATT?
4. **Systems:** When the kids first came depending on the day of the week it was I would probably have to collect some kind of lunch money in the third grade. So, I didn't know what the procedure would be.
5. **Transformations:** Composition, I wonder what I was supposed to do there? I guess this (picking up worksheet from in-basket) can be used for language and also for that (composition).
6. **Implications:** There is nothing here in the plan book about social studies but I noticed they have social studies so I looked at the book and I'm familiar with the theories so . . . I can do that.

4

Developing Creative Productivity Through the Enrichment Triad Model

Joseph S. Renzulli
Sally M. Reis

I would argue that the starting point, indeed the bedrock of all studies of creativity, is an analysis of creative products, a determination of what it is that makes them different from more mundane products.

—MacKinnon, 1987, p. 12

In the several years during which the Enrichment Triad Model (Renzulli, 1977) has been used as the basis for educational programs for high-potential students, we have witnessed an unusually large number of remarkable examples of creative productivity on the part of young people whose educational experiences have been guided by this plan. Like most other people involved in the development of theories and generalizations, we did not fully understand at the outset of our work the full implications of the model. These implications relate most directly to teacher training, resource procurement and management, product evaluation, and a host of theoretical concerns (e.g., motivation, task commitment, self-efficacy) that probably would have gone unexamined, undeveloped, and unrefined without the favorable results that were reported to us by early users of the model. This is a nice way of saying that we were really flying by the seat of our pants in the early days and probably should have been satisfied with the positive results that seemed to be accruing. But contrary to the popular philosophy—if it ain't busted, don't fix it—we were heady with initial results and intuitively followed the Japanese concept of Kaizan—look for every possible way to introduce better ways of doing it. If teacher A consistently produced high levels of creative productivity in students, how could we capture that technology and replicate it in teachers B through Z? And if a particular category of resources proved to be consequential in promoting desirable results, how could we generalize that category and make it available to larger numbers of teachers and students? And, of course, we became increasingly interested in why the model was working and how we could further expand the theoretical rationale underlying our work. Thus, several years of research and field testing, and an examination of the work of other theorists has brought us to the point of tying together the material presented in this chapter.

The chapter is divided into three parts. In Part I we provide a brief description of the Enrichment Triad Model and two case studies that illustrate the model in action. This section also includes a summary of research studies that have been carried out on various aspects of the model. In Part II we discuss the work of selected theorists who have contributed to the further development of the rationale underlying the model. In Part III we focus our attention on research related to product evaluation because that is the dimension of the model that represents what is considered to be the pure payoff of our workcreative productivity. This part includes our own efforts to develop a set of criteria for evaluating the creative products of young people.

THE ENRICHMENT TRIAD MODEL: AN OVERVIEW AND CASE STUDIES

The Enrichment Triad Model (see Figure 4.1) has been field tested and used in various types and sizes of school districts across the country for the last 15 years. It was designed to encourage creative productivity on the part of young people by exposing them to various topics, areas of interest, and fields of study; and to further train them to *apply* advanced content, process-training skills, and methodology training to self-selected areas of interest. Accordingly, three types of enrichment are included in the Enrichment Triad Model.

Type I enrichment is designed to expose students to a wide variety of disciplines, topics, occupations, hobbies, persons, places, and events that would not ordinarily be covered in the regular curriculum. In schools that use this model, an enrichment team consisting of parents, teachers, and students often organizes and plans Type I experiences by contacting speakers, arranging minicourses, demonstrations, or performances, or by ordering

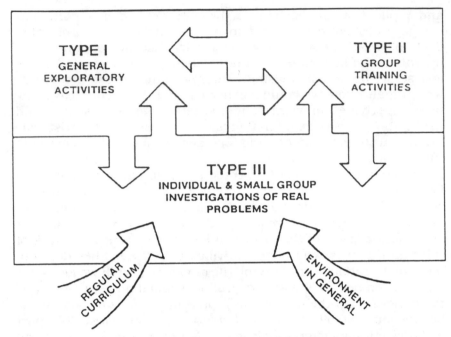

Figure 4.1. The Enrichment Triad Model

and distributing films, slides, videotapes, or other print or non-print media.

In one school district that uses the Enrichment Triad Model, a speaker from the State Department of Environmental Protection gave an informative and exciting presentation about acid rain to elementary students in grades three through five. All students in those grade levels attended the lecture. Three young girls from one third-grade classroom became very excited about the topic and the dangers posed by acid rain to their environment. At the conclusion of the speech, they rushed up to the speaker and asked how they might learn more about the topic and what they could do to address the environmental threats posed by acid rain to their community. At this point, without further training or appropriate methodological skills, these students would probably not have been able to continue with their newly discovered interest. Unfortunately, we believe this is the inevitable result of the didactic style of teaching and "batch processing" of students that occurs in many classrooms throughout our country. Fortunately, in this case, a classroom teacher observed the interest and documented the experience on a form called an Action Information Message (see Figure 4.2). In this way, the interest was recorded on this form

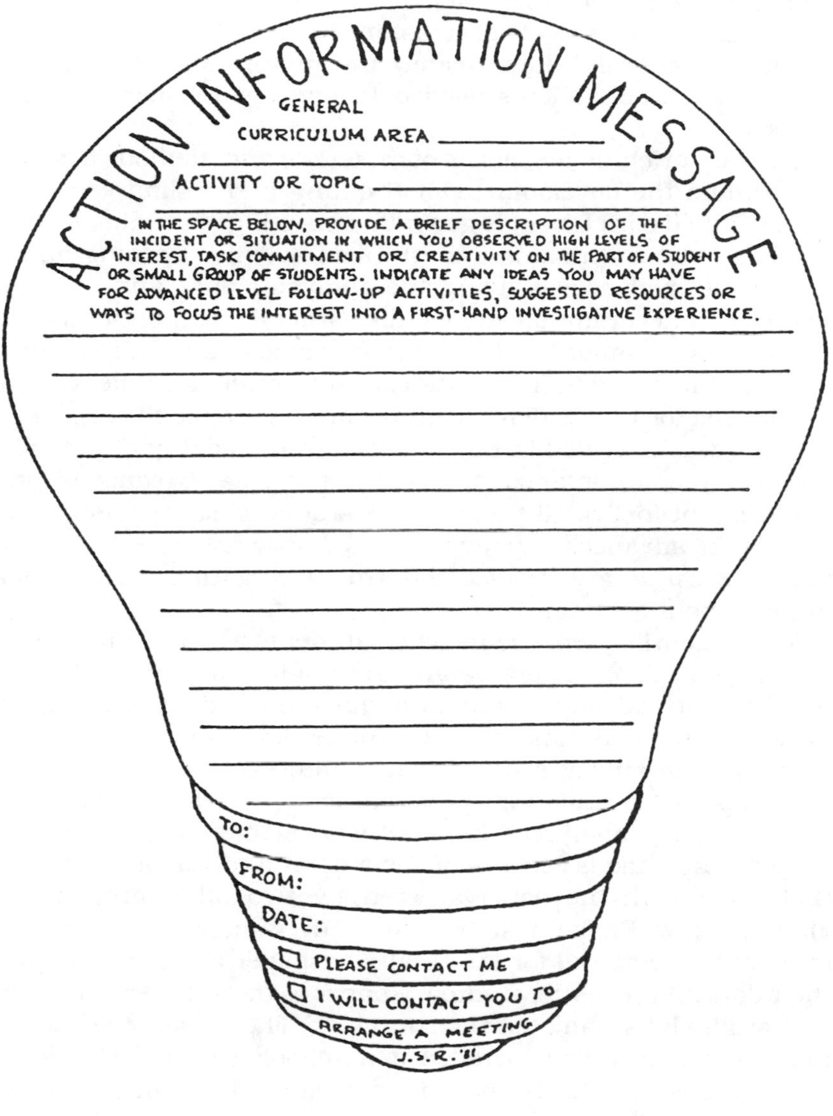

ACTION INFORMATION MESSAGE

GENERAL
CURRICULUM AREA _____

ACTIVITY OR TOPIC _____

IN THE SPACE BELOW, PROVIDE A BRIEF DESCRIPTION OF THE INCIDENT OR SITUATION IN WHICH YOU OBSERVED HIGH LEVELS OF INTEREST, TASK COMMITMENT OR CREATIVITY ON THE PART OF A STUDENT OR SMALL GROUP OF STUDENTS. INDICATE ANY IDEAS YOU MAY HAVE FOR ADVANCED LEVEL FOLLOW-UP ACTIVITIES, SUGGESTED RESOURCES OR WAYS TO FOCUS THE INTEREST INTO A FIRST-HAND INVESTIGATIVE EXPERIENCE.

TO:

FROM:

DATE:

☐ PLEASE CONTACT ME

☐ I WILL CONTACT YOU TO ARRANGE A MEETING

J.S.R. '81

Date Received_____
Date of Interview
with Child_____
Date Child
Was Revolved In_____

Figure 4.2. Action information message

and later transmitted to a teacher trained in the Triad Model who served as an enrichment specialist in the school. This teacher was primarily responsible for providing the appropriate Type II enrichment that these students needed to investigate their newfound interests.

Type II enrichment consists of materials and methods designed to promote the development of thinking and feeling processes. Some Type II enrichment is general, consisting of training in areas such as creative thinking and problem solving, learning how to learn skills such as classifying and analyzing data, and advanced reference and communication skills. Other Type II enrichment is specific, as it cannot be planned in advance and usually involves advanced instruction in an interest area selected by the student. In the case of the students who became interested in acid rain, training was provided in how to analyze the acidity of precipitation and how to organize and record the data. Because of prior involvement in Type II training, the students had previous experiences in advanced reference skills and were able to use the *Reader's Guide to Periodical Literature* to gather current information about acid rain.

Type III enrichment occurs when students become interested in pursuing a self-selected area and are willing to commit the time necessary for advanced content acquisition and process training in which they assume the role of a first-hand inquirer. For example, the students who became interested in acid rain collected specimens each time precipitation fell in their city for eight months. They analyzed the acidity level of that precipitation, keeping meticulous records of their data, and further compared their data with the data gathered by two other groups from another New England state and from Canada. The students prepared an editorial for the local newspaper and sent a copy of their data and resulting summary paper to the speaker whose talk had originally stimulated their interest. They also developed an interest center which included a notebook of articles collected from various periodicals, the students' data, a log of their activities and various information, photos, and other material. Use of the interest center might be helpful in stimulating other students' interests in the topic. The completed Type III investigation was evaluated using the procedures discussed in Part III of this paper.

The enrichment experiences that are included in the Triad Model do not always have to be used chronologically; that is, we do not always begin with Type I, proceed to Type II, and conclude with Type III investigations. Many students have become inter ested in pursuing a Type III study during a Type II training experience. A group of upper elementary students from Windsor, Connecticut, for example, became interested in the overcrowding of prisons while working on a practice problem for the Future Problem Solving state program. This problem-solving process (an example of excellent Type II training) and the introduction of the real problem (the overcrowding of prisons) led directly to the development of a Type III: the investigation of local solutions to this national problem.

In districts using the Enrichment Triad Model, students who are identified as above average or who display the potential to develop high levels of task commitment or creativity are identified as a talent pool and provided with regular Type I and II experiences. Many of these enrichment opportunities are also periodically extended to a broader spectrum of the population. In this way, students who are not formally identified are involved in enrichment experiences which may lead them to pursue various interests that they would probably not ordinarily pursue. Students who are identified are also eligible to receive additional services as a part of their enrichment program, including an analysis of their interests, learning styles, and a thorough review of how the regular curriculum can be modified to meet their individual needs. This curriculum modification, entitled curriculum compacting, often results in the elimination of hours of work that students have previously mastered. The time saved by curriculum compacting is often used for Type III investigations initiated by the student (Renzulli & Reis, 1985).

The following four Type III investigations are representative of the work of thousands of students who have completed these studies during the last 15 years.

When Both Parents Work

Lisa Grune Baum   Peter Noyes School
Grade 4   Sudbury, Massachusetts

Brief description:

Lisa was concerned because her mother was returning to school to become a lawyer. This meant that both her parents would be away from home and eventually working during the day. Lisa wanted to help herself and other kids cope with this situation and also to find out how other kids felt about it.

Lisa spent seven months on her Type III. Initially she interviewed and surveyed numerous fourth graders. She also worked with local guidance center personnel who became so interested in her work that they helped her with the layout and eventually published her pamphlet.

Lisa's teacher, Linda Aksamit Walsh, indicated that

> the most difficult time for Lisa was organizing her information for her product. She had such a wealth of knowledge to share that she didn't know where to begin and was becoming discouraged. Lisa eventually wrote down random thoughts that she felt were important and we cut the ideas into strips. We then made 'idea piles' in the various categories. From there, Lisa was able to see the total picture of the project coming together. This renewed her enthusiasm.

Child Abuse: It's Not What You Think

Jim Kraai   Janet Rauh   Winterset Middle School
Lisa Martin   Mark Roach   Winterset, Iowa
Ryan Nelson   Jill Rodish
Stacey Nicholl
Grades 7 & 8

Brief description:

Child abuse was a topic in the 1982 Future Problem Solving Program. The students in Winterset became so interested in the problem that they dropped out of the Future Problem Solving competition and concentrated on the local aspects of child abuse. While doing their research, the students found that among all child abuse materials available through the Iowa Department of Social Services, nothing had been written for *kids*. Over the next six months, the students completed their research and also accomplished the following:

1. Students studied newspaper ad formats and successfully suggested a more visible "To Report Suspected Child Abuse" ad for a local paper.
2. Students conducted a survey of their peers to determine what middle school students needed and wanted to know about child abuse, then drafted a pamphlet.
3. In addition, they wrote a play and minilectures on child abuse which they presented to all middle school students.

Mrs. Linda Parker, the students' teacher, indicated that the students' energy and task commitment was amazing. Yet since this was their first Type III, she found that the students could sometimes only see the end and not how to get there. As she explained,

> There were times I was tempted to become very directive and say, "You work on this section; you survey these people; you rewrite this scene," and so forth. I tried to guide quietly with questions, with "let's decide" goal setting, "who could" responsibility sharing, "how about" idea generating, and so forth. That patience, out of determination that the products would be truly theirs, plus the reinforcing positive responses the students receive, established an attitude and pattern for our whole Enrichment Program: one of questioning, problem solving, responsibility, caring, quality, and sharing.

Koalas

Stephanie Zinger   Killingly Memorial School
Grade 2   Danielson, Connecticut

Brief description:

Stephanie had an idea for a Type III even before she started seeing her resource teacher, Alane Starko, in September. She knew she wanted to study koalas and spent the next several months researching the topic. As her Type III, she eventually developed a slide show. She used books from different libraries, wrote to the Australian embassy, and completed many note cards. She organized her information and wrote the first draft of her script. Before completing the project, Stephanie was to rewrite her script three times, select and photograph pictures to illustrate her slide show, and record a taped narration that accompanies the slides. Her Type III required six months of work and became a permanent part of her school library's audiovisual collection.

A Children's Museum for Tuscaloosa County

Third Graders   Regional Education Center
Target Program   Northport, Alabama

Brief description:

While a group of students was studying historical homes in Tuscaloosa County in order to create a coloring book for all third graders in the county, they learned about a historical home that might be demolished. The students were very upset at the prospect of a beautiful old home being torn down and suggested that the home be used as a children's museum. After learning that this home could not be used for the museum, they started an organized effort to have a children's museum built or developed elsewhere in the county. The students brought their idea to the Tuscaloosa County Commission in a well-organized and entertaining short skit. Many adults joined in the effort and the teachers involved, Karen Thompson and Judith Taylor, report that the museum is now a reality.

Research on the Enrichment Triad Model

The effectiveness of the Triad Model has been documented by a series of research studies and field tests in schools with widely varying socioeconomic levels and program organizational patterns. Using a population of 1,162 students in grades one through six in 11 school districts, Reis and Renzulli (1982) examined several variables related to the effectiveness of the model. The talent pools in each district and at each grade level were divided into two groups. Group A consisted of students who scored in the top five percent on standardized tests of intelligence and achievement. Group B consisted of students who scored between 10 to 15 percentile points below the top five percent. Both groups participated equally in all program activities.

The Student Product Assessment Form (SPAF; Renzulli, Reis, & Smith, 1981) was used to compare the quality of products from each group. An analysis of variance indicated there were no significant differences between Group A and Group B with respect to the quality of students' products. These findings verify the three-ring conception of giftedness (above-average abilities, task commitment, and creativity) underlying the model and clearly support the effectiveness of the model in serving a group that is somewhat larger than the traditional top five percent.

Questionnaires and interviews were used to examine several other factors related to overall program effectiveness. The data—gathered from classroom teachers, administrators, students in the talent pools, and their parents—indicated that feelings about the program were generally positive. Many classroom teachers reported that their high level of involvement in the program had favorably influenced their teaching practices. The opinions of parents whose children had been in traditional programs for the gifted did not differ from those of parents whose children had been identified as gifted under the expanded criteria. Resource teachers, many of whom had been involved previously in traditional programs for the gifted, overwhelmingly preferred the identification procedure used in the Enrichment Triad Model to the traditional reliance on test scores alone.

Additional research (Delisle & Renzulli, 1982) examined academic self-concept and locus of control. This study established the importance of nonintellective factors in creative production and verified earlier research related to the three-ring conception of giftedness. Using a step-wise multiple regression technique to study the correlates of creative production, Gubbins (1982) found that above-average ability is a necessary but not sufficient condition for high-level productivity. The roles of task, time commitment, and the importance of student interests were verified. Several factors related to improved productivity were identified. A study of student, parent, and classroom teachers' attitudes toward the model (Delisle, Reis, & Gubbins, 1981) revealed support for this approach and a high degree of cooperation among all persons involved in the implementation of a Triad program. A comprehensive study of administrators' attitudes toward programs based on the Triad Model was conducted by Cooper (1983). The findings indicated that, although the programs had not been integrated into the school curriculum as thoroughly as had been anticipated, the model was effective in serving talent pool students; it helped to minimize attitudes of elitism; and it promoted a "radiation of excellence" (Ward, 1962) throughout the schools in which the model was implemented.

Starko (1986) studied the effects of participating in a Triad program. She examined the effects of the Triad Model on both student productivity and feelings of self-efficacy connected with creative productivity. This research compared students who participated in Triad programs for at least four years with students who qualified for such programs who received no services. Questionnaires were used to determine the number of creative products produced by both groups, within school programs and in independent activities outside of school. They were also used to gather information about attitudes and skills associated with creative productivity. Information on self-efficacy was collected using an original instrument based on Bandura's self-efficacy theory and the components of creative productivity as presented in the Schoolwide Enrichment Model. Hierarchical multiple regression and qualitative analyses of open-ended questionnaire items was used for data analysis. Results indicated that students who became involved in independent study projects in the Triad program more often initiated their own creative productivity outside of school than did students in the control group. Starko also found that participation in this enrichment program had an increased positive effect on students' attitudes toward school when compared to the control group.[1]

The research summarized above and experiences growing out of widespread use of the model lead to a number of conclusions. First, although the model provides special services to larger numbers of students than do traditional programs for the gifted, the greater involvement of classroom teachers and the rotation of students in and out of Type III enrichment activities actually increase, rather than decrease, services to gifted children.

Second, special programs that have traditionally been restricted to students who score in the top 5% on standardized tests can effectively serve other high-ability students, if we take such factors as action information into account when we identify participants and establish program activities. By doing so, we also minimize concerns about elitism and help to do away with the you-have-it or you-don't-have-it approach to giftedness.

Third, programs for the gifted that rely on traditional identification procedures may not be serving the wrong students, but they are certainly excluding large numbers of well above-average pupils who, given the opportunity, are capable of producing an equally high level of work. High levels of productivity can only occur when above-average ability interacts with other factors such as task commitment and creativity. It is these other factors that enable students to create products of exceptional quality.

Finally, the flexibility that characterizes our model can help to insure more appropriate identification of high-ability students and more appropriate programs to meet their individual needs. In a larger context, it also provides an alternative to traditional approaches that have made programs for the gifted the veritable ping-pong balls of educational priorities.

---

[1] A detailed technical report (Renzulli, 1989) describing studies dealing with all aspects of the Triad/Revolving Door system is available from the Bureau of Educational Research at the University of Connecticut.

RESEARCH AND THEORY UNDERLYING THE ENRICHMENT TRIAD MODEL

The rationale underlying this model is divided into the following three parts: a brief theory of knowledge; studies of highly creative and productive individuals; and an application of the educational philosophy of John Dewey, especially as it relates to his concern for educational experiences that focus on the pursuit of real problems.

A Brief Theory of Knowledge

Untold numbers of books have been written about theories of knowledge, and various authors have posed several organizational systems for classifying knowledge and studying it in a systematic manner. Although any one of these organizational systems might serve as the rationale underlying a particular approach to creative productivity, the theory of knowledge that we have selected as a rationale for the Triad Model is one that focuses on both levels and functions of knowledge within any given content field.

The theory of knowledge underlying the model is based on three levels of knowing first suggested by the American psychologist and philosopher William James (1885). These levels are: knowledge-of, knowledge-about (also referred to as knowledge-that), and knowledge-how. Before going on to describe these levels, it must be pointed out that each of the three levels, and especially the second and third levels, also exist on a continuum from the simple to the complex. It remains the responsibility of teachers and curriculum developers to determine the degree of complexity within each level that might be appropriate for a given age or ability group.

Knowledge-of. This entry level of knowing might best be described as an awareness level, and it is most compatible with the Type I enrichment dimension of the Triad Model. Knowledge-of consists of being acquainted with, rather than familiar with an area of study, a piece of information, a person, place, object, or event. James (1885) referred to this level as "knowledge by acquaintance" to distinguish it from more advanced levels, which he referred to as "knowledge by systematic study and reflection." Thus, for example, a person may be knowledgeable of a field of study called astrophysics, and might even add that he or she knows a little bit about what astrophysicists study. But it would be inaccurate to say that this person is knowledgeable *about* astrophysics in any way other than on a very superficial or awareness level.

Knowledge-of involves remembering (storage of knowledge), recollecting (retrieval of knowledge), and recognizing, but this level does not ordinarily include more advanced processes of mind that will be described below when we discuss knowledge-about. Most curriculum development efforts automatically begin with the knowledge-of level, but they proceed quickly to the knowledge-about level because this level represents the systematic study and reflection that James used to distinguish between lower and higher levels of knowing.

Knowledge-about. Knowledge-about represents a more advanced level of understanding than merely remembering or recalling information that has been learned. This area of knowledge is reflected in the Type II dimension of the Triad Model. Knowledge-about builds on remembering and recalling, but it also includes more advanced elements of knowing such as distinguishing, translating, interpreting, and being able to explain a given fact, concept, theory, or principle. Being able to explain something might also involve the ability to demonstrate it through physical or artistic performance (e.g., demonstrating a particular dance movement) or through a combination of verbal and manipulative activities (e.g., demonstrating how a piece of scientific apparatus works).

Knowledge-how. This level represents types of knowledge that enable persons to make new contributions to their respective fields of study. It deals mainly with the *application* of investigative methodology to the generation of the knowledge-about aspects of a given field of study. Scholars generally view knowledge-how as the highest level of involvement in a field. It represents the kind of work that is pursued by researchers, writers, and artists who are making new contributions to the sciences, humanities, and the arts. In the Enrichment Triad Model, knowledge-how is reflected in the procedures used for the development of Type III enrichment.

The theory of knowledge represented by James's three levels is used in this rationale in harmony with Alfred North Whitehead's (1929) concepts of romance, technical proficiency, and generalization. According to Whitehead, we first develop an interest or romance about a particular field or topic (Type I). A young person might, for example, develop a romance with the field of medicine as he or she explores the field or selected topics within the field at the knowledge-of level. Second, some people follow up this romance by pursuing a field or career to the point of becoming a proficient practitioner in one of the medical professions. The development of content and process skills range along a continuum of complexity, and within the Triad Model, they are most reflective of our concept of Type II enrichment. Most professionals within a field reach their maximum involvement at this level, however there are some persons who go on to the generalization level. It is these persons who say, in effect, "I want to add new information and contribute new knowledge to the field of medicine." This third level is, in many respects, consistent with one of the major goals of Type III enrichment. The rationale underlying this goal is that special educational programs should contribute to the development of persons who will be the inventors, leaders, and creative producers of the next generation. The Triad Model has been developed in a way that places a premium on both the organization and pursuit of authentic knowledge, and the application of investigative methodology to problem areas within various content domains.

In view of the general goals of the model set forth above, we are not as concerned with the issue of knowledge-as-product as we are with the process objectives that have broader transfer value such as application, appreciation, self-actualization, and improved cognitive structures. In other words, this model views representative topics as vehicles for process development. The structural dimensions and key concepts mentioned above provide the learner with tools for examining any or all of the vast number of topics in a given discipline. This model views the learner as one who is developing, practicing, applying, and (hopefully) gaining an appreciation of a particular segment of knowledge by studying topic A so that the learner may then use the same strategies to examine any one or a combination of topics B through Z. We do not expect the young learner to "declare a major" at an early age, although in certain cases (mostly in mathematics, selected sciences, and arts) early declarations are not uncommon. Rather, the goal is to create the conditions that result in the formation of an investigative modus operandi on the parts of the developing learner.

This model also places a large amount of emphasis on the appropriate use of methodology within content fields. All content fields can be defined, in part, by the research methods and investigative techniques that are used to add new knowledge to a given field of study. Most knowledge experts consider the appropriate use of methodology to be the highest level of competence in a content field. Indeed, this is the level at which research scientists, composers, authors, and academicians who are making new contributions to their fields typically operate. Although this level undoubtedly requires advanced understanding of a field, and sometimes requires the use of sophisticated equipment, young students can successfully learn and apply some of the entry-level methodologies that are associated with most fields of knowledge (Bruner, 1960). The methodology dimension is also an important consideration for the development of differentiated curriculum because one of the major goals of education for the gifted is to develop a positive attitude toward the creative challenges of investigative activity and knowledge production. A focus on the acquisition and application of methodology also forces the issue of more active learning and a hands-on involvement with a content field.

Finally, the Enrichment Triad Model is based on the belief that learning experiences for highly able students should result in both concrete and abstract products. These outcomes are reflected below.

Table 4.1. Categories of Instructional Products

CONCRETE PRODUCTS	ABSTRACT PRODUCTS
• Knowledge	• Cognitive Structure
• Written Products	• Problem-Solving
• Spoken Products	Strategies
• Artistic Performances	• Values
• Leadership Behaviors	• Appreciations
	• Self-Actualization

These two kinds of products generally work in harmony with one another and are separated here only for analytic purposes. The concrete products consist of the acquisition of specific segments of knowledge plus a broad range of tangible things that are actually produced by students (e.g., reports, stories, time lines, dances, musical compositions, etc.). It is important to emphasize that these concrete products are not considered to be ends in and of themselves. Rather, they are viewed as means or vehicles through which the various abstract products can be developed and applied (Renzulli, 1988b).

The abstract products consist of more enduring and transferable outcomes of the learning process. In most cases, the abstract products take many years to reach full maturity; however, each circular experience should make a contribution to one or a combination of these more enduring goals of instruction. The abstract products include improved cognitive structures and problem-solving strategies (Renzulli, 1977, pp. 64–68); the development of a value system (including new appreciations for knowledge, methodology, and the aesthetic aspects of knowledge); and the development of self-actualization. This final category includes specific affective components of development such as self-concept, self-efficacy (Bandura, 1977), and social and emotional adjustment. Taken collectively, concrete and abstract products represent the overall goals of providing special programs for high potential students.

Studies of Highly Creative and Productive Individuals

A large body of accumulated research (Renzulli, 1978) clearly indicates that persons who have been recognized because of their unique accomplishments and creative contributions possess a relatively well-defined set of three interlocking clusters of abilities. These clusters consist of above-average, though not necessarily superior, general ability; task commitment; and creativity. No single cluster makes giftedness, but rather it is the interaction among the three clusters that is the necessary ingredient for creative and productive accomplishments. This interaction is represented by the shaded portion of Figure 4.3. Each cluster plays an important part in contributing to the display of gifted behaviors; however, it is important to point out that the general ability cluster is usually a constant factor in those persons whom we consider to be well above average in intelligence and achievement. The other two clusters are not either always present or always absent, as is usually the case in traditionally measured general abilities. Research has clearly shown that creativity and task commitment can be developed in certain persons, at certain times, and under certain circumstances. Accordingly, these clusters should not be viewed as the criteria for entrance into gifted programs, but rather as traits which gifted programs should attempt to develop and to bring into interaction with one another and with the traits included in the above-average general ability segment of the model. A detailed description of the relationship among the clusters and the importance of the interactions between and among them can be found in Renzulli (1986).

Space does not permit a detailed review of the research underlying the three-ring conception of giftedness; however, the interested reader can find the studies that support this concept in the two references cited above and commentary on reactions to the concept in a more recent publication (Renzulli, 1988a). This publication also includes a step-by-step description of how we select students for special services. For purposes of the current discussion, we would like to present a small number of generalizations about the gifted and talented that emerged from the large body of studies that were reviewed on this subject. We will also include the definition of giftedness that underlies all of the programming recommendations contained in the Triad Model.

The first generalization is the need to make a distinction between traditional indicators of academic proficiency and creative productivity. A sad-but-true fact is that special programs have favored proficient lesson learners and test takers at the expense of persons who may score somewhat lower on tests but who more than compensate for such scores by having high levels of task commitment and creativity. It is these persons that research has shown to be the ones who ultimately make the most

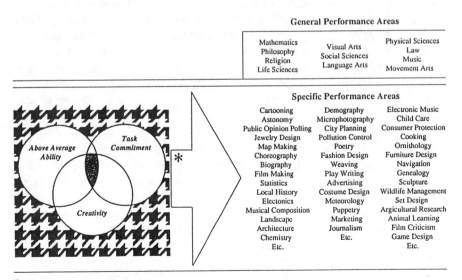

General Performance Areas

Mathematics	Visual Arts	Physical Sciences
Philosophy	Social Sciences	Law
Religion	Language Arts	Music
Life Sciences		Movement Arts

Specific Performance Areas

Cartooning	Demography	Electronic Music
Astonomy	Microphotography	Child Care
Public Opinion Polling	City Planning	Consumer Protection
Jewelry Design	Pollution Control	Cooking
Map Making	Poetry	Ornithology
Choreography	Fashion Design	Furniture Design
Biography	Weaving	Navigation
Film Making	Play Writing	Genealogy
Statistics	Advertising	Sculpture
Local History	Costume Design	Wildlife Management
Electonics	Meteorology	Set Design
Musical Composition	Puppetry	Argicultural Research
Landscape	Marketing	Animal Learning
Architecture	Journalism	Film Criticism
Chemistry	Etc.	Game Design
Etc.		Etc.

Above Average Ability · Task Commitment · Creativity

* *This arrow should be read as " ... brought to bear upon"*

Figure 4.3. Graphic representation of the three-ring definition of giftedness

creative/productive contributions to their respective fields of endeavor.

A second generalization is that an operational definition should be applicable to all socially useful performance areas. The one thing that the three clusters discussed above have in common is that each can be brought to bear on a multitude of specific performance areas. As was indicated earlier, the interaction or overlap among the clusters makes giftedness, but giftedness does not exist in a vacuum. Our definition must, therefore, reflect yet another interaction, but in this case it is the interaction between the overlap of the clusters and any performance areas to which the overlap might be applied. This interaction is represented by the large arrow in Figure 4.3.

A third and final generalization is concerned with the types of information that should be used to identify superior performance in specific areas. Although it is a relatively easy task to include specific performance areas in a definition, developing identification procedures that will enable us to recognize these areas of superior performance is a more difficult problem. Test developers have thus far devoted most of their energy to the development of measures of general ability, and this emphasis is undoubtedly why these tests are relied upon so heavily in identification. However, an operational definition should give direction to needed research and development, especially as these activities relate to instruments and procedures for student selection. A defensible definition can thus become a model that will generate vast amounts of appropriate research in the years ahead.

Although no single statement can effectively integrate the many ramifications of the research studies described above, the following definition of giftedness attempts to summarize the major conclusions and generalizations resulting from this review of research.

Giftedness consists of an interaction among three basic clusters of human traits—these clusters being above-average general and/or specific abilities, high levels of task commitment, and high levels of creativity. Gifted and talented children are those possessing or capable of developing this composite set of traits and applying them to any potentially valuable area of human performance. Children who manifest or are capable of developing an interaction among the three clusters require a wide variety of educational opportunities and services that are not ordinarily provided through regular instructional programs. A graphic representation of this definition is presented in Figure 4.3.

John Dewey and the Concept of Real Problems

In many ways, the ideas put forth in the Enrichment Triad Model are based on both an interpretation of the educational philosophy of John Dewey and our desire to translate this philosophy into a practical plan for program development. Although we would like to believe that all educational experiences should be built around the pursuit of real problems, we have long since come to realize that efficiency in the learning process is more easily achieved if we make some use of contrived problems or exercises and if we employ certain methods of teaching that are not necessarily associated with the discovery of a solution to real problems. Simply stated, there is nothing wrong with teaching children multiplication tables or vocabulary words using methods that may involve memorization, repetition, and other contrived exercises, such as using words in a sentence, looking up their meanings in a dictionary, and alphabetizing a spelling list. Ultraliberal educators may disagree with this traditional stance, but the fact remains that these methods have served us well for hundreds of years in providing mass education for the general population.

Our concern in this model, however, is not with general education, but rather with qualitative differences in the education of high-potential youngsters. In this regard we would like to suggest that one of the major ways we can guarantee such differences is to make real problems the central focus of any plan for enrichment-based education. Before attempting to develop a definition of "real problems," let us examine the rationale for giving these problems such a prominent role in our model.

If there are any two overriding factors that have brought the need for enrichment-based models into existence they are that (a) nature has not made every human being a carbon copy of every other, and (b) civilization has continuously produced men and women who have done more than merely learn about or replicate existing knowledge.

If such were not the case, the growth of civilization would be totally dependent upon the *accidental* discovery of new knowledge. Civilization does not glorify the copyists or the high-level replicators of knowledge and art, and only rarely does history remember people who have made accidental discoveries. Rather, our focus has been on men and women who have purposefully made it their business to attack the unsolved problems of mankind. It is for this reason that scholars in creativity and cognitive study constantly invoke such names as Einstein, Edison, Curie, Beethoven, Duncan, and a host of others who have made creative contributions to their chosen fields of endeavor. If society's creative producers and solvers of real problems are constantly held up before us as idealized prototypes of the gifted person, then it seems nothing short of common sense to use their modus operandi to construct a model for educating our most promising young people. This is not to say that we should minimize the importance of providing gifted youngsters with the most advanced courses or experiences involving existing knowledge. Good old-fashioned book learning of the accumulated, organized wisdom of the ages helps to provide the stuff out of which new ideas and breakthroughs in knowledge will occur. But a major focus within such courses (or independent from any course) should be on the production of new knowledge. Such production is a function of both mastery of the concepts and environment that purposefully and unequivocally tell youngsters that they can be creative producers. People sometimes seem skeptical when our colleagues describe case after case involving outstanding examples of creative and productive work emanating from students participating in Triad-based programs. There is a very simple reason for the quantity and quality of this productivity. From their earliest years in the program, our students are constantly stimulated to explore new and interesting topics and ideas. They are encouraged to develop creative problem-solving techniques and research skills. They understand that they are in this special program because we expect them to develop not only the techniques, but also the attitude and task commitment for going beyond existing knowledge. Attitudinal development, a strong belief in one's ability to be a creative producer, is as important as the learning content. For example, there were probably a thousand people who knew as much about the theory of flight as the Wright brothers, but Wilbur and Orville built the airplane and made it fly.

Let us now turn our attention to the definition of a real problem. The word "real," like so many other concepts in education, gets tossed around so freely that after a while it becomes little more than another piece of useless jargon. Our research on the meaning of a real problem did not produce a neat and trim definition, but we were able to come up with the following list of characteristics which will serve as a set of parameters for analyzing this important concept. Please review the following list with an eye toward determining whether or not you are in agreement with each statement.

Characteristics of a Real Problem

1. A real problem must have a personal frame of reference, since it involves an emotional or effective commitment as well as an intellectual or cognitive one.
2. A real problem does not have an existing or unique solution.
3. Calling something a problem does not necessarily make it a real problem for a given person or group.
4. The purpose of pursuing a real problem is to bring about some form of change or to contribute something new to the sciences, the arts, or the humanities.

At the beginning of this section, an argument was introduced that equated real problems with qualitative differences in learning. We would like to close by proposing a series of questions, we call the Qualitative Differential Education for the Gifted (Q-DEG) Quiz. The questions were designed to be somewhat of an acid test for qualitative differences in learning and can be raised in connection with any particular piece of work a youngster does in a special program. You might want to keep in mind one or more of the sample Type III projects described earlier as you review these questions.

The Q-DEG Quiz

		YES	NO
1.	Did every student do it?	___	___
2.	Should every student do it?	___	___
3.	Would every student want to do it?	___	___
4.	Could every student do it?	___	___
5.	Did the student do it willingly and with zest?	___	___
6.	Did the student use appropriate sources and methodology?	___	___
7.	Was the work directed toward having an impact upon an audience?	___	___

In almost all of the sample Type IIIs described above, the answers to the first four questions are NO; the remaining three are YES. These answers represent for us the characteristics of a qualitatively different learning experience and the makings of a real problem.

PRODUCT EVALUATION RESEARCH AND
PRACTICE

The evaluation of creative products can provide insight into the creative potential of students who participate in gifted and talented programs. It may also provide input into the process which is used to complete products. Little research has been conducted in the area of product evaluation in gifted and talented programs. In fact, a review of numerous instruments for product and process evaluation of completed student products in a gifted program reveals a paucity of research in this area. Few instruments are available for perusal and even fewer have been evaluated in terms of reliability, validity, or field test data.

Recently, product evaluation forms have been developed by Callahan (1980), Tuttle (1980), Besemer and Treffinger (1981), and Westberg (1990). All four forms have been utilized in research and evaluation studies. Tuttle's form was designed to provide a rater with a valid basis for assessing the quality of the work and the implementation of research and communication skills. Tuttle also noted that his form is appropriate only for certain types of products—those involving research skills and the sharing of the product with an audience.

Callahan's *Product Evaluation Form* was specifically designed to evaluate Type III investigations in a gifted program based on the Enrichment Triad Model (Renzulli, 1977). Callahan devised the form to determine whether the student had become familiar with the problems, techniques, methodologies, environment, product, and audience of the interest area that was selected for the investigation. There is no distinction between process and product skills in either Tuttle's or Callahan's instruments.

Westberg (1990) used Amabile's (1983) consensual assessment technique to develop an instrument for assessing the creative productivity of inventions made by elementary and middle school students. Westberg's *Invention Evaluation Instrument* is used to evaluate student inventions. The interrater reliabilities on the 11 items ranged from .69–.92 with a median rating of .82. The interrater reliability for the instrument as a whole was .96.

Besemer and Treffinger (1981) developed the *Creative Product Analysis Matrix* (CPAM), proposing that groups of related attributes cluster along three different, but interrelated, dimensions: (a) novelty, (b) resolution, and (c) elaboration and synthesis. Later research was conducted on whether or not subjects would evaluate creative products in a manner consistent with the proposed model. Selecting a variety of creative products, a judging instrument based on CPAM and called the *CPAM Adjective Checklist* was developed, containing 110 adjectives and adjectival phrases describing the three dimensions of novelty, resolution, and elaboration and synthesis. Based on this research, 12 subscales were constructed from the 110 different words under the three dimensions. Reliability and validity studies conducted on CPAM are reported by the authors as quite positive.

Development of the Student Product Assessment Form

Content Validity.
Description of the Student Product Assessment Form.   The first stage in the development of the *Student Product Assessment Form* (SPAF; Renzulli & Reis, 1985, pp. 470–476) was to establish content validity. Program coordinators and teachers throughout the country were asked to provide the researchers with any forms or instruments used to evaluate student products. Every response indicated that formal product evaluation rarely occurred; when it did, the instruments used were locally developed and lacked reliability and validity information. Most of the product rating forms were very brief and sketchy, consisting of questions students were asked to answer on completion of a project, such as: What did you learn by doing this project? A review of literature was also undertaken in an effort to identify methods of evaluating student products completed in gifted programs, and a shortage of instruments designed for this purpose was found. Few of the instruments available were evaluated in terms of reliability, validity, or field-test research.

Based upon the examination of the literature and our years of familiarity with the outstanding products developed by gifted students, a new form was designed (see summary of form in Figure 4.4) to provide raters with a valid and reliable basis for assessing the quality of products completed in gifted and talented programs. Fifteen items were generated which assess both individual aspects as well as the overall excellence of the product.

Name(s) _____ Date _____

District _____ School _____

Teacher _____ Grade _____ Sex _____

Product (Title and/or Brief Description) _____

_____

Number of Months Student(s) worked on Product _____

FACTORS	RATING*	NOT APPLICABLE
1. Early Statement of Purpose...................	_____	_____
2. Problems Focusing	_____	_____
3. Level of Resources	_____	_____
4. Diversity of Resources.........................	_____	_____
5. Appropriateness of Resources.............	_____	_____
6. Logic, Sequence, and Transition	_____	_____
7. Action Orientation	_____	_____
8. Audience	_____	_____
9. Overall Assessment.............................	_____	_____
A. Originality of the Idea	_____	
B. Achieved Objectives Stated in Plan...	_____	
C. Advanced Familiarity with Subject....	_____	
D. Quality Beyond Age/Grade Level	_____	
E. Care, Attention to Detail, etc.	_____	
F. Time, Effort, Energy	_____	
G. Original Contribution............................	_____	

Comments:

Person Completing this Form _____

*Rating Scales: Factors 1–8   Factor 9A-9G
  5 - To a great extent   5 = Outstanding
  3 - Somewhat   4 = Above Average
  I - To a limited extent   3 = Average
                                    2 = Below Average
                                    1 = Poor

Figure 4.4. Student Product Assessment Form summary sheet

Each item represents a single characteristic on which raters should focus their attention (see Figure 4.5). Items 1 through 8 deal with particular aspects of product development, while item 9 has seven different components which deal with an overall assessment of the product. No examples of students' work are provided for item 9.

DIVERSITY OF RESOURCES

Has the student made an effort to use several different types of resource materials in the development of the product? Has the student used any of the following information sources in addition to the standard use of encyclopedias: textbooks, record/statistic books, biographies, how-to-do-it books, periodicals, films and filmstrips, letters, phone calls, personal interviews, surveys or polls, catalogs and/or others?

For example, a fourth grade student interested in the weapons and vehicles used in World War II reads several adult-level books on this subject which included biographies, autobiographies, periodicals, and record books. He also conducted oral history interviews with local veterans of World War II, previewed films and filmstrips about the period, and collected letters from elderly citizens sent to them from their sons stationed overseas.

5	4	3	2	1	NA
To a great extent		Somewhat		To a limited extent	

Figure 3.5. Sample characteristic from the Student Product Assessment Form

When completing the ratings for the overall assessment of a student's product, raters should attempt to evaluate the product in terms of their own values and certain characteristics that indicate the quality, aesthetics, utility, and function of the overall contribution. In other words, raters are encouraged to consider the product as a whole (globally) in item nine and to use their own judgment and rely on their own guided subjective opinions when rating this item.

To further examine content validity, the form was submitted for evaluation to several recognized national authorities in the field of education of the gifted, as well as in the area of educational research. It was further distributed to 20 experienced teachers of the gifted in Connecticut. The authorities were asked to carefully assess the content of the form for omissions, clarity, and duplications. They were also asked for suggestions which would improve the form. Very few suggestions or omissions were mentioned by the experts in the field and the form was, accordingly, modified only very slightly.

Reliability.

Interrater agreement. Interrater agreement (see Table 4.2) was determined in two separate phases. In the first phase, 19 raters with familiarity to the field of education of the gifted (many of the raters were resource room teachers of the gifted) rated the product of a primary grade student. The percentage of interrater agreement on the items during the first and second phases ranged from 54.5% to 100%. Lower items were eliminated and a revision of SPAF was undertaken.

Items 2, 6, and 7, which did not receive an agreement percentage of 80% were revised and refined; one key concept in item 9 was eliminated and replaced with an item that three raters had listed as an omission. In phase two, 22 raters (19 of the phase one group and three additional teachers of the gifted) rated a second and a third product. On the second product, interrater agreement of 100% was achieved for 12 of the 15 items. The other three items achieved agreement percentages of 86.4, 90.9, and 95.5.

Stability and interrater reliability. An additional consideration addressed was the extent that ratings would be stable over time. The same raters assessed a second product approximately

Table 4.2. Percentage of Interrater Agreement on the Student Product Assessment Form

ITEM	PRODUCT 1			After Review PRODUCT 2			PRODUCT 3			
	5-4	3	2-1	5-4	3	2-1	5-4	3	2-1	NA
1	100.0			86.4	13.6		90.9	9.1		
2	63.2	26.3		100.0			86.4	9.1		4.5
3	94.7	5.3		90.9	9.1		68.2	27.3	4.5	
4	89.4	5.3	5.3	95.5	4.5		54.5	27.3	9.1	9.1
5	100.0			100.0			77.3	18.2		4.5
6	68.4	21.0	5.3	100.0			81.8	13.6		4.5
7	63.2	15.8	21.0	100.0			95.5	4.5		
8	94.7		5.3	100.0			90.9	9.1		
9	4-3		2.1	4-3		2-1	4.3		2.1	
A	78.9		21.0	100.0			95.5			4.5
B	100.0			100.0			100.0			
C	94.7		5.3	100.0			100.0			
D	100.0			100.0			100.0			
E	100.0			100.0			100.0			
F	100.0			100.0			100.0			
G	100.0			100.0			100.0			

two weeks after the first assessment. A correlation of +.96 was achieved between the first and second assessment of product two (see Table 4.3).

A final phase of the reliability check was the generation of inter-rater reliabilities for 20 different products in five different domains. The products were submitted for assessment to staff members in three public school programs for gifted students in Connecticut. Four experienced teachers of the gifted were asked to evaluate the products using the *Student Product Assessment Form.*

To obtain the interrater reliabilities, the technique described by Ebel (1951) was utilized, intercorrelating the ratings obtained from different raters as the approach to the reliability of ratings (Guilford, 1954, pp. 395–397). Interrater reliability results of the mean reliability for one rater as well as four raters on the nine different items ranged from .718 to 1.000. The mean interrater reliability for one rater was .961 and for four raters was .990.

Using the Student Product Assessment Form. We strongly discourage the formal grading of students' creative prod

Table 4.3. Student Product Assessment Form Interrater Reliability of One Rater and Four Raters on Individual Items and Tools

Items	1 Rater	4 Raters
1. Early Statement of Purpose	1.000	1.000
2. Problems Focusing	1.000	1.000
3. Level of Resources	.973	.993
4. Diversity of Resources	.963	.990
5. Appropriateness of Resources	.983	.996
6. Logic, Sequence and Transition	.779	.934
7. Action Orientation	.913	.977
8. Audience	.533	.820
Subtotal Key Components 1-8	.994	.998
9. Overall Assessment		
A. Originality of the Idea	.778	.993
B. Achieved Objectives Stated in Plan	.789	.937
C. Advanced Familiarity with Subject	1.000	1.000
D. Quality Beyond Age/Grade Level	.912	.971
E. Care, Attention to Detail, etc.	1.000	1.000
F. Time, Effort, Energy	.875	.966
G. Original Contribution	.390	.718
Subtotal Key Concepts 9A-G	.924	.980
Total of All Items on SPAF	.961	.990

ucts. No letter grade, number, or percent can accurately reflect the comprchcnsive types of knowledge, creativity, and task commitment that are developed within the context of a creative product. At the same time, however, evaluation and feedback are an important part of the overall process of promoting growth through this type of enrichment experience and, therefore, students should be thoroughly oriented in the procedures that will be used to evaluate their work. The best way to help students gain an appreciation for the ways in which their work will be evaluated is to conduct a series of orientation sessions organized around SPAF. Two or three examples of completed student products that highlight varying levels of quality on the respective scales from the SPAF instrument will help students to have an appreciation for both the factors involved in the assessment and examples of the manifestation of each factor.

CONCLUSION

The development of creative productivity is a complicated and elusive process. While our years of field testing and conducting research about the Enrichment Triad Model have convinced us that teachers can indeed help students to complete outstanding examples of creative and productive work, many questions remain unanswered, but they will serve as guideposts to guide our future research agenda. For example, some of our first groups of students who took part in an elementary school Triad program for three or four years are currently completing college and entering careers or graduate school. Will the experiences they had in elementary and junior high school as a part of this model have any impact on their adult creative productivity? Did the experiences provided for them under the auspices of the Enrichment Triad Model have an influence on their decisions to attend a graduate school or to select a career? One of the students who started an original elementary school newspaper as her Type III project in fifth grade is now pursuing a career in journalism. Another student who studied astronomy for two years in elementary school is entering graduate school in this area. Would these decisions have been made if the program did not exist or if it had been guided by a model that placed more emphasis upon accelerated learning rather than creative productivity? We hope that follow-up studies now in progress and ones that will undoubtedly emerge as we examine other ramifications of the model will help us to both establish some cause-and-effect relations and provide guidance for modifications that any dynamic plan for creative productivity must surely undergo.

REFERENCES

Amabile, T.M. (1983). *The social psychology of creativity*. New York: Springer-Verlag.

Bandura, A. (1977). Self-efficacy: Toward a unifying theory of behavioral change. *Psychological Review, 84*, 191–215.

Besemer, S.P., & Treffinger, D.J. (1981). Analysis of creative products: Review and synthesis. *Journal of Creative Behavior, 15*, 159–178.

Bruner, J. (1960). *The process of education*. Cambridge, MA: Harvard University Press.

Callahan, C.M. (1980). *Unpublished student product rating scale*.

Cooper, C. (1983). *Administrator's attitudes towards gifted programs based on the enrichment triad revolving door identification model: Case studies in decision making*. Unpublished doctoral dissertation, University of Connecticut, Storrs.

Council for Exceptional Children. (1979). *Sample instruments for the evaluation of programs for the gifted and talented* (pp. 11–17). Storrs, CT: University of Connecticut, Bureau of Educational Research.

Delisle, J.R., Reis, S.M., & Gubbins, E.J. (1981). The revolving door identification and programming model. *Exceptional Children, 48*, 152–156.

Delisle, J.R., & Renzulli, J.S. (1982). The revolving door identification and programming model: Correlates of creative production. *Gifted Child Quarterly, 26*, 89–95.

Ebel, R.L. (1951). Estimation of the reliability of ratings. *Psychometrics, 16*, 407–424.

Gubbins, E.J. (1982). *Revolving door identification model: Characteristics of talent pool students*. Unpublished doctoral dissertation, University of Connecticut, Storrs.

Guilford, J.P. (1954). *Psychometric methods*. New York: McGraw-Hill.

James, W. (1885). On the functions of cognition, *Mind, 10*, 27–44.

MacKinnon, D.W. (1987). Some critical issues for future research in creativity. In S.G. Isaksen (Ed.), *Frontiers of creativity research: Beyond the basics* (pp. 120–130). Buffalo, NY: Bearly Limited.

Reis, S.M., & Renzulli, J.S. (1982). A research report on the Revolving Door Identification Model: A case for the broadened conception of giftedness. *Phi Delta Kappan, 63*, 619–620.

Renzulli, J.S. (1977). *The enrichment triad model: A guide for developing defensible programs for the gifted*. Mansfield Center, CT: Creative Learning Press.

Renzulli, J.S. (1978). What makes giftedness? Re-examining a definition. *Phi Delta Kappan, 60*, 180–184.

Renzulli, J.S. (1986). The three ring conception of giftedness: A development model for creative productivity. In R.J. Sternberg & J. Davidson (Eds.), *Conceptions of giftedness*. New York: Cambridge University Press.

Renzulli, J. S. (1988a). A decade of dialogue on the three-ring conception of giftedness. *Roeper Review, 11*, 18–25.

Renzulli, J.S. (1988b). The multiple menu model for developing differentiated curriculum for the gifted and talented. *Gifted Child Quarterly, 32*, 298–309.

Renzulli, J.S., & Reis, S.M. (1985). *The schoolwide enrichment model: A comprehensive plan for educational excellence*. Mansfield Center, CT: Creative Learning Press.

Renzulli, J.S., Reis, S.M., & Smith, L.H. (1981). *The revolving door identification model*. Mansfield Center, CT: Creative Learning Press.

Starko, A. (1986). *The effects of The Revolving Door identification model on creative productivity and self-efficacy*. Unpublished doctoral dissertation. The University of Connecticut, Storrs.

Tuttle, F.B. (1980). *Evaluation report for Concord, MA: Project Gather and Project Lift*. Concord, MA: Concord School System.

Ward, V. (1962). *The gifted student: A manual for program development*. A Report of the Southern Regional Project for Education of the Gifted. Atlanta, GA: Southern Research Educational Bureau.

Westberg, K.L. (1990). *The effects of instruction in the inventing process on students' development of inventions.*Unpublished doctoral dissertation, University of Connecticut, Storrs.

Whitehead, A.N. (1929). The rhythm of education. In A. N. Whitehead (Ed.), *The aims of education*. New York: Macmillan.

5

Issues on Stimulating Creativity in the Schools: A South American Perspective

Solange Wechsler

CREATIVITY IN SOUTH AMERICA

The importance of studying creativity in South America has been recognized for the last two decades. Results from systematic studies done in this area indicate that there is a possibility for applying basic creativity principles in the Southern American cultures. The 13 countries have diverse social, economic, and educational development and it is important to consider the characteristics of their diversity when studying the present nature of knowledge about creativity in South America.

This chapter will examine the status of knowledge about creativity in Brazil, the largest country in South America. Some important peculiarities about this country will be presented from a historical perspective for better understanding of the main questions raised by Brazilian researchers. This approach will stress the important role that the development of creativity research has in the solutions of Brazilian problems. Limitations and gaps of this research will be pointed out to suggest directions and areas in which further investigation is most needed for the countrys benefit.

Brazil is a large country, occupying nearly half of South America with 3,286,470 square miles. It was first visited by Pedro Alvarez Cabral in 1500 and remained a Portuguese colony until 1822. The name Brazil was derived from the Portuguese word for the red color of Brazilwood (*brasa* = glowing coal), which the early visitors gathered. The country's national language is Portuguese, with no existing dialects.

The Portuguese colonizers main aim was the development of

sugar plantations for later crop exportation to European countries. However, the natives could not adapt to the back-breaking labor of the cane fields, and slaves were imported from Africa in large numbers. The slave trade existed until 1850 and a law for gradual emancipation of the slaves was passed in 1871.

Brazil is a society which has many races that have been derived from the intermarriages of whites, blacks, Indians and other immigrant races. The population now is 54% white, 38.45% mulatto, 5.89% black, 0.63% Asian, and a few others. The main immigrants to Brazil were from Portugal (31%), Italy (29%), Spain (12%), Germany (5%), and Japan (4%). A small number of natives (3%) still live in the Amazon region of Northern Brazil (Abril, 1990). Because of the low proportion of other races like the Japanese, Germans, or Indians, their influence on the Brazilian culture is considerably small.

The combination of different cultures brought a great diversity of values, traditions, and religions to Brazil. European culture and Catholic values (mainly from Portuguese, Italian, and Spanish people) merged with African rites, beliefs, and music. It is easier to understand Brazilian habits and behaviors from the theme of integration: The culture integrates the expansive Latin American attitudes with a sense of rhythm and an enjoyment for movement from its African ancestors.

Brazils present population is estimated to be 150 million, with 20% living in rural areas. The annual birthrate is 2.8% and approximately 47% of all Brazilians are below the age of 20, indicating that this is a young country (UNICEF, IBGE, 1987).

Brazil is a developing country. Wealthy cities like Rio de Janiero, Sao Paulo, Curitiba, Porto Alegre, and the capital, Brasilia, exist in the eastern and southern areas. However, there are very poor cities located in the dry and forest regions of the north and northeastern states, such as Amazonas, Para, and Alagoas.

BRAZIL'S EDUCATIONAL SYSTEM

The Brazilian education system is divided into three levels: a primary level consisting of the first eight grades (i.e., for children between ages 7 and 15), a secondary level of three grades, and the tertiary level for postsecondary education. Public school attendance consists of 86% primary students; 42% go on to secondary school, 40% of whom receive higher education. The quality of primary and secondary education differs considerably between public and private schools—the former is generally inferior. Students from middle- and high-class socioeconomic families typically attend private schools, while those from lower class socioeconomic homes have few options other than public schools (Oakland & Wechsler, 1988).

The School Dropout Problem

Brazilian public education is facing a serious crisis due to the high dropout rate and grade retention. Nationally, among 100 pupils who enter the first grade, 38 reach the fourth grade, 12 finish the ninth grade, 5 finish high school, and fewer than 3 go to college. The dropout rates are even higher in the northern and poorer Brazilian states, where only 23% of the students finish the fourth grade and 10% reach the ninth grade (IPLAN/IPEA, UNICEF, SUDENE, 1986).

Analysis of school dropouts during the elementary years shows that the most difficult grades to pass are the first (primary grade level) and the fifth (junior high school). Between the first and second elementary grades dropout and repeating grade rates reach as high as 56% at the national level, and almost 75% in the northern Brazilian states.

Grade repetition is related to academic failure. In fact, after repeating a grade more than twice, the lower class children tend to quit school. If we consider that it is only at the fourth elementary grade that students reach the minimum writing level, we can conclude that those who drop out of school before the fourth elementary grade will regress into illiteracy. Thus, the possibility of breaking the cycle of poverty by educating the population is considerably unlikely if children do not remain in schools long enough to become independent and productive citizens.

Several studies have been done by Brazilian researchers to investigate the possible causes of dropping out of school. Their results indicate that a complex problem exists, which stems from the family, school, and teacher, as reviewed by Wechsler and Oakland (1988). Families that are low on the socioeconomic scale do not value education, and their children are considered more important when contributing to the family income than they are when attending school. Brazilian public schools in the poor northern regions do not offer adequate physical conditions for learning, such as number of desks, ventilation, potable water, teaching materials, and so on. The regular 4-hour daily class schedule is sometimes shortened to 3 hours, due to the high number of school-age children in some areas.

The high student-to-teacher ratio, plus the irrelevance the school curriculum has in these childrens lives, increases the difficulty of sustaining motivation in the classrooms. In many rural regions, we can find teachers who have not completed the fourth elementary grade. Poor teaching methodologies are common problems among most teachers in Brazil, where pencil-and-paper is the preferred strategy and there is little space for the development of creativity, curiosity, and internal motivation for learning.

The serious crisis that the Brazilian education system is facing calls for urgent and creative solutions. There is no doubt that a country can be fully developed when there is a large investment in its human potential. Brazilian researchers are concerned with these facts and have been directing their investigations to search for solutions to solve this grave educational situation.

The amount of research being done by educators and psychologists exploring the development of creativity in schools is increasing and researchers are considering the various dimensions of the cognitive, emotional, and social effects of developing creativity. A review of these studies suggests that creativity is emerging as a discipline in Brazil as a result of the application of its basic principles and methodologies to the Brazilian school settings.

STAGES FOR THE DEVELOPMENT OF CREATIVITY IN BRAZIL

There are steps to follow when examining the development of psychology in any country (Azuma, 1984). If we adapt Azumas model to creativity, we would follow these steps toward the growth of creativity as a science in a specific country:

1. A pioneering stage, in which the relevance of creativity is realized
2. An introductory stage, in which creativity is accepted as an important discipline
3. A translation and modeling stage, in which attempts are made to fully apply Western concepts and technologies to the culture

4. An indigenous stage, in which new concepts and technology appropriate to the culture are developed
5. An integration stage, in which the science of creativity is freed from an exclusively Western influence and develops orientations consistent with the dominant cultural characteristics

The development of creativity in Brazil can be located in the third stage and moving into the fourth stage, if we follow the above sequence.

The relevance of creativity has already been recognized in Brazil, and an increasing number of studies have been emerging from the graduate centers located in the most developed cities of Brasilia, Sao Paulo, Rio de Janeiro, Porto Alegre, and Pernambuco. This indicates the importance of creativity as a discipline to study.

The trends observed in these studies consist of applying Western creativity principles (mainly from the U.S.) or adapting them to Brazilian reality, and searching for new technologies and methodologies that are more adaptable to the Brazilians social, economic, and educational characteristics. The transition of the study of creativity from the third to the fourth stage in Brazil is consistent with the overall advancement of the research in educational and school psychology (Oakland & Wechsler, 1988).

Conditions for Research in Brazil

Four conditions are regarded as being highly important for the development of educational and psychological research in a country. They are: (a) the existence of graduate programs dedicated to the studies of specific areas. (b) availability of outside support for research on relevant issues, (c) existence of publications where the research is disseminated, and (d) presence of professional associations committed to the promotion of research (Oakland & Wechsler, 1988).

Graduate programs and research. There has been an increasing amount of creativity research produced since 1968 by the faculty and graduate students associated with four main universities: University of Brasilia, Federal University of Rio Grande de Sul, Pontifical Catholic University of Rio de Janiero, and the Federal University of Pernambuco. The programs are usually at the Master's level and associated with education and psychology departments.

The absence of creativity research in other areas, even those typically related to creativity such as art, literature, drama, music and so forth, indicates that the education and psychology disciplines were the ones given the responsibility of investigating the nature and applicability of the principles of creativity to the Brazilian culture.

Availability of publications. Meager support for research in Brazil endangers the quality of investigations carried on at the universities and prevents extramural studies by the professional community. Because there are no journals dedicated exclusively to creativity, education, and school psychology, the major findings in creativity research have been published in a general way in psychology and education journals or have been confined to university libraries in thesis format.

Nine main journals feature the writings of Brazilian educators. Nevertheless, economic difficulties interrupt the regular publication of these journals. Recently, efforts have been made by Brazilian research granting agencies, as well as graduate psychology and education associations, to edit abstracts, reviews of papers, theses, and dissertations written by Brazilian researchers. The total absence of these materials has added considerable roadblocks to an accurate estimation of the research trends, developments, and progress in Brazil.

Brazilian professional associations. Two major professional associations are trying to promote the importance of creativity in the country, and especially in Brazilian education. They are the Brazilian Association for the Gifted (founded in 1978) and the Brazilian Association for School and Educational Psychologists (founded in 1988 by the author). These associations are directing their activities at parents, teachers, school counselors, educational supervisors, and school directors to convey the message that it is important to invest in Brazilian childrens' creative talents as a solution to the countrys educational crisis.

The Brazilian Association for the Gifted has already established regional sections in more than seven states and promoted annual conventions and seminars since 1975. There has been hope of increasing the awareness of the various dimensions of the gifted, and calling attention to the traditional confusion between creativity and intelligence through these events. Some programs for the gifted have been initiated at the private and the public level, like the one maintained in the public education system of Brasilia for the elementary children, which has been in place for 13 years.

Brazilian federal law, passed in 1971, assured the rights of exceptional children to a special educational program that included the gifted. However, social bias has hampered the necessary funding for these programs. Higher priority has to be given to the poor and deficient children so that Brazil can reduce the high illiteracy rate and solve the school dropout problem. Therefore, accumulating sufficient research data on the benefits that creativity brings to school achievement has been the main objective of Brazilian researchers in an effort to convince the countrys educational authorities of the importance of creativity in the schools.

THEORETICAL KNOWLEDGE ON CREATIVITY IN BRAZIL

The theoretical knowledge about creativity in Brazil has been mainly influenced by well-known North American educators and psychologists such as Alex Osborn, J. P. Guilford, and Paul Torrance. Carl Rogers's and Rollo May's humanistic approach, and the behaviorist framework of B. F. Skinner have also had an impact, in different ways, on the study of creativity in Brazil.

Until recently, few foreign books specifically related to creativity have been translated into Portuguese. They are: *O Poder Criador da Mente* (*Applied Imagination*; Osborn, 1981); *A Coragem de Criar* (*The Courage to Create*; May, 1982); *Criatividade: Testes, Medidas e Avaliacoes* (*Guiding Creative Talent*; Torrance, 1976); *Pode-se Ensinar Creatividade?* (*Is Creativity Teachable*; Torrance & Torrance, 1974); *Arte e Ciencia da Criatividade* (*The Arts and Sciences of Creativity*; Kneller, 1978); and *Criatividade: Progresso e Potencial* (*Creativity: Progress and Potential*; Taylor, 1976).

Brazilian educators and psychologists have also been reporting their theoretical knowledge about creativity through several papers and books. Although their production is not considerably high yet, we can cite five major books dealing with this theme: *Psicologia da Criatividade* (*Psychology of Creativity*; Novaes, 1972); *Criatividade e Orientacao Educacional* (*Creativity and Educational Supervision*; Assumpcao, 1981); *Criatividade* (*Creativity*; Campos & Weber, 1987); *Identificacao e Desenvolvi-*

mento da Criatividade (*Identification and Development of Creativity*; Wechsler, 1992); and *Psicologia da Criatividade* (*Psychology of Creativity*; Alencar, 1986a).

The importance of stimulating the creatively gifted, as well as other dimensions of the gifted, has also been a concern of Brazilian educators. Three main books have been influencing the development of this area in Brazil: *Desenvolvimento Psicologico do Superdotado* (*Psychological Development of the Gifted*; Novaes, 1979); *Psicologia e Educacao de Superdotado* (*Psychology and Education of the Gifted*; Alencar, 1986b); and *Os Superdotados: Quem Sao? Onde Estao?* (*The Gifted: Who Are They? Where Are They?*; Santos,1988). Experiences originating from gifted programs have also been accumulating in this area and are being reported in the proceedings of the annual conferences, sponsored by the Brazilian Association for the Gifted.

RESEARCH FINDINGS ON CREATIVITY IN BRAZIL

Research on creativity in Brazil is increasing, mainly through the contributions of graduate centers in psychology and education. Most frequently, the theoretical basis for the hypothesis of these studies has come from Guilfords definition of creativity, equating creativity with divergent thinking. They have also come from Torrances conception of creativity as a process of sensing gaps in information, forming new hypotheses about the missing elements, testing them, and communicating their results. Therefore, Brazilian researchers affirm that creativity is definable, measurable, and can be developed.

Cognitive and emotional dimensions of creativity, as well as their interrelationships with the social dimension, have been researched in this country. Most of the studies have emphasized the low social value of creativity with samples from low socioeconomic environments, as they constitute a major portion of the Brazilian population. Researchers have also aimed their research at the comprehension of the public school education system, where the main problems related to academic failure are located.

The major findings of Brazilian creativity research, published in paper or thesis format, can be put into four broad categories: the creative person, the creative process, the creative product, and the creative environment. The following presentation of the Brazilian research results will refer to these classifications to provide a clear picture of our current state of knowledge about each one of these aspects.

The Creative Person

The identification of the most important traits or characteristics associated with creative persons has received attention from innumerable researchers. The great interest in this area probably results from the possibility of predicting creative production, if there are common personality traits related to creativity and the need to know if these characteristics are universal or if they only appear in a specific culture. Research in this area has focused on the assessment of the Brazilians creative strengths, creative women's attitudes and conflicts, and creative children's adjustment in the classroom.

Brazilian's creative characteristics. Investigations carried on to identify Brazilian's creative characteristics have been based on assessing creative people's strengths through their drawings or written responses.

The work of Torrance and Ball (1980) and Torrance and Wu (1981) indicated that there were certain characteristics of North American children's drawings that were highly related to their adult creative achievements. These creative strengths, assessed through the figural forms of the Torrance Tests of Creative Thinking (TTCT; Torrance, 1974), were: expression of movement and emotions, combination of ideas, expressiveness of titles, unusual and internal visual perspective, elaboration, fantasy, humor, extension of boundaries and articulation in telling stories.

Wechsler (1981) assessed North American written responses. Subjects demonstrated the existence of creative verbal skills that might also imitate their adult creative achievements. These strengths are: expression of emotions, fantasy, unusual perspective, elaboration, and analogy. The instrument used for this assessment was the verbal form of the TTCT (Torrance, 1974).

The concurrent validity of these creative verbal strengths was verified in our study with Brazilian adults of both sexes (Wechsler, 1985a). The high number of relationships observed among these verbal strengths and the subjects creative achievements, not only in the United States but also in Brazil, indicates the possibility of existing universal traits that could distinguish the creative person's behavior in any culture (Wechsler, 1985b).

The creative figural strengths of Brazilian and U.S. children were also compared (Wechsler & Richmond, 1982). The results obtained in this study called our attention to the diversity of ways to express creativity through drawings. While Brazilian children have a higher preference to demonstrate their creativity through the expression of emotions, unusual perspective, and extending the boundaries of their drawings, the U.S. children have a higher frequency of humor and richness of imagery in their figures. These findings indicate the existence of tendencies toward preferable ways of creating in each culture, which have been considered when comparing each countrys creative production.

While educators have to be aware of a child's creative strengths to help the child's full development, there is also a need to consider children's weaknesses that may hinder the expression of their creative potential. In our study with creatively gifted children (Wechsler, 1987a), we observed their difficulties in planning and their dislike for critical thinking. For every minute of planning activities, they leaped to several minutes of divergent thinking. If we consider that divergent thinking has to be followed by convergent thinking to improve a product after its creation, we can conclude that there is a need to work with Brazilian children on both divergent and convergent thinking abilities to increase their chances of creative production (Wechsler, 1988).

The results from these studies also indicate that programs for the gifted can not be transplanted from one culture to another without considering cach countrys learning and thinking preferences. Our observations of gifted programs for Brazilian children indicate the strong effect of socioeconomic class on the way these children react to the proposed activities. Children who come from medium and high socioeconomic classes can work well during sit-in situations, but this does not necessarily occur with children from low socioeconomic environments. These children tend to prefer activities involving expression of emotions and movement. We believe that more research is needed about the creative strengths of Brazilians to improve existing programs for the gifted in this country (Wechsler, 1987a).

Creative Brazilian women. The absence of studies of creativity in Brazilian women and the concern for the repression of their creative potential was the theme of another study by Wechsler and Guerreiro (1986). The picture that emerged from this investigation was of someone with several conflicts: fear of being original and not assuming the conforming role prescribed to

her by society, fear of actualizing herself and risk losing her
femininity, and fear of freeing her curiosity and not being able to
fit the mother's role.

Many Brazilian women occupy leading positions in the country.
It can be inferred that their personal conflicts inhibit them from
fully demonstrating their creative potential. Similar to the majority of women in the world, Brazilian women have suffered from
a long history of suppression of their creative talents. Researchers
urgently need to investigate the best methodologies to help creative women develop their self-esteem so as to fully actualize their
creative possibilities.

The creative characteristics of Brazilian women in elementary
school teaching roles were also investigated by Guerreiro (1987)
using the verbal and figural forms of the TTCT (Torrance, 1974).
These teachers' highest creative strengths, as demonstrated by
their written and drawing responses, were expression of emotions,
elaboration, extension of boundaries, and unusual perspective.

Using Torrance's (1979) explanation for the possible meanings
of these creative strengths, we can infer that Brazilian teachers are
nonconforming persons, ready to break rules and limits, with
great capability to express their feelings and emotions and to
implement their ideas. When we consider the sad picture of
Brazilian school dropouts, we come to the conclusion that these
teachers are not able either to express their full creative potential
in their classrooms or develop creative thinking in their students.
Brazilian researchers are aware of these constraints and have been
investigating several methodologies to help the teachers manifest
their creative talents in the classrooms.

Creative childrens school adjustment.   What relationship
exists between creative Brazilian children, their teachers and
peers? What influence does social class, grade, gender, and intelligence have on the expression of their creative abilities? These
were some of the questions raised in the studies of Alencar (1984)
and Wechsler and Richmond (1984).

The study conducted by Alencar tried to answer the first
question. Children were rated by their teachers as having high,
medium, and low levels of creativity. They were then given
descriptions of students having various qualities and were asked
to choose those characteristics they would want for themselves or
for their friends. Interesting findings came from their responses,
since the children rated as being creative did not prefer the same
quality for themselves, although they did indicate that it was a

quality they would like in friends. The highly rated creative children would rather be popular, honest, and intelligent to gain social acceptance and possibly be held in high regard by their teachers than to be generators of new ideas.

A creative person's pressure to conform and to receive love from their significant others is a common point in most of the cross-cultural studies. Societies tend to discriminate and punish uncommon or unexpected behavior, and researchers need to investigate ways to change this universal tendency to repress creativity.

The adjustment of Brazilian children, as perceived by their teachers, does not depend on their gender, intelligence, or creativity level (Wechsler & Richmond, 1984). Only the grade level seems to influence the perception of adjustment. It is observed that the children at the first and last years of elementary school are the most difficult to handle.

Another finding from Wechsler and Richmonds study with Brazilian children confirms Torrance's (1963) observation from U.S. samples about the fourth-grade slump. Brazilian students from three different socioeconomic levels enter the first elementary grade presenting no differences in relation to their creative potential. However, by the fourth elementary grade there is a considerable decline in these children's creative abilities, the highest loss for those coming from low socioeconomic environments.

We do not have sufficient data now to affirm whether the fourth-grade slump is altered in later school grades. There seems to exist, in most of the schools around the world, a total absence of knowledge on how to develop the great potential children bring to schools. If researchers do not focus their efforts to change this common trend, we are heading toward a world where the greatest talents are killed just by entering school.

The Creative Process

Various methods for developing creative thinking and behavior have been tested by Brazilian researchers. The overall conclusion resulting from these studies is that creativity is possible to assess and develop through different procedures for different age groups and in various types of environments.

A new research trend in Brazil explores methods of processing information and their relationship with creativity. Results from these studies have called attention to cultural differences in preferred ways of learning and thinking. The need for methodologies that will capitalize on the predominant thinking styles in each country so that creative production is enhanced has been pointed out.

Following is a series of Brazilian investigations on process and methodologies that are capable of developing creativity. We will compare these findings with data from other countries.

Oral and written language. Studies involving creative expression through oral and written languages have used different strategies. Wiedmann (1976) used various stimuli in different situations—individual text readings, text discussions, text titles, and free associations—and investigated their effects on fluency and flexibility in compositions. This author's findings indicated that all of the stimuli could enhance creativity in written language, but the largest effect resulted from student discussions of the texts.

Two main reading methods have been used in the Brazilian elementary schools: the synthetic and the analytic. The first one teaches reading through the recognition of letters, phonemes, and their combinations. The second method teaches reading through the total structure or synthesis of a text and sentences. The combination of these methods has been used in most of the Brazilian schools. Garcia (1979) tried to investigate which one could have the most impact on language fluency, flexibility, and originality. Her results showed that only flexibility was significantly influenced by the analytic method, probably due to its emphasis on the word unit.

Gender influences were only observed in the first study; therefore, they did not confirm the traditional assumption of women's superiority in language. More research is needed in this area, along with an investigation of learning styles and preferences when approaching reading or writing materials.

Student-centered teaching methods. The influence of Carl Rogers' theory on centering teaching methods around students' needs and objectives was the basis for the studies of Medeiros (1977) and Papa (1975). The first author investigated the effects of two teaching procedures: student-centered methods and teacher-centered methods. Her results indicated that both methods can bring positive results to students achievement, either by evaluating them through Bloom's taxonomy (knowledge, comprehensions, application, analysis, and synthesis) or through Guilford's conception of originality.

Punitive and rigid teaching procedures are usually not considered conducive to students' creative thinking. This was the question raised in Papa's (1975) study, which compared the effects on children's artistic productivity when using pressure and punishment as a teaching method on one hand, and a nonevaluative and free classroom atmosphere on the other. Interesting results were obtained by this author, as his data indicated there were no significant differences between the two teaching methods in relation to the children's creative production.

These studies illustrated the need for being cautious when classifying teaching methodologies as creative and noncreative. Apparently, some students might need external motivation and more structured situations to be productive. We still have to clarify in future studies whether these differences are related to culture, socioeconomic classes, gender, or individual personality characteristics.

Reinforcement, mediation, and modeling procedures. The behaviorist approach made various contributions to the study of creativity in Brazil. The effect of social reinforcement on children's verbal creativity, for example, was the theme of a study carried on by Maia (1976). Her findings indicated that this procedure was effective for children from high and middle socioeconomic classes, increasing their verbal fluency and originality. However, for those children coming from low socioeconomic environments, social reinforcement did not seem to be sufficient to develop their creativity, indicating the need to investigate combinations of different types of reinforcement for the poor students.

Mediation strategies seemed to have positive effects on verbal creativity. This was the conclusion of two studies carried on by Santos (1975) and Guhur (1976). The first investigation revealed significant gains in verbal creativity when written instructions and oral training were given before presenting the stimulus situation. The second study combined modeling with instructions, which obtained positive results on fluency and flexibility of ideas. Findings from these studies indicate the positive effects of reinforcement and mediation strategies on creative production. However, more investigation needs to be done to ascertain the most effective strategy, as well as specific content areas for people in the low socioeconomic environments.

Incubation and information searching procedures.   Incubation is considered to be an important period preceding the insight phase. Nevertheless, incubation time is seldom given to students in the classroom to enhance the possibility of coming out with creative solutions. This theme concerned Negreiros (1978), who investigated the effects of incubation on the solution of complex visual problems. Her positive results demonstrated that this strategy is powerful and possible to use in regular school situations.

The absence of creative behavior in the schools might also be due to the lack of students training in information searching procedures. This was the hypothesis tested by Osowski (1976). She experimented with new solutions through teaching strategies which promoted uncertainty, curiosity, and willingness. Her findings indicated that these strategies can only be effective for those who already have some degree of creative thinking.

The creative disposition is a factor affecting most of the studies done by international researchers on ways to develop creative behaviors. A commonly mentioned limitation on training procedures that increases creativity is time. Therefore, we need to focus our future investigations on how much time is necessary for working with persons who have low dispositions toward creative thinking.

Art and science education.   Are art and science teachers enhancing creative thinking in their students? This question was answered by observing and interviewing art teachers and evaluating the books used in science education at the elementary school level.

The first study done by Fonseca (1978) verified that art teachers are not making use of the potential offered in this area, since they are more concerned with artistic techniques than with enhancing creative expression through arts. Unfortunately, in art education, quick production is emphasized more often than the creative process, thus denying an excellent opportunity to release the students creative potential.

Science education is not contributing to scientific creativity either. The evaluation of science books used in Brazilian schools by Alencar (1989) indicated that most of them require only copying, memorizing, and comprehension of the contents.

The conclusion from these studies demonstrates that Brazilian schools are directed at reproducing facts and thoughts rather than enabling students to be productive thinkers. The books, as well as the teachers, do not allow for process beyond the given information. After all the passive years in the elementary and high school grades, we can hardly expect our college students to be able to think and behave creatively.

Learning and thinking styles. The importance of learning and thinking preferences and their relationships with creative production have recently concerned international researchers. The question raised in these cross-cultural investigations refers to the universality of the learning styles concept and its effect on each culture's creative production and school achievement.

Several studies have been conducted by this author and collaborators, aimed at responding to this question. One of these investigations referred to the construct validity of the Brazilian population using the Learning Styles Inventory (Dunn, Dunn, & Price, 1984), which proposes 22 influential factors on learning and thinking preferences (Wechsler, Polonia, & Torres, 1988). Our results indicated the existence of only 15 factors affecting Brazilian adolescents' learning styles, which relate to the following variables: sociological (learning with peers vs. learning alone, adult motivated, authority figures present), physical (tactile preferences, required intake, needs mobility, late morning vs. early morning, afternoon vs. morning), environmental (noise level, temperature, light, design), and emotional (motivation, persistence, responsibility).

A comparison of these results with those obtained from North American samples indicated that some learning styles do not seem to be important to the Brazilian culture, as we did not observe the following styles in our students: ability to learn in several ways; auditory, visual, and kinesthetic preferences; and evening vs. morning factors. Nevertheless, it is interesting to observe that visual, oral, and kinesthetic activities are the main teaching strategies used by Brazilian teachers, and are also the ones that seem to be the most inadequate for the Brazilian students. This justifies the urgency to research students' learning styles and to orient teaching methodologies to their main preferences.

The possible relationships among learning styles and academic achievement were also investigated in our studies (Wechsler, Torres, & Polonia, 1989; Wechsler, Torres, Polonia, & Pasquali, 1990). Concerning overall academic achievement, there was only a significant relationship between the variable and students' responsibility. As for the prediction of reading and math achievement, specifically, the greater influence came from the following styles: learning with peers, motivation, persistence, and temperature.

Sociological, emotional, and environmental factors seem to be very important in predicting Brazilian students' achievement. This does not necessarily occur with U.S. higher achievers in math and reading (Dunn & Dunn, 1978), who seem to prefer working alone. Preference to work or be with groups is usually observed among Brazilians, as well as most of the Latin American cultures. Therefore, better use of group strategies is needed to increase motivation in the classrooms.

The relationship among learning styles and creative characteristics was the theme of another investigation (Wechsler, Fialho, Wanderly, & Trestini, 1988). By observing Brazilian adolescents' drawings, we were able to verify their high frequency of responses expressing emotions, internal and unusual perspective, and their influence upon emotional and sociological learning and thinking preferences. Findings from these studies are confirming the importance of our previous investigations on Brazilian creative characteristics. If we consider Torrance's (1976) affirmation of the importance of using the strengths of culturally different children, we can conclude that the Brazilian schools should provide students with more group activities involving expression of emotions and feelings, and allow them more opportunities to express their nonconforming ideas. Our future studies intend to clarify the relationship between learning styles and creative achievements, aiming specifically at gifted children.

The Creative Product

Investigations aimed at enhancing creative production have used different procedures with samples of various age groups and experiences. The overall conclusion of these studies was that creative production is identifiable, measurable, and observable in innumerable ways.

Diverse techniques have been employed in workshops for increasing creative thinking and behaviors such as brainstorming, guided fantasy, forced combinations, attribute listing, sociodrama, creative reading and written exercises, creative problem solving, and so forth. The main objective for the use of these strategies was not to verify the effects of each one of them but to trace out their overall impact on the different dimensions of the creative production.

Student's cognitive abilities and behaviors. Most of the Brazilian research related to creativity has verified the positive effect of different procedures upon the cognitive creative abilities of fluency, flexibility, and originality using Guilford's or Torrance's frameworks. Although these authors' tests were frequently used as instruments to assess creative dimensions, we can also find investigations evaluating these creative aspects through the analysis of an individual's behaviors, attitudes, or production.

As remarked in the previous section, our findings have indicated there are specific creative processes that can be enhanced and measured through their impact on fluency, flexibility ,and originality of ideas. Studies combining different creative strategies also confirmed their positive effects not only on students cognitive creative abilities but also on behavior.

However, influential variables affecting the degree that these creative abilities can be increased were reported by several authors. Socioeconomic class, for example, is frequently mentioned in Brazilian studies, as children from lower socioeconomic families have difficulty responding to testing situations. Gender influence on cognitive creative abilities is not conclusive, since it seems to interact with socioeconomic class. For example, poor girls have higher scores than boys from the same social class, and the contrary seems to happen for the boys from middle and upper socioeconomic families (Alencar, 1974; Rodrigues, 1979).

Preschool childrens behavior and cognitive abilities can be affected by various creative training strategies, as concluded by Silva (1978) and Alves (1985). Creative dramatic play is a powerful tool to use with preschool children, since it can help them to increase not only their divergent and convergent thinking abilities, but also their expression of leadership and socializing behaviors.

On the other hand, high school and college students can benefit from creative training exercises tied to their academic content or vocational guidance procedures. Creative techniques can help these students to be more conscious and receptive to their internal lives and surrounding environment, as well as improve their confidence in risk taking when choosing new career fields (Assumpcao, 1978; Rosas, 1988).

Children's futuristic perceptions. Torrance (1979) affirmed that if children can be prepared to think about the world's future problems, they will be able to solve them more creatively when adults.

The results obtained from our studies with Brazilian children who came from different regions showed that they can think about their future, combining their fantasies with their immediate needs (Novaes et al., 1981). However, the cognitive developmental stage and the socioeconomic class are important variables to consider when observing children's futuristic perceptions expressed through their drawings. Children from lower socioeconomic environments have different concerns than those from wealthy regions. For example, in this study Brazilian children from poor states mentioned future problems related to habitation and hunger, while those living in richer states were more concerned with pollution and the collapse of the traffic system.

International comparisons of children's perception of future problems, carried out by the research team at the University of Georgia, also indicated the strong impact of each country's economic development on children's proposed solutions for the future. Children from well-developed nations were more concerned with the impact of the most recent scientific discoveries upon men's lives. Children from Second and Third World nations revealed their preoccupation with their own country's development, such as the nonexistence of food or sufficient money to buy it, overpopulation, and so forth.

The above findings direct our attention to the influence socioeconomic variables have on children's perceptions of the future. Appreciation of this component is necessary to understand the creative production in several nations.

Children's school achievement.   What are the effects of creativity training procedures on students' grades? How can creative strategies affect behaviors conducive to high achievement in school? These were the main questions posed by Brazilian investigators concerned with the serious school failure problem occurring in this country. Studies measuring school achievement, through pre-post designs, were unanimous in affirming the positive effects that creative training exercises can bring to the students, not only related to their cognitive creative abilities but also to increasing their motivation to learn (Cunha, 1979; Magalhaes, 1972).

Undoubtedly, school achievement can be dramatically increased if we consider the students' thinking and learning styles. Using the brain-hemisphericity concept, Guerreiro (1987) tested the hypothesis of using right-brain strategies to increase the

school achievement of disadvantaged children who were repeating the first grade for the third time. Training programs on
ways to adapt right-brain strategies to the regular academic
content were given to teachers. The positive results obtained
demonstrated the importance of capitalizing on children's hemis-
phericity preference while teaching them. These students increased not only their grades but also their motivation and
curiosity to learn more.

The use of right-brain strategies with the Brazilian gifted is
usually refuted by the idea that creative thinking is good for all
children. We tested this assumption in a 3-month program for
gifted and regular children (Wechsler, 1987b). Our results indicated that all children can benefit from creative thinking activities, though their gains occur in different ways and degrees. The
gifted children had higher gains on measures of classroom participation, while the regular children increased their motivation to
learn, as well as their fluency and originality of ideas. In conclusion, there is a need to offer different opportunities for the gifted as
well as the average student to optimize the full use of Brazilians
talents.

Teachers' behaviors.   Ways to help Brazilian teachers in
developing and expressing their creative thinking potential in the
classroom have been a main concern of Brazilian researchers.
Various training programs were tested with teachers, and the
results were evaluated not only through the teachers' behavior
but also the students'.

One important variable affecting school achievement is related
to the teachers' expectations of their pupils. The influence of this
variable upon students behaviors is a common finding of international researchers. A teacher's reinforcement of certain types of
behaviors will cause these behaviors to appear more frequently,
according to behavior psychologists. Children want to receive
attention and be loved by their teachers, so they behave in the
teacher's preferred way, according to the humanist psychologists.

Considering the following affirmations, we can understand why
creative behavior seldom appears in the classrooms, since
teachers do not seem to like or value it. For example, 95% of
Brazilian teachers from an elementary school declared that they
prefer students who are obedient, sincere, courteous, hard-
working and popular with their peers. Characteristics usually
associated with creativity, such as high intuition, curiosity, and

independence of thought were considered by teachers as not being as important or relevant in the classrooms as the former (Alencar & Rodrigues, 1978).

However, research on creativity training programs with teachers showed us the possibility of changing repressive attitudes against creative behavior in the classrooms. Our studies with Brazilian teachers indicated the need to start working with them while they are still taking courses at the normal school (teacher preparation schools). Creativity training programs can be beneficial to teachers at the normal school in several ways: informing them about the importance of creativity in the classroom, developing their cognitive creative abilities, and helping them to come up with their own suggestions in adapting creative thinking techniques to their academic content (Fleith, 1990).

The effects of teachers training programs can also be verified on their students behavior, as some researchers have demonstrated (Ott, 1975; Wechsler, Torres, & Polonia, 1989). If teachers prefer an inductive methodology rather than a deductive one, they will be able to increase their students fluency, flexibility, and sensitivity to problems. However, none of these methodologies seem to be sufficient to increase students original thinking.

Teaching methodologies need to be combined with teachers personality characteristics within an environment that respects students learning preferences if we want to elicit creative behaviors. This seems to be the result we are heading toward in our progressing research on Brazilian teachers' styles and their relationships with students' creativity and achievement.

The Creative Environment

To understand the functioning of an institution, we have to observe it through various aspects: philosophy of work (overt or covert), social climate, relationships among its members, contact with the surrounding community, financial resources, existing facilities, and so forth.

In the same way, to comprehend a functioning school, we have to investigate using the principles of organizational psychology, considering it as a large institution with its own rules and characteristics.

Although teachers and students are an important component of the school institution, their relationships do not explain the total of school functioning. Therefore, if we want to understand why creativity is absent from Brazilian schools, we also have to investigate the other school professionals' perceptions of the importance of creative thinking and behavior for education.

There seems to be a general wish for something called creativity in many Brazilian public and private schools. However, Novaes (1989) concluded from her interviews and observations of various schools that a considerable distance exists between the wish and the real act. The professionals most concerned with creative thinking and behaviors were the psychologists in Novaes's (1989) study. The school supervisors were more concerned about pacing the academic content, and the directors were concerned with administrative duties. Most of the professionals in the schools tended to relate creativity to arts and leisure activities. Therefore, perhaps we need to shift our focus from the teachers and students, and invest our efforts in working with the other influential people in the school.

Another important factor to consider when analyzing an institution is the degree to which it respects the characteristics and values of its surrounding community. Our school institutions can hardly be perceived as attending to the communitys peculiarities. Instructional programs that have been preprepared, as well as books, are sent through the state and municipal education departments to all schools, regardless of their locations. Students' cultural characteristics are seldom understood by the school staff, who tend to emphasize uniform evaluation procedures and rigid behavioral rules for all students. Therefore, little space is granted for creativity in most schools, and they are located either in the cities or in the poor rural areas (Gomes, 1985).

Investigations related to creativity in organizations other than the schools are rare in Brazil. Only one study was located in our review; it was conducted by Hesketh (1985) on the importance of creativity and self-concept to industrial management. Her findings indicated that creativity could influence the relationships in an organization, while self-concept could affect managers' efficiency. Limitations of this research can account for the sampling procedure that did not include the top range executives, but included those who were immediately subordinate. Thus, our future studies have to inquire if creative thinking in the Brazilian industries is left to administrators and no one else.

The few studies done in Brazil related to creative environment in institutions or organizations do not permit us to make general conclusions. Compared with the quantity of research done in relation to the teacher, the student, and student–teacher relationship, we still know very little about how to make an impact on school dynamics and to make them more sensitive to a creative functioning. Our future studies will have to focus on the total school structure rather than working on its isolated units, such as the teacher or the students.

CONCLUSIONS

Our review of Brazilian research confirms that creativity is emerging as an important discipline to study in this country. Considering the stages for the full development of creativity as a science, which are based on Azuma's model (1989), we noted previously that Brazil's creativity knowledge is at the transition from stage three to four. This shows that attempts to translate and model Western concepts of creativity to Brazilian culture are turning into efforts to develop new concepts and technologies that are more appropriate to Brazil.

Taking into account the serious educational crisis occurring in this country, it is easily understood why creativity research in Brazil has focused almost exclusively on the school situation. However, perceiving the schooling problem as only one part of the great economic and social problem of this country, we recognize that creativity research has to spread to other areas to have a full impact on Brazilian development.

Philosophic Considerations

From a philosophical standpoint, we could situate Brazilian creativity studies in the following dimensions: ontology (the nature of its reality), epistemology (the nature of its knowledge), and axiology (the nature of its value), as recommended by Isaksen and Murdock (1988).

Concerning the ontology question, which deals with the nature of the creativity phenomenon, we can acknowledge from our Brazilian research finding that creativity is real and universal, and its effects can be observed through peoples cognitive abilities, personality, and production.

The epistemology question, related to the nature of the creativity knowledge, can be answered mostly through our research on the creative person and process. Our data indicated the existence of some cross-cultural traits and processes that can identify the creative personality and help individuals think and act more creatively. Granted, not all the traits related to the creative personality can be verified in all cultures. In the case of Brazil, the most frequently observed creative characteristics were related to preferences in demonstrating feelings and emotions and nonconforming behaviors. As these creative strengths are not the highest ones in other countries, such as the United States, we can conclude that cross-cultural differences about the nature of creativity knowledge exist.

As for the creative process, Brazilian studies have indicated the power of specific techniques and their combinations on various aspects of cognitive creative abilities (fluency, flexibility, and originality) as well as on behaviors conducive to creative production. A variety of theoretical approaches have been used in creativity research in Brazil, such as the humanistic, behaviorist, psychodynamic, and so forth. All of them were able to produce positive results in several dimensions of creative thinking and behavior, thus pointing in the direction of a universal process related to creativity.

Research on learning styles and creativity in Brazil signaled the existence of cultural differences on preferred ways of approaching information. Although there are some common styles related to various cultures, such as Brazil and the United States, our data indicated the strong Brazilian emphasis on styles related to emotional, sociological, and environmental factors. Thus, it is important that these styles be considered when planning any creativity training activity for the Brazilian population.

The axiological question indicates the existence of subcultural values related to creativity in Brazil, since most of our data are influenced by socioeconomic variables. Our main educational problems are occurring at the public schools, which are attended by the majority of lower class children. We have to focus our investigations on people from poor environments, and find ways to develop their creative potential and raise their motivation to finish at least the elementary and secondary education levels and overcome the school dropout tendency.

Limitations

Current limitations to delineate a more accurate profile of Brazilians' creative personality, process, and product are due to several factors.

Brazilian researchers often mention one main difficulty surrounding the identification and measurement of creativity: the absence of creativity assessment procedures that have been created or validated in Brazil. Although Torrance's (1974) and Guilford's creativity tests are frequently used by Brazilian researchers, these measures are always validated in the research sample, because there is not a complete validation study for samples of all ages. The author is currently involved in a large validation study with the verbal and figural forms of the TTCT (Torrance, 1974), as well as investigating their relationships with learning style factors through the use of Dunn, Dunn, and Price's Instrument (1984) to counteract this limitation. We also have to mention the work of Rosas (1978) who developed a figural creativity test and studied its validity with an experimental sample.

In some areas, the scarcity of investigations does not permit us to draw general conclusions with respect to the Brazilians. The creative environment has seldom been researched under the reference frame of organizational psychology. Therefore, we need to focus our future studies in this area to have a better understanding of its dynamics in the country.

The investigators' concerns with the elementary school problems have prioritized studies with children from 7 through 14 years old and with teachers. However, we have to direct our view to other types of samples, such as Indians or blacks, to understand Brazilians' thinking and behavior. The creative adult, when working in roles other than that of teacher, also needs to be investigated more thoroughly; for example, musicians, writers, scientists, executives, and so forth.

It is also necessary to call attention to the need for more experimental research with Brazilian creative gifted children. Most of the Brazilian reports in this area are limited to experiences with gifted programs that were conducted without a systematic research methodology. Therefore, gifted education in this country has been based on intuition rather than on a scientific view.

We also note that Brazilian research findings cannot effectively contribute to the improvement of the country's educational system unless there is a political decision to invest more in the public schools. Brazilian governmental leaders are not yet able to acknowledge the great waste of human talents in the public schools. As soon as this happens, we then will be able to make decisive contributions to the solution of the schools' failure.

This chapter has outlined the status of knowledge on creativity in Brazil, attempting to bridge the country's historical, social, and educational characteristics with the research findings on creativity using Brazilian samples. An effort was made to propose future areas for investigation, as well as to stress important Brazilian characteristics to consider in future studies. In conclusion, we suggested the importance of combining research efforts with political willingness, to make effective contributions to the solution of the educational problems and increase the chances of having creative and capable Brazilian citizens.

REFERENCES

Abril, E. (1990). *Almanaque Abril: A enciclopedia em um volume* [*April Almanac: The encyclopedia in one volume*]. Sao Paulo, Brazil: Editora Abril.

Alencar, E.M.L.S. (1974). Efeitos de um programa de criatividade em alunos da quarta e quinta serie [Effects of a creativity training program on fourth and fifth grade students]. *Arquivos Brasileiros de Psicologia Aplicada, 26*, 59–68.

Alencar, E.M.L.S. (1984). Caracteristicas psico-sociais de criancas mais ou menos criativas [Psychosocial characteristics of creative children]. *Interamerican Journal of Psychology, 18*, 87–99.

Alencar, E.M.L.S. (1986a). *Psicologia da criatividade* [*Psychology of creativity*]. Porto Alegre, Brazil: Artes Medicas.

Alencar, E.M.L.S. (1986b). *Psicologia e educacao do superdotado* [*Psychology and education of the gifted*]. Sao Paulo, Brazil: Editora Pedagogica e Universitaria.

Alencar, E.M.L.S. (1989). *A contribuicao dos livros de ciencias para o desenvolvimento das habilidades criativas* [*The contribution of sciences books for the development of creative abilities*]. Unpublished manuscript.

Alencar, E.M.L.S., & Rodrigues, C.J.S. (1978). Relacao entre tempo de ensino, localidade da escola e caracteristicas comportamentais consideradas desejaveis e indesejaveis por professores do ensino do I grau [Relationships among teaching experience, school location and desirable characteristics perceived by first grade elementary teachers]. *Arquivos Brasileiros de Psicologia Aplicada, 30*, 75–93.

Alves, S.M.A. (1985). *Efeitos das tecnicas de jogos dramaticos na criatividade, socializacao, lideranca, raciocinio divergentes e convergentes de pre-escolares superdotados e economicamente carentes* [*Effects of dramatic plays on gifted and disadvantaged children in relation to socialization, leadership, convergent and divergent thinking abilities*]. Unpublished master's thesis, Universidade Estadual do Rio de Janiero, Brazil.

Assumpcao, J.A.M. (1978). *Desenvolvimento da criatividade na orientacao educacional* [*Creative development through vocational guid-*

ance]. Unpublished master's thesis, Pontificia Universidade Catolica do Rio de Janeiro, Rio de Janeiro, Brazil.

Assumpcao, J.A.M. (1981). *Criatividade e orientacao vocacional [Creativity and vocational guidance]*. Sao Paulo, Brazil: Editora Cortez.

Azuma, A. (1989). Psychology in a non-western country: Stages through which psychology develops. In P. Saigh & T. Oakland (Eds.), *International perspectives on psychology in the schools* (p. 3). Hillsdale, NJ: Erlbaum.

Campos, D.M.S., & Weber, M.G. (1987). *Criatividade [Creativity]*. Rio de Janeiro, Brazil: Editora Sprint.

Cunha, R.M.M. (1979). *Programa de treinamento experimental para desenvolvimento de habilidades criadoras [Experimental program for creative development]*. Unpublished master's thesis, Pontificia Universidade Catolica do Rio de Janeiro, Brazil.

Dunn, K., & Dunn, R. (1978). *Teaching students through their individual learning styles*. New York: Reston.

Dunn, R., Dunn, K., & Price, G. (1984). *Learning styles inventory*. Kansas: Price Systems.

Fleith, D.S. (1990). *Efeitos de um programa de treinamento de criatividade em estudantes normalistas [Effects of a creativity training program in students at normal school]*. Unpublished master's thesis, Universidade de Brasilia, Brazil.

Fonseca, A.A.S. (1978). *Arte/Educacao. O professor e as condicoes de ensino de educacao [Arts education: The teacher and his/her condition for education]*. Unpublished master's thesis, Universidadae Federal da Bahia, Bahia.

Garcia, M.L. (1978). *O desenvolvimento da capacidade criativa da crianca e o papel dos metodos empregados no ensino da linguagem [The development of childrens' creative potential and its relation to language teaching methodologies]*. Unpublished master's thesis, Fundacao Getulio Vargas, Rio de Janeiro, Brazil.

Gomes, V.L.T. (1985). *Cultura, criatividade e desempenho escolar [Culture, creativity and school achievement]*. Unpublished master's thesis, Universidade Estadual do Rio de Janeiro, Brazil.

Guerreiro, M.C.R. (1987). *Efeitos do treinamento de professores em tecnicas criativas no rendimento escolar de alunos repetentes da primeira a quarta serie [Effects of teachers' creative training programs on school achievement of repeating grade students]*. Unpublished master's thesis, Universidade de Brasilia, Brazil.

Guhur, J.V.M. (1976). *Efeitos da modelacao e instrucoes sobre o comportamento criativo em adolescentes [Effects of modeling and instructions on adolescents' creative behavior]*. Unpublished master's thesis, Universidade Federal do Rio Grande do Sul, Porto Alegre, Brazil.

Hesketh, M.M.A. (1985). *Criatividade e auto conceito: Fatores determinantes no desempenho gerencial [Creativity and self-concept: Influential factors on management]*. Unpublished master's thesis,

Universidade de Brasilia, Brazil.

IPLAN/IPEA, UNICEF, SUDENE (1986). *O menor e a pobreza* [*The young and the poverty*]. Serie instruments para a acao, n. 5- Brasilia: UNICEF.

Isaksen, S.G., & Murdock, M.C. (1988, March). *The outlook for the study of creativity: An emerging discipline?* Paper presented at the American Association of Higher Education, Washington, DC.

Kneller, G.F. (1978). *Arte e Ciencia da Criatividade* [*The art and science of creativity*]. Sao Paulo: Instituicao Brasileira de Difusao Cultural. (Original work published in 1965).

Magalhaes, R.H. (1972). *O desenvolvimento do pensamento criativo atraves do treinamento pedagogico* [*The development of creative thinking through teachers' training*]. Unpublished master's thesis, Pontificia Universidade Catolica do Rio de Janeiro, Brazil.

Maia, I.R.R.R. (1976). *Efeitos do reforco no desenvolvimento da criatividade verbal em escolares* [*Effects of reinforcement procedures on students' verbal creativity*]. Unpublished master's thesis. Universidade Federal do Rio Grande do Sul, Porto Alegre, Brazil.

May, R. (1982). *A coragem de criar* [*The courage to create*]. Rio de Janeiro, Brazil: Nova Fronteira. (Original work published in 1975).

Medeiros, G.K. (1977). *O ensino centrado no aluno e suas relacoes com o desempenho e a criatividade* [*Student-centered teaching methodology and its relation with achievement and creativity*]. Unpublished master's thesis, Universidade Federal do Rio Grande do Sul, Porto Alegre, Brazil.

Negreiros, T.C. (1978). *Relacao entre periodo de incubacao e pensamento produtivo na solucao de problemas* [*Relationship between incubation and productive thinking on problem solutions*]. Unpublished master's thesis, Pontificia Universidade Catolica do Rio de Janeiro, Rio de Janeiro, Brazil.

Novaes, M.H. (1972). *Psicologia da criatividade* [*Psychology of creativity*]. Rio de Janeiro, Brazil: Vozes.

Novaes, M.H. (1979). *Desenvolvimento psicologico do superdotado* [*Psychological development of the gifted*]. Sao Paulo, Brazil: Atlas.

Novaes, M.H. (1989). Processos criativos no ensinoaprendizagem: Uma contribuicao da psicologia escolar [Creative process on learning and teaching: a contribution of school psychology]. *Arquivos Brasileiros de Psicologia Aplicada, 41,* 46–55.

Novaes, M.H., Seidl, L., Carvalho, J., Fidalgo, I.H., Damasceno, C.F., Pelegrini, L.F., & Almeida, P.M.P. (1981). Capacidade antecipatoria da crianca e sua percepcao da realidade futura [Children's forecasting abilities and futuristic perceptions]. *Arquivos Brasileiros de Psicologia Aplicada, 33,* 82–101.

Oakland, T., & Wechsler, S. (1988, August). *School psychology in Brazil: An examination of its research infrastructure.* Paper presented at the annual meeting of the American Psychological Association, Atlanta, GA.

Osborn, A.F. (1981). *O poder criador da mente [Applied imagination].* Sao Paulo, Brazil: Ibrasa. (Original work published in 1957).

Osowski, C.I. (1976). *Estrategias para buscar informacoes e atitudes criadoras [Searching information strategies and creative attitudes].* Unpublished master's thesis, Universidade Federal do Rio Grande do Sul, Porto Alegre, Brazil.

Ott, M.B. (1975). *Influencias das estrategias de ensino no desenvolvimento da criatividade [Effects of teaching strategies on creative development].* Unpublished master's thesis, Universidade Federal do Rio Grande do Sul, Porto Alegre, Brazil.

Papa, J. (1975). *Estudo quasi-experimental para testar a eficacia de um metodo de pressao como meio de aumentar a criatividade artistica [Quasi-experimental study to test the effects of a pressure method upon artistic creativity].* Unpublished master's thesis, Pontificia Universidade Catolica do Rio Grande do Sul, Porto Alegre, Brazil.

Rodrigues, C.J.S. (1979). *Um estudo do pensamento criativo entre alunos do primeiro grau [A study on elementary students' creative thinking].* Unpublished master's thesis, Universidade de Brasilia, Brasilia, Brazil.

Rosas, A.C.S. (1978). *Construcao do teste de aptidao criativa TAC-versao experimental [Construction of a creative aptitude test TAC-experimental version].* Unpublished master's thesis, Fundacao Getulio Vargas, Rio de Janeiro, Brazil.

Rosas, A.C.S. (1988). *Ativacao de comportamentos criativos em estudantes universitarios [Eliciting creative behaviors on college students].* Unpublished manuscript, Universidade Federal de Pernambuco, Brazil.

Santos, L.M. (1975). *Remediacao em criatividade verbal: um estudo comparatorio de criterios e procedimentos [Remediation on verbal creativity: Comparison study of procedures and criteria].* Unpublished doctoral dissertation, Universidade de Sao Paulo, Sao Paulo, Brazil.

Santos, O.B. (Ed.). (1988). *Os superdotados: Quem sao? Onde estao? [The gifted: Who are they? Where are they?]* Sao Paulo, Brazil: Editora Pioneira.

Silva, T.F. (1978). *Desenvolvimento da criatividade atraves das estrategias de ensino criativo na pre-escola [Creativity development in the preschool through creative strategies].* Unpublished master's thesis, Pontificia Universidade Catolica do Rio Grande do Sul, Porto Alegre, Brazil.

Taylor, C.W. (1976). *Criatividade: Progresso e potencial [Creativity: Progress and potential].* Sao Paulo, Brazil: Instituicao Brasileira de Difusao Cultural. (Original work published in 1964).

Torrance, E.P. (1963). *Education and the creative potential.* Minneapolis, MN: The University of Minnesota Press.

Torrance, E.P. (1974). *Torrance tests of creative thinking: Directions manual and scoring guide. Verbal Test A, Figural Test A.* Lexington, VA: Ginn.

Torrance, E.P. (1976). *Criatividade: Medidas, testes e avaliacoes* [*Guiding creative talent*]. Sao Paulo, Brazil: Instituicao Brasileira de Difusao Cultural. (Original work published in 1962).

Torrance, E.P. (1979). *The search for satori & creativity.* Buffalo, NY: The Creative Education Foundation.

Torrance, E.P., & Ball, O.E. (1980). *Scoring and norms: Technical manual for the streamlined scoring of the Torrance tests of creative thinking, Form A.* Athens, GA: Georgia Center for Studies of Creative Behavior.

Torrance, E.P., & Torrance, P.J. (1974). *Pode-se ensinar criatividade?* [*Is creativity teachable?*] Sao Paulo, Brazil: Editora Pedagogica e Universitaria. (Original work published in 1973).

Torrance, E.P., & Wu, T.H. (1981). A comparative longitudinal study of the adult creative achievements of elementary school children identified as highly intelligent and as highly creative. *Creative Child and Adult Quarterly, 6,* 71–76.

UNICEF/IBGE. (1987). *Criancas e adolescentes: Indicadores sociais* [*Children & adolescents: Social indicators*]. Rio de Janeiro, Brazil: Fundacao Instituto Brasileiro de Geografia e Estatistica.

Wechsler, S. (1981). Identifying creative strengths in the responses to the verbal forms of the Torrance tests of creative thinking. *Dissertation Abstracts International 42,* 3521A (University Microfilms No. 82–01588).

Wechsler, S. (1985a). Assessment of verbal creative strengths in Brazilian adults. *School Psychology International, 6,* 133–138.

Wechsler, S. (1985b). A identificacao do talento criativo nos Estados Unidos e no Brasil [The identification of creative talent in United States and Brazil]. *Psicologia: Teoria e Pesquisa, 1,* 140–147.

Wechsler, S. (1987a). Brazilian gifted children chart new courses. *Gifted, Creative and Talented, 10,* 29–30.

Wechsler, S. (1987b). Efeitos do treinamento de criatividade em criancas bem-dotadas e regulares [Effects of creativity training on gifted and regular children]. *Arquivos Brasileiros de Psicologia Aplicada, 39,* 95–111.

Wechsler, S. (1988). Problematica da identificacao de superdotados/talentosos [Problems on identifying the gifted and the talented]. In O.B. Santos (Ed.), *Os superdotados: Quem sao? Onde estao?* (pp. 55–63). Sao Paulo, Brazil: Editora Pioneiras.

Wechsler, S. (1992). *Identificacao e desenvolvimento da criatividade.* [*Identification and development of creativity*]. Campinas, Brazil: ABRAPEE.

Wechsler, S., Fialho, A.C.N., Wanderley, F.S., & Trestini R.L. (1988). Caracteristicas criativas de adolescentes e sua produtividade na vida real [Creative characteristcs of adolescentes and creative production in real life]. *Proceedings of the XVIII Reuniao Anual da Sociedade de Psicologia de Ribeirao Preto.* Sao Paulo, Brazil: Ribiero Preto.

Wechsler, S., & Guerreiro, M.C.R. (1986). Fatores biograficos influenciantes na criatividade da mulher brasileira [Biographical influential factors on Brazilian creative women]. *Educacao e Realidade, 11,* 81–87.

Wechsler, S., & Oakland, T. (1988, July). *Preventive strategies for educating low income Brazilian children.* Paper presented at the XI International School Psychology Colloquium, Bamberg, West Germany.

Wechsler, S., Polonia, A.C., & Torres, P.L. (1988). Estilos de pensar e aprender e suas implicacoes educacionais [Learning and thinking styles and their educational implications]. *Proceedings of the XVIII Reuniao Anual da Sociedade de psicologia de Ribeirao Preto* (p. 265). Sao Paulo, Brazil: Ribeirao Preto.

Wechsler, S., & Richmond, B. (1982). Creative strengths of Brazilian and American children. *Interamerican Journal of Psychology, 16,* 27–32.

Wechsler, S., & Richmond, B. (1984). Influencias da dotacao intellectual e criativa no ajustamento em sala de aula [Influences of intellectual and creative capabilities on classroom adjustment]. *Arquivos Brasileiros de Psicologia Aplicada, 36,* 138–147.

Wechsler, S., Torres, P.L., & Polonia, A.C. (1989, June). *Estilos de aprender de estudantes brasileiros e suas relacoes com os estilos de seus professores* [Learning and thinking styles of Brazilian adolescents and their relationships with their teachers' styles]. Paper presented at the XXII Interamerican Congress of Psychology, Buenos Aires, Argentina.

Wechsler, S., Torres, P.L., Polonia, A.C., & Pasquali, L. (1990). *Influencias dos estilos preferenciais de aprender pensar sobre o rendimento em portugues e matematica* [Learning styles influences on portuguese and math achievement]. Unpublished manuscript, University of Brasilia, Brasilia, Brazil.

Wiedmann, L. (1976). *Influencia de diferentes situacoes estimulo na criatividade em redacoes* [Influences of different stimuli-situation on creative compositions]. Unpublished master's thesis, Universidade Federal do Rio Grande do Sul, Porto Alegre, Brazil.

PART II

STIMULATING CREATIVITY: ORGANIZATIONAL PERSPECTIVES

6

Barriers to Creativity and Their Relationship to Individual, Group, and Organizational Behavior

Les Jones

The existence of barriers that limit an individual's creative output is a widely held assumption in the field of creativity. It is also generally accepted that some of these barriers relate to characteristics of the creative person and others to the environment in which a person exists. These assumptions are derived from both theoretical considerations and practical experience, with the latter as the primary source of support. Although a variety of material about the subject exists in creativity literature (Adams, 1974; Majaro, 1988; Parnes, 1967; Van Gundy, 1987), there is much overlap in both concepts and interpretation. One way to improve this situation is to take a more systematic approach to research about the nature of barriers to creativity. The importance of further understanding the nature of barriers to creativity should not be neglected if we wish to strengthen our effectiveness in making creativity useful in applied situations.

There are a variety of reasons why research on barriers to creativity has not kept pace with the recognition of their importance:

1. The topic is complex and does not lend itself to quick answers.
2. The variables need to be viewed interactively, rather than in isolation.
3. Similarities and differences in concepts and definitions have not been carefully examined.
4. Effective methods of assessment have not been developed.
5. Collaboration on the topic has been limited.

This chapter will address the above issues, focusing particularly on the development of effective methods of assessment via the research of myself and my colleagues (Jones, 1987; Rickards, 1991) in the Creativity Unit at Manchester Business School. The discussion will include comments on the relationship between creativity and barriers, an overview of the major definitions of barriers to creativity and issues for further consideration.

DEFINITIONS OF CREATIVITY

Creativity definitions vary from the general humanistic description to the rigid operational statement. Rickards (1985) commented on the difficulties experienced in finding definitions which agree, citing two researchers (Ackoff & Vergara, 1981; Freedman, 1976) who had found several hundred different definitions.

Dauw and Fredian (1971) reported that Torrance (1965) had defined creativity as:

> the process of becoming sensitive to problems, deficiencies, gaps in knowledge, missing elements, disharmonies, and so on; identifying the difficulty; searching for solutions, making guesses or formulating hypotheses about the deficiencies: testing and retesting them; and finally communicating the results. (p. 28)

Contrast this definition, which is essentially a description of a particular type of problem-solving process, with that of Newell, Shaw, and Simon (1962). They adopted a criterion-based approach, which suggested that any problem solving may be creative:

> To the extent that one or more of the following conditions are satisfied:
> 1. The product of the thinking has novelty and value;
> 2. The thinking is unconventional, requiring modification or rejection of previous ideas;
> 3. The thinking requires high motivation and persistence over a long span of time (continuously or intermittently) or at a high intensity;
> 4. The problem as initially posed was undefined, so that part of the task was to formulate the problem itself. (Newell, Shaw, & Simon, 1962, pp. 65–66)

While both of these definitions focus on the process, the latter more so than the former, there are a number of implications which suggest the involvement of other factors. Torrance's references to "becoming sensitive" and "disharmonies" refer to characteristics of the person, as does Newell's requirement for "high motivation and persistence." "Communicating the results" suggests Torrance had a product in mind and Newell specifically refers to the product having novelty and value. Torrance also refers to "testing and retesting," which implies some feedback from the environment. However, despite these implications, neither author focuses attention on the importance of the interaction between process, person, product, and press.

Without committing myself to a specific definition of creativity, I am basing my arguments in this chapter on four premises. The first is that creativity is a process needed for solving particular types of problems which are not clearly bounded or have not previously been encountered by the problem solver. The second is that creativity is not a special gift enjoyed by a few but is a common ability possessed by most people which can be developed or suppressed as a result of their individual experiences.

In the context of the first premise, psychological barriers or blocks to creativity would be seen as interfacing with the creative person. In the third case not only might the press directly impose barriers to creativity, through rules and policies, but it may reinforce the psychological barriers by giving feedback. The fourth premise is that the cumulative outcome of all these other effects would then influence the quality of the product. These effects are demonstrated in Figure 6.1, which is derived from a diagram produced by the Product Working Group at the 1990 Buffalo Conference.

This interactive model of creativity is the key to understanding both the nature of creativity itself and the nature of the barriers which inhibit it. A theory of creativity which focuses narrowly on the creative process without regard to the style and abilities of the people involved or the climate in which they are operating is itself imposing barriers which may affect the quality of the creative product.

The same is likely to be true of those theories which focus only on the person or the press. Not only does an interactive model help to identify the range of barriers that need to be taken into account, but an understanding of these barriers may help us to refine our concepts of creativity.

Isaksen and Murdock (1990) suggested that for creativity to become a discipline, it must concern itself with the philosophical categories of ontology (the nature of its reality), epistemology (the nature of its knowledge), and axiology (the nature of its its value).

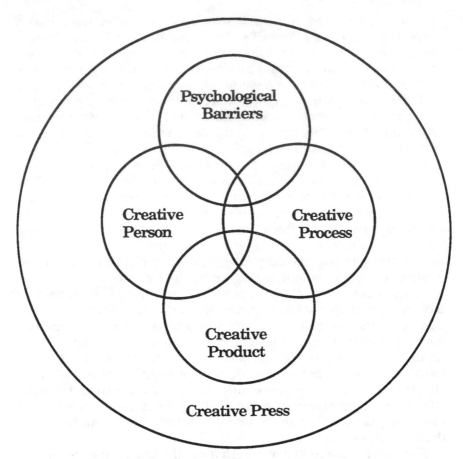

Figure 6.1. Interaction of psychological barriers with the 4 Ps

Any study of barriers to creativity must therefore address these same issues.

In terms of reality, any measure of barriers must be demonstrably examining factors which are accepted as relevant to creative behavior. From the epistemological viewpoint, Zais (1976) referred to ways of knowing as:

1. Knowing by insight with no empirical basis;
2. Knowing by authority;
3. Knowing by uncovering through the senses or perceptions;
4. Knowing by intersubjective verification or common sense;
5. Knowing by logic; and
6. Knowing by constructing.

Each of these ways is likely to have its own set of barriers and these need to be examined.

The axiological field provides the most difficult area for the study of barriers. Are we examining the effect of values or beliefs on the ability to act creatively or are we concerned with the way in which our values decide what is creative?

When designing the research project into barriers to creativity, I did not expressly consider these philosophical factors, but I shall return to them in discussing the validity of the research model.

BARRIERS TO CREATIVITY

Figure 6.1 shows the psychological barriers as being influenced by the press which Rhodes (1987) described as "the relationship between human beings and their environment." However, the person as a whole is influenced by the press, not only in present circumstances but historically, back to the day of birth (or even earlier). Without entering the nature/nurture debate, it seems likely that the greater part of an individual's behavior is the result of a lifetime's exposure to the outside world.

Most writers on creativity refer to the personal blocks or barriers which tend to get in the way of creating new ideas. Although each writer tends to have his or her own list of favorite blocks, many of the same ones occur in most lists. Sometimes the lists of barriers are not categorized, while at other times they are. Some of the categories reoccur in different lists although the same individual barriers may not always occupy the same category. Adams (1974) used four categories:

1. Perceptual blocks
2. Cultural and environmental blocks
3. Emotional blocks
4. Intellectual and expressive blocks

Dauw and Fredian (1971) referred to three types of blocks that they linked to the pressure on children to conform to established patterns of thought and behavior. They mentioned the categories defined by Arnold (1962) who, in reflecting on the factors essential to a creative individual's personality, suggested that they may not be developed to their full potential because of:

1. Perceptual blocks, which prevent a person from getting a true, relevant picture of the outside world;
2. Cultural blocks which result from the influences of society; and
3. Emotional blocks such as fear, anxiety, and jealousy.

Simberg (1964) used the same three categories and Raybould and Minter (1971) also used the perceptual, cultural, and emotional categories but included an additional category which he described as a lack of "knowledge and fluency in the language of the problem." He suggested that illiteracy, or lack of fluency with words, could be a bar to creativity.

Gregory (1967) referred to "roadblocks to scientific problem solving" which he categorized under five headings:

1. Functional
2. Psychological
3. Sociological
4. Physical-Environmental
5. Physiological

He listed 134 different blocks under these headings.

Morgan (1968) listed, under the general heading of emotional blocks or defense mechanisms, six blocks, three of which he then subdivided further:

1. Personal feelings of insecurity
2. Need for superficial security
3. Inability to use the unconscious freely
4. Inability to use the conscious mind effectively
5. Work-oriented barriers
6. Environmental barriers

Parnes (1967) differentiated between internal and external blocks to creativity. He likened the internal blocks arising from hereditary and past environmental factors to a governor on the engine of a car, preventing the engine from achieving its full potential power. He compared the external blocks due to present environmental conditions to obstructions on a freeway which prevent the car from using its full power effectively.

Van Gundy (1987) organized barriers into the following categories:

1. Structural
2. Social/Political
3. Procedural
4. Resource
5. Individual

These labels appear to link up with the inputs he describes in his systems model of the organizational innovation process. Isaksen (1988) spoke of three broadly overlapping categories of blocks to creative thinking:

1. Personal
2. Problem-solving
3. Situational

He then linked these to a number of organizational obstacles to creativity found by research at the Center for Creative Leadership.

Majaro (1988) seemed to put most of the blame for barriers to creativity on organizational factors. He suggested that while some of these could be removed, others are an integral part of the firm's history and tradition and can only be circumvented. The final list considered here is that of Danzig, Nevis, and Nevis (1970), which formed part of a questionnaire and training package. It consists of 14 blocks:

1. Fear of failure
2. Reluctance to play
3. Resource myopia
4. Overcertainty
5. Frustration avoidance
6. Custom-bound
7. Impoverished fantasy life
8. Fear of the unknown
9. Need for balance
10. Reluctance to exert influence
11. Reluctance to let go
12. Impoverished emotional life
13. Unintegrated Yin-Yang
14. Sensory dullness

None of these lists are supported by evidence of validity, other than a subjective face validity, and with the exception of the

Danzig-Nevis list, there does not appear to have been any attempt to measure the extent of the various blocks. Furthermore, many of the categories are not very meaningful since they tend to categorize the causes of the blocks and barriers rather than the barriers themselves. Parnes's (1967) division into internal and external barriers seems a more useful focus since it enables the separation of those barriers which are related to more enduring personality characteristics and long-term cultural influences from those which may be of a more temporary nature or related to specific current circumstances.

It has been suggested that since these blocks are generally accepted, measurement is not really necessary and it is sufficient to make people aware of the barriers which may affect their performance. There are two serious drawbacks to this approach. First, without evidence of validity we may be wrongly diagnosing the problems and any suggested cures may be ineffective, if not harmful. Second, without reliable evidence that they might have problems, why would anyone wish to do things differently?

The motivation for this research was the need for a measure which would enable me to give valid and confidential feedback to individuals on their own personal barriers. This would enable them to decide whether they felt a need to try to overcome them, and if so, would be useful in deciding what remedial action might be appropriate. The most appropriate starting point for developing such a measure would be the Danzig-Nevis listing, because it focused on the internal blocks and the authors had produced a questionnaire to measure the blocks.

The reason for focusing on the internal blocks was not to ignore the external ones but to separate them. Having identified an individual's personal barriers, these data can be used to examine the external environmental factors which may be influencing the individual. Similarly, the recognition of group differences in the level of particular barriers may be used to investigate the causes of such differences. Only through the consideration of all these factors can the effectiveness of the problem-solving process be optimized, as demonstrated in Figure 6.1.

This list contains many blocks mentioned by other writers and the authors have produced a questionnaire to measure the blocks, so I have used it as the basis for my research. This is not to imply that these blocks make up the best list published or that they cover all the possible barriers. Rather, it is sufficiently consistent with the literature to warrant experimental trials.

THE DANZIG-NEVIS TRAINING PACKAGE

This package is based on the questionnaire, mentioned above, designed some years ago by Sonia and Edwin Nevis and Elliot Danzig of Danzig-Nevis International, Inc. and included by Roger Harrison in his "Laboratory in Initiative, Autonomy and Risk Taking" workshop. The questionnaire covered the 14 "Blocks to Creativity" mentioned above, and contained 15 questions on each block. In addition to the questionnaire, there were essays describing each block together with a number of exercises for each one. My company (ICI) purchased the package and it was used for creativity training. It was partially successful because those students who were already committed to improving their creativity found the questionnaire useful in highlighting their particular blocks and further increased their self-knowledge by tackling the exercises. With less committed managers there was a resistance to the length of the questionnaire, some difficulty in distinguishing between some of the block definitions, and a feeling of unreality about the exercises.

The information obtained from managers who completed the questionnaires did suggest that the instrument was measuring factors relating to managerial problem solving and creativity. The evidence of the nature of the blocks and some integrating framework to justify and explain them in terms which suggested remedies was lacking. It was the development of such a framework that I took as the theme for my research (Jones, 1987).

Developing an Inventory for Individual Blocks to Creativity

When the accumulated data were analyzed, it was found that half of the 14 blocks could be combined into one major category (later labeled the strategic category) whose subblocks were highly related. The other seven blocks, however, showed very little correlation with these strategic blocks though some showed significant correlation with one another.

After considerable cluster analysis, it was found possible to extract four independent groups of items, each of which suggested a different type of blocking mechanism.

The four independent factors arising from these studies were eventually labeled as strategic, values, perceptual, and self-image barriers to problem solving.

Strategic barriers are connected with the individual's preferred approach to the problem-solving process. They include aspects such as imagination, ability to tolerate uncertainty and openness to new ideas. *Values barriers* reflect personal values, beliefs and attitudes and the degree of flexibility displayed in applying them. *Perceptual barriers* indicate sensual acuity and awareness of the environment. *Self-image barriers* relate to preparedness to assert oneself and make use of the resources available.

To describe how these mechanisms interact and affect the way information is processed, I devised a model based on the Atkinson-Shiffrin (1971) information-processing model. My model proposed four levels of information-processing filters (see Figure 6.2). The different blocks arose out of different information-processing deficiencies.

The *physical perceptual filter* represents the physiological limits on our ability to recognize signals from the environment. The *mental perceptual filter* is the process by which the brain selectively registers and interprets data. The *short-term store* is the working memory which has a very limited data-handling

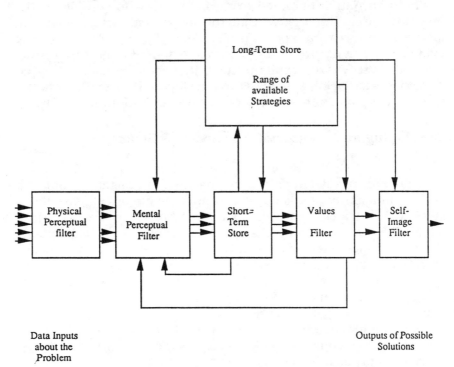

Figure 6.2. Information processing model of problem-solving barriers

capacity and which influences the amount of data passing through the mental perceptual filter. The *long-term store* is where all our knowledge and past experience is stored. The wider the range of problem-solving strategies we are aware of, the greater will be the number of responses we can make to the stimuli from the short-term store. The *values filter* reduces the available problem-solving options in line with our personal values and beliefs. It also influences the way in which incoming data are interpreted. The *self-image filter* further attenuates the range of possible solutions in line with our ability to get our ideas accepted by others.

Data from the environment impinge upon the sensory registers that make up the physical perceptual filter, and only those which are within the capacity of those registers (i.e., within the sensitive frequency range for hearing or sight) are passed on to the mental perceptual filter. Here, data are encoded or excluded according to feedback from the long-term store, either directly or via another filter, or the ability of the short-term store to cope with the quantity of data involved. The information progressing to the short-term store is then compared with that already held in the long-term store and a range of response options are generated. These response options may be reduced as they pass through the values and self-image filters that are controlled by information held in the long-term store. The output from the self-image filter then results in a behavioral response.

The validity of this model was investigated by developing an inventory which measured the four barriers. The outcome was a short (30-item) inventory with 12 items measuring strategic blocks and six items testing each of the other three blocks.

In its final version, entitled *The Jones Inventory of Barriers to Effective Problem-Solving* (since abbreviated to JIB), an individual's scores were presented, with those of the population and the sample to which he or she belonged in a personal profile (see Figure 6.3). The higher the score, the more blocked the subject is on that particular barrier.

This profile may then be used as the basis for a personal feedback discussion with the individual concerned.

If JIB is examined in the context of the philosophical factors mentioned by Isaksen and Murdock (1990), it can be seen that from the ontological perspective it seems to be testing the generally perceived reality of creativity. This is confirmed by the comparative studies discussed below.

Epistemologically, the questions used address all six of the

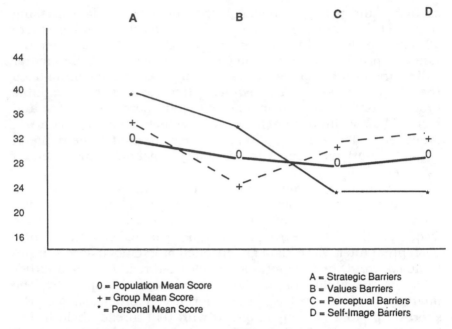

Figure 6.3. The feedback form permitting individual, group and population score comparisons

"ways of knowing" listed by Zais, while the values barriers are clearly related to the axiological category.

Analysis of Data Obtained

The inventory has been administered to about 1,300 subjects in the United Kingdom, mainly in the managerial and technical fields. The results show that the correlations between the barriers are low and that the variation between individuals is large. This indicates that subjects with equal total scores can be blocked in quite different ways, which enables feedback to be focused on the particular needs of an individual. This also helps to explain why the more usual forms of creativity training, which tend to focus on the strategic barriers, are not as effective in producing practical results as we might expect. Experience with a wide range of organizations suggests that it is not the lack of creative ideas which stands in the way of innovation, but the lack of the ability or determination to get those ideas listened to and understood.

The self-image barrier seems to be the greatest impediment to successful implementation of new ideas, a view that appears to be confirmed by the research into the personality characteristics of creative people where high ego strength, independence, and enthusiasm are regularly quoted (Barron, 1968; Gregory, 1967; MacKinnon, 1962).

Group Scores

The inventory was designed to investigate the barriers experienced by individuals, but some interesting differences in group scores were noted. Each of the groups below had mean scores which were significantly high or low. High scores indicate that the groups are relatively blocked and the low scores indicate that they are unblocked.

35   newly qualified architects low on perceptual barriers ($p < 0.1$)

45   young graduate engineers low on self-image barriers ($p < 0.01$)

58   Open University students high on self-image barriers ($p < 0.001$)

125   accountants high on perceptual barriers ($p < 0.001$)

27   bankers low on self-image barriers ($p < 0.1$)

100   technical sales staff low on self-image barriers ($p < 0.01$)

37   technical managers high on perceptual barriers ($p < 0.1$)

18   rail managers low on perceptual barriers ($p < 0.01$)

14   trainers and consultants low on both strategic ($p < 0.001$) and self-image barriers ($p < 0.01$)

52   health service senior managers low on strategic and values barriers ($p < 0.1$), perceptual barriers ($p < 0.01$) and self-image barriers ($p < 0.001$)

All of the significant differences listed above are in relation to the total test population—currently about 1,300 subjects—consisting mainly of managers and professional staff in industrial, commercial, and public service organizations in the U.K.

Although it is not possible to generalize from these results, they were sufficiently intriguing to stimulate further research to explore whether the barriers exhibited by particular occupations or organizations are markedly different from the general test population.

Comparisons with Other Measures

There are a number of measures which cover similar areas to the JIB. Strategic barriers appear to be measured by the Kirton Adaptor-Innovator inventory (KAI; Kirton, 1985) and the Human Information Processing Survey (HIPS; Torrance, Taggart, & Taggart, 1984).

Trials have been carried out to compare the JIB with both of these. A comparison between JIB and KAI carried out on 17 engineering graduates showed significant negative correlations between strategic barriers and innovator behavior, which had been predicted. The correlations were, with the total KAI score ($p < .01$ and with the three KAI subgroups, originality ($p < .01$), efficiency and rule conformity ($p < .1$). What was not predicted was the correlation of the total JIB score with the total KAI score ($p < .001$). Further, there was a correlation between the self-image barrier and the KAI total ($p < .01$). This suggests that the KAI is measuring the same factors as the JIB but without differentiating them in the same way. A comparison between JIB and the HIPS involved 47 part-time MBA students. In this case there was the expected negative correlation ($p < .001$) between strategic barriers and the right-brain scores, but there were also significant correlations ($p < .1$) between rightbrain and both barriers total and values barrier. The correlation between right-brain and perceptual barriers was zero, which is consistent with all previous data which have shown hardly any correlation between perceptual barrier scores and any other measure. However, in this case, this was rather surprising since right-brain behavior is associated with a visual, holistic style of thinking which one might expect to be associated with a lack of perceptual barriers.

Two attempts have been made to compare scores on the JIB with those on the Kolb (1976) Learning Style Inventory. The first involved 20 MBA students. Perceptual barriers correlated significantly with abstract conceptualization ($p < .1$) and self-image barriers correlated positively with reflective observation ($p < .1$) and negatively with active experimentation ($p < .1$). However, in the second experiment with 15 accountants, no significant correlations were found.

CURRENT RESEARCH PROGRAM

A research program is being carried out at Manchester Business School to examine to what extent the four barriers measured by the JIB vary within and between organizations. It is planned to carry out surveys within six organizations looking at variables such as sex, hierarchical level, occupation, age, and location. The research will be funded by the organizations involved in the research. The benefit to the organization will be an awareness of the strengths and weaknesses of different parts of the organization in problem-solving terms and their level compared to other organizations. However, the need for confidentiality means that individual scores will only be given to the person concerned, and data about organizational scores will be given anonymously to other organizations unless the donor organization decides otherwise.

The first study has been carried out in the company to which the graduate engineers, mentioned above, belong. JIB was completed by 122 members of the mechanical engineering group and the results were analyzed in terms of functional groupings, grade, location, and age. Gender was not studied because only three women were included in the sample.

The sample consisted of staff across the whole range of the organization, from technical clerks to senior managers, with ages ranging from 22 to 60. The total sample was divided, roughly equally, into two groups working in the Northeast and Northwest of England. There was no significant difference between the scores of the two geographical groupings, nor were there any appreciable differences between different job groupings within the mechanical engineering function. There were, however, differences related to age and grade. The total sample was more blocked than the test population on strategic barriers ($p < .01$) and less blocked on self-image barriers ($p < .01$).

Correlations were carried out between age, grade, and the four barriers, and the results are shown in Figure 6.4.

Age correlated positively with grade ($p < .001$) as one might expect. Age also correlated positively (i.e., the level of blockage increases with the age of the subject) with strategic barriers ($p < .01$), value barriers ($p < .1$), and self-image barriers ($p < .1$). The only significant correlation between grade and barriers was a negative correlation with self-image ($p < .1$).

The second study used a marketing division of a large electrical components company, and 80 employees (approximately two-thirds of the total labor force) were tested. The sample consisted of 49 men and 31 women, between the ages of 17 and 62, and covered the whole range of employees—from directors to junior clerical and secretarial staff. They belonged to two major functional groupings, marketing and administration, which comprised

	Age	Grade	S	V	P
Grade	0.45				
Strategic	0.28	− 0.04			
Values	0.22	− 0.01	0.45		
Perceptual	0.06	− 0.05	0.12	0.12	
Self-Image	0.20	− 0.15	0.25	0.34	0.23
Significance Level			0.1	0.01	0.001
Value of r (n = 122)			0.15	0.24	0.30

Figure 6.4. Correlations of JIB scores for 122 engineers ($n = 122$)

the more senior staff, and a third group, support services, which consisted of the junior staff concerned with both of the other functions.

In addition to the JIB, all participants completed the KAI inventory. There were no significant differences between the mean scores of the sample ($n = 80$) and the population means for any of the KAI or JIB elements. In fact, none of the relevant means differed by more than one point for any of the scores. The correlations between age, grade, and the scores on the two inventories are shown in Figure 6.5.

As in the first study, there was a predictable correlation between age and grade. The relationships of both age and grade with the four barriers were very similar except that the positive correlation between age and strategic barriers was even more significant ($p < .001$). The internal correlations between the four barriers were lower than in the first study. Those between the three KAI subscores were all significant ($p < .001$) but in no case

	Age	Grade	O	E	R	T	S	V	P
Grade	.35								
KAI-O	− .36	.22							
KAI-E	− .15	.25	.42						
KAI-R	− .08	.28	.49	.39					
KAI-T	− .27	.31	.86	.69	.80				
JIB-S	.43	− .07	− .49	− .42	− .37	− .54			
JIB-V	.28	.01	− .34	− .18	− .24	− .33	.08		
JIB-P	.09	− .11	− .23	.04	.05	− .09	− .06	.02	
JIB-SI	.13	− .28	− .51	− .32	− .22	− .46	.23	.24	.21
Significance Level			.1	.01	.001				
Value of r (n=80)			.19	.29	.35				

Figure 6.5. Correlations of JIB and KAI scores for 80 commercial staff

exceeded the 25% level of covariance. As was noted earlier, there appear to be clear relationships between some of the barriers and elements of KAI.

Examination of the means for the functional subgroups showed that the administration sample ($n = 32$) was significantly more blocked ($p < .1$) than the group mean on strategic and self-image barriers, while the marketing sample ($n = 19$) had significantly lower blocks on self-image ($p < .1$) and significantly higher scores on KAI originality ($p < .01$), efficiency ($p < .1$) and total ($p < .01$). The senior management grade (six men including two directors) scored significantly higher than the total group on KAI originality ($p < .01$) and total ($p < .1$).

Comparing the samples of men ($n = 49$) and women ($n = 31$), the JIB showed no significant differences on any of the barriers, but on the KAI the male group mean scores were significantly higher ($p < .1$) than the female on efficiency, rule conformity, and total. The only other significant gender difference was on grade, where men were significantly more highly graded than women ($p < .001$).

Although it is expected that the research outlined above will help to identify where differences in psychological barriers to problem solving exist within and between organizations, it is unlikely to explain why they exist.

In the first study, the sample is less blocked on self-image, but we do not know whether this is the result of being engineers, the recruiting policy of the company, the work environment, or some other factor. It is intended to see if a sample of electrical engineers from the same company would produce similar results. In both studies, older subjects seem more blocked on strategic, values, and self-image barriers. Is this due to changes as people get older or is it a consequence of different environments or recruitment criteria at the time of their appointment? Grade seems to have little effect on any of the barriers but given the high correlation between age and grade, it may be that the positive correlations with age are masking a negative correlation with grade. Further analysis of the data should reveal if there is any significant relationship between grade and any of the barriers within the different age bands.

FUTURE RESEARCH

More research will be needed to decide whether these barriers are situationally dependent, whether they are indicative of organiza tional choice, or whether they are the unintended consequences of organizational climate.

The situational dependency calls for studies such as those carried out by Talbot (1984) on learning style, and by Rosenfeld (1989) and Puccio (1990) on the KAI. Work has already begun on comparing JIB scores with those on climate measures produced by Ekvall (1986), Rickards and Bessant (1980), and Francis and Woodcock (1975). However, I am increasingly concerned that the investigation into climate has so far only taken into account the human perspective of organizations, concentrating on the fit between the individual and the organization. Perhaps we need to extend the barriers model to take account of the structural, political, and symbolic perspectives of the organization described by Dr. Luke Novelli, Jr. (1993).

Professor M.K. Raina (1993) challenged the limitations of the Western view of creativity and this has obvious implications for the types of barriers which might exist in markedly different cultures. Even within our own culture the vast majority of the test population for JIB consists of students, managers, and professionals. In the few instances where we have tested subjects from the lower levels of organizations, we have encountered the need to explain some of the wording of the test items and if we were to extend the range of the test population we would need to drastically redesign the instrument.

Most creativity theory has come from a psychological perspective. Professor Magyari-Beck (1993) stressed the need for an interdisciplinary approach. The matrix which he proposed suggests a framework for a much broader investigation into barriers to creativity than is possible using JIB alone. Magyari-Beck is currently using JIB in Hungary and I look forward to seeing whether this reveals any differences from the pattern of scores produced by subjects in Western Europe.

Another interesting field of study is the comparison of JIB scores with behavior in specific interpersonal situations. This holds out the hope of using JIB to predict behavior in such circumstances. Murdock (1989) described the comparison of JIB scores with the types of conflict in which individuals are typically involved. Recent observations on counseling courses for Ward Sisters at a U.K. hospital suggest that problems with counseling style are related to scores on the JIB. Other areas where this approach will be tested are management style, stress, and communications. A major application of this approach is projected to be in the area of career guidance and the JIB is already being tested, in an interactive computer form, by an executive place-ment agency.

The final area of new research we are undertaking will expand our domain into the field of creative writing. In a joint research project between Manchester Business School and Buffalo State College we are investigating the impact of training in the use of root metaphors, as described by Professor Robert C. Burkhart (1990), on JIB scores. This project is using a split-half version of JIB and it is intended to replicate the experimental design using the MBA Creativity Option at Manchester.

CONCLUSION

Better understanding of barriers to creativity, via the JIB and other mechanisms, must be aimed primarily at benefitting the individual by developing the creative person. This is the purpose for which the JIB was developed and despite its other uses, it is the one for which it is best suited. It is already perceived by partici-pants as a way of obtaining new insights into their own behavior and development needs, and there is potential for doing much more in this field. However, as we understand more about indi-vidual psychological and physical barriers, we can utilize this knowledge to produce more effective group problem solving through teams built on a better mix of creative abilities, and thus enhance the creative process.

The concept of barriers might also be used to reduce those organizational barriers which limit the expression of creativity. This might lead to a climate which encourages individuals and teams to find new and exciting ways of meeting the organization's goals. It should, however, take account of not only those barriers that impact immediately upon the individual but also the more insidious barriers which operate at the political and structural levels.

As we live more and more in a world of multinational organiza-tions and international suppliers and customers, we need to be more aware of the different cultural barriers that may be hin-dering our attempts to improve our effectiveness. Even within our own society, people have different levels of need which may influence the type of barrier to which they are likely to be subjected. By considering such factors we may have a better understanding of what constitutes the creative press.

This conference has confirmed my belief that a unidimensional approach to creative problem solving is likely to prove ineffective. Only a contingency approach which takes account of the people involved (person), the type of outcome that is being sought (product), the selection of an appropriate approach (process), and the cultural and organizational climate (press) is likely to achieve a satisfactory outcome.

At a time when most organizations and societies are undergoing rapid change, the interest in creativity and innovation is very strong. We have an opportunity to demonstrate that creativity research can contribute to successfully coping with the challenges we all face. I believe that we will only succeed if we can successfully convert our academic knowledge into practical approaches which are seen by managers and workers to be both relevant and attractive.

REFERENCES

Ackoff, R.A., & Vergara, E. (1981). Creativity in problem solving and planning: A review. *European Journal of Operational Research, 7,* 1–13.

Adams, J.L. (1974). *Conceptual blockbusting: A guide to better ideas.* San Francisco, CA: W. H. Freeman.

Arnold, J.E. (1962). Education for innovation. In S.J. Parnes & H.F. Harding (Eds.), *A sourcebook for creative thinking.* New York: Charles Scribner.

Atkinson, R.C., & Shiffrin, R.M. (1971). The control of short-term memory. *Scientific American,* p. 225.

Barron, F. (1968). *Creativity and personal freedom.* Princeton, NJ: Van Nostrand.

Danzig, E., Nevis, E., & Nevis, S. (1970). *Blocks to creativity* (Unpublished training workshop package). Danzig-Nevis International, Inc.

Dauw, D.C., & Fredian, A.J. (1971). *Creativity and innovation in organizations.* Dubuque, IA: Kendall/Hunt.

Ekvall, G. (1986). *Creative climate questionnaire.* Stockholm: FA Radet - The Swedish Council for Management and Organizational Behaviour.

Francis, D., & Woodcock, M. (1975). *People at work.* San Diego, CA: University Associates.

Freedman, B.L. (1976). *Relationships between theoretical constructs of creativity and two major practical techniques of creative problem solving.* Unpublished thesis, University of Manchester, Manchester, UK.

Gregory, C.E. (1967). *The management of intelligence: Scientific problem solving and creativity.* New York: McGraw-Hill.

Isaksen, S.G. (1988). Concepts of creativity. In P. Colemont et al. (Eds.), *Creativity and innovation: Towards a European network.* Deventer, Netherlands: Kluwer.

Isaksen, S.G., & Murdock, M.C. (1990). The outlook for the study of creativity: An emerging discipline? *Studia Psychologica, 32,* 53–77.

Jones, L. (1987). *The development and testing of a psychological instrument to measure barriers to effective problem solving.* Unpublished masters thesis, University of Manchester, Manchester, UK.

Kirton, M. J. (1985). *Kirton adaption-innovation inventory.* Hatfield, England: Hatfield Polytechnic.

Kolb, D.A. (1976). *Learning style inventory technical manual.* Boston, MA: McBer.

Mackinnon, D.W. (1962). The personality correlates of creativity: A study of American architects. In G.S. Neilson (Ed.), *Proceedings of Fourteenth Congress on Applied Psychology, 2,* 11–39.

Magyari-Beck, I. (1993). Creatology: A potential paradigm for an emerging discipline. In S.G. Isaksen, M.C. Murdock, R.L. Firestein, & D.J. Treffinger (Eds.), *Understanding and recognizing creativity: The emergence of a discipline* (pp. 48–82). Norwood, NJ: Ablex.

Majaro, S. (1988). *The creative gap.* London: Longman.

Morgan, J.S. (1968). *Improving your creativity on the job.* New York: American Management Association.

Murdock, M.C. (1989, December). *Identifying blocks and barriers for managing conflict creatively.* Paper presented at Second European Conference on Creativity and Innovation, Noordwijk, Netherlands.

Newell, A., Shaw, J.C., & Simon, H.A. (1962). The processes of creative thinking. In E.H. Gruber, G. Tyrell, & M. Wertheimer (Eds.), *Contemporary approaches to creative thinking.* New York: Atherton Press.

Novelli, L. (1993). Using alternative perspectives to build more robust theories of organizational creativity. In S.G. Isaksen, M.C. Murdock, R.L. Firestein, & D.J. Treffinger (Eds.), *Understanding and recognizing creativity: The emergence of a discipline* (pp. 281–295). Norwood, NJ: Ablex.

Parnes, S.J. (1967). *Creative behavior guidebook.* New York: Charles Scribner.

Puccio, G.J. (1990). *Person-environment: Using Kirtons Adaptor-Innovator theory to determine the effect of stylistic fit upon stress, job satisfaction and creative performance.* Unpublished doctoral thesis, University of Manchester, Manchester, UK.

Raina, M.K. (1993). Ethnocentric confines in creativity research. In S.G. Isaksen, M.C. Murdock, R.L. Firestein, & D.J. Treffinger (Eds.), *Understanding and recognizing creativity: The emergence of a discipline* (pp. 235–253). Norwood, NJ: Ablex.

Raybould, E.B., & Minter, A.L. (1971). *Problem solving for management.* London: Management Publications Limited.

Rhodes, M. (1987). An analysis of creativity. In S.G. Isaksen (Ed.), *Frontiers of creativity research: Beyond the basics* (pp. 216 - 222). Buffalo, NY: Bearly Limited.

Rickards, T. (1985). *Stimulating innovation.* London: Frances Pinter.

Rickards, T. (1991). Creativity and innovation: Woods, trees and pathways. *R&D Management, 21,* 97–108.

Rickards, T., & Bessant, J. (1980). The creativity audit: Introduction of a new research measure during programmes for facilitating organizational change. *R & D Management, 10*(2), 467–475.

Rosenfeld, R. (1989, December). *Creative styles: Harnessing and focusing creativity.* Paper presented at Second European Conference on Creativity and Innovation, Noordwijk, Netherlands.

Simberg, A. (1964). *Creativity at work: The practical application of a complete program.* Boston, MA: Industrial Education Institute.

Talbot, R.J. (1984, September). *Situational influences on learning style.* Paper presented at International Conference on Development, Learning and Organisational Change, Bradford University, UK.

Torrance, E.P. (1965). Scientific views of creativity and factors affecting its growth. *Daedalus, 94* , 663–682.

Torrance, E.P., Taggart, B., & Taggart, W. (1984). *Human information processing survey.* Bensenville, IL: Scholastic Testing Service.

Van Gundy, A.B. (1987). Organizational creativity and innovation. In S.G. Isaksen (Ed.), *Frontiers of creativity research: Beyond the basics* (pp. 358–379). Buffalo, NY: Bearly Limited.

Zais, R.S. (1976). *Curriculum principles and foundations.* New York: Harper & Row.

7

Creativity From a Business School Perspective: Past, Present, and Future

Tudor Rickards

INDUSTRIAL CREATIVITY: A FRAGMENTED FIELD OF INQUIRY

The intention of this chapter is to present some state-of the-art conclusions about the body of work from the Manchester Business School (MBS) Creativity Research Unit, using creative product as a unifying theme. In order to do so, five differing kinds of outputs (products) are described, arising from literature surveys, training experiences, action research work, laboratory experiments, and networking activities. Together they suggest a research agenda for the future work of the unit.

Rationale for Creativity in Business School Settings

In the late 1950s, few practicing managers gave much thought to creativity as a process which might have practical significance in their work. By the late 1980s, industrial consciousness about the importance of creativity had been raised through newspaper articles, popular books, management gurus, and a general recognition of the importance of flexibility in turbulent industrial environments.

However, in the early 1990s, a visit to any English-language business school revealed a disturbing reality. In the management literature there are a large number of "how to do it" books and articles on stimulating creativity at individual, team, and organizational levels. However, in those publications which require submitted material to be examined through blind peer-review systems, there are far fewer research papers. The field of manage ment education is growing rapidly. There is an increasing number of practitioners offering creativity training, predominantly as short components within general educational programs. Yet very few business schools throughout the world offer creativity as a core subject within their undergraduate and master's level programs.

These observations suggest that at present, creativity has earned some credibility in the practical world of business. However, in contrast with topics like finance, accounting, marketing, strategy, operations research, and industrial psychology, they also indicate that the subject is not yet one which has gained legitimacy for business scientists.

Manchester Business School: An Educational Innovation

Two major business schools, one in Manchester and the other in London, were founded as the premier U.K. postgraduate institutions in the 1960s. Supported by industry and government, they were charged with developing a new kind of business education appropriate for the emerging European business community of the last quarter of the 20th century. One difference from earlier schools was a high proportion of work in training, consulting, and research modes for practicing managers.

The second director of the Manchester school, Tom Lupton, the distinguished British business academic, argued that the earlier established structures and research practices of business schools had failed to bridge the gap via applied theory, and as a result, scientific discoveries and product development were loosely coupled. Lupton (1984) suggested that one way for business studies to close the gap would be by developing more applied activities within which businesses, academics, and business practitioners could work together. He cited action research methodologies as being particularly suited for the challenge, that is to say, research which aimed to contribute to the practical concerns of the business community and the academic researchers.

In the 1970s and 1980s, Lupton's ideas helped in the development of a unique approach to management education. His emphasis on action research was reinforced by an MBA program that concentrated on industrial projects, which substituted for the better-known Harvard Business School case study approach. He encouraged staff to develop action research methodologies, particularly in modeling and influencing sociotechnical systems in order to gain international recognition (Morris, 1984; Mumford, 1981, 1983).

A series of research groupings flourished in this atmosphere, including the R&D Research Unit, which sponsored research into creativity as early as 1972, and later spun off the Creativity Research Unit as a discrete entity. Professor Lupton and Professor Grigor McClelland, the previous director of the School, were instrumental in obtaining faculty appointments in two subjects that had not previously been considered appropriate for research and teaching within a major business school: entrepreneurship and creativity.

In the early 1970s, the academic challenge for the Creativity Unit was to study, develop, and legitimize the subject of creativity in business. From the outset, the work responded to the demands of the business world. Guided by a group of senior industrialists, the emerging research unit began to explore the managerial literature in search of theoretical frameworks that could be applied in industrial contexts. Training programs were developed for assorted audiences, often of multicultural composition, and driven by the demands of the marketplace. Strong academic and industrial links were forged through Lupton's action research methods, and extended to include creative problem-solving methodologies (Rickards, 1974). Where possible, extensive contacts with managers permitted more controlled laboratory conditions for assessing instruments and personal differences. In addition, attention was paid to communicating with the growing numbers of industrial contacts through networking activities.

Between 1972 and 1989, an estimated 30,000 managers and professionals from 16 different countries became involved in the creativity training and action research programs associated with the Manchester Business School (Rickards, 1990).

THE MANCHESTER EXPERIENCES: FIVE KINDS OF PRODUCT

Literature Studies (1972–1990)

In light of the fragmented state of the field of industrial creativity, it became an important task to review the literature from related fields at intervals, and to attempt a partial synthesis for research and practical audiences. Four of these studies were carried out between 1972 and 1990. It is a valuable exercise to review them for changes in emphasis and for clues regarding the theoretical influences of workers within the MBS Creativity Research Unit. The group was in an influential position, particularly in the 1970s, which provided a major source of practical and theoretical information on industrial creativity for organizations in the U.K. and other Western European countries.

Historical sources to 1974.   It was observed in an annotated review of key texts on "techniques and underlying principles" (Rickards, 1974) that "techniques seem in many cases to be described more often than they have been practised" (p. 192). Jantsch (1967) and McPherson (1969) were cited as important early documents; Osborn (1949) was noted for his seminal studies of brainstorming and for anticipating later studies of motivational psychology; Gordon (1961) and Prince (1970) for their work on the synectics system; deBono (1971) for lateral thinking; and Zwicky (1948) and Allen (1952) for contributions to morphological methods of analysis and structured idea generation. Haefele (1962) was mentioned for his industrial experience and his classification of barriers to creativity in organizations; Vernon (1970) was taken as an important collection of research papers, within which Guilford's work was singled out for its pioneering importance; and Koestler (1964) was noted as offering a framework for studying the act of creation. The importance of redefinition in industrial problem solving was emphasized and linked with references to insight experiments (Duncker, 1926) and personal construct theory (Bannister & Fransella, 1971).

A state-of-the art review (1980).   A second literature survey (Rickards, 1980) confirmed that literature on industrial creativity was far less codified and of a more variable quality compared with the psychological and educational materials. In order to scan the field for important techniques and concepts, a sample of key texts was identified and content analyzed. The sources were selected after citation evaluation of available material and consultation with practitioners (mostly European) and researchers (mostly North American).

Five families of techniques were mentioned in all nine sources: brainstorming, synectics, morphological analysis, use of analogies, and check lists. The first three were given more major coverage than the latter two (Rickards, 1980). The author noticed the few references to lateral thinking, although this appeared to be better known to European managerial audiences than most of the technique systems mentioned in the texts.

Key managerial and creativity texts (1988, 1990).   In two recent reviews a similar analytical process was followed to derive a set of more broadly based managerial readings to support creativity training programs (Rickards, 1988) and subsequently to update the creativity material reported in the earlier reviews. Here, it will be necessary only to outline the material that is not well documented elsewhere in this collection of conference papers.

The North American change management literature (Blanchard & Johnson, 1982; Morgan, 1986, 1989; Peters & Waterman, 1982) nicely reflected the European views of Handy (1988) and Adair (1989). Both groups emphasized the critical importance of flexibility and problem solving in turbulent managerial environments. Belbin (1981) and Larson and LaFasto (1989) made excellent empirical observations of the nature of individual differences and mechanisms for reconciling the differences as creative outputs in managerial teams. European practitioners of structured innovation approaches included Carson (1989), Geschka (1983, 1986), Rickards (1985, 1988), Carson (1989), and Hill (1988).

In the 1980s, reports from other cultures were noted, enriching a literature which had been strongly biased toward North American sources (Khandwalla, 1984; Magyari-Beck, 1988; Richardson, 1988; Yamada, 1987). These workers demonstrated that creativity should not be treated as a culture-free concept.

The reviews reveal the kinds of literature that were influencing the work of the Creativity Unit at MBS. In the 1970s and 1980s, the emphasis was on understanding the scope and limitations of creativity-spurring techniques. It was important to codify and study the predominantly North American work, which tended to be theoretically grounded (e.g., with a rationale for a technique) or practitioner-oriented, but rarely both at the same time. In the late 1980s, interest had broadened to include creativity implicit in the more general managerial texts. European and other cultural influences were collated and studied to provide contrasts with the early North American work directly related to creativity.

Training "Products" (1972–1989)

The emerging demand for creativity training.   Manchester Business School provides two distinct categories of management education: graduate education within master's and doctoral degree programs, and courses for a wide range of professionals and managers nominated for development training ("postexperience education"). One common feature of both kinds of training is great pressure to deliver the designated topics in a time-efficient way. This is a trend that developed through the 1980s. Within the graduate programs, creativity training competed with other, longer established topics. In postexperience programs, the time pressure was even more intense. Cost-conscious program directors sought the minimum contact time believed compatible with delivering training objectives.

In the early 1970s, creative education was only offered to participants whose jobs were considered to demand creativity. Participants were typically research and development managers, or marketing and project executives. Gradually, however, the material was integrated in to every course within the school, including MBA and doctoral programs. One highly successful series of creativity sessions is now offered during international banking courses. Versions can also be found in retail management courses, senior executive programs, small business development programs, and local government and health administration courses.

The objectives of the creativity training programs. The agreed objectives for the shortest (one-day) programs are:

- to raise awareness among participants about the nature of industrial creativity
- to dispel some widespread assumptions regarding the
- immutability of creative performance
- to illustrate how creative performance at work can be enhanced

In longer programs, an important additional objective is added:

- to provide basic skills in creative problem solving

Content and contexts of the programs
The 1-day postexperience programs. Participants (10–30) receive a mix of short exercises with a minimum of formal presentational material. In the space of a day, learning gains are likely to be at the level of temporary heightened awareness of personal capacity for creative action. Without some reinforcing factors back

in the workplace, the benefits are likely to decline rapidly. It is usually not practical to devote time to implementation planning, as the creativity training is typically part of a longer, intensive educational experience.

The 3-day training programs. This has become the most common length of program for in-house requirements, often as a module repeated across a selected group receiving targeted development. In 3-day programs, after several hundred experiences, a stable and robust design has emerged. Material was originally developed from the pioneering programs at the Creative Problem Solving Institute, Buffalo (Parnes, Noller, & Biondi, 1977). The theme of Day 1 is awareness. Day 2 concentrates on skill acquisition, including work on important job-related issues brought by the participants. Day 3 is a workshop which includes issues of implementing change. The European modifications also include a less established format (each course is partially redesigned by the trainers), less emphasis on a stage-by-stage delivery of a process framework, and more opportunities for personal awareness and development work (Rickards, 1987, 1988; Rickards & Freedman, 1979; Talbot & Rickards, 1984).

The 10-day "Acquiring Creative Problem-Solving Skills" programs. In their second term, (or semester) first-year MBA students at Manchester Business School may elect to take a 10-day optionAcquiring Creative Problem-Solving Skillsone day a week, which reinforces the messages of their introductory project, provides intensive contact with industrial clients and their problems, and seeks to integrate practical experiences with the body of knowledge about industrial creativity. The option can be seen as an extended version of the 3-day program, with greater scope to include background materials. Two required sets of reading are Rickards (1985) on stimulating innovation and Rickards (1988) on industrial problem solving.

The general format of this option has mornings reserved for training exercises and concept discussions, and afternoons for projects and library work, culminating in a project working for industrial clients. For example, in 1990, one team worked with an inner-city task force for ideas on urban renewal; another team helped an advanced robotics institute develop fresh thinking for marketing possibilities to counter increasing competitive pressures. Guest speakers from industry are also invited either to bring "challenges" to the group, or to present their own experiences. It has also been found valuable to invite the graduates to give presentations based on their own previous job experiences.

Conclusions from the short (1–10-day) creativity training programs. Reactions from participants who brought their real-life problems to workshops suggest that the experience has given them fresh perspectives on their problem, indicated by regular requests for a record of the process including the flip chart materials.

Longer term and more tangible results have also been reported. Hill (1988) reported how participants in a major oil company went on to produce patents, new strategies and new products for the organization. Talbot and Rickards (1984) reported tangible products within a major engineering company. The triggering mechanism was a strategy of encouraging technical professionals from previous courses to return and to pose their own problems for the course and to report their own successful follow-up actions. This "benign cycle" was subsequently found to lead to technological and organizational innovations (Talbot, this volume).

From a large number of experiences it can safely be reported that our 1-day programs rarely lead to follow-up work and tangible products. Three-day programs for industrial clients may achieve valuable results, as reported above (Hill, 1988; Talbot, this volume). However, in order to achieve results these programs may first require the development of a critical mass of trained people in contact through formal or informal networking.

Outputs from the 10-day programs included tangible products such as contributions to corporate innovation success, and, in addition, included evidence of changes in the behaviors and problem-solving strategies of participants.

Internalization of skills leading to industrially valuable discoveries may require repeated reinforcement of the technique systems on real-life problems which, in our range of training contact times, can only be acquired by participants exposed to the longer 10-day programs. Other factors may also contribute to the observed benefits; for example, the longer programs are the only ones which included nonexperiential work such as private study and the production of written reports to include reflection of the theoretical implications of any creative experience.

Action Research Products (1975–1990)

The last two decades have seen a substantial shift within organizations toward more flexible structures and strategies. The shift has been attributed to increased environmental turbulence associated with the pervasive influence of new technology. Over time it has influenced increasing numbers of organizational sectors and transcended national boundaries.

There has been a growing recognition of the importance of innovation—the process of change which produces novel responses to environmental needs. The requirements for change include needs for new processes and techniques for stimulating change. The action research response is for researchers to collaborate on real-life projects. Collaboration is usually for a sufficient period of time in order to introduce and study the change processes. This is so that the organization deals with its immediate needs, and over time researchers build up generalized knowledge.

This is the process which characterizes the industrial projects that have been carried out in conjunction with the Creativity Research Unit. An early example, and some recent action research projects, are summarized below.

The SCIMITAR studies (1972–1989). Perhaps the best-known work with which the Manchester Creativity Unit has been associated was undertaken by a team led by John Carson in a primary chemicals conglomerate in the 1970s and early 1980s. A structured approach to a new product development evolved and was given the acronym SCIMITAR (Structured Creativity and Integrated Modeling for Industry, Technology, and Research).

Approximately 1 product reached the marketplace successfully for every 100 product ideas generated. The statistic remained surprisingly stable in later work, reported at one stage as 100 new products reaching the marketplace, from a total of 100,000 product ideas recorded over a period of approximately 6 years (Carson & Rickards, 1979). Eight of the 100 commercialized products were considered significant contributors to the company's revenues, and took the project comfortably beyond a break-even position. Commercial successes included an asbestos substitute with a particular application in fire barrier doors and a delayed-release fertilizer.

Hybrid PII-SCIMITAR trials (1985–1990). The PII project took place in the Netherlands contemporaneously with the SCIMITAR work (Buijs, 1984, this volume). A hybrid PII/SCIMITAR model was tested in the U.K., with six Manchester-based process consultants in six small, inner-city companies offering a maximum of ten days of "free" consultancy. Four out of the six firms claimed some tangible benefit from the project, one of which was rated a significant innovation for the company (Rickards, 1988).

One company retained their consultant for further work on a fee-paying basis (one of the criteria of perceived value of an exercise). Further work continues in the inner city, where community leaders have received creative problem-solving training and have worked closely with the Creativity Unit.

Coordinating innovation efforts in a major organization (1988–1990). In 1987, the process engineering division of a multinational division set up a series of change programs. An innovation manager coordinated the execution of the programs, working closely with the Creativity Unit in an action research mode. The "product" goal was for each engineer or engineering manager to return to a follow-up day (six to eight weeks later) with tangible evidence that he had achieved progress in the role of a facilitator of some innovation process. A number of commercially valuable results were reported on the follow-up day, including implementation of a new-technology monitoring system which brought considerable investment savings during the project-formulation stage of innovation.

Creating a culture change in government agency (1989–1990). A regional government agency was engaged in a major culture shift to encourage more innovative behaviors from all its staff. The chief executive sponsored creative problem-solving training at four levels, spanning from the directorate to the front-line managers. A 2-day problem-solving training program was designed and delivered by the trainers from the Creativity Research Unit. Initial evidence showed that the "cascade" approach helped set up a common language for change. Potential conflicts could be tackled in a constructive problem-solving mode which overcame some of the serious communication barriers within each level of the organization and across hierarchical levels that existed prior to the program.

Conclusions from the action research activities. It is the nature of action research that hypotheses emerge gradually, and that confirmation is slow and oblique (many uncontrolled variables). Conclusions tend to be generalizations, incorporated with uncertainties about their scope beyond the actual boundaries of the conducted work. However, the entire body of experience supports a view that complex industrial situations can be supported through a creative problem solving approach. The specifics of situations demand that the structures, techniques, roles, goals, and so on emerge through the problem-resolving process. Nevertheless, each experience confirms a systems similarity within any complex problem-solving process. The participants are well advised to explore their initial viewpoints and possible alternatives (reframing procedures). Search procedures can be enhanced through structures which keep divergent and convergent stages distinct (e.g., some version of the Osborn-Parnes five-stage problem-solving model). Diagnostics applied through survey-feedback methods (Rickards & Bessant, 1980) help individuals and groups understand and improve the climate for change. Techniques and creativity training provide mechanisms for challenging and overcoming assumptions. They can also provide a common language which supports change initiatives when extensively applied.

The action research work has been intimately connected with the progress of the Creativity Unit. It enables the unit to explore theoretical issues and the empirical reports of other practitioners in practical trials; it confirms the general paradigmatic position that creativity can be supported and enhanced through structured interventions; and it is a long-term dialogue between the academic and practical worlds, enriching both communities.

Products of Laboratory Experiments

There appears to be continual interest about research in the assessment of creative behaviors (e.g., Hocevar & Bachelor, 1989; Kirton, 1989). Training courses provide a rich source of data collected by application of self-report inventories with managerial audiences. Data are available in our archives from courses conducted since the early 1970s, and a thorough codification of the data on a computerized form has begun.

Communications "Products"

The MBS Creativity Unit was one of the earliest European research units to be concerned with creativity for the MBA and other managerial audiences. Bulletins have been produced since the mid-1970s, under the titles *Creativity Network* (1975–1982); *Creativity & Innovation Network* (1982–1987); and *Creativity & Innovation Yearbook* (1988–1989). In 1992, in-house efforts were converted into a major new quarterly journal, *Creativity and Innovation Management*. The networking publications have helped pull together the strands of industrial research and training activities, initially in the United Kingdom, and later internationally.

KEY ISSUES FOR ACTION AT THE CREATIVITY RESEARCH UNIT

In this section the viewpoints which characterize the Manchester approach, and the key action issues for the Creativity Unit which emerge from those viewpoints are considered.

A Systems View of Creativity

As early as Rickards (1974), a systems approach was put forward to explain how predetermined structures such as creative problem-solving techniques help in the generation of outputs which are not predetermined. The principle, termed creative analysis, invoked a metasystem mediating the individual's problem-solving routines. The concept of creative analysis was itself influenced by the management cybernetics of Beer (1966, 1972, 1979). It permitted an explanation of "set to break set" (Parnes, 1981) in terms of a metasystem which "controls" the individual's problem-solving system, enabling an individual to escape from habitual thinking through challenging assumptions. (By applying another systems principlethat of the recursive nature of systems components at differing levels of generalitycreative analysis can be similarly applied to model the mechanisms whereby teams and organizations may develop sets to break sets.)

Another key systems concept is variety or complexity control. Rickards and Freedman (1978); Rickards (1985); and Rickards and Puccio (1989) examined the divergence/ convergence stages of creative problem solving as processes for balancing of the complexity within and across each stage (subsystem) in problem solving.

A simple to understand, yet powerful systems model has been incorporated into the training programs described above. It models creativity as a process of "going beyond the obvious" (Figure 7.1), proposing two kinds of blocks which inhibit creativity, each requiring differing approaches for overcoming them:

- a potentially self-reinforcing "stuckness" loop, escape from which requires the challenging of assumptions (Ackoff & Vergara, 1981)
- a "satisficing" block noted by business theorists (Simon, 1960)

Various approaches have been suggested for dealing with the satisficing tendency in organization systems (Crosby, 1989; Deming, 1986; Rickards, 1981). The methods require the adoption of new techniques and structures within the organization, leading to incremental innovation and total quality performance.

The systems approach to creativity has become an intrinsic part of the consultancy and training provided by the Manchester group. It provides researchers with a methodology for exploring the nature of creativity. In the context of this conference, the four

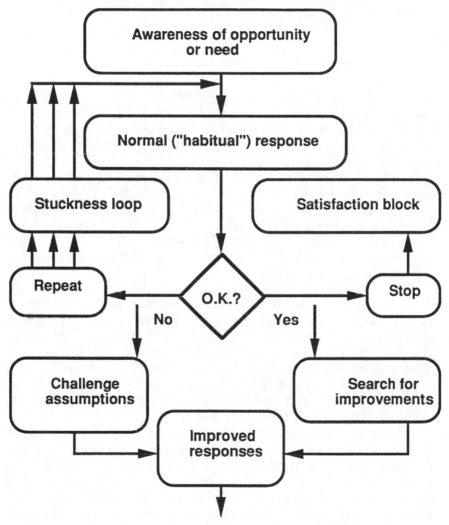

Figure 7.1. Systems model of problem solving indicating the "stuck-ness" loop, satisfaction block, and mechanisms for "going beyond the obvious."

dimensions of person, process, product, and press became the elements for a systems approachprovided each is studied in the framework implied by the totality of four interacting components (Rhodes, 1961). Such an approach points the way forward: We will continue to collect data on individuals, processes, products, and climate. Our interpretations, however, will require us to seek the interrelationships among the dimensions. It is a view gaining support from other researchers including Magyari-Beck (1985, 1988) and Csikszentmihalyi (1988).

Implementation

Within the stage models of creative problem solving developed by, among others, Parnes, Noller, and Biondi (1977), and Isaksen and Treffinger (1985), several diverge/converge sequences end in some version of implementation of ideas or solutions as acceptance finding.

Managers encountering such models in our training programs generally indicate that the models have high face validity. However, in action research situations dealing with technological problems (Rickards, 1973), innovation problems (Carson & Rickards, 1979), and strategic issues (Rickards, 1988), implementation is frequently a process of continued managing of a problem rather than resolving it completely.

A sophisticated theoretical rationale was given by Churchman and Scheinblatt (1965) who described a "dialectic" of implementation, which is in essence a model of information exchange across two knowledge systems (theoretical possibilities anticipated by the researchers and practical knowledge of the problem owners). This is an important point. In less formal terms, implementation is a process in which outside facilitators and problem owners interact to discover more and more possibilities emerging from the situation through joint problem solving.

An issue for action is for the emerging creativity paradigm to test the proposition that creative problem solving does not "solve" complex problems, but makes them more manageable. The product is primarily committed actions for making progress. If managers expect problems to be completely solved, their basic assumption is appropriate to simple, but not complex problems. As their problems are complex, creative problem solving will not produce complete resolution, and will be evaluated by the managers as having failed. Here we have a promising and testable hypothesis, amenable to investigation within action research studies. In essence, we need more information about the attitudes, beliefs, and expectations of managers when dealing with complex situations.

Training Issues

The possibility of developing creative potential through training is a basic assumption of the creative problem-solving paradigm. Far fewer studies have been reported on the impact of industrial training, in contrast with reports of the impact of exercises in various high school and college courses (Torrance, 1987).

The following propositions emerge from a consideration of Manchester experiences with industrial participants (1972–1989) and were reported recently (Rickards, 1990). They offer promising areas for research investigations:

- Measurable impacts can be achieved through creativity training with managerial/professional audiences.
- Such courses are excellent testing grounds for creativity training, in that they almost always include feedback to the course administrators of perceived value of the material.
- Creativity training has survived in such environments over a period of years. The ratings are comparable with more traditional components of management education such as marketing, strategy, and finance.
- The evidence for permanent learning gains is harder to assess. The very short (1/2- to 1-day inputs) probably assist consciousness raising, although in a few cases they may trigger action as evidenced by follow-up requests for further information or training.
- A substantial majority of participants at the outset of training present conflicting and confused ideas about creativity. Creativity is believed to be a fixed, possibly innate characteristic, yet creativity techniques may be accepted as a possible route to improved problem solving.
- Three-day and 5-day programs of an experiential form can lead to personal learning gains and progress on real problems (flip chart material taken away to be processed in the client organizations). However, noticeable organizational impacts (Hill, 1988, Talbot, 1990) seem to require the emergence of a critical mass of trained people, and even when these occur, seem to

follow a dormant period after training has started, perhaps of several years.

- The 10-day (1 day per week) programs have consistently shown changes in attitudes and skills of the participants some of whom go on to apply learned skills and techniques in their work environments.
- The courses should confront participants with real open-ended problems with which individuals are personally involved. Techniques which are simply mastered on realistic but model problems are harder to use on real problems. This reality trough seems to be a necessary part of the learning process. In the absence of such encounters, longer term behaviors remain uninfluenced.

Potential Research/Training Dilemmas

There are specific difficulties in collecting research data within management training programs. Participants expect some recognizable payoff for their contribution to a longer term research project. International audiences present problems concerning the validity of instruments that have not been thoroughly validated cross-culturally. Issues of confidentiality of data may conflict with benefits from sharing data. The trainer/researcher faces a potential dilemma. For research purposes it would be desirable to administer a range of validated instruments to each participant, and also collect biographical information, whereas there are pressures to minimize application times, focus on a small number of instruments, and provide rapid and personalized feedback.

The research issue becomes how to pursue research and training goals in mutually reinforcing ways. This requires working out a code of conduct which goes beyond the legal requirements of the situation. In the short training programs at Manchester, psychometric measures which take longer than 15 minutes to administer are eschewed, and developmental efforts are concentrated on measures which are easy to understand and apply. Data are collected only when the process permits direct feedback offering potential personal learning gains for each respondent. (In addition, in the U.K. it is legally necessary to remove names and other individual identifiers from all data stored electronically.) Nevertheless, selective presentation of psychometric material from our database enriches subsequent training by offering assorted benchmarks for individual and team behaviors associated with creativity and creative problem solving.

Laboratory and Real-World Practices

In several careers since his school days the author has found himself engaged in research intended to yield real-world (i.e., practical) results. It has been a repeated discovery that the laboratory experiment is a wonderful source of new ideas and a means of challenging old ideas. It also keeps the training up to date, and the trainers aware of the nature of their uncertainties. In systems terms, however, there is a rather loose coupling between the laboratory trial and real-world issues and strategies for dealing with them. As Roweton (1989) put it, referring to creativity research, his team "anguished all day and sometimes late into the night about the social value of trivial research with clean research designs" (p. 251).

An identified need is to find ways of enabling well-designed laboratory studies and less controllable real-life encounters to enrich each other's findings. One action possibility is for any grouping which has strengths in one domain to seek out partners with strengths in the other, for mutual creative venturing and accomplishments. This ideal suggests increased collaboration among previously isolated university departments, business schools, and the world of work outside those privileged groves of knowledge.

The Whole-Brain Metaphor

Various themes of interest to managerial researchers may be contained within a broad whole-brain metaphor (Taggart, 1984). These include the nature of intuition (Ainsworth-Land, 1982; Shallcross & Sisk, 1989) and visual imagery leading to product innovations or corporate missions/visions (Geschka, 1986; Parker, 1987). A key research issue for the unit is how to characterize the preverbal processes which assist in the generation of novel conceptual products. Current work (Rickards, 1988) is centering on exploring the processes of generating analogical material, drawing on the early work of Gordon (1956, 1961). A medium-term research goal is to apply expert systems methodology to make explicit the decision-making mechanisms taking place when facilitators are engaged in synectics-type metaphoric generation.

A Reorientation Toward Studies of Product

The work on this chapter prior to the conference served to collect together a great deal of material which has been summarized above. The literature surveys cited above were carried out strongly conditioned toward finding ways of enhancing industrial creativity. It might be expected that such a mindset would have unearthed literature with a focus on the creative product, yet the absence of product orientation in the selected material, once observed, is remarkable. The influential practitioners and researchers identified in the literature studies were far more occupied with the process—the how and the why of creativity—than with its outputs.

However, the intensive exploration of the product theme by the working team during the research conference helped in a personal reframing of the material. The rewriting of this chapter has taken place with greater attention to the importance of product (which enriches but does not replace a systemic approach to creativity research).

Some conclusions arise directly from a refocusing of attention on to the creative product:

- In training programs, efforts should be redoubled to carry out careful follow-up or impact studies which will investigate the emerging products (Basadur, 1988). These will include self-reported changes in behaviors and knowledge, as well as tangible real-world products. The pioneering work of Besemer and O'Quin (Besemer & O'Quin, 1987; O'Quin & Besemer, 1989) on creative product instruments offered a starting point for such efforts. Runco (1988) also indicated the importance of product attributes for analyzing creative outputs (in the context of publications for a new creativity journal).
- In action research, the required facilitative or process skills required will benefit from renewed efforts to help create products such as "shared visions" of goals which sustain task motivation (Buijs, 1988; Parnes, 1988). In these ways research into the creative product will become more important for the Manchester group, permitting better integration of the fragmented theoretical and practical knowledge of person, product, and press.

REFERENCES

Ackoff, R.L., & Vergara, E. (1981). Creativity in problem-solving and planning: A review. *European Journal of Operational Research, 7,* 1–13.

Adair, J. (1989). *Great leaders.* Guilford, UK: Talbot Adair Press.

Ainsworth-Land, V. (1982). Imaging and creativity: An integrating perspective. *Journal of Creative Behavior, 16(1)*, 5–28.

Allen, M. (1952). *Morphological creativity.* Englewood Cliffs, NJ: Prentice-Hall.

Bannister, D., & Fransella, F. (1971). *Inquiring man.* Harmondsworth, UK: Penguin.

Basadur, M. (1988). Needed research in creativity for business and industrial applications. In S.G. Isaksen (Ed.), *Frontiers of creativity research: Beyond the basics* (pp. 390–416). Buffalo, NY: Bearly Limited.

Beer, S. (1966). *Decision and control.* Chichester, UK: Wiley.

Beer, S. (1972). *Brain of the firm.* Chichester, UK: Wiley.

Beer, S. (1979). *The heart of the enterprise.* Chichester, UK: Wiley.

Belbin, M. (1981). *Management teams: Why they succeed or fail.* London: Heinemann.

Besemer, S.P., & O'Quin, K. (1987). Creative product analysis: Testing a model by developing a judging instrument. *Journal of Creative Behavior, 20,* 115–126.

Blanchard, K., & Johnson, S. (1982). *The one minute manager.* New York: William Morrow.

Buijs, J. (1984). *Innovation en interventie.* Deventer, Netherlands: Kluwer.

Buijs, J. (1988). Innovation and vision. In P. Colemont, P. Grholt, T. Rickards, & H. Smeekes (Eds.), *Creativity and innovation: Towards a European network.* Deventer, Netherlands: Kluwer.

Carson, J.W. (1989). *Innovation: A battleplan for the 1990s.* Farnborough, UK: Gower Press.

Carson, J.W., & Rickards, T. (1979). *Industrial new-product development.* Farnborough, UK: Gower Press.

Churchman, C.W., & Scheinblatt, A.H. (1965). The researcher and the manager: A dialectic of implementation. *Management Science, 11(4),* B69 - B87.

Crosby, P.B. (1989). *Let's talk quality.* New York: McGraw-Hill.

Csikszentmihalyi, M. (1988). Society, culture and person: A systems view of creativity. In R.J. Sternberg (Ed.), *The nature of creativity: Contemporary psychological perspectives* (pp. 325–339). New York: Cambridge University Press.

deBono, E. (1971). *Lateral thinking for management.* London, UK: McGraw-Hill.

Deming, W.E. (1986). *Out of crisis.* Cambridge, MA: MIT Press.

Duncker, K. (1926). A qualitative study of productive thinking. *Journal of Genetic Psychology, 33,* 642–708.

Geschka, H. (1983). Creativity techniques in product planning and development: A view from West Germany. *R & D Management, 13(3),* 169–183.

Geschka, H. (1986). Creativity workshop in product innovation. *Journal of Product Innovation Management, 3(1),* 50–56.

Gordon, W.J.J. (1956, November/December). Operational approach to creativity. *Harvard Business Review*, pp. 41–51.

Gordon, W.J.J. (1961). *Synectics: The development of creative capacity.* New York: Harper & Row.

Haefele, J.W. (1962). *Creativity and innovation.* New York: Reinhold.

Handy, C.B. (1988). *The age of unreason.* London: Hutchinson.

Hill, P. (1988). Innovation using creative problem-solving techniques. *Creativity & Innovation Yearbook, 1,* 106–111. Manchester, UK: Manchester Business School.

Hocevar, D., & Bachelor, T. (1989). A taxonomy and critique of measurements used in the study of creativity. In J.A. Glover, R. Ronning, & C. Reynolds (Eds.), *Handbook of creativity.* New York: Plenum.

Isaksen, S.G., & Treffinger, D.J. (1985). *Creative problem-solving: The basic course.* Buffalo, NY: Bearly Limited.

Jantsch, E. (1967). *Technological forecasting in perspective.* Paris: OECD.

Khandwalla, P.N. (1984). *The fourth eye.* Allahabad, India: Wheeler and Co.

Kirton, M.J. (1989). *Adaptors and innovators: Styles of creativity and problem-solving.* London: Routledge.

Koestler, A. (1964). *The act of creation.* London: Hutchinson.

Larson, J., & LaFasto, F.M.J. (1989). *Teamwork: What must go right/ what can go wrong.* Beverly Hills, CA: Sage.

Lupton, T. (1984). University Business Schools: Looking to the future. *Creativity & Innovation Network, 10*(2), 57–65.

Magyari-Beck, I. (1985). Creatological studies. *Budapest University of Economics Papers on Labor Economics, 6,* 1–76, Budapest.

Magyari-Beck, I. (1988). New concepts about personal creativity. *Creativity & Innovation Yearbook, 1,* 121–126. Manchester, UK: Manchester Business School.

McPherson, J.H. (1969). *Structured approaches to creativity* (Rep. No. 385). Stanford, CA: Stanford Research Institute Long-Range Planning Service.

Morgan, G. (1986). *Images of organization.* Beverly Hills, CA: Sage.

Morgan, G. (1989). *Creative organization theory: A resource book.* Beverly Hills, CA: Sage.

Morris, J. (1984, October). *Getting the learning spiral to work.* Development Learning and Organizational Change Conference, Bradford University, Yorkshire, UK.

Mumford, E. (1981). *Values, technology, and work.* The Hague, Netherlands: Martinus Nijhoff.

Mumford, E. (1983). *Designing human systems.* Manchester, UK: Manchester Business School.

O'Quin, K., & Besemer, S.P. (1989). The development, reliability, and validity of the revised creative product semantic scale. *Creativity Research Journal, 2,* 267–278.

Osborn, A.F. (1949). *Applied imagination.* New York: Charles Scribner.

Parker, M. (1987, December 13–16). *Let's share some experiences on organizational visioning.* First European Conference on Creativity and Innovation, Noordvijk, Netherlands.

Parnes, S.J. (1981). *The magic of your mind.* Buffalo, NY: Creative Education Foundation.

Parnes, S.J. (1988). The creative studies project. In S.G. Isaksen (Ed.), *Frontiers of creativity research: Beyond the basics* (pp. 156 - 188). Buffalo, NY: Bearly Limited.

Parnes, S.J., Noller, R.B., & Biondi, A.M. (1977). *A guide to creative action.* New York: Charles Scribner.

Peters, T., & Waterman, R. (1982). *In search of excellence.* New York: Harper & Row.

Prince, G.M. (1970). *The practice of creativity.* Cambridge, MA: Harper & Row.

Rhodes, M. (1961, April). An analysis to creativity. *Phi Delta Kappan,* pp. 305–310.

Richardson, J. (1988). The historic boundlessness of the creative spirit. In *Windows on Creativity and Invention* (pp. 298 - 321). Maryland: Lomond.

Rickards, T. (1973). Brainstorming in an R & D environment (1969–72). *R & D Management, 3,* 137–144.

Rickards, T. (1974). *Problem-solving through creative analysis.* Farnborough, UK: Gower Press.

Rickards, T. (1980). Designing for creativity: A state of the art review. *Design Studies, 1(5),* 262–272.

Rickards, T. (1981). Innovation in tiny increments. *International Management, 7,* 114.

Rickards, T. (1985). *Stimulating innovation.* London: Pinter.

Rickards, T. (1987). Closing down: A classification of creative decision-making aids. *Journal of Managerial Psychology, 2(3),* 11–16.

Rickards, T. (1988). *Creativity at work.* Farnborough, UK: Gower.

Rickards, T. (1990). Innovation and creativity, woods, trees, and pathways. *R&D Management Conference.* Manchester, UK.

Rickards, T., & Bessant, J. (1980). The creativity audit: Introduction of a new research measure during programs for facilitating organizational change. *R&D Management Journal, 10(2),* 467–475.

Rickards, T., & Freedman, B.L. (1979). A reappraisal of creativity techniques in industrial training. *Journal of European Industrial Training, 3(1),* 3–8.

Rickards, T., & Puccio, G. (1989). Creative problem-solving and general systems theories: Towards an integration of two paradigms. *Proceedings of the 33rd Annual Meeting of the International Society for General Systems Research,* Edinburgh, Scotland.

Roweton, W.E. (1989). Enhancing individual creativity in American business and education. *Journal of Creative Behavior, 23,* 248–257.

Runco, M. (1988). Creativity research: Originality, utility, and integration. *Creativity Research Journal, 1,* 1–8.

Shallcross, D., & Sisk, D.A. (1989). *Intuition: An inner way of knowing.* Buffalo, NY: Bearly Limited.

Simon, H.A. (1960). *Administrative behavior* (2nd ed.). London: Macmillan.

Taggart, W.M. (1984, October). *A 'whole brain' model of human information processing.* Development Learning and Organizational Change Conference, Bradford University, Yorkshire, UK.

Talbot, R., & Rickards, T. (1984). Developing creativity. In C. Cox & J. Beck (Eds.), *Management development: Advances in theory and practice.* Chichester, UK: Wiley.

Torrance, E.P. (1987). Teaching for creativity. In S.G. Isaksen (Ed.), *Frontiers of creativity research: Beyond the basics* (pp. 189–215). Buffalo, NY: Bearly Limited.

Vernon, P. (1970). *Creativity: Collected readings.* Harmondsworth, UK: Penguin.

Yamada, K. (1987). Creativity in Japan. *Creativity & Innovation Network, 12,* 33–40.

Zwicky, F. (1948). *Morphological method of analysis and construction.* New York: Interscience.

8

Creativity in the Organizational Context: Implications for Training*

R. J. Talbot

Practice and experience are important aspects of learning about creativity. My own experiences as a creativity trainer have been significant in stimulating my interest in the organizational context in which people are (or are not) creative. In particular, these experiences have stimulated my inquiry into and application of the features of organizations that inhibit or facilitate a person's creativity and in how an understanding of these features can be used to improve creativity training effectiveness for individuals and organizations. This chapter will describe some of those significant experiences and their implications for using creativity in an organizational context. It also contains a description of some pertinent organizational theories and research and an exploration of their relevance to creativity training.

THE STEP-BY-STEP COURSE: BEGINNING EXPERIENCES AND INSIGHTS

I began my involvement in designing and running creativity courses in 1978 as a guest tutor for a Manchester Business School course, Creativity Step-by-Step, run by Tudor Rickards and his colleagues (see Rickards, this volume). I was full of enthusiasm for Creative Problem Solving (CPS) and other creativity processes and techniques. I saw people from a variety of backgrounds success

*The stimulus for this chapter was provided by participation in the 1990 International Conferences on Creativity in Buffalo, NY. I am very grateful to Peter Wesenberg and his colleagues of the Norwegian Center for Leadership Development in Oslo, Norway for their generous financial support. Without them, I could not have attended.

fully using what they had learned. Conversely, I also heard about many of the difficulties they encountered or anticipated when trying to practice these skills back at work.

For example, some participants left our course with what might be called a high "euphoria quotient": They couldn't wait to get back to work and try things out. Some of them reported at course follow-up meetings being severely deflated by the negative responses of some of their colleagues. Others reported more successful attempts at introducing creative approaches into their work situations. These latter responses seemed to me to have been more realistic about the merits of the techniques, so my first response as a trainer was to try and help all participants get a more realistic view of what was possible in the work situation. This was done by getting them to compare the sorts of problems, people, activities, or atmosphere encountered in the course with those pertaining at work and to use these comparisons as a basis for deciding what was and was not transferable (Talbot & Rickards, 1984).

I noticed other differences between the more and less successful, although their significance did not register at the time. For example, a manager of a research and development laboratory had reported a successful introduction of brainstorming sessions to his team, whereas a junior officer in local government had considerable difficulties. These differences seemed to involve power, leadership skills, and type of organizational setting.

CREATIVITY IN ENGINEERING AND SCIENCE: ADDITIONAL LEARNING FROM PRACTICE

A few years later, colleagues from UMIST and I were invited to deliver a 3-day course in creativity for young engineers and scientists as part of their induction program into a large, publicly funded research and development organization. After the first four courses, an investigation into the impact of the course was conducted (Wesenberg, 1983; Wesenberg & Talbot, 1984) that yielded the following recommendations:

1. Course participants should be helped to see that it is the attitudes and behaviors associated with the use of CPS techniques which determine the creative act and not just the techniques themselves. Such behaviors and attitudes included open-mindedness, postponing judgment, being positive rather than critical and negative, being more patient and

tolerant, being more flexible with other people, seeing others' points of view, trying to listen to others, trying to be less dogmatic, trying to be less conventional, and discussing more with others about one's work problems.

2. As important preconditions for creative attitudes and behavior, the course should facilitate an increase in participants' self-esteem and self-confidence.

3. Individual psychological, organizational, and structural aspects of the reentry problem should be confronted in a supportive manner.

4. In order to be more effective, a creativity course should be based on an explicit "philosophical" framework.

5. A follow-up course might be a good forum for dealing with some of the problems associated with past participants' attempts to become more creative at work.

All of the recommendations within our control were implemented effectively. My impression of the impact of changes resulting from this research was that people developed not only CPS skills but also a greater awareness of relevant features of their working situations and of the need to improve relationships with colleagues, bosses, and subordinates. We had little doubt that it was possible to effectively learn to apply the CPS approach to the technical problems participants encountered at work. Parnes (1967), for example, had described a variety of studies indicating the effectiveness of training, and our own experiences showed that participants had used the CPS approach effectively on our courses.

To illustrate this, it is necessary to say a little about our course. Its design was centered around core teaching of some basic divergent techniques for defining and redefining problems, generating ideas, and developing solutions (P-I-S procedures), together with some techniques for convergence and for selecting promising ideas. The focus was on thinking skills involved in using techniques. For practice we used puzzles, often specially selected or designed to illustrate various principles. As participants became more skilled in the use of the techniques, they practiced on more realistic problems—problems which might occur, but which none of the participants owned or were involved in. A realistic problem was used for practicing a run-through of the full P-I-S procedure. Then followed a whole day during which two real-world problems were tackled. For the first of these sessions, a client from the organization identified a real problem to be worked on. On several occasions, ideas from these sessions were taken up by this client and incorporated into his own work. In fact the course, which was run four times per year, almost became his private think tank. For the other session, some course participants acted as clients for their own technical problems and often reported progress in their thinking.

This design principle—practicing on puzzles, then realistic, then real problems—developed independently of, but not dissimilar to that underlying Treffinger's Creative Learning Model (Treffinger, 1988). It enabled participants to use the techniques and to work together before having to deal with the additional complexities of ownership of problems and the real-world pressure to produce solutions by yesterday.

Anticipated Inhibitors

Participants made the approach work on the course, but again they reported it as difficult to adopt in their work situations. To deal with this problem we introduced a session into the course on "The Organizational Context" that focused on helps and hindrances to creativity at work.

Many of the difficulties participants described centered around the way other people treated them at work, and particularly on how they were treated by their immediate superiors. What also became apparent in discussion was their belief that they could not do much about this treatment. Table 8.1 shows, in their own words, what participants on one course believed to be the main external sources of creativity inhibition.

My interpretation of these difficulties centered around the idea that engineers and scientists in particular were not strongly endowed with what might be called "people-handling" skills. Although eminently competent at technical aspects of their work, they tended to take for granted or treat as a given the way they were treated by others. Discussion of organizational context drew their attention to the impact of the nature of their relationships with others on their capability to be more creative in their technical problem solving. This somewhat unexpected conclusion and the raised awareness stimulated by it was by no means always welcomed by participants. For some, it opened up issues they would have preferred to avoid. This information about context implied that to be more creative at work, they had to do more than just go back and use the skills they learned and used

Table 8.1.   Behaviors of Others Hindering Creativity: Comments from Creativity Course Participants

• Boss providing solution with problem • Boss that doesn't like novelty • Working to time and cost • Boss that overrides your decisions • Playing people off against each other • Taking the piss (peer pressure) • Boss' indecision • Overwork • Lack of confidence (of boss in you, in particular) • Boss taking credit for your ingenuity • General problems of morale • Lack of choice of work • Someone who is a know-all • Boss/client not supporting idea	• No cooperation from other dept's • Flexi-time (great disgruntlement) • Bosses not confident in themselves • Scottish Development Dept. • Being told to go and consult expert (and therefore think along same lines) • Being told to take responsibility (unfairly) • General low public esteem (or even antipathy) towards one's endeavors • Need to know policy - information withheld • Being told idea is not safe (worried because boss won't like it)

successfully during the course. Concentrating only on the technical aspects of their work was not enough. Somehow they had to spot or create opportunities for using their skills in what they saw as less than favorable circumstances, and that meant treating people differently and getting others to treat them differently.

The boss as inhibitor.   As can be seen from Table 8.1, "the boss" was a frequently reported source of difficulty. Course participants did not seem enamored with their bosses, yet bosses were among those people that needed to be treated differently. In parallel with these courses for engineers and scientists, I had been running a half-day session on leadership in a course for managers in the same organization. Most of the managers were people who would be the bosses of the creativity course participants.

On-course assessment of bosses' leadership styles indicated marked differences between the way in which they saw themselves and how they were seen by subordinates. We used LEAD-Other (Hersey & Blanchard, 1981) with creativity course participants for their bosses, and LEAD-Self with the managers. These assessments suggested that bosses saw themselves as much more adaptable, much more supportive, and only slightly more directive than they were seen by subordinates. Managers also showed a marked reluctance to delegate appropriately to subordinates. The data confirmed that subordinates saw bosses in an unfavorable light. Only the most self-confident subordinates were likely to dare to attempt to get bosses to treat them better, particularly if bosses thought they were leading well already.

Colleagues as inhibitors. Some of the inhibition of creativity was related to the behavior of colleagues. Generally, however, participants felt more able to improve their working relationships with colleagues. They had found the structured "Problems-Ideas-Solutions" approach, together with the principle of deferred judgment, particularly helpful in facilitating a disciplined and constructive group climate, and frequently reported pleasure and amazement at how well they had worked together. One particular source of surprise was the fact that nonexperts could make useful contributions to problem solving. (To a physicist, a chemical engineer is a nonexpert.) There still remained the problem, however, that not all of their workmates had been through the course. Some of the participants were not entirely confident of being able to or even being permitted to teach their colleagues the techniques, but they were more confident that they could influence them by treating them more positively.

The system as inhibitor. A third source of external creativity inhibition alluded to by participants was the "system"the organization, its rules, and control systems. They reported working conditions reminiscent of those described in the literature as inhibiting creativity; for example, Reitz (1981) described managerial practices and organizational policies which foster fear, anxiety, and defensiveness (all inhibiting of creativity) such as: (a) an oppressive organizational climate, manifested by close, punitive supervision; (b) a stress on the consequences of failure rather than the rewards for success; (c) organizational instability; (d) excessive formalization of rules, policies, relationships, and procedures; (e) a highly centralized organizational structure; and (f) little time for thinking and experimenting.

There was little the young engineers and scientists felt they could do about the organization, although they frequently suggested that their bosses should attend our creativity course (in the belief that their bosses could and should do something). They believed they had little power to affect the way things were done in the organization, and given their relatively junior positions—most of them were recent graduates—they were probably right.

However, a second study by Wesenberg (1986) suggested that this feeling of powerlessness need not be confined to the lower levels of the organizational hierarchy. His major insight resulting from a series of companywide, in-depth interviews in a different engineering company was that members of the organization unintentionally and unknowingly contributed to the production and maintenance of the organizational conditions that they reported as inhibiting their creativity. His respondents did have a sophisticated understanding of the nature of creativity, and they did very much want to realize their creative potential in their work, but they tended to blame the organization for their frustration at not being able to do so. They reported several inhibiting factors: (a) an ambiguous organizational structure related to recent and not-so-recent rationalization and mergers; (b) little apparent evidence of a business plan, strategic thinking, or technical development for the future; (c) short-term management thinking; (d) a widespread "them and us" attitude; (e) a rigid hierarchical structure; and (f) a stringent financial control system. Wesenberg (1986) summarized, "All in all, they reported frustration in satisfying needs for identity, meaning, purpose, and belonging, together with a penetrating feeling of uncertainty and ambiguity."

These reported inhibitions on creativity were not confined to any particular level nor to any particular part of the organization. Everybody seemed to be inhibited by "the others." A logical consequence of this fact was that everybody inhibited everybody else's creativity, or even more interestingly, that individuals inhibited their own creativity. They did this by joining in those activities which for themselves produced the creativity-inhibiting conditions. For example, striving for, obtaining, and jealously guarding visible proofs of their individual success in the organization (e.g., promotion, office furniture of ever-increasing luxury, or a personal parking space) seemed to satisfy some aspects of people's needs. However, this striving for status and position was one of several factors that seemed to contribute to the production and maintenance of a rigid hierarchical structure and was also cited as a cause of creativity inhibition.

Another widespread strategy for satisfying needs for identity, meaning, purpose, and belonging was to be a member of a tightly and exclusively defined work group and to fight for the group's success in the organization. The existence of such groups was often cited as one of the factors contributing to the penetrating "them and us" attitude.

The interviewees did not realize that they contributed to the production and maintenance of an organizational structure and ideology that inhibited their own creativity. Most of them perceived "the organization" as a powerful entity which moved in wondrous ways, independently of its members, to impose on, constrain, or coerce them. Existentially, they saw themselves only as objects at the mercy of a reified entity—The Company. The only way to satisfy any needs at all was to do the organization's bidding, to devote their efforts to being seen, to conform, or to be loyal group members. All these strategies, however, were based on dependency and led to defensiveness of one's subordination to the organization or blaming "the organization" for whatever went wrong.

Self as inhibitor. One way out of this predicament is for individuals to accept responsibility for the part they play in producing and sustaining the organization in its current form and then create things to do that will begin to change their work circumstances.

When confronted with the negative influence of their behavior, some course participants were able to see and accept responsibility for their own creativity-inhibiting actions and made plans for changing their behavior on return to their work. Typically, such plans focused on something participants felt was within their control, such as ways of improving interpersonal relationships.

End of Course Action Plans

End of course action plans contained suggestions that might be pertinent to a variety of contexts. Participant actions are listed below.

Things to do more of:

Spend more time with people you work with	Share problems with and bounce ideas off others
Set aside time for collating ideas	Be more expressive in groups
Encourage others	Be supportive of others
Be honest with people	Accept criticism
Clarify with manager what s/he wants/what is needed	Promote interest and enthusiasm
Criticize constructively	Be more assertive and more cooperative

Things to do less of:

Holding back ideas	Being impulsive
Blindly accepting tasks set by managers	Insulting and humiliating people who make mistakes
Being intolerant of people who antagonize you	Interrupting people

This list of resolutions, if successfully implemented, would produce a climate not unlike that described by Ekvall and Tängeberg-Andersson (1986). There has long been a consensus on the characteristics of the creative situation. As early as the late 1970s, recommendations concerning the fostering of creativity in subordinates were being made. For example, MacKinnon recommended that a manager should

> show respect for and confidence in the ability of the younger person to act autonomously and responsibly; the granting of considerable freedom of action; a plentiful supply of models of effective, resourceful and innovative behavior on the part of managers with whom the younger employees can identify; a variety of challenging assignments; encouraging rather than forcing the development of skills and interests for effective and creative performance in a managerial role. (Freedman, 1976–1977)

Also, see MacKinnon (1978) for his fascinating set of accounts of explorations of creativity.

Ekvall's study of a newspaper office describes a creative climate and an editor behaving in a manner similar to that described by MacKinnon. Nolan (1981) is another who described the characteristics of the creative climate in an interesting way. Five themes are highlighted: (a) action responsibility—we are uniquely responsible for what we do and not responsible in the same way for what others do; (b) change—to change, people need to be able to invent new things to do; (c) working effectively with others—people who can take responsibility for themselves and can invent new ways to get things done make good team members; (d) communication—using inventive skills requires open-mindedness, open-mindedness allows ideas in; and (e) learning and change—people learn by doing new things; even if something new isn't successful, the chances for change will be greater the next time.

Behaving Creatively in an Organizational Context: The Challenge

To summarize, course participants had demonstrated to themselves and to each other their ability to work creatively on real, technical problems in the course. They were generally willing to try out creative approaches to problems back at work, but they anticipated problems in getting the opportunity to do so. Much of the difficulty seemed to be associated with their bosses, though colleagues, the organization, outside agencies, and occasionally themselves were also sometimes blamed.

The difficulty was not in describing the appropriate climate for creativity, but in generating such conditions. Participants in the courses described came from an already existing, and, reportedly, largely creativity-inhibiting context. Their problem was not to produce a creative climate from scratch, but to try and change what already existed into something more receptive to their attempts at creativity.

An alternative way of formulating this problem might be how to spot and take opportunities for creativity in the existing situation without deliberately attempting to alter the climate. There must be times when ideas for improvement, or even for more radical change, would be acceptable, even needed. The challenge is to pick one's moment and method of introduction (perhaps armed with some knowledge of likely responses to new ideas). Anticipating reactions to new ideas was a part of the earlier Manchester Business School courses, as well as the current one, and is dealt with as "acceptance finding" by Isaksen and Treffinger (1985).

Whether one is trying to operate more creatively within an existing context, or trying to change it to be more receptive to creativity attempts, it seems clear that the more one understands about the situation and about why things happen the way they do, the more effective is one likely to be.

PERSPECTIVES ON CREATIVITY IN THE ORGANIZATIONAL CONTEXT

In an earlier paper (Talbot, 1982) I argued that if they are to be successful, designers need an understanding of the context in which they are operating, and of the human context at which their designs are aimed. The same is true for any problem solver. For creativity course participants, the problem confronting them can be expressed as how to get more opportunities for creativity in the job. Tackling *that* problem effectively requires domain relevant knowledge and skills, where the domain is the organizational context.

Organizations are complex phenomena. There are many different types of organizations. They can be large or small, stable or changing, formal or informal, public or private, product or service oriented, profit-making or non-profit-making. In addition, as Magyari-Beck's Creatology Matrix (Magyari-Beck, 1993) reminds us, organizations themselves exist in a societal context.

National/cultural assumptions, beliefs, and customs will affect what goes on in organizations. We cannot really generalize about creativity in organizations. It depends on whose creativity we mean and in what sort of organization and in which society. Novelli (1993), points out that current creativity theory does not have the requisite variety to cope with organizational complexity and needs extending beyond its psychological and social-psychological roots. Magyari-Beck (1993) concurs.

My particular focus has been on the challenge facing participants in creativity courses in the United Kingdom. Mostly, they are engineers and scientists involved in technical problem solving, managers of technical subordinates, and more recently, managers seeking more creative approaches to managerial problems. As a trainer, I would like to be able to provide them with enough understanding of their organization to help them read their organizational context, and perhaps, help them develop skills suitable for taking action to improve the chances for realization of the creative potential of themselves and others in their workplace.

PERSPECTIVES ON CREATIVITY IN THE ORGANIZATIONAL CONTEXT: DISCUSSION AND IMPLICATIONS

A number of authors have relevant things to say about creativity in the organizational context that might be useful for trainers to consider. Novelli (1993) describes four perspectives from which organizations can be viewed—the humanist, the structural, the political, and the symbolic—and shows how differently issues concerning organizational creativity may be seen from each perspective.

Morgan (1986) provided a neat encapsulation of the benefits of postponing judgment and diverging in problem defining and also suggested that a variety of perspectives are required to aid understanding of organizations. He argues that effective managers and professionals need to be skilled in the art of "reading" situations in which they are involved:

> Skilled readers have the capacity to remain open and flexible, suspending immediate judgements whenever possible, until a more comprehensive view of the situation emerges. They are aware of the fact that new insights often arise as one reads a situation from "new angles" and that a wide and varied reading can create a wide and varied range of action possibilities (p. 12)

He further notes:

> Less effective managers and problem solvers, on the other hand, seem to interpret everything from a fixed standpoint. As a result, they frequently hit blocks that they can't get around; their actions and behaviors are often rigid and inflexible and a source of conflict. When problems and differences of opinion arise, they usually have no alternative but to hammer at issues in the same old way and try to create consensus by convincing others to "buy into" their particular view of the situation (p. 12)

(See Jones, this volume, for a more extensive treatment of blocks to creativity in an organizational context.)

Morgan invites us to contemplate organizations from a number of perspectives, each based on a particular metaphor; for example, organizations as machines, organisms, brains, cultures, political systems, psychic prisons, flux and transformation, and instruments of domination. The key feature of a metaphor is its tendency to highlight certain features of a phenomenon and ignore others. Looking at life as an obstacle course produces rather different images than seeing it as a visit to a favorite restaurant or toy shop. Looking at an organization as though it were a machine focuses our attention on such features as smooth running, components working in coordination, and so on, and might give rise to a tendency to see people as parts—repairable when defective, replaceable when worn out or when obsolete. Viewing an organization as an organism, however, might highlight the effects of environment on organizational survival. Morgan does not argue for one metaphor in preference to another, but suggests that they all have value, and that they are all limited in different ways by virtue of the fact that metaphorical thinking always produces a one-sided insight. It is the deliberate use of many metaphors that produces a multifaceted view of an organization—a skillful "reading" of an organization.

Both Novelli's and Morgan's sets of perspectives are rich sources of ideas for understanding the relatively intangible aspects of organizational life. They provide ways of understanding why people in organizations do the things they do and are the way they are. Such conceptualizations—theories—are essential bases for informed action, particularly action aimed at enhancing the creativity of oneself and others. Of course, these are not the only ways of looking at the organizational context. Developments in understanding of organizational culture, and in particular two typologies of organizational culture due to Harrison (1987a) and Ekvall (1988), are strongly relevant.

ORGANIZATIONAL CULTURE: AN OVERVIEW

Corporate culture is usually taken for granted and tends to remain outside of conscious awareness. It is the product of long-term social learning and reflects what has worked well enough in the past to be taken for granted and to be passed on to succeeding generations of employees.

There have been many attempts at defining culture (see Rousseau, 1988, for example), and not surprisingly, some disagreements among researchers. For my purposes, a useful way of describing culture is based on Uttal (1983): "Shared values (what is important), shared beliefs (how things work), that interact with an organization's structure and control systems to produce behavioral norms (the way we do things around here)." To these components I would add

> Basic assumptions: unconscious, taken for granted, nonconfrontable and nondebatable assumptions about how organizational problems should be solved;
> Artifacts: visible manifestations of the other levels of cultural elements, including observable behaviors of members, as well as the structures, systems, procedures, rules, and physical aspects of the organization (Cummings & Huse, 1989).

Cummings and Huse (1989) also suggested that cultural elements exist at different levels of cultural awareness. Basic assumptions exist at the deepest level, and artifacts at the highest.

In between come values, beliefs, and norms. Thus the easiest aspects of culture to see and to change are the artifacts, and the hardest are the basic assumptions.

An Overview: Characteristics of Organizational Culture

Intensity of culture.   We can talk about cultures as having intensity and direction. Intensity is related to the degree of influence on organizational members and is a function of the degree of consensus regarding appropriate and inappropriate behavior. The greater the intensity of a culture, the stronger and more commonly held are its assumptions, values, beliefs, and norms; thus the more agreement there is on *what constitutes a problem*, on what sorts of *actions are permissible* to solve it, and what sorts of *solutions are desirable*.

New circumstances, for which there is no tried, trusted, and agreed solution, may well present opportunities for culture change or threats to the organization's survival if they are not considered. New solutions, especially those which are incompatible with basic assumptions and fundamental values, are likely to be unacceptable. New solutions which do not violate basic assumptions and values will be more acceptable.

The greater the intensity of an organizational culture, the more constrained and protected individuals are, as long as they conform. When there is disagreement about the desirability of solutions or about permissibility of actions (especially to new problems), the characteristic means by which such conflict is resolved will depend on what sort of culture pertains, or the direction of it.

Direction of a culture.   The direction of a culture refers to the particular set of assumptions, values, beliefs, and norms that distinguish one type of culture from another. Harrison (1987a) describes four types of organizational culture: power, role, achievement, and support cultures.

Power cultures.   A good boss is decisive and firm but fair, and protective and indulgent to loyal subordinates, who in turn are hard working in their boss's interests. The organization treats individuals as though their time and energy were at the disposal of persons higher in the hierarchy.

The power-oriented organization is authoritarian and hierarchical. It is dominated by a strong leader or a coalition, who often run the organization for their own benefit, as though they owned it (often they do). People in the organization strive for status and influence, and they endeavor to build close relationships with power figures. Political skill is important in getting ahead. (Harrison, 1987a, p. 6)

Role cultures. A good boss is impersonal and correct, demanding of subordinates only that which is required by the formal system. In return, good subordinates are responsible and reliable and do not do things surprising or embarrassing to their superior. Individuals are treated as though their time and energy were available to the organization through a contract with rights and obligations on both sides.

> The role-oriented organization is hierarchical also, but power is exercised through rules, systems, and procedures. Personal power is replaced by formal, legalistic structures. Written or unwritten rules and contracts specify job requirements, rewards, and disciplinary procedures. Those who stay within the rules (or at least don't get caught breaking them) are usually safe from the arbitrary exercise of power. (Harrison, 1987a, p. 6)

Achievement cultures. In an achievement culture, a good boss is egalitarian and influenceable in matters concerning the task, and uses authority to get the resources needed to get on with the job. Good subordinates are self-motivated and open with ideas and suggestions, but will give the lead to others if they show greater expertise.

> The achievement-oriented organization is directed toward 'making a difference' in the world. Its thrust is toward some valued goal or ideal. The organization provides opportunities for its members to use their talents and abilities in ways that are intrinsically satisfying, and that advance a purpose or a goal to which the individual is personally committed. Thus, people are internally motivated rather than being controlled from the outside by rewards, punishments, or rules and systems. (Harrison, 1987a, pp. 6–7)

Support cultures. A good boss is concerned and responsive to the personal needs and values of others, and uses his or her position to provide satisfying and growth-stimulating work opportunities for subordinates. The good subordinate is deeply interested in developing his or her own potentialities and is open to learning and receiving help, as well as to helping others develop their potential.

The support-oriented organization motivates and bonds people through close, warm relationships. People learn to trust and care for one another and for the organization. They trust the organization to take care of them, to be responsive to their needs, and in turn they are responsible for taking care of the organization. (Harrison, 1987a, p. 7)

Harrison (1987b) described both positive and negative sides of these types of cultures. In the power-oriented organization, the positive side is that the strong protect and take responsibility for the weak (so long as the weak do as required). The dark side is the danger that those who are dependent will be exploited by those who are in positions of power.

In the role-oriented organization, the positive side is order, rationality, fairness, and efficiency. The darker side is rigidity, impersonality to the point of inhumanity, and a preoccupation with the internal workings of the organization (as manifested in the stereotyped view of the bureaucracy).

The positive side of the achievement orientation centers around the commitment of individuals to their work. It engages them totally, they feel they are working for something bigger than themselves, and "give their all"; they supervise themselves; there is high morale, teamwork, and a sense of camaraderie; people feel special and elite; and there is a sense of urgency to achieve the goal of the organization. However, there is a darker side to the achievement orientation which stems from its strengths:

In their single-minded pursuit of noble goals and an absorbing task, people lose their sense of balance and perspective; the end can come to justify the means. The group or organization exploits its environment, and its members—to the detriment of their health and quality of life—willingly exploit themselves in the service of the organization's purpose. Further the achievement-oriented organization is frequently underorganized; it relies on high motivation to overcome its deficiencies in structure, systems and planning. In addition, although it evokes enthusiasm and commitment, it may not have a heart: employees and their needs are subordinate to the organization's mission and its needs. After a time, people realize this and may begin to mistrust the organization—or they may remain committed but suffer high levels of emotional and physical stress. (Harrison, 1987b, p. 12)

The positive aspects of the support orientation are that people help each other, communicate a great deal, enjoy spending time together, are viewed as basically good, value harmony, do not let each other down, and so on. On the downside, individuals tend to avoid conflict so as to preserve harmony—postponing tough decisions about people so as not to hurt their feelings, or the organization might value consensus so highly that decisions take too long to make. Avoidance of conflict, particularly in the sense of suppressing negative feelings, tends eventually to lead to a breakdown in communication (Bienvenu, 1971). The basic challenge facing members of a support culture stems from possible competing demands of attention to the job and attention to relationships. In addition, there are always likely to be some people with rather deep-seated personal problems (to do with a negative self-concept, for example), that are too personal or too unpleasant to share with colleagues, or just too difficult for them to handle, however supportive the culture.

ORGANIZATIONAL CULTURE AND CREATIVITY: IMPLICATIONS FROM RESEARCH AND PRACTICE

It seems reasonable to suggest that individuals belonging to different organizational cultures will have different experiences relating to creativity. I put it this way because I do not want to fall into the trap of identifying only with the (relatively) powerless. In all organizational cultures, there is scope for someone to be creative. In a power-oriented culture, creativity is limited to the powerful, namely those in control of resources and with the say-so on who is and who is not allowed to be a member of the organization, and to those with the ear of and patronage of the powerful.

In a role-oriented organization, creativity may well be confined to those with the power to devise (or improve) the rules, that is, those with position power—and to those whose role is to be creative in the service of the organization. It might be the case that those lower down in the hierarchy of both types of culture devote their creativity to circumventing, or even undermining the system. Managerial creativity in these sorts of organizations might well manifest itself in devising managerial control systems for exploiting those lower in the hierarchy, or in devising or selecting technology that reduces the dependency of the organization on its workers. Harrison (1987b) puts it very clearly:

> The history of modern business and industry is the story of efforts by creative managers and technical experts to minimize the influ-

ence workers' choices about how much "personal energy"—the capabilities an individual brings to the workplace each day—to commit to work. The strategy for productivity improvement has been to develop technology and to design systems that require a minimum of commitment from workers, and then to ensure that they put in that minimum by providing multiple layers of supervision and tight systems for controlling costs, quality and output. (p. 5)

People respond to such close control by either complying with minimum effort needed to do their jobs or by rebelling overtly or covertly. Management, in turn, responds with more close control. Workers then withdraw commitment, and so the cycle continues—McGregor's "Theory X" in operation (McGregor, 1960). In such circumstances, the managed are most unlikely to be creative.

Another way of expressing this is to say that the powerful in some organizations seek to minimize the opportunity for creativity of their workers in order to maintain control of operations, which in turn reduces the intrinsic motivation of workers and possibly results in the atrophying or nondevelopment of the relevant skills. In our courses, managers from such cultures, though they usually espouse achievement and support, which bear close resemblance to McGregor's "Theory Y," often behave in a highly controlling manner, because "that's the way things are done around here." At best, a manager in such a culture can seek ways of protecting his subordinates from the hierarchy, and generate and maintain a creativity-encouraging microculture. The newspaper office described by Ekvall and Tängeberg-Andersson (1986) seemed to be a good example. The team survives as long as the leader can ward off pressures to conform to the organization's dominant culture, and, most importantly, as long as the team comes up with what the powerful in the organization want.

In an achievement-oriented organization there would seem to be much opportunity for creativity. People are intrinsically motivated; they are interested in the work itself. However, if an individual's interests differ from what is required for one reason or another, the lack of fit between individual and organization is likely to reduce creative performance and job satisfaction, and to increase stress (Puccio, 1990), or lead to a parting of the ways, initiated by one side or the other. Differences may exist because of errors in recruitment procedures, or because the goals of the individual change, or because the work changes due to changes in organizational goals. Even if individual and organizational goals remain compatible, the demands that a high-intensity achievement culture can place on individuals may result in premature burnout.

In a support culture, people's primary motivation is again intrinsic, though the emphasis shifts toward personal development, and may not be particularly compatible with business goals, as Harrison suggests:

> The pure support culture tends not to thrive in business unless it is balanced by a drive for success—an achievement orientation. The achievement orientation releases and focuses the personal energy that a love of doing and a high sense of purpose evokes from us; the support orientation taps into personal energy that ties of love and trust evoke from us. (Harrison, 1987b, p. 14)

The following table is a summary of the opportunities for creativity for various people in the pure versions of the four organizational cultures. As can be seen, none of the culture types is inhibitive of everybody's creativity (though the price paid may be high in some circumstances).

Clearly, the ideal culture for the creativity of all members of an organization, in Harrison's terminology, is a mixture of an achievement culture and a support culture.

Swedish Culture Patterns

Ekvall (1988) reached a similar conclusion. He described four "culture patterns" that he observed in Swedish industry. These culture patterns are described in terms of how much emphasis is placed on each of three value orientations, which are labeled *structure*, *people*, and *change*.

Value-orientation and culture patterns observed in Swedish industry. The *structure orientation* is articulated in Taylor's "scientific management" concept and in Weber's bureaucratic principles.

- Leadership is task-oriented and controlling
- "Mechanistic"
- People are mainly seen as parts of a well-oiled machine.

The *people orientation* is based on human relations ideas as exemplified by McGregor's Theory Y.

Table 8.2. Creativity in Different Organizational Cultures

Culture	The Creators	Their Products
Power	Those with resource power and in control of organizational membership.	Organizational goals, etc., and prescriptions for who does what, when they do it, and how they do it.
	Those sponsored by or prepared to submit to the powerful.	What the powerful prescribe; namely, the procedures, services and/or products chosen by the powerful.
Role	Those with the power to devise or change the rules and procedures.	New or improved rules, namely, administrative procedures for regulating what people do, and how and when they do it.
	Those willing and able to work within the rules (or at least, to appear to do so).	Products and/or services prescribed by the rules.
Achievement	Those with the relevant expertise and commitment to organizational goals.	Products and/or services appropriate to the expertise of organizational members.
Support	Those with commitment to people, and with the ability to relate to others.	Self-developmental service to themselves and others in (and served by) the organization.

- People are naturally active and interested in their work.
- Management enables rather than controls.
- Higher commitment results from worker participation in decision making.

Of all the value orientations, the *change orientation*

is the youngest and it is gaining ground. Leadership terms such as "entrepreneurial" and "transformational" leaders mirror this orientation. The modern distinction between leader and manager, between the person who creates meanings and goals for others and the one who administrates information and decisions, is clearly a result of this value-orientation being strong. (Ekvall, 1988, p. 7)

This orientation is characterized by:

- "entrepreneurial" and transformational leadership
- leader who creates meanings and goals for others.

Ekvall then goes on to describe four organizational culture patterns—Types A, B, C, and D—based on the degree of emphasis placed on these value orientations.

In the *Type A* culture:

- Most emphasis is placed on structure.
- There is bureaucratic culture with an authoritarian face.
- Employees keep their ideas to themselves.

The *Type B* culture has the following traits:

- It emphasizes structure, but has a marked people orientation.
- There is a bureaucratic culture with a human face.
- It has a weak change orientation.
- Improvements of process and product will emerge, radically new concepts will not.

In the *Type C* culture:

- There is a classic entrepreneurial culture, almost wholly change oriented.
- Innovation is highly valued.
- Innovations must be in directions approved by the leader.

In the *Type D* culture:

- There is strong orientation toward people, some emphasis on change, and little on structure.
- Innovation is vital for the survival of the organization.
- People have the interests of the organization as well as their own at heart.
- Improvements and new concepts will emerge.

This mention of "improvements and new concepts" is reminiscent of Kirton's Adaptor-Innovator style distinction (Kirton, 1976, 1984, 1989). Adaptors seek improvements to existing systems, whereas innovators typically suggest more radical solutions to problems. From Ekvall's descriptions of the four culture patterns, it would seem that, for the workforce at least, Type A offers scope for neither creative adaptors nor creative innovators; Type B offers scope for creative adaptors, but not creative innovators; Type C favors creative innovators; and Type D offers opportunities for both styles of creativity.

There does not seem to be a perfect fit between Harrison's four culture types and Ekvall's four culture patterns. Type A looks like a role culture ("a bureaucracy") with a strong leavening of the power culture ("an authoritarian face"). Type B seems also to be a role culture, with a bit of support culture ("a bureaucracy with a human face"). Type C seems to be an achievement culture, but one that is overlaid with strong power culture connotations. Type D seems to be a combination of a support culture and an achievement culture. This is where Ekvall says we have "the best conditions for a successful idea-handling system." The Harrison and the Ekvall perspectives both lead us to the same conclusion: To get the opportunity to realize creative potential, a person needs to be working in a culture of achievement and support, where change (a condition needing and produced by creative problem solving) and people (the creative problem solvers) are valued.

In such a culture it should be possible for both those with adaptive styles and also those with innovative styles to flourish. That is, the degree of "stylistic fit" between individual and organization can be high. Puccio (1990) used the design of a modified version of the Kirton Adaption-Innovation Inventory called the Kirton Adaption-Innovation Adjustment Scale. It was designed to reveal peoples' perceptions of what style they are required to adopt, what style they adopt, and what style they would like to adopt in their jobs. From these results, various indicators of stylistic fit can be obtained. The study showed that a lack of fit was associated with various outcomes: higher levels of stress, and lower levels of job satisfaction and creative performance. In general, the participants in his study saw their jobs as requiring them to be more adaptive than was their preference. In one of his organizations for which we have data (in a study underway) the prevailing culture is seen as a power/role combination, while the general preference is for an achievement/support combination. A tentative conclusion from these studies suggests some support for the Ekvall-Kirton connection described above.

MOTIVATION AND CREATIVITY

Mention has already been made of differences in motivation between the various culture types. Amabile's (1987) research strongly suggests that intrinsic motivation—more a feature of achievement and support cultures than of power or role culturesis conducive to creativity, whereas extrinsic motivation—the main tool of authority—is not.

> The unifying theme in all my own research is that people will be most creative when they are motivated primarily by passionate

interest in their work. This passionate interest is called intrinsic motivation—the motivation to work on something primarily for its own sake, because it is enjoyable, satisfying, challenging, or otherwise captivating. By contrast, extrinsic motivation is the motivation to work on something primarily because it is a means to an end; the work only represents a way to earn money, gain recognition, satisfy someone else's orders, or meet a deadline. According to the intrinsic motivation hypothesis of creativity, intrinsic motivation is conducive to creativity and extrinsic motivation is detrimental. Moreover social factors in the work environment can influence intrinsic/ extrinsic motivation and, as a consequence, can influence creativity as well. (Amabile, 1987, p. 224)

Among such social factors she includes evaluation expectation, surveillance, reward expectation, competition, and restriction of choice—conditions particularly visible in power and role cultures.

However, most human actions, including creativity, take place in a social context; it is equally obvious that many people in the past, in the present, and undoubtedly in the future, have been, are being, and will be creative. Either creative people are somehow immune to or have ways of dealing with inhibitory social factors, or they must somehow find themselves in (or intuitively gravitate toward) situations where the inhibitory factors are absent or not strong enough to destroy their intrinsic motivation. In Harrison's terms, a balanced achievement/support culture is the least inhibitory of intrinsic motivation. However, individuals with a very strong interest may well be able to survive in a power or role culture if they have the power to pursue these interests.

It is clear that creativity of some kind is possible in very different social settings or culture types, and that different sorts of people are successful in the different settings. It may be that there is such a wide range of personality traits of creative people (Freedman, 1976–1977) because, in part at least, there is a wide variety of social settings. To be creative in one social setting requires different traits than in another. Some pursuits, such as architecture, require the management of teams of people to help realize the designs of the architect's creative product. A poet, however, works alone. It would be surprising to find any great similarity between the personalities of successful architects and poets.

High creatives are also more complex (Reitz, 1981). Maybe they have had to cope with a greater variety of social situations before finding or creating the social setting that gives them time and space to realize their creative potentials. Gowan (1977) says:

We have used as creative only those persons who stubbornly remained so despite all efforts of the family, religion, education, and politics to grind it out of them. . . . As a result of these misguided efforts, our society produces only a small percentage of its potential of creative individuals (the ones with the most uncooperative dispositions). (Treffinger, 1987, p. 104)

Apart from implying that seeking to identify personality traits of creative people without taking social context into account might produce biased results, this suggests that a different, less "misguided" society might contain more creative persons: "If we learn to domesticate creativity—that is, to enhance it rather than deny it in our culture—we can increase the number of creative persons in our midst by about fourfold" (Gowan, 1977, p. 89).

In such a society, we might not have to resist the efforts of others to make one conform in order to be creative (but maybe creativity in such a society would be defined differently, and still be confined to those uncooperative with the norms of that culture). Raina (1993) argues that creativity is defined and understood differently in cultures other than that in the developed Western countries: "Once we come out of ethnocentric confines, I believe our concepts may become wider, richer and probably more challenging and unified. We have to realize that some idea of creativity is present in the thinking of all cultures" (p. 144).

CULTURE CHANGE: CHALLENGES AND SUGGESTIONS

Information on organizational culture offers yet another way of describing the conditions necessary for creativity. It can also offer ideas about what is involved in creating or changing to a culture conducive to everyone's creativity. Changing a culture means that basic assumptions need to be identified and challenged. Ackoff and Vergara (1981) actually define creativity as the ability to modify self-imposed constraints where one form of constraint is assumptions. Values, beliefs, norms, and behavior also need to be changed.

Given these elements, problems likely to be encountered in attempting such change become clearer. People are likely to resist having their basic assumptions and values challenged. Many of the people reading this chapter no doubt see creativity as basically a good thing—something to be identified, nurtured, and promulgated. Some of them may be offended, or at least made to feel uneasy, at the suggestion that creative behavior has destructive as well as constructive effects. To the extent that an innovation displaces what was previously there, the creative behavior that gave rise to the innovation was also destructive. The arrival and development of the motor car, for example, had a direct impact on the lives and work of those involved in maintaining horses as the major power source for transportation. Holding a deep-rooted belief or basic assumption in the benefits of progress may be a way of protecting ourselves from considering the destructive aspects of creative behavior.

In the same way, an individual or group trying to promote an achievement/support culture in an organization with a current power/role culture in which all members have a stake will come up against resistance to change. People working in the field of organizational development and change (Huse & Cummings, 1985; Ivancevich & Matteson, 1990) and organizational design (e.g., Daft, 1989) have realized this and suggest some means of dealing with it. Daft (1989) includes planning to overcome resistance to change in his recommendations for managing change. He suggests that: (a) change needs to be in the interests of members and for the good of the organization; (b) good communication is essential so that people understand the change; (c) people should be involved as early as possible in the implementation of the change (participation enhances commitment); and (d) as a last resort, people should be forced or coerced into accepting the change. Though this last reason may cause anger or even sabotage, it may be needed when speed is essential.

For those considering culture change, Huse and Cummings (1985) offered interesting, practical advice: (a) clear strategic vision to provide purpose and direction; (b) top management commitment to manage and create a constant pressure for change; (c) symbolic leadership to communicate the new culture through action; (d) supporting organizational structure modification to make people aware of and encourage the performance of new and required behaviors; (e) change in organizational membership through selection and elimination so as to produce the proper alignment of people, especially key leaders, with the new culture; and (f) selection and socialization of newcomers and removal of deviants to influence the fit to new values and behaviors.

Both Daft and Huse and Cummings aim their recommendations at management, assuming that management has the power to effect organizational change and that the support of top management is essential for the successful implementation of any change. There is more than a whiff of paradox within each set of suggestions, especially when one is considering how to change from a power/role culture to a support/achievement culture. If all else fails, management should *impose* the new culture by coercion (Daft, 1989), or by "selection and socialization of newcomers and termination of deviants" (Huse & Cummings, 1985). These appear to be examples of using the power appropriate to power/role cultures to try and create a support/achievement culture. Presumably management does not relinquish its power after the change. In that case has a culture change really taken place?

Understanding Individual Creativity in Organizational Settings: Psychological Contracts

The key to understanding individual creativity in an organizational setting is provided by the concept of the psychological contract. In any organization there is an implied psychological contract between a member and the organization. Handy (1976) described this psychological contract as essentially a set of expectations. The individual expects to satisfy certain needs by being a member of the organization; in return that person will expend some energy and talent. Similarly an organization has its set of expectations of the individual and a list of payments or outcomes. Since most individuals have more than one kind of psychological contract with more than one organization (family obligations, leisure pursuits), it is not necessary for them to seek to satisfy all their needs under any one contract. A manager cannot assume, for instance, that all subordinates have put their needs for creativity into a contract with the organization. Further, if a contract is not perceived identically by both parties, it can become a source of trouble or conflict and cause difficulties in understanding people's motivation.

Any attempt by management to change the culture of an organization, in whatever direction, also involves a change in at least one side of the psychological contracts the organization has with its members.

Types of psychological contracts.   Handy (1976) described three basic types of psychological contract: (a) coercive, (b) calculative, and (c) cooperative. Coercive contracts where people are held against their will are predominant in custodial institutions, coercive unions, and concentration camps. In this nonvoluntary psychological contract, the individual is controlled by the rule and punishment of a small group, and conformity is essential to avoid punishment. Calculative contracts usually result in an explicit exchange of goods or money for services rendered. Entered voluntarily, control is retained by management by providing fulfillment for the individual's desires. In cooperative contracts, individuals voluntarily tend to identify with and creatively pursue organizational goals. While management retains ultimate control through personnel selections and the allocation of resources, individuals gain input into goal setting and responsibility for day-to-day operations.

Using psychological contracts to create change. According to Handy (1976), there is a distinct trend on the part of many managements to try to move the psychological contracts of their organization toward cooperative contracts (a similar move to that from power/role to achievement/support culture). But not everyone wants a change in this direction. Being creative and sharing responsibility for goals and decisions brings cares as well as delights. Not all individuals will want those cares as part of their psychological contract for that part of their life. Change means uncertainty—abandoning the certainty of whatever satisfactions they now obtain for the uncertainty associated with the new way of doing things.

In short, you cannot impose a psychological contract on anyone without it coming to be seen as coercive. Freedom of entry into the contract is one of the prerequisites of the cooperative contract. Thus trying to change to a creativity-supporting culture or contract has its problems. Not everybody wants to be creative at work or, perhaps, not in the mode—adaptive or innovative—required by the organization. It may be necessary to force the new culture/contract onto people, turning what was intended to be a cooperative contract into a coercive one, or at least reminding people that too great a lack of compliance with the new culture might result in termination of employment. This analysis suggests that there is an inherent tension between individual creativity and organization.

Organizational subcultures. Handy (1985) suggested that organizations can have several subcultures. For "steady state" activities—those activities which are routine or programmed—

such as the accounting system, office services, and much of production and sales, he suggested that a role culture is appropriate. For innovation activities—those directed at changing the things that the organization does or the ways that it does them—such as research and development, parts of marketing, the developmental side of production, or corporate planning, an achievement culture is appropriate. For dealing with crises or breakdowns and for policy activities such as setting of priorities, establishing standards, direction and allocation of resources, and the initiation of action, a power culture is appropriate. This might indicate that most organizations have a power subculture at the top. To be creative lower down in the hierarchy, one must either be protected to some extent by one's own manager, be unconcerned if aware of or confident in one's ability to participate effectively in the political struggles characteristic of power cultures.

IMPLICATIONS OF ORGANIZATIONAL CULTURE FOR CREATIVITY TRAINING

The main concern of this chapter is related to the different significance of creativity training to people from different organizations or from different parts of one organization, and to the opportunity they have for realizing their creative potentials in their particular context. These ideas on organizational culture can be employed to help training participants gain awareness of important features of themselves and of their work situation.

This awareness is very similar to what Tonge and Cox (1984) called "perceptual sensitivity." or the perceiving of behaviors or feelings in social situations. To operate in a social context they also suggest that an individual needs "diagnostic abilities," the explaining of reasons for behavior and feelings, and "action skills," the ability to behave effectively in active situations (Tonge & Cox, 1984).

In other words, a person needs to know what is happening, why it is happening, and how to do something about it. These are reminiscent of problem-solving skills applied to the social domain. I would insert a fourth, for completeness, between diagnostic ability and action skill, namely *planning skill*—the ability to make plans, based on one's diagnosis, for taking action.

These skills are not dissimilar to those described by Kolb in his theory of experiential learning (Kolb & Fry, 1975). We base much of our training on Kolb's model, and in recent creativity course designs we are incorporating more sessions on social skills. These types of skill are applicable at five levels in a hierarchy of social skills, ranging from personal skills, to the interpersonal, group, intergroup, and organizational levels. As Tonge and Cox put it:

> Effective performance at any one level involves skills at all the earlier levels. For example, effective interpersonal skill involves also high levels of personal skills, and so on to the organizational level where being effective involves skills at all other levelspersonal, interpersonal, group, and intergroup. (Tonge & Cox, 1984, p. 19)

However, even if, after attending one of our training courses, participants' creative problem-solving skills and social skills had been enhanced, and they did accept responsibility for the part they played in creating and maintaining the culture, they still may not be able to generate opportunities for creativity. They may well be able to improve relationships with those with whom they have direct contact, but their ability to affect more distant individuals will be limited by the type and amount of power they have.

Therein lies one of the frustrations of being a creativity trainer. One can create a course climate in which people can be creative, knowing at the same time that some of them at least will be unable, for one reason or another, to reproduce that experience in their jobs. Indeed, the more they enjoy the experience, the worse the perception of their jobs might become. One could be partly responsible for decreasing the fit between the individual and his organization, which might in turn lead to an increase in stress and decreases in job satisfaction and performance.

AN ORGANIZATIONAL FRAMEWORK FOR CREATIVITY TRAINERS

Although there is a great deal more material on aspects of organizational context that is relevant and available, what is needed by creativity trainers and researchers, and certainly what course participants need, is a framework to help impose some coherence on the material.

One of Wesenberg's recommendations for improving our course for engineers and scientists (Wesenberg & Talbot, 1984) related to the development of an explicit and coherent course philosophy. Our response to this recommendation holds promise as a framework for understanding creativity in organizations and for clarifying the potential role of creativity training in them as well.

Philosophical aspects of creativity are based on the common belief among those involved in the emerging discipline of creativity (see Isaksen & Murdock, 1990) that everyone has creative potential to some degree or another and that certain preconditions are necessary to realize creative potential. Borrowing, slightly ironically, from the detective novel "Whodunnit?" format, I developed a formulation of these preconditions for creativity. Essentially, an individual needs the *motive*, the *means*, and the *opportunity* in order to be creative. The detective is looking for the perpetrator of the crime, hence the irony, since the impression that one could get from course participants was that creative behavior was sometimes something of a crime.

Represented below is a formulation of the preconditions required for creativity. A key factor of the formulation is the interdependence of the three preconditions: The absence of one component means the absence of creativity; changes in one component can affect the other two components.

Motive describes a person's desire to be creative and to go beyond previous solutions to problems. For example, the belief that one could be creative is related to self-confidence and self-esteem. *Means* includes domain-relevant knowledge and skills, together with creative problem-solving skills. *Opportunity* consists of awareness of opportunities—being able to spot them, being ready to grasp them, being aware of pressures against creativity, being

Table 8.3. Preconditions Required To Realize Creative Potential

The Precondition	Motive	Means	Opportunity
is character-ized by ...	a desire to be creative; to go beyond previous solutions	domain-relevant knowledge and skills; creative problem solving skills	an awareness of an opportunity; having the time and space
In the absence of....	Motive	Means	Opportunity
one needs....	encouragement to assist in improvement of self-belief	direction, guidance, training, or experience; CPS training	ways of coping with frustration; influential organizational power and the skill to use it

able to cope with these pressures, and being able to create opportunities for creativity. Subsequently, I have modified the definition of opportunity to include "having the time and space." Getting opportunities or getting the time and space for creativity depends on social skills, to some extent, and, as we shall see below, power.

As far as the course was concerned, we saw our role as trainers as helping people to acquire or reawaken the motive by having creative experiences; helping people acquire the means—creative problem-solving skills (they already possessed the domain-relevant knowledge, or, to put it another way, we could not teach them anything about their technical subjects, though they might learn from each other); and by helping them become aware of the various aspects of opportunity. This last aspect was dealt with through discussions and exercises relating to the organizational context and re-entry. Opportunity is thus closely tied to organizational context.

A key feature of this formulation is that all three components are necessary for creativity to occur. The absence of one or more means the absence of creativity, just as the absence of motive, means, or opportunity eliminates a suspect from the detective's considerations. A second noticeable feature is that changes in one component can have effects on the others; lack of opportunity may lead to atrophying of skills, for example, or to loss of desire. What might happen when just one or another of the necessary ingredients is missing is described below.

Motive Lacking . . . Uncommitted to Being Creative

If individuals have the means and the opportunity but not the motive, what they need is encouragement or support to help improve self-belief, or perhaps a successful creative experience to help (re)awaken the desire to be creative. A look at the various aspects of working conditions which might be affecting his/her motive might also be useful.

Lacking the Means . . . Unable to be Creative

If individuals have the motive and the opportunity, but not the means, some sort of direction, guidance, training, or experience could be appropriate. Assuming an individual did have the domain-relevant knowledge and skills, creative problem-solving skills training would be appropriate.

No Opportunity . . . Frustrated

If individuals have the motive and the means but not the opportunity, they are likely to feel pretty frustrated, and need to find ways of coping with those feelings. A reading of the situation could indicate what might realistically be done. This might result, at one extreme, in an individual decision to leave the organization, or to give up any hope of being creative in their work because the requirement is to do the job in a prescribed manner, no more and no less. On the other hand, the reading might suggest that it is possible to develop means of creating and then preserving and defending opportunity. To achieve this, individuals need power in a form that works in their organizational context, and the skill to use it. If individuals are attempting to change their situation, the change does not happen by itself. They must have sufficient power to be able to influence others in the direction of the desired change.

Power

To get and keep the time and space for creativity we need power of some kind, and the skills to use whatever power we have in order to exert influence on others. To some extent, we are all dependent on others (and on our ability to influence them) for opportunities to be creative.

Handy (1985) describes several sources of power:

Physical power. This is derived from the possession of superior physical force. Characteristics include:

- does not have to be used for it to be effective
- is often sufficient to endow considerable influence
- is expressed through straightforward coercion
- is rarely seen in work organizations

Resource power. This derives from control of resources. Characteristics include:

- physical (e.g., money or materials)
- psychological resources (e.g., the ability to confer status through such things as promotion)
- influence is found in exchange of action for resources

Position power.   This derives from the position or role occupied by the individual. Characteristics include:

- managers, by position, control their subordinates
- relies on being backed up by resource or physical power
- influenced primarily through the rules and procedures of the organization
- depends on everybody accepting the rules
- challenged rules necessitate a backup source of power

Expert power.   This derives from one individual having greater knowledge or expertise than others. Characteristics include:

- the possession of information or expertise which is not available to others
- is wielded by a process of persuasion
- ranges from logical to emotional support of desired action.

Personal power.   This is derived from sheer force of personality, and often referred to as charisma. Characteristics include:

- religious leaders and some political leaders are good exponents
- high personal power, coupled with high expert power, real or assumed, could give the individual the status of "guru"
- influence is by inspiration.

Negative power.   This is referred to as the power to disrupt.

Using the Motives, Means, Opportunity Framework in Creativity Training

The motive-means-opportunity framework can provide some useful insights for educators, particularly creativity trainers, who might be interested in diagnosing the training needs of potential or actual course participants. It does suggest that in some cases CPS training, though of intrinsic value, could be a source of frustration to people when they lack the opportunity to practice their newly developed creative skills, and lack the power or skill to create such opportunities. Technical personnel often express this frustration. For recent graduates who are still learning the job, part of the cause is their relative lack of expert power. For more established people, whose expertise is acknowledged, the issue appears to be an unwillingness or an inability to use their power (or to develop other sorts of power) in order to get opportunities.

People often feel trapped in their jobs, and have no other outlet for creativity. They have lost the urge to be creative at work, they have let their skills atrophy, and are just marking time until something else turns up or until retirement. When they leave employment, their departure passes unnoticed. When they come to review their life or, as Lesner and Hillman (1983) put it, enter the stage of creative self-evaluation, there may not be much to review.

Leadership and Followership Implications

Operating effectively in the technical domain requires effective operation in the social domain. Or, to put it another way, creating and defending opportunities for creativity, particularly in a work situation where they do not currently exist, requires the motive, plus the means, and, of course, the opportunity to create such opportunities. The more participants understand about the organization of which they are a member, and the better their skills at actually influencing the course of events, the better their chances of creating or maintaining opportunities for their own creativity.

They may not always be successful, of course. Understanding and skills, though necessary, are not sufficient for generating opportunities for creativity. For example, other, perhaps more powerful individuals may not wish one to be creative and may be able to successfully resist one's attempts to create or maintain opportunity (and they might be justified in doing so, especially if they regard the consequences and predictable outputs from you as being inimical to the interest of the organization).

For some people, there is the additional responsibility of creating and maintaining opportunities for others to be creative, notably their subordinates. Managers have responsibility not only for getting the best *out of* their subordinates, but also getting the best *for* their subordinates. Managers who are good at this aspect of their jobs will, in effect, be a major source of opportunities for creativity for their subordinates. The editor described in Ekvall and Tängeberg-Andersson (1986) appears to be just such a manager.

The MOM (Motive-Opportunity-Means) framework bears some

resemblance to Situational Leadership Theory (SLT; Hersey & Blanchard, 1981). From this perspective, managers are supposed to behave toward subordinates based on readiness to perform a particular task. This readiness depends upon how able or competent they are and upon how willing or committed they are to do the task. One provides direction for the less than wholly competent, and support for the not totally committed. As leader, it is assumed that one is in control of the opportunities one's subordinates have for doing various tasks. As a leader, one has the responsibility to develop subordinates to a level of readiness to do a task where they need neither support nor direction. At this level tasks can be delegated to them.

It is at this level of readiness that the potential for creativity emerges. The subordinate knows how to do the task, is keen to do it, and might begin to think of better ways of doing it or of different ways of achieving the same task goals. Clearly the response of the manager to such possibilities is going to matter quite a lot. In some organizations, particularly those with power or role cultures, managers are often reluctant to delegate for fear of giving up too much power to their subordinates and losing control of them. They thus withhold opportunities for creativity.

CONCLUSION

Creativity training can take into account more than just creative problem-solving skills. Creativity in an organizational context requires an individual to possess the motive, the means, and the opportunity. Organizations essentially are the sources of opportunity. Different cultures may be found in different organizations, or in different parts of the same organization. These different cultures vary in the extent to which they offer opportunities for creativity (of either the adaptive variety or of the innovative variety), and to whom it is offered. Spotting, getting, and keeping opportunities depends in part on how much of what sort of power one can exercise. Typically, technical people have to rely mainly on their expert power. Opportunity also depends in part on social skills, the possession of which can help an individual either tap the power of others or obtain it for themselves.

An important feature of creative behavior is that there is some degree of novelty about its product. Creativity leads to change. The nature, degree, and direction of such change, however, is not entirely predictable by either the creator or others.

Creativity training, especially if it is effective, enables people to better generate change and cope with change. However, people not in receipt of or not amenable to such training are likely to resist the changes wrought by others. Creativity training does not produce people who hold the same views and values. People exist mainly in a context consisting of other people: They create their context and are created by it. A lack of awareness, diagnostic, planning, and action skills in the social domain could make the consequences of trying to be more creative less than wholly delightful. I have on occasion wrapped up a creativity training course by answering the question "Can a person become more creative at work?" as follows: "Yes; if he/she wants to, if he/she is able to, if he/she has the chance to, and if he/she is prepared to live with the consequences."

This response might well serve as a challenge to those who want to learn more about creativity and as a challenge to those who are training without considering the importance of context in their design and delivery.

REFERENCES

Ackoff, R.L., & Vergara, E. (1981). Creativity in problem solving and planning: A review. *European Journal of Operational Research, 7,* 1–13.

Amabile, T.M. (1987). The motivation to be creative. In S.G. Isaksen (Ed.), *Frontiers of creativity research: Beyond the basics* (pp 223–254). Buffalo, NY: Bearly Limited.

Bienvenu, M.J., Sr. (1971). An interpersonal communication inventory. *The Journal of Communication, 21,* 381 - 388.

Cooper, C.L., & Robertson, I.T. (1988). *International review of industrial and organizational psychology.* London: Wiley.

Cummings, T.G., & Huse, E.F. (1989). *Organization development and change* (4th ed.). New York: West Publishing.

Daft, R.L. (1989). *Organization theory and design.* New York: West Publishing.

Ekvall, G., & Tängeberg-Andersson, Y. (1986). Working climate and creativity: A study of an innovative newspaper office. *Journal of Creative Behavior, 20*(3), 215–225.

Ekvall, G. (1988, August/September). *The organizational culture of idea management.* Paper presented at the International Congress of Psychology, Sydney, Australia.

Freedman, B. (1976–1977, Winter). MacKinnon on Creativity. *The Manchester Business School Review, 3.*

Gowan, J.C. (1977). Some new thoughts on the development of creativity. *Journal of Creative Behavior, 11,* 77–90.

Handy, C.B. (1976). *Understanding organizations* (1st ed.). Harmonds-worth, UK: Penguin Books.

Handy, C.B. (1985). *Understanding organizations* (3rd ed.). Harmonds-worth, UK: Penguin Books.

Harrison, R. (1987a). *Organization culture and quality of service: A strategy for releasing love in the workplace.* London: Association for Management Education and Development.

Harrison, R. (1987b, Autumn). Harnessing personal energy: How companies can inspire employees. *Organizational Dynamics,* 5–20.

Hersey, P., & Blanchard, K.H. (1981). *Management of organizational behavior: Utilizing human resources.* Englewood Cliffs, NJ: Prentice-Hall.

Huse, E.F., & Cummings, T.G. (1985). *Organization development and change* (3rd ed.). New York: West Publishing.

Isaksen, S.G., & Murdock, M.C. (1988). The outlook for the study of creativity: An emerging discipline? *JANUS.* Buffalo, NY: State University College at Buffalo, Center for Studies in Creativity.

Isaksen, S.G., & Treffinger, D.J. (1985). *Creative problem solving: The basic course.* Buffalo, NY: Bearly Limited.

Ivancevich, J.M., & Matteson, M.T. (1990). *Organizational behavior and management.* Boston, MA: Irwin.

Kirton, M.J. (1976). Adaptors and innovators: A description and measure. *Journal of Applied Psychology, 61,* 622–629.

Kirton, M.J. (1984). Adaptors and innovatorsWhy new initiatives get blocked. *Long Range Planning, 17(2),* 137–143.

Kirton, M.J. (1989). *Adaptors and innovators: Styles of creativity and problem-solving.* London: Routledge.

Kolb, D.A., & Fry, R. (1975). Towards an applied theory of experiential learning. In C.L. Cooper (Ed.), *Theories of group processes* (pp. 33–58). London: Wiley.

Lesner, W.J., & Hillman, D. (1983). A developmental schema of creativity. *Journal of Creative Behavior, 17(2),* 103–114.

MacKinnon, D.W. (1978). *In search of human effectiveness: Identifying and developing creativity.* Buffalo, NY: Bearly Limited.

Magyari-Beck, I. (1993). *Creatology: A potential paradigm for an emerging discipline.* In S.G. Isaksen, M.C. Murdock, R.L. Firestien, & D.J. Treffinger (Eds.), *Understanding and recognizing creativity: The emergence of a discipline* (pp. 48–82). Norwood, NJ: Ablex.

Makin, P.J., Cooper, C.L., & Cox, C.J. (1989). *Managing people at work.* London: British Psychological Society/Routledge.

McGregor, D. (1960). *The human side of enterprise.* New York: McGraw-Hill.

Morgan, G. (1986). *Images of organization.* London: Sage.

Nolan, V. (1981). *Open to change.* Bradford, UK: MCB Publications Ltd.

Novelli, L., Jr. (1993). Using alternative perspectives to build more robust theories of organizational creativity. In S.G. Isaksen, M.C. Murdock, R.L. Firestien, & D.J. Treffinger (Eds.), *Understanding and recog-*

nizing creativity: The emergence of a discipline (pp. 281–295). Norwood, NJ: Ablex.

Parnes, S.J. (1967). *Creative behavior guidebook*. New York: Charles Scribner.

Puccio, G.J. (1990). *Person-environment fit: Using Kirton's adaptor-innovator theory to determine the effect of stylistic fit upon stress, job satisfaction and creative performance*. Unpublished doctoral thesis. Manchester, UK: School of Management, UMIST.

Raina, M.K. (1993). Ethnocentric confines in creativity research. In S.G. Isaksen, M.C. Murdock, R.L. Firestien, & D.J. Treffinger (Eds.), *Understanding and recognizing creativity: The emergence of a discipline* (pp. 435–453). Norwood, NJ: Ablex.

Reitz, H.J. (1981). *Behavior in organizations*. Homewood, IL: Irwin.

Rousseau, D.M. (1988). The construction of climate in organizational research. In C. L. Cooper & I. T. Robertson (Eds.), *International review of industrial and organizational psychology* (pp. 139–158). London: Wiley.

Talbot, R.J. (1982). Problems and change: Some thoughts on the human context of designing. In B. Evans, J.A. Powell, & R.J. Talbot (Eds.), *Changing design* (pp. 99–108). London: Wiley.

Talbot, R.J., & Rickards, T. (1984). Developing creativity. In C.J. Cox & J.E. Beck (Eds.), *Management development: Advances in theory and practice* (pp. 93–121). London: Wiley.

Tonge, B., & Cox, C.J. (1984). *A taxonomy of educational objectives in the social domain: For use in management development* (Occasional Paper No. 8702). Manchester, UK: Manchester School of Management.

Treffinger, D. (1987). Research on creativity assessment. In S.G. Isaksen (Ed.), *Frontiers of creativity research: Beyond the basics* (pp. 103–119). Buffalo, NY: Bearly Limited.

Treffinger, D. (1988). Model for creative learning: 1988 update. *Creative Learning Network Newsletter, 2*(3).

Uttal, B. (1983, October). The corporate culture vultures. *Fortune, 17.*

Wesenberg, P. (1983). *Creativity as a human potential: An inquiry into human creativity*. Unpublished masters dissertation, School of Management, The University of Manchester Institute of Science and Technology (UMIST), Manchester, UK.

Wesenberg, P. (1986). *Creativity in organizations: A contradiction in terms?* Unpublished doctoral thesis, School of Management, UMIST, Manchester, UK.

Wesenberg, P. (1988). Creativity in organizations: A contradiction in terms? *Creativity and Innovation Network, 12, 3–4.*

Wesenberg, P., & Talbot, R.J. (1984). *An assessment of a creativity course*. Manchester, UK: Manchester School of Management, UMIST.

9

The Development and Assessment of Creative Thinking Techniques: A German Perspective

Horst Geschka

PRELIMINARY REMARKS

I have worked in the field of creativity techniques since 1965, and I was part of the European development that has taken place in the last 25 years. Most of what is presented is drawn from personal experience, so although an objective view is attempted, a subjective perspective and judgment cannot be avoided. Moreover, experience and insight into the development refers mainly to Germany, Austria, and Switzerland. Through contacts and collaborations, the developments in other European countries have also been observed, but the statements given in this chapter are primarily valid for the countries mentioned.

CREATIVITY TECHNIQUES: HOW THEY DEVELOPED IN EUROPE

The first courses in brainstorming can be traced back to the early 1960s. In 1965, Bernd Rohrbach started with short 1-day seminars on creative problem solving, in which he presented brainstorming and synectics. These seminars gained remarkable public and company interest. The new methods were considered exciting unconventional approaches with a certain mystic character. In these early years, companies tried to apply brainstorming, but the results were disappointing. The rules were unusual, open communication unknown; skilled moderators were not available. As a reaction to these difficulties, Rohrbach invented brainwriting, namely Method 635.

In 1966 Fritz Zwicky's book *Entdecken, Erfinden, Forschen im morphologischen Weltbild* (Discovering, inventing, and researching in morphological view) was published. In this book he described the morphological methods. Zwicky's book was well received in Germany and even moreso in Switzerland. His "morphological box" was adopted rather quickly by technical planners and methodologists in machinery design.

In 1970, I initiated an extensive study of idea generation methods at the Battelle Institute in Frankfurt. Ninety European companies, mainly German, cooperated in this project. Known methods worldwide were collected and tried out in 170 experimental sessions. Participants in these experimental sessions, as well as the problems they considered, came from the participating companies themselves. The problems were real business-world tasks, most of a technical nature. With respect to obvious weaknesses and gaps, the Battelle team developed approximately 10 new techniques. After this basic project, Battelle-Frankfurt started training courses in creativity techniques, which served some 4,000 participants from German industry until the programs were terminated in 1989.

In the mid-1970s, other seminar organizations began also to offer courses on creativity techniques. In other European countries early trainers and developers of structured approaches to creative problem solving included:

- Tudor Rickards at the Manchester Business School in the UK (since 1971)
- The Innovation Group (Jan Buijs, Hans Smeekes, and others) at TNO in the Netherlands (since 1975)
- Ulf Perning (SIPSI Creaform) in Sweden (since 1977)
- Hans Graverson and Herluf Trolle at the Technological Institute in Denmark (since 1980).

Today creativity techniques are taught at most universities as part of marketing or innovation management courses. Morphological methods are, in general, considered elements of the methodology of machinery design and are also part of the university education. It is typical that European authors or trainers are not stuck with one technique but recommend or work with a variety of different techniques.

Creativity techniques are now rather widely used in German, Austrian, and Swiss industry. It seems that the level of application is higher there than in other European countries. Conversely, these techniques are nearly unknown in public and social institutions. In the United States and Canada, such institutions seem to be much more open to management techniques; creativity training and creativity techniques play a greater role in this sector in North America than in Europe.

A recent empirical study by Gemünden (1990) showed that successful product innovations are correlated with intensive idea generation activities, which essentially means applying creativity techniques. A study by Mica (in preparation) in the Netherlands indicated that applying structured approaches for creative problem solving led to a higher rate of innovation in a company.

In Germany, Austria, and Switzerland, creativity techniques are mostly applied by strictly following explicit procedures and directions. It is not common to modify or alternate the basic principles or to mix methods in a rather unconcerned way. This rather formal application of techniques appears to be another difference from other European countries and North America.

Specific European Methods: Their Origin and Their Concept

Brainwriting. In the 1960s, Bernd Rohrbach observed several difficulties with brainstorming in German companies:

- not enough time for mulling an idea and thinking it over; the Brainstorming rule to listen to the ideas of others does not allow considering and developing one's own ideas
- unskilled moderators not able to avoid or reduce negative group dynamic effects
- inadequate minutes; ideas were not described precisely and consequently not really understood in the later refinement, development, and evaluation process.

Rohrbach (1969) proposed "Method 635" in the late 1960s. This method requires a group of six people. They generate three ideas on a sheet of paper, then the sheets are passed to the neighbor, who tries to further develop them. The sheets are passed around five times (see Figure 9.1). Time for idea generation in one section of the process is limited to approximately 5 minutes.

Method 635. Method 635 is quite well known and often applied by marketing and advertising people. It is especially

Figure 9.1. Method 635

well-suited for creating names or slogans, problems for which brainstorming has turned out to be less productive. One has to turn around various formulations in the mind, composing one which is especially humorous, pithy, or rhyming. One is disturbed in this thinking process by the contributions of the others in the group—especially under the rule of listening to each other. The individual idea development process can be interrupted.

Brainwriting techniques, especially Method 635, give room for individual idea development, but also force the participants to consider the solutions of the others and to work under time pressure. Another typical field of application of Method 635 is the variation and differentiation of basic solution concepts. One can assume that by the 635 procedure a given concept is changed and detailed in various directions. It ensures that the participants work on the initial ideas, which is not guaranteed in a brainstorming session.

I extended Method 635 by integrating an evaluation procedure and a selection and a conception phase. I call this further development the ring-exchange technique (Ringtauschtechnik), as the term Method 635 is often not easily understood or misinterpreted.

The Battelle team observed that participants working with the 635 method sometimes felt stressed or did not like to wait until the next exchange. Two techniques were introduced to avoid these shortcomings: the brainwriting pool and Kartenumlauftechnik (card-exchange technique). Both techniques have no fixed time mechanism for exchange.

The brainwriting pool. In the brainwriting pool method, individuals write ideas on a sheet of paper. When they run out of ideas they exchange their own sheet with one in the pool in the middle of the table (see Figure 9.2). The ideas on the new sheet are read, and new ideas are generated in response which are then written down on the same sheet. Of course the pool has to be filled in advance by some idea sheets to allow the exchange process. This can be done in several ways. One is to stop the idea production after approximately 3–4 minutes and to put the sheets into the pool. Another way is to prepare a few sheets with ideas in advance. The exchanges with the pool can be done whenever the individuals choose.

Card-exchange technique.   The card-exchange technique uses the advantages of pincards. Here the ideas are written on cards with thick markers. The cards are passed to the neighbor who picks them up when he or she wants new stimuli. The cards circle around the table (see Figure 9.3). After about 20 minutes, idea generation may be stopped. The cards are then sorted and clustered on a table and then pinned on a board. Finally a first evaluation is done by sticking adhesive dots to the most promising ideas.

Use of this card technique has spread rather fast in German industry in recent years, probably since the communication technique Metaplan is well known and widely used in Germany and other European countries. Basic elements of the Metaplan technique are specific pinwalls, cards in different shapes and colors, adhesive dots, and other working materials. These materials which are used in the card-exchange technique are available in

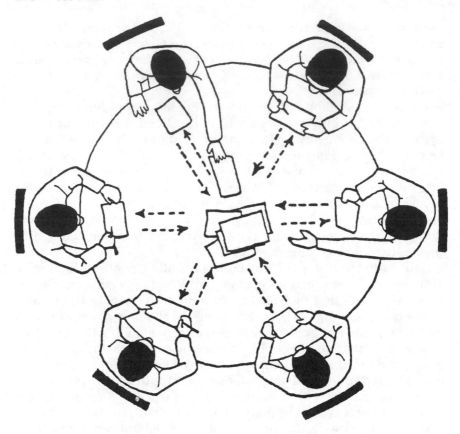

Figure 9.2. Brainwriting pool

most companies and people are used to working with them. Thus, there are no technical barriers to applying the technique.

The advantages of the card technique include: (a) the flexibility to work with cards which can easily be sorted, changed, or eliminated; and (b) the visualization that is facilitated by posting the cards.

Confrontation techniques. Bernd Rohrbach and the Battelle group also introduced synectics into the German scene. The basic element of this methodology has been considered to be an excursion by a series of analogies. Although this method has been presented in seminars it has never seemed to be widely applied in companies. There were barriers to the excursion process requiring that the participants play very unusual and strange parts. The

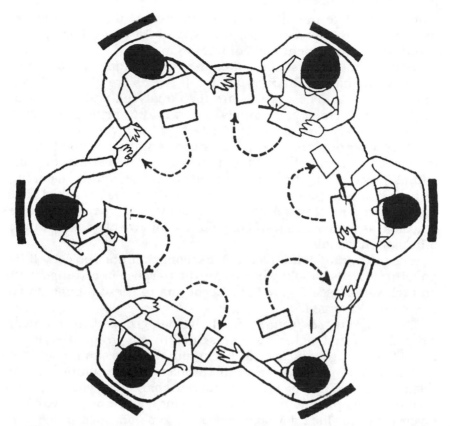

Figure 9.3. Card-exchange technique. (Write one idea on a card and put the cards to the right. Pick neighbor's card, read, associate, and put all cards to the right.)

process takes a rather long time (two hours or more) and many participants were already mentally tired when the essential part of idea generation (force-fit) began.

In response to these difficulties, the Battelle group created two new confrontation methods and Rohrbach also developed a more specific approach. The idea-generating principle in synectics is the force-fit. The problem solver is supposed to derive from the characteristics and principles hidden in a word ideas to solve the problem. We call this phenomenon confrontation. A number of creativity techniques are based on the confrontation principle (e.g., catalogue technique, forced relationship). The Battelle team considered two directions to cope with the above-mentioned difficulties: (a) delete the difficult and lengthy excursion procedure, but preserve the force-fit with words; and (b) find other mechanisms for estrangement and confrontation.

Omitting the excursion resulted in the technique called stimulating word analysis (Reizwortanalyse). Words are generated in a random process. These words are then analyzed with respect to their typical elements, functions, and working principles. From these characteristics, ideas are derived for the given problem.

To discover other mechanisms for confrontation, several experiments were conducted. After a number of experiments with stimuli perceived by the other senses (touching objects, listening to noises, looking on pictures) the conclusion was reached that pictures are a most powerful stimulus of ideas. This result is quite plausible as we live in a world of pictures, and we all pick up much information visually.

When working with pictures as confrontation objects it is opportune to also apply pictures for the purpose of estrangement and relaxation (see Figure 9.4). According to these thoughts two techniques emerged.

Visual group confrontation. In visual group confrontation, carefully selected pictures are presented to the group. A series of about five pictures and specific background music should help the participants to get away from the problem and to plunge into a relaxed mood. Then pictures of another character, with more individual elements and details, are used for confrontation with the given problem. Idea development is done as an open process of group communication. The idea-generation phase normally lasts for 30–40 minutes, during which six to seven pictures are presented and analyzed.

Picture folder brainwriting. This method combines the advantages of the visual confrontation with those of the card-exchange technique. The structure of the process is the same as described above, but the idea development from pictures is done individually with the help of picture folders which consist of 10 selected pictures (three pictures for estrangement and relaxation, seven pictures for analysis and idea generation). The ideas are written down on pincards. After about 20 minutes, the idea development with pictures is stopped, and the cards are passed around to serve as additional stimuli for ideas. As in the card-exchange technique, the cards are then clustered on the table, transferred to a pinboard, and evaluated with dots.

The visual confrontation approach has proved to be a powerful approach to trigger unusual ideas. The ideas are typically of a very

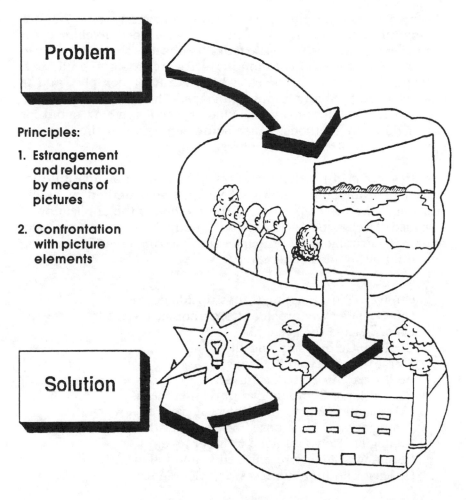

Problem

Principles:

1. Estrangement and relaxation by means of pictures

2. Confrontation with picture elements

Solution

Figure 9.4. Visual confrontation

different nature: Some are very general, while others are very vague, just proposing a solution direction. Still others present very concrete suggestions for detailed solutions.

Basic synectics.   Bernd Rohrbach also started with synectics but further developed it into a step-by-step problem-solving methodology which he called *basic synectics*. Typical elements of this methodology are: standardized questions and answers, different defined functions in the group (problem poser, moderator, resource persons), and a precise time structure which has to be observed rather strictly. It is a straightforward procedure for generating a few innovative solutions with good likelihood for implementation. The famous excursion phase is no longer a fixed part of the methodology. Computer software exists to guide participants through the process, which is rather complex and is characterized by many jumps and loops. (The terms basic synectics and *excursion synectics*, or just *synectics*, which stand for rather different methods, cause some confusion in the German literature as well as under appliers.)

Quickstorming.   Hans Morowa, president of an institute involved in leadership training, developed the method of quickstorming. The basic approach of the method is the application of so-called "archetypes of creative thinking." As archetypes, Morowa has formulated 12 principles for fostering creative thinking and stimulating idea generation:

> Gulliver: Turn existing things upside-down!
> Off: Consider the problem from another level!
> Off-off: Leave the system!
> Domino: Go one step ahead!
> Step-by-step: Avoid big leaps!
> Additives: Integrate a catalyst!
> Bisociations: Combine two unrelated ideas!
> Polysociations: Integrate different parts to a whole!
> Atomization: Decompose and consider the parts separately!
> Analogies: How is it done in other areas?
> Here now: Detect present trends and follow!
> Do less! Eliminate unnecessary elements!

The archetypes are formulated as questions which have to be answered very quickly. The whole process should be run through within 20 minutes. There is also software available which leads and supports the procedure.

Morphology.   The basic approach of morphology is the division of a complex problem into elements (parameters), the collection of solution ideas for the parameters, and finally the combination of the parameter solution ideas into an overall solution. For this general approach two techniques exist.

Morphological tableau. The morphological tableau (also called morphological box) takes a number of parameters into consideration (see Figure 9.5 as an example). An overall solution is a line through the table.

One difficulty in forming the morphological tableau is to find and properly formulate the parameters. They have to represent all essential elements of the problem and should be—as much as possible—independent of each other.

A morphological tableau yields a large number of possible solutions (in principle, all possible combinations). The number of overall solutions is thus very often in the range of 10,000 to 100,000. To find the best solution is rather difficult; several approaches can be applied.

Sequential morphological solution development. The sequential morphological solution development proposed by Geschka and Schlicksupp (1972) first ranks the parameters according to their impact on the overall solution. Then a new and effective combination of ideas of the two highest ranked parame-

Problem: New ideas for criminal stories

Parameter	Options			
The person murdered	wealthy widow	valuable racehorse	head of a seminar	prostitute
The cause of death	shock	shooting	unascertainable	(English) ale
The scene of action	London in the smog	nightclub in Paris	golf course	Frankfurt Stock Exchange
The murderer	heir	priest	Aunty Mary	participant in a seminar
The motive	greed for money	blood-lust	habit	to eliminate the person in on the secret
The case is cleared up by	coincidence	self-denunciation	traces in the snow	idea generation
The hero	James Bond	foreign worker	journalist	Jimmy Carter

Figure 9.5. The morphological tableau: An example

ters are formed. To this core combination an idea from the following parameter that fits very well is added. Then the same is done with the next parameter, and so on. In this way good overall solutions are built up. (This approach is applied in the PC software MOSEL which supports the process of developing a morphological tableau and finding several good solutions; Geschka, 1988.)

Morphological matrix. The morphological matrix reduces the problem to two parameters. This allows us to design a matrix instead of a tableau (see Figure 9.6). In a matrix, every field is a potential solution instead of a line as in the morphological tableau. With a matrix one can work much more clearly. Furthermore, entrances indicating solution ideas or exclusive factors can be made in the matrix fields.

The morphological matrix is especially suited to discover "white fields," solution fields that have never been considered before.

Sometimes it is argued that morphological methods are approaches of system analysis and systematic combination, but not techniques that enhance creative thinking. Of course the morphological approach gives an analytically derived framework. The challenge is then to identify original combinations and to interpret the combinations in a creative way (How can element A1 and element B7 be combined to form an innovative solution? What does it mean to combine element A2 with element B2?). Morphology can be considered a creativity technique when the users apply the system as a framework for combinative creative thinking processes.

In industrial practice most problems must fit into given structures. Highly creative suggestions resulting in dramatic changes of the conditional framework are very often not acceptable. The morphological tableau is very well suited to support idea generation in a well defined set-up. It fits very well, for example, the familiar thinking patterns of engineers, who have shown high preference for this technique in our experience.

Diffusion and Application of Creativity Techniques

Several surveys about the knowledge and diffusion of creativity techniques in German industry have been undertaken (Geschka, 1983, 1987; Geschka & Yildiz, 1990). The number of subjects whose questionnaires were analyzed in all three surveys was between 103 and 115.

Cooling in the Home

P1 / P2	food		electrical devices	persons	pets	plants
	solid	liquid				
living room				C		I
bedroom						
bathroom	X	X	I			
kitchen	C	C	I			
children's room						
store rooms	I	I		X	X	
car		I				
garden						
balcony					I	
picnic						

P1 = What could be cooled? (object)   C = covered
P2 = Where could be cooled? (locations)   I = interest
                                           X = not possible, not to
                                               be considered

Figure 9.6. The morphological matrix: An example

Knowledge of creativity techniques in West Germany.
Figure 9.7 shows the actual knowledge of creativity techniques.
Brainstorming is really broadly known. The brainwriting techniques are now in second place. The morphological methods are
as widely known as the brainwriting techniques, but they did not
diffuse as fast as these in the last decade. Confrontation tech-

niques (excursion synectics, visual confrontation methods, etc.) are much less known.

Application of creativity techniques in West Germany.
Of course, application of the techniques is lower than knowledge (see Figure 9.8). Nevertheless, only 26% of the questioned firms declare that they never apply brainstorming. The difference between knowledge and application (columns "Good knowledge" and "Comprehensive knowledge" in Figure 9.7 against "Occasionally" and "Frequently" in Figure 9.8) is highest for brainstorming. The more complex and difficult it is to apply the methods the more knowledge and application go together; for the confrontation techniques there is no difference between these two aspects.

Considering developments since 1973, one can state that there has been a great increase in application of creativity techniques from 1973 to 1980 (see Figure 9.9) For brainstorming and the brainwriting techniques a certain polarization can now be observed: The "frequent appliers" show a rather high percentage but the "never appliers" also are relatively high. An explanation of this result may be that many companies tried the techniques but have found out that they are not applicable for the tasks of their operations (e.g., mostly routine work) or they are in contrast to the company culture (procedures, style, behavior, etc.). These companies know that the techniques do not fit to them.

Comparison of the surveys in 1973, 1980, and 1987. The application of the confrontation techniques seems to be at about

	Totally unknown	Only known by name	Some knowledge	Good knowledge	Comprehensive knowledge
Brainstorming	1	1	11	55	32
Brainwriting techniques	20	11	20	32	17
Morphological methods	20	13	23	31	13
Confrontation techniques	31	22	25	16	6

In percent of the answers (107)

Figure 9.7. Knowledge of creativity techniques in Germany

	Never	Occasionally	Frequently
Brainstorming	26	25	49
Brainwriting techniques	54	35	11
Morphological methods	59	35	6
Confrontation techniques	80	16	4

In percent of the answers (107)

Figure 9.8. Application of creativity techniques in Germany

	Never			Occasionally			Frequently		
	1973	1980	1987	1973	1980	1987	1973	1980	1987
Brainstorming	17.5	12.8	26	61.5	44	25	21	43.2	49
Brainwriting techniques	89.5	44	54	9	47.7	35	1.5	8.3	11
Morphological methods	73.5	54.1	59	19	30.3	35	7.5	15.6	6
Confrontation techniques	80	68.1	81	17.5	29.4	17	2.6	2.5	2

In percent of the answers (107)

Figure 9.9. Application of creativity techniques: Comparison of the surveys in 1973, 1980, and 1987

the same level as in the 1970s, with a certain peak in between (see Figure 9.9). The confrontation techniques, especially excursion synectics, are in general considered very difficult, so high diffusion can not be expected. These methods are the domain of specialists.

The diffusion of the morphological methods has reached a remarkable level, but in recent years a certain saturation or even decline can be observed. These methods appear much easier when described in the literature or demonstrated in seminars than they are in practice. It is rather difficult to identify and formulate a meaningful set of parameters and to extract superior solutions. These negative experiences may have resulted in more reluctance to apply the morphological approach.

The sources of ideas have changed from 1973 to 1987 (see

Figure 9.10). Teamwork with creativity techniques has increased to 26%, while 34% of the companies declare work without using formal methods as a source of successful ideas. This means 60% of successful ideas are generated in groups. The contributions of individuals are much lower, at 27%. It seems that these characteristics have not changed very much in the last 10 years. In the

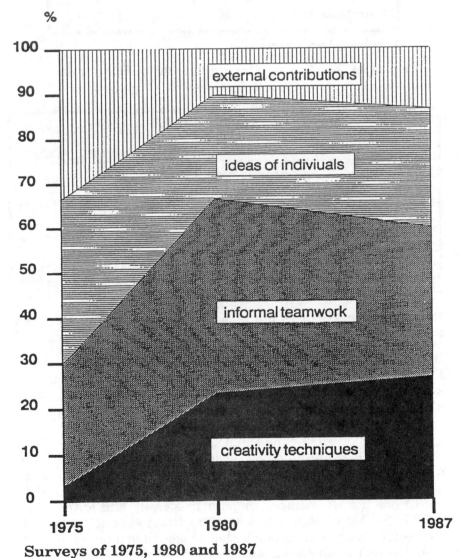

Surveys of 1975, 1980 and 1987

Figure 9.10. Sources of succesful ideas

1970s, however, the group as a source of successful ideas roughly doubled from about 30% to about 60%.

CREATIVE THINKING AND BEHAVIOR OF MANAGERS

Concept of the Survey

In 1985 I carried out a survey among German, Swiss, and Austrian managers about creative thinking and behavior. The questionnaire was developed in cooperation with the Japanese SOKEN Research Institute in Tokyo (Takahashi, 1985). (One aim was to come up with an intercultural comparison.) In the three countries, 1,224 managers were addressed; 340 questionnaires were returned. In the Netherlands the same investigation was done by Wim Vaags (University of Eindhoven) in 1986, from which additional questionnaires were analyzed.

Survey Results

Many of the managers repeated that they pursue the generation of ideas quite consciously. They think about the problem, look for specific information in specialized literature, and obtain stimuli through technical discussions and relevant professional conferences. This preliminary phase is characterized by inner unrest, but at the same time also by concentration even up to sensations of stress. They subject themselves to pressure to produce results. This stress, however, is embedded in a prevailing positive mood (high interest in solutions).

Ideas can then be generated at any time and anywhere. However, it can be seen that there are times when idea generation is more frequent: early in the morning and late at night. In all the countries, idea generation happens more frequently in the evening and at night (after return from work) than in the morning (before going to work):

When do ideas emerge most frequently?

	German	Swiss	Austrian
Early morning	47.8	49.1	61.0
Evening/at night	77.6	73.6	74.3

During the day, namely, at work, when one's attention is fully required by other matters, fewer creative ideas are generated.

There is a tendency for older managers to have their ideas more in the morning and for younger managers to have them more in the evening. Managers repeated noticeably more ideas while using some means of transport mainly, when driving their car. The drive to work in the morning and on the way home in the evening are typical prethinking and contemplating phases. Some managers report that they have a dictaphone in the car to record ideas that come up suddenly.

Once the creative idea has come up, a feeling of relaxation, relief, satisfaction, and even happiness follows. Usually the idea is written down immediately. Many of the questioned people said that they keep thinking it through and talk about it to someone who happens to be there at the time. After that, measures are taken in order to organize and translate into action the idea in detail.

Only a small number of managers are in favor of playful and spontaneous activities. Purposeful and technically relevant activities are predominant. This is especially true for younger managers.

Many managers consciously stimulate the generation of ideas. Many statements could be out of a textbook on the subject of promoting creativity: Analyzing the problem, relaxing and thinking about something else, subjecting oneself to new stimuli, positively influencing one's own mood, even up to purposeful use of creative thinking principles, and formal creativity techniques.

Comparison with the Japanese Survey

On comparing the results of the European poll with the Japanese survey, many agreements and many clear differences are obvious. The more rational and purposeful behavior of the European managers is the thread that is common to all the questions. The Japanese expose themselves to situations that are not strictly relevant to the problem, they inform themselves broadly, and have relaxed talks with friends. Idea generation is more spontaneous and has more intuitive elements. The following comparison serves to further clarify this tendency:

1. Japanese managers prefer to a far greater extent a bustling environment when thinking about ideas than the European managers.
2. The Japanese have the majority of their ideas in bed (52%).

3. While Europeans expect stimuli through relevant lectures, seminars, visits to other companies, fairs, and exhibitions, the Japanese businessmen go into the city centers; for example to book shops and libraries, to supermarkets, theaters, and entertainments.
4. The European managers study mainly specialized literature. The Japanese colleagues on the other hand inform themselves through magazines of a more general nature, through TV, radio, and daily newspapers. They also read technical journals.
5. In the preliminary phase of idea generation, European managers have talks with external and internal experts, colleagues, and staff working on the same subject. The Japanese frequently talk to private acquaintances of the same age.
6. The majority of the Japanese questioned state that ideas come spontaneously. The Europeans mainly work their way from a presentiment to a solution to a final formulation of the solution.
7. In order to make progress when they are stuck, European managers talk to someone or think more about the matter, whereas drinking coffee or tea and listening to music are the means for Japanese to cope with this situation.

Even after an idea was born, purposeful behavior dominates in European managers. The idea is written down, further developed, completed and secured by further information, planned, and translated into action. Spontaneous activities in order to divert one's thoughts or distance oneself from the problem are rarely mentioned.

Contributions of the Eastern Countries

In Eastern European countries, especially in the former German Democratic Republic and in the former Soviet Union, the methodology of inventions has a long tradition. In fact, the design methodology has its origin in works at technical universities in East Germany (i.e., Lohmann in Dresden and Hansen in Halle) and can be traced back into the early 1950s.

The Russian Genrich S. Altschuller analyzed about 40,000 "strong" inventions and developed a general theory of the solution of technical problems (TRIS; Altschuller, 1984). A special algorithm (procedure) was built up (ARIS) which leads nearly automatically to qualified solutions. One essential step in the procedure is the analysis of the problem in such a way that the search area is reduced drastically. Then the task is precisely defined, especially the technical contradiction of the task is worked out. Solutions are developed through applying a number of rules, principles, and tactics. Altschuller has formulated 40 heuristic solution principles. A few examples may illustrate the type of principles:

1. principle of underlayed cushions
2. principle of a countereffect achieved before
3. principle of a mediator
4. principle of self-supply
5. principle of thin layers
6. principle of changing the states of aggregation
7. principle of composite materials

Altschuller's list has been further developed in East Germany and there are now about 50 principles available.

Johannes Müller (Chemnitz), a philosopher, developed in the late 1960s the *systematic heuristic*. It is a methodology of scientific and technical problem solving worked out very systematically in great detail. It uses special terms and structures quite different from the problem-solving methodologies in Western countries. It is basically a system of standardized procedures and methods which covers all aspects and phases of scientific and technical problem solving. High emphasis is given to the analysis and formulation of the problem.

The systematic heuristic was taught on a broad scale by the chambers of technology in so-called "inventor schools." Characteristics of the Eastern methodologies are: (a) principles on different levels of abstraction, (b) systems broken down in hierarchies, and (c) logical and consequently pursued procedures.

Psychological insights of the process of idea generation at the level of the individual are not considered much. In general, the advice is given to work through the methodological steps in a group (collective) but here again group dynamic effects stimulating or hampering creative thinking are not taken into account.

Better insight into practice, strengths, and weaknesses of the systematic heuristic will be gained in the near future through personal contacts and common work with the experts in East Germany. Communication did not exist in the past; even the literature of the socialistic countries was not observed in the European countries of the West.

OVERVIEW

Creativity techniques are widely known and applied in Western Europe. In many countries they are taught, although not in detail, in the frame of academic education. Public training courses are organized by quite a number of institutions. Many large companies offer courses in creativity techniques regularly in their vocational training programs. The trainers mostly stem from the second generation.

In the literature and in the training seminars usually a number of techniques are presented. The prevailing philosophy emphasizes a mix of creativity techniques (there are very few "gurus" who preach only one methodology).

European schools of creative thinking principles are manifested in brainwriting, morphology, and systematic heuristic. They are all rational approaches. Morphology and systematic heuristic focus to a high degree on abstract and analytic thinking. The brainwriting techniques suppress spontaneity and lessen stimulating effects for others.

Methods built on the psychology of the creative process are not typical for Europe (with one exception: visual confrontation). Some methods even neglect knowledge of individual creative processes or group effects enhancing creative thinking (e.g., methods stressing quick procedures or giving no room to further develop ideas of others).

These methodological developments are in a certain contrast to the results of the survey of managers on their creative thinking. They do many things which are in accordance with the theory of the creative process. Ideas come up everywhere and at any time with a certain predominance of the times early in the morning and late at night. Another interesting fact is that driving in the car is an activity favorable for idea generation. Comparing the survey results in detail with those of Japanese managers, a difference can been seen: European managers are less spontaneous and intuitive in all conscious activities before and after the idea flash occurs than their Japanese colleagues.

REFERENCES

Altschuller, G.S. (1984). *Erfinden - Wege zur Lösung technischer Probleme*. Berlin: VEB Verlag Technik.
Battelle-Institut. (1972). *Methoden und Organisation der Ideenfindung in der Industrie*. Frankfurt, Germany: Battelle.

Gemünden, H.-G. (1990). *Effizienz von Forschung und Entwicklung.* Unpublished report, University at Karlsruhe, Germany.

Geschka, H. (1983). Creativity techniques in product planning and development: A view from West Germany. *R & D Management, 13*(3), 169–183.

Geschka, H. (1987). Kreativitätstechniken in Produktplanung und -entwicklung. In J. Löhn (Ed.), *Der Innovationsberater* (pp. 1151–1154). Freiburg, Germany: Haufe.

Geschka, H. (1988). Development of morphological solutions using a personal computer program. In P. Colemont et al. (Eds.), *Creativity and innovation: Towards a European network* (pp. 197–200). Dordrecht: Kluwer.

Geschka, H., & Mägdefrau, H. (1992). How businessmen generate ideas: Results of a European survey and comparison with a Japanese poll. *Creativity and Innovation Management, 1*(1), 14–19.

Geschka, H., & Yildiz, A. (1990). Probleme in den Griff bekommen. *Gablers Magazin, 4,* 36–40.

Mica, A. (in preparation). *Results of a research into the use of creative problem solving in Dutch product development.*

Rohrbach, B. (1969). Kreativ nach Regeln. *Absatzwirtschaft, 1,* Oktoberausgabe, 73–76.

Takahashi, M. (1985). *Research on the idea generation pattern of contemporary businessmen.* Unpublished report, SOKEN Research Institute, Tokyo.

Zwicky, F. (1966). *Entdecken, Erfinden, Forschen im morphologischen Weltbild.* München-Zürich: Droemer Knaur.

10

Creativity and Innovation in the Netherlands: Project Industrial Innovation and its Implications

Jan Buijs

In the past 20 years, innovation has emerged as one of the major factors contributing to the economic success of countries and organizations. Although much time and effort has been spent on defining the topic, the term *innovation* remains fuzzy. Simply defined, innovation means the introduction of something new. However, a number of semantic problems arise when using this simple working definition. When something new is introduced, some preliminary action is necessary to come up with the idea. This leads to the initial confusion between invention (coming up with something new) and innovation (the successful introduction of the new idea). It also links creativity (finding something new) with innovation (accepting and introducing something new).

What is a successful product introduction? If a consumer buys a new product but throws it away after a couple of hours, is the product a success? Does success mean reaching the sales figures and profit margins predicted by the marketing plans? Does success mean positive reactions in the business press? Is it enough that the company that manufactured the product learns something from its introduction?

An additional problem concerns the concept of *new*. For whom is the product new? Is the product new for the world, new for the market, new for the business, new for the company, or new for the consumer? When a child learns something new at school it is new for them, but is the school system in which they learned it innovative? Introducing a new technology could be an innovation, but what about the introduction of an old technology in a developing country?

Another major area of confusion in the field of innovation is its application. Introducing a new product could be innovation, but what about a new piece of technological equipment, a new procedure in the accounting department, or a new marketing campaign? All these examples are introductions of something new, but are they considered innovations?

Finally, it is important to make the distinction between innovation as a result (the successful introduction of something new) and innovation as a process (finding and developing something new that hopefully leads toward a successful introduction).

Consider the situation in which one company spends enormous amounts of time and money to develop a new technology, only to become number two in its field with a 10% market share. Contrast this company with the approach of one of its competitors that introduced something less refined and technical several months earlier and consequently has attained a market share of 80%. The first corporation has not introduced an innovation, because its competitor has received the initial credit, and most of the customers. Let us consider the process for a moment. Was not the process of innovation in one company similar to the process in the other company? The results of the innovation process differ, but the innovation process is the same. From my standpoint as a management consultant, focusing on the process of innovation is a more useful approach than focusing only on the result.

On a conceptual level there is as much confusion about innovation as there is about creativity. From my point of view, developed over 10 years of management consulting and recently refined in four years of academic experience, innovation is the process of finding and developing something new for an organization.

There is a distinction between innovation on the level of objectives and innovation on the level of means. There is a chain running from objectives to means and vice versa; but this distinction is important to me. Finding new businesses, designing new products, or penetrating into new markets is innovation of the first kind (innovation on the level of objectives). Some examples of the second type of innovation (innovation of means) are: introducing new technologies (particularly when they are developed by others) and introducing new procedures or new organizational structures. My interest is primarily oriented toward the first type of innovation—innovation processes that lead to new product or market combinations for an organization. To develop these new product or market combinations, I concentrate on the process aspect of creativity.

This creative process approach was used to stimulate innovation in small and medium-sized industrial companies in the Netherlands. The Netherlands is about as large as greater Los Angeles, with almost the same number of inhabitants (14–15 million people). Agriculture is an important business in the Netherlands. Using less than 6% of the work force, it produces about 25% of the country's export value. It is the second largest exporter of agricultural goods in the world. (The United States is first.) Traditionally the Netherlands has been a country of farmers and traders, and industrial experience is limited. The industrial revolution in the Netherlands began after the World War II. Although some well-known multinational companies, like Philips, Royal Dutch Shell, Unilever, DSM, and AKZO are headquartered in the country, most of the industrial population consists of small and medium-sized companies, with fewer than 500 employees, most without research and development facilities.

A HISTORICAL OVERVIEW OF RESEARCH ON INNOVATION IN THE NETHERLANDS

In an industrial structure like the Netherlands, where the majority of companies employ fewer than 500 people and manufacture and sell relatively simple products, the main emphasis for governmental industrial support should be on the design and development of new products.

Traditionally the Dutch government has been responsible for support of a good educational system, an effective infrastructure, good relations with other countries to maintain exports, good industry-labor relations for keeping costs down and morale high, and research and development facilities for small and medium-sized enterprises (SMEs). Additionally the government has provided a system of grants to assist in defraying the costs of high-risk product development carried out inside companies.

In the early 1930s, a national organization, TNO (the Netherlands Organization for Applied Scientific Research), was established to apply results from international scientific research to stimulate industrial activities in Dutch companies. Since its formation, TNO has developed into a large and significant research institute. It has been compared to the Battelle Memorial Institute and the Stanford Research Institute. In the late 1960s, both government efforts and the work conducted by TNO was becoming ineffective. TNO became an objective in itself and most SME's were oriented toward a fast return, selling existing products at low prices rather than developing new ones. It was in this context that the interest for industrial innovation in the Netherlands began.

INNOVATION PROCESSES IN THE NETHERLANDS (1972–1974)

TNO conducted the first research project on industrial innovation in the early 1970s. This study was influenced by the results of the famous SAPPHO study in the United Kingdom. The SAPPHO study compared pairs of innovations. Each pair consisted of a successful innovation and a failure. By tracing the histories of these innovations, some interesting findings for stimulating innovations were discovered (Robertson, 1972). From a research perspective, it is noteworthy that this research began with the creative product and traced back to other variables which included the creative process and the creative person.

The TNO researchers modified this design and focused on characteristics of innovating and noninnovating companies. TNO investigated a typical industry sector that manufactured internal transportation equipment (elevators, conveyer belts, fork lift trucks, etc.). All 134 companies of this industry sector were interviewed and a number of organizational company characteristics were examined. Innovative companies were defined as companies in which 20% of present revenue was based on products introduced in the preceding two years. By comparing the most innovative companies with the least innovative, TNO researchers discovered several important results (Beckers, 1974):

1. Innovative companies have an explicit strategy for innovation and have established a structure to achieve this strategy. They have also dedicated money and human resources to innovation.
2. Innovative companies are more externally oriented; not only do they have better relations with their customers, but they also have more information about their competitors. Additionally, they know more about relevant work in government laboratories and in universities, and have better contacts with their labor market, their local communities, and the like.
3. Innovative firms have an "open" management style, and are more likely to exhibit participative leadership.

4. Innovative firms are not afraid to make mistakes, because they learn from them. They encourage their employees to experiment and reward taking risks.
5. Innovative companies spend more time, money, and energy in training and developing their human resources.

It is important to note that these results were reported nearly 20 years ago. It seems that they are as valid now as they were then.

THE SCHOOL OF INDUSTRIAL DESIGN ENGINEERING (1969–PRESENT)

At approximately the same time TNO conducted the landmark study on innovating organizations, Delft University of Technology opened the School of Industrial Design Engineering. This school was established to provide Dutch industry with well-trained design engineers that specialized in new product development. The school's program was designed to combine design skills with manufacturing knowledge, ergonomics, and management sciences.

One of the early studies conducted at the School of Industrial Design Engineering resulted in an extensive methodology for new product development (Eekels, 1973). Since 1971, more than 1,100 professional industrial design engineers have graduated from the school. In addition to producing young engineers, the school provides Dutch society with results of research projects conducted on innovation and creativity (Buijs, 1988; Buijs & Nauta, 1989; Eekels, 1981; Roozenburg & Eekels, 1991; Vink, 1989; Zweers, 1988).

THE INNOVATION CONSULTING GROUP (1976–PRESENT)

After completing the study of innovative companies in 1974, TNO collaborated with the Netherlands government to begin a new research project to determine if noninnovative companies could be transformed into more innovative ones. A small project was scheduled for 1975 through 1979.

After a year, there was no visible progress on the project. As a result, a number of individuals inside TNO took the initiative to begin a new commercial consulting activity in the field of industrial innovation. After some market research on the viability of this venture, I was asked to become their first innovation consultant. In 1976 I founded the Innovation Consulting Group. The purpose of this group was to help companies innovate.

The basic method used to create innovations was an adaptation of the methodologies developed earlier at the Delft School of Industrial Design Engineering. The primary methodology is a simple step-by-step model of the innovation process. It begins with the strategic analysis of a company to determine its reasons for innovating and concludes with the introduction of a new product to the marketplace (Buijs, 1984; Eekels,1973; Roozenburg & Eekels, 1991). In the original model (1973) a number of creative problem-solving methodologies were introduced at a very basic level. Over the years these methodologies have been refined and currently form an essential part of the innovation consulting method.

Use of the term "creative problem-solving methodologies" may create some problems. I use the term to label idea-generating techniques as well as idea-selection techniques. Both of these techniques are essential in all stages of the innovation process. Traditionally, CPS techniques have been viewed as methods to stimulate divergence in idea finding. However, my experience has been that converging is as important as diverging. Diverging is only one step in getting ideas; it is essential to converge to transform an idea into a workable solution. Divergence without convergence is useless. Both of these steps must be executed throughout all stages of the innovative process.

An additional aspect of the TNO innovation consulting method is process consulting. There are two different consulting styles (Greiner & Metzger, 1983; Schein, 1987). The most common approach is *expert consulting*. Consultants using the expert consulting style solve the problems of their clients by giving them the one correct solution. In most cases this is an appropriate way of dealing with a problem. However, the weakness of this method is that implementing the solution is the clients' task. Quite often we find that the "correct" solutions are not being implemented, because the client organization does not accept the solution.

In contrast to the expert consulting approach is *process consulting*. Process consulting originated in the fields of social psychology, organizational behavior, and group dynamics. It is designed to involve the client maximally in finding the solution to their own problem. Consultants using process consulting teach clients to solve their own problem. The client's implementation of their solution is the natural end in this type of consulting project. The consultant using this approach acts as a facilitator.

The consulting styles above are described as an opposing pair. In reality, consulting approaches are much more complicated and a blend of these two approaches is possible. An elegant metaphor to describe expert consulting and process consulting is the following: *Give a man a fish and he eats for a day* (expert consulting); *teach a man to fish and he eats for a lifetime* (process consulting).

This metaphor also indicates the overlap possible in the two consulting methods. Sometimes you have to feed people before you can teach them how to fish. This approach is similar in consulting: Sometimes it is best to give a company a bright solution and sometimes it is best to teach them to find their own.

Process consulting focuses on the problem-solving process, but it is essential that a solution is developed for the problem (the product). If you teach people a new way to fish and they never catch one, it is unlikely that they will find your method of fishing useful. It is essential that process consultants help their clients create real results.

Process-Oriented Innovation Consulting Method

The accepted consulting style at TNO is the expert approach. However, the Innovation Consulting Group was committed to a process approach. Initially it was difficult for the clients and other members of TNO to accept this method as a way for moving companies from noninnovative to more innovative. However, there was a commitment to this approach and it was included as an important element in the forthcoming Project Industrial Innovation. The process-oriented innovation consulting method is based on five basic elements. Those elements are:

1. Process-consulting skills
2. The step-by-step model of the innovation process
3. A multidisciplinary innovation team from inside the company
4. Use of CPS techniques to stimulate the creative talents of the team members
5. Development of information-gathering skills for the team members.

The first element in this method was process consulting. The second aspect of the method was designed to teach the client about the innovation process. The model was described in simple terms, contrary to the original model that was developed at the School of Industrial Design Engineering. The use of academic terms was limited (Buijs, 1987a). The model also combined ideas about strategic planning with methodologies for new product development.

The third element was used for gaining acceptance of the results of the innovation process. Additionally, the innovation teams were multidisciplinary. Innovation cannot be limited to marketing, product design, or manufacturing; it needs the involvement of top management, purchasing, human resources, and administration. The fourth element of the model was used to stimulate idea generation by the innovation team members. Creativity techniques were used in the project to help the team members overcome their fear of saying "strange" things or their unwillingness to express their daydreams about the future of the company. As stated earlier, creativity techniques include both divergent thinking methods and convergent thinking approaches.

The last element of process-oriented innovation consulting was designed to assist the innovation team members in developing skills for gathering external information. Most team members look inward—even top management and marketing departments of small and medium-sized companies have a very limited view of their outside world. Usually the company has knowledge of only direct competitors and suppliers. Contacts with universities, consulting firms, government agencies, or international chambers of commerce are usually nonexistent. The task of the innovation consultant is to stimulate the team members to step into the outside world and get necessary information. Bridging the gap from inside the company world into the outside world is one of the most important stimuli for improving innovation (Buijs, 1987b). It is important to note that the results of the original TNO research from 1974 are clearly an important part of this method.

THE EXPERIMENTAL PROJECT INDUSTRIAL INNOVATION (1976–1979)

In 1976, the small-scale project mentioned above was finally started. This research project was designed to develop ways to change noninnovative firms into more innovative firms. The study was originally pilot tested with 15 companies. Half of these companies were mature businesses with obsolete products and declining markets. The other half were entrepreneurial firms with innovative high-tech ideas but with no actual commercial activity.

This mixture of mature companies and start-up companies was influenced by the Netherlands' political climate. TNO petitioned the government to pay for this research project. The economic situation in the Netherlands was poor, unemployment was high, and many mature firms were declaring bankruptcy. Other major firms were experiencing financial difficulties and the opportunities for full employment were almost nonexistent. In this depressed climate, it was very easy for the government to assume that citizens that started their own business would be the ultimate solution to the problem.

To contrast the Netherlands with the United States, Dutch people are considerably less entrepreneurial. If there is an entrepreneurial spirit, it is usually limited to starting a speciality restaurant, an import agency, or a one-person consulting firm.

Industrial and high-tech firms were not being started in the Netherlands. The government hoped that if TNO could develop a method for improving the entrepreneurial situation, particularly for industrial, high-tech start-ups, the economic condition of the country would also be improved.

Due to the influence of the Dutch government, TNO was forced to direct the research at two objectives. The first was to change noninnovative mature firms into innovative firms. The second objective was to develop entrepreneurial ideas into viable industrial businesses.

The research project target group for mature businesses was also the commercial target group of the Innovation Consulting Group. Due to limited resources, it was determined by TNO that the Innovation Consulting Group would cooperate with the research project in the mature business area. This cooperation led to the involvement of an additional 15 cases. The research group also adopted the process-oriented innovation consulting method of the Innovation Consulting Group as their principal method for transforming noninnovative firms into innovative firms.

The major focus of the TNO research group was toward start-up operations. Conducting research with start-ups was a new and consequently rewarding experience for TNO researchers. Science-oriented researchers were helping entrepreneurs reach venture capitalists, commercial, and technological experts within months. They also assisted in completing administrative jobs, participating in sales meetings, and in some cases in cosigning contracts. The research facilities of TNO were sometimes used to solve technological problems. All these services were free of charge to the entrepreneurs.

At the conclusion of the 3-year project, the TNO research group reported the following conclusions (Beckers, 1978; During, 1986):

1. External consulting helps both mature firms and entrepreneurial firms.
2. The consulting style for helping mature firms differs from the consulting style for entrepreneurial firms. Mature firms need process consulting, and entrepreneurial firms need expert consulting
3. The process-oriented innovation consulting method developed by the Innovation Consulting Group is a good method and should be transferred to the Netherlands' consulting world.
4. Helping entrepreneurial firms is still in its infancy, no "standard" method is yet available, and therefore the project should be continued on a larger scale.

These results may appear to be more politically oriented than scientific. It was important for the research group to continue their assistance to start-up ventures, and TNO wanted to be the leader in innovation consulting. The researchers themselves behaved as expert consultants. The best way to continue to work with start-up ventures was to emphasize a difference between their consulting style and the process-oriented consulting style of the Innovation Consulting Group.

The conclusion regarding the nonexistence of a "standard" method for helping entrepreneurs is also suspect. All researchers were originally scientists or engineers. Because they had no psychological or behavioral knowledge, their focus on the entrepreneur created some tension in their consulting approach. For them every entrepreneur was unique and therefore it was impossible to have a "standard" method. From subsequent personal experiences, I believe that it is possible to help start-ups with a standard approach to process consulting.

PROJECT INDUSTRIAL INNOVATION (1980–1985)

TNO and the Dutch government initiated another project in late 1979. This project was called Project Industrial Innovation (PII project). PII was designed to transfer the process-oriented consulting method to Dutch management consultants and to develop a consulting approach for entrepreneurial firms. The government showed support by providing a budget large enough to assist 150 companies and to train more than 50 management consultants. They also provided a budget for helping start-up firms. The rest of this chapter is limited to the assistance of the mature firms; the results of the start-up help are reported elsewhere (van Goch, 1984). PII began in 1980 and continued until 1985. A total of 155 mature industrial companies were involved, together with 64 management consultants from about 40 different private management consulting firms.

The Organization of the Project

PII was organized in such a way that a steering committee held all political responsibility. A small project bureau conducted the project organization and training, and the consultants and the companies did the practical work.

The project bureau's task was to select the companies and train the management consultants. The most important criterion for selecting companies was the nature of their innovation problem in relation to its timing. Because the process consulting style was used exclusively for all the consulting projects inside Project Industrial Innovation (PII), companies with short-term innovation problems were excluded from participation. A short-term innovation problem is one in which solutions had to be implemented within a very short time. In addition, these companies did not have the financial resources to survive the normal duration of a 2- to 4-year innovation project.

Most of the companies that were accepted had problems with obsolete products, declining markets, aggressive competitors, or out-of-date technology. Four hundred companies applied to participate in the PII project. After the initial screening, 185 were invited to join the project. Thirty companies failed during the first preliminary steps. In total, 155 companies were partners in the PII project.

The Training of the Consultants

The second task of the project bureau was to provide training for the private management consultants. One of the objectives of the PII project was to transfer knowledge of process-oriented innovation consulting to the Netherlands' management consulting world. Participating consultants were given the opportunity to test out these methods in real-life situations. The participating consultants were to become the "teachers" of the participating firms. The consultants were learning process-oriented innovation consulting by doing process-oriented innovation consulting.

Before the consultants were allowed to begin actual work, they were required to participate in several workshops, in which the new method was explained and illustrated with case studies. Part of the program consisted of special workshops on creativity techniques and conflict management. Overall, more than 200 consultants were interested in joining this program. One hundred and twenty participated in the training program and 64 were involved in an innovation project inside a participating firm. Most consultants carried out two different projects during the 4 years of existence of PII. In this way it was possible to get more information about consultants' learning processes.

In addition to the extensive consultant training program, PII also provided participating companies with a subsidy of approximately 50% of the consultants' fee. For the consultants, PII served as an acquisition tool; for the companies PII served as a quality house; for TNO, PII acted as a large test market for the innovation consulting method; and for the Netherlands government, PII acted as its major innovation support scheme of the 1980s.

The Concrete Results of the PII Program

Project Industrial Innovation was designed to achieve three results. First, it was necessary for the participating companies to achieve some concrete results. After completing the program, the companies should have been able to describe the results of their innovation project in terms of which new product they wanted to develop, how much money they wanted to spend, what market they intended to penetrate, how they planned to manufacture and distribute the product, and how many months it would take to bring the new product to the marketplace.

The second result focused on the learning effect inside the participating companies. Were these companies able to continue their innovation process without the help of the PII consultant? Were they able to start a new innovation project in the immediate years following the first one?

The third result focused on the learning effect of the management consultants. Did they apply the method as was intended? Did they make methodical improvements? Did they implement innovation consulting in their normal commercial practice?

It is quite easy to detect the concrete results of the PII project. Part of the PII model is a description of the "design objective." This is a written statement developed by the company describing the new product idea and its intended market objectives. From the 155 companies participating, 110 completed their PII project with a design objective (71%).

It is a bit more difficult to measure the internal learning effect in the companies. After completing their PII project, all the companies were interviewed. Several questions on the interview dealt specifically with this learning effect. Although the answers are subjective, 117 of the companies were very positive about the learning effect (76%).

Consultant learning has been exemplified by presentations at international conferences and the merging of two existing consulting firms after the principals met during one of the PII training workshops. Additionally, in 1980 only two consulting firms mentioned innovation consulting as one of their core activities; in 1986 more than 20 did.

Finally, the step-by-step model used to structure the innovation process by PII resulted in the following findings: 28% of all the innovations were product innovations, 12% were market innovations, 41% were product or market innovations, and only 19% were technology innovations in December 1984. The term product innovation is used to identify a specific result of the innovation process, namely a new product on the present market. A market innovation means the entrance of a new market with a present product. Product or market innovations are the most radical ones—new products in new markets. Technology innovations are limited to innovations in the manufacturing process. According to the introduction, new is always related to the company involved.

If we compare these results with the well-known product-market matrix of Igor Ansoff (1968), the PII participants developed more high-risk innovations than would have been theoretically predicted. It is also interesting to examine these results in terms of the innovations' newness. Forty-eight percent of the PII results in the PII project companies were very new, 40% were new to the company, and 12% reached marginal innovations. It seems clear that PII accomplished its objectives.

Scientific Results of the PII Program

In addition to the concrete results attained by the participating companies and the learning gains achieved by the firms and the consultants, it is important to consider another outcome of PII. This outcome focuses on the two principal methods of consulting used—expert consulting and process consulting.

Process consulting was an integral part of the PII method. In the early days of the Innovation Consulting Group at TNO, it was difficult to gain acceptance for this approach. It was also difficult to show the viability of this approach to the PII steering committee. In the 17-member steering committee, two members represented the Netherlands' consulting world. Both were expert consultants. The two representatives of the Ministry of Economic Affaires (the sponsor of PII) were not convinced of the viability of process consulting. Only the representatives of TNO and the academic world (a well-known academic with much management consulting experience, who had published several books on process consulting) were in favor of the process consulting approach. The majority of the steering committee, including the chairman, were representatives of Dutch industry, and did not have a clear preference.

The original approach was to require proven experience in process consulting from every participating consultant. Due to the consulting style debate in the steering committee, a compromise was formulated. Process-oriented innovation consulting was the official method of the PII project (for helping mature firms), but consultants without any process experience were also allowed to join the program. However, they had to agree to behave like process consultants during their PII work.

As a result of this compromise, the population of participating consultants consisted of three types: consultants with previous process consulting experience, expert consultants, and an "in-between" group called "programmatic" consultants. These consultants behaved like program managers.

By using this diverse consultant population, it was possible to relate the overall results of the project to the type of consulting approach. Consultants with previous process-consulting experience were significantly more successful than expert or programmatic consultants, using the measures identified in Buijs (1984).

The average success score for all the projects was 55%. The process consultants were successful in 80% of the cases, the programmatic consultants in 60%, and the expert consultants in

25% of the cases. This was particularly striking because most of the process consultants had no experience in subjects like technology, marketing, or new product development. It was also noteworthy that some of the expert consultants, whose expertise was technological innovation, had success scores of zero.

Another interesting result of this aspect of the project was the duration of the consulting process. Process consultants used fewer consulting days to achieve their successes than the programmatic consultants. The average amount of consulting days was 38. The expert consultants used 32 days, the programmatic consultants, 40 days and the process consultants 37 days.

The amount of human energy expended in the innovation processes by companies varies by the different success categories. The most successful innovation teams invested more than 1,600 man hours in their project; the least successful ones invested only 1,060. The average amount of man-hour investment was 1,380.

Expert consultants required limited energy from their client (940 hours), process consultants required 1,300 hours, and programmatic consultants required of their clients more than 1,500 hours. These results refute the common prejudice that process consulting takes an extreme amount of client time and energy. The findings convinced even the most skeptical expert consultant in the Netherlands that process consulting was a better approach to assist clients with their innovation problems than the expert consulting method.

In addition to the results mentioned above, a number of other findings emerged. One of the findings concerned the relationship between the size of the innovation team and the achievement of the internal learning effect. The PII program found that the larger the team, the better the learning effect.

Specific creativity techniques were useful stimulants for generating and selecting ideas. The addition of creativity techniques to the original innovation method (Eekels, 1973) led to more successful innovations. It was also found that the more ideas generated the greater the results in overall innovation.

Finally, external information was essential to the success of the innovation process. The more external sources investigated, the greater the result of the innovation process (Buijs, 1984, 1987b).

Longer Term Effects of PII

It is important to ascertain the long-term effects of a program as large as PII. The PII results were measured one year after the project was completed and again two and one half years later (Bubberman, Buijs, & van Klaveren, 1987; Buijs, 1986, 1987b).

One hundred and twenty-nine companies (83%) achieved concrete results in the formulation of a "design objective" in December 1985. The internal learning effect grew from 117 cases to 146 cases, which was an increase of 25%. It is also interesting to examine the number of market introductions based on ideas generated during the PII project. In December 1984 only 21 innovations reached the market, and in December 1985 this number increased to 43 market introductions.

It is also interesting that 19 of the 45 firms that had not formulated a design objective in December 1984 had indeed developed a design objective one year later. They developed the design objective independently, without the expertise of the PII consultants (because the program was terminated in December 1984).

If we examine the innovations in terms of type of innovation and degree of newness, we find that 43% of the innovations are product innovations (up 15% from 28% in 1984), 8% of innovations are market innovations (down 4% from 12% in 1984), 35% are product or market innovations (down 6% from 41% in 1984), and 14% are technological process innovations (down 5% from 19% in 1984). The dominance of the product innovations is now clearly visible. In terms of newness, the December 1985 results showed an overall score of 50%.

Additional follow-up interviews were scheduled with all PII participants in the spring of 1987. We found that some of the firms had spun off as independent units, some were acquired by other firms, some went out of business, and some had moved without leaving a forwarding address. One hundred and twenty-seven firms were contacted and 116 of them were willing to talk about their past PII experiences.

The findings of these follow-up interviews are interesting. Fifty-one product introductions occurred as a result of the PII consultancy. Additionally, 62 other innovations reached the market as a result of the continuing innovation processes inside the companies. The result is an astonishing 113 market introductions from the 116 companies interviewed.

Sixty-six percent of the companies interviewed reported that they used the step-by-step innovation consulting model in one way or another. Sixty-four percent reported that they were still working with the internal multidisciplinary innovation team established during the PII project.

Creativity techniques were one of the basic methods used in the PII method. When PII began, only 5% of the companies had heard about these techniques, and there were no experienced users. Thirty percent of the participants stated that they were using creativity techniques for both developing innovations and for solving other types of business problems in December 1985. In April 1987, 49% were using them.

The final aspect of the PII method investigated was the emphasis on external information. In April 1987, 47% of the companies stated that they were more oriented toward external information and were gathering this information on a more intensive basis than before they joined the PII project.

These results indicate that four of the five key elements of the process-oriented innovation consulting method have become a major part of the participating organizations. This learning effect is largely the result of the fifth element, which is the process-oriented consulting behavior of the participating consultants.

Key Discoveries from PII

Considering the results reported above, Project Industrial Innovation was a success. Operating on a budget of about $6 million over a 4-year period, the Dutch government had a major effect in stimulating innovation in small and medium-sized industrial firms.

What can we learn from this program? It is possible to examine key learning from several perspectives. However, before examining these discoveries, it is important to summarize some of the most important reasons for the success of PII. The most important factors of the PII success include:

1. A well-described and tested method supported by an independent research institute
2. Support for the project on the highest level in government and industry (SMEs)
3. A very small project bureau
4. Introduction of market mechanisms to manage the budget
5. Participation of private management consultants
6. Involvement of a limited number of policy makers during all the stages of the project (preliminary study, experimental project, operational project)
7. The project approach.

Let us now turn to some of the key discoveries of PII. Although the innovation method used in this project proved to be successful, other methods in different situations could probably have created similar results. It is important, however, to have a specific method and to make this method as transparent as possible to all the participants.

Another important aspect of the innovation method is the fact that the approach was explicitly tested under scientific circumstances. All the participants knew they were part of an experiment, and that failure could add valuable information to the project. The quasiexperimental design of the project stimulated thinking about the methods used and the limits of their application.

The training workshops conducted in the project were particularly useful for discussing the process-oriented innovation consulting method. The constant comments obtained through this approach gave detailed insights into the innovation processes. The award-winning book written about this method is now in its second printing and continues to sell well.

Another key discovery from PII was the importance of the belief in the innovation process by key government officials. In the early 1970s, no one had any detailed knowledge of how to change noninnovative companies into more innovative ones. After the reports of the initial research findings were released, a TNO director contacted the chairman of the most important industrial association in the Netherlands. Together these individuals convinced the newly appointed minister of economic affairs (a former member of the board of that industrial association and presently Prime Minister) to start the experimental Project Industrial Innovation.

Additionally, by organizing the program as a project with fixed objectives and a fixed termination date, it was assured that no one would attempt to extend the project, or begin a new governmental or TNO agency. In December 1984, the results of the project were presented in a 1-day event. Additionally, some of the participating companies presented their new products resulting from PII. Three months later all the administrative work was completed and the project was terminated.

Finally, based on the studies that examined the success of PII as an innovative tool for government (Van Dijk et al., 1986; Zwaan, 1989) there was no single critical success factor. The integrative approach (including industry, government, consultants and research institutes) used in conjunction with the participative cooperation between the consultants and the company team members, and the focus on stimulating innovation from inside the organization all played major roles in stimulating innovation.

Although PII was a success, there were also some areas in which the program could be improved. Unfortunately, there were considerable political interests involved in the program. The government, civil servants, the industrialists, and various company objectives all needed to be considered. A steering committee with 17 members also provides a major political challenge. During the 12-year duration of this project, four different government administrations with at least two different political views were involved.

Another area of concern in this project was the double role of TNO. On one hand, TNO invented the process-oriented innovation consulting method; on the other hand consultants of the Innovation Consulting Group were active as consultants under the PII regime. It would have been better to have worked with TNO as a kind of control group, instead of allowing full participation in the experimental group. Unfortunately because of this involvement, researchers and the sponsors were sometimes so intent on creating new product innovations, that sometimes they forgot to look at the process influences. As such, the PII program became more of a consulting program than an objective research program.

The final concern was the decision to maintain a low-profile approach to this project. Direct marketing toward the target group of companies was not allowed. All acquisitions were achieved through lectures at industrial clubs, Rotary Clubs, and so on. The public relations of the program should be conducted on a more professional, strategic basis.

Is it possible to transfer a program like PII to other countries or other situations? I believe it is. However, so far it has proven difficult to accomplish. Several small-scale experiments in the United Kingdom and Norway have been discussed, but little action has occurred.

Stimulating innovation inside a company means that one is involved in the most strategic aspects of that organization. Very intimate and delicate information about the company's future is considered. This can appear very threatening to an organization.

Another element that could create problems in a project of this nature is governmental involvement. Most industrialists do not like the idea that the government is looking over their shoulder and government agencies usually are not equipped with the best possible professionals. It is very important to keep the government at arm's length and hire the best consultants available. Quality, flexibility, a firm belief and a strong emphasis on achieving results are important ingredients for success.

PII was a government-sponsored private initiative, but other sponsors could also initiate such a project. In the Netherlands it took 12 years years to learn. Hopefully others will learn from that experience and achieve success a little bit sooner.

REFERENCES

Ansoff, H.I. (1968). *Corporate strategy.* Harmondsworth, UK: Penguin Books.

Beckers, P.J.M. (Ed.). (1974). *Innovatieprocessen in de Nederlands industrie* [Innovation processes in the Netherlands industry]. Apeldoorn, Netherlands: TNO/COP.

Beckers, P.J.M. (1978). *Eindrapport van de werkgroep van het Project Industriële Innovatie* [Final report of the working group of Project Industrial Innovation]. Apeldoorn, Netherlands: PII.

Bubberman, R.T., Buijs, J.A., & van Klaveren, H.J.J. (1987). *Innoveren op de lange termijn* [Innovation in the long run]. Delft, Netherlands: Delft University of Technology.

Buijs, J.A. (1984). *Innovatie en interventie* [Innovation and intervention]. Deventer, Netherlands: Kluwer.

Buijs, J.A. (Ed.). (1986). *De lange termijn effecten van het Project industriële innovatie* [The long-term effects of Project Industrial Innovation]. Delft, Netherlands: TNO.

Buijs, J.A. (1987a). Innovation can be taught. *Research Policy, 16,* 303–314.

Buijs, J.A. (1987b). *Innovatie en interventie, tweede geheel herziene druk* [Innovation and intervention, 2nd ed.]. Deventer, Netherlands: Kluwer.

Buijs, J.A. (1988). Innovatie, een bijzonder verschijnsel [Innovation is an extraordinary phenomenon]. *M & O, 42,* 209–233.

Buijs, J.A., & Nauta, K.L. (1989, December 10–13). *Creativity training at the Delft School of Industrial Design Engineering.* Paper presented at the Second European Conference on Creativity and Innovation. Noordwijk, Netherlands.

Dijk, J.W.A. (1986). *Innovatie en overheidsbeleid* [Innovation and government policy]. Amsterdam: VU Uitgeverij.

During, W.E. (1986). *Innovatieproblematiek in kleine industriële bedrijven* [Innovation problems in small industrial companies]. Assen, Netherlands: Van Gorcum & Comp.

Eekels, J. (1973). *Industriële Doelontwikkeling* [Industrial goal setting]. Assen, Netherlands: Van Gorcum & Comp.

Eekels, J. (1981). Strategie van de produktontwikkeling [Product development strategy]. *Markeur, 3e.*

van Goch, H.A.P. (1984). *Conclusies en aanbevelingen ter bevordering van jonge innovatieve bedrijven op basis van PII-a-ervaringen* [Conclusions and recommendations based on the PII-a experiences, to stimulate new technology-based firms]. Apeldoorn, Netherlands: PII.

Greiner, L.E., & Metzger, R.O. (1983). *Consulting to management.* Englewood Cliffs, NJ: Prentice-Hall.

Robertson, A.B. (1972). *Success and failure in industrial innovation.* SPRU: University of Sussex.

Roozenburg, N.F.M., & Eekels, J. (1991). *Produktontwerpen, struktuur & methoden* [Product design, structure, and methods]. Utrecht, Netherlands: Lemma.

Schein, E.H. (1987). *Process consultation* (Vol. 2). Reading, MA: Addison Wesley.

Vink, N.J. (1989, October 11–14). *Innovation: Some aspects of under-management.* Paper presented at the 9th International Strategic Management Conference, San Francisco, CA.

Zwaan, A.H. (1989). Innovatie-onderzoek en Beleid [Innovation research and policy]. *M & O, 43*, 354–365.

Zweers, A. (1988, December 5–6). *The entrepreneurial element and innovation.* Paper presented at the Second Workshop on recent research on entrepreneurship (EIASM), Vienna.

PART III

STIMULATING CREATIVITY: OUTCOMES

11

The Power of Product*

Roger L. Firestien

I would argue that the starting point, indeed the bedrock of all studies of creativity, is an analysis of creative products, a determination of what it is that makes them different from more mundane products.

—Donald MacKinnon (1978)

Making the complicated simple, awesomely simple, that's creativity.

—Charlie Mingus (cited in Besemer, 1984)

There is probably no one single definition of the wonderful human phenomenon called creativity. There is also probably no one single definition of the creative product. However, when studying creativity it is helpful to look at the field through an organizing framework. Rhodes (1961) developed such a framework. In his search for a unifying approach to creativity, Rhodes examined 56 different definitions that were present in the literature at that time. Rhodes found those definitions clustered around four overlapping and interrelated strands. Those strands were the creative person, the creative process, the creative product, and the creative press, or environment. Isaksen (1987) extended Rhodes's approach when he introduced the concept of the "4 Ps" of creativity as an overlapping Venn.

Researchers at the 1990 International Creativity Research Conference approached their work from these perspectives. Four groups of researchers focused their deliberations in the areas of

*A major portion of this article is the result of the deliberations of the Creative Product Research group at the 1990 International Research and Networking Conference. Members of the group included Min Basadur, Susan Besemer, Jan Buijs, Roger Firestien, Karen O'Quin, Joe Renzulli and Tudor Rickards. Special thanks to Hedria Lunken and Dennis Carter who facilitated the working sessions of the product group and Suzanne Vosburg and Paul Guthart for their valuable assistance in the preparation of this chapter.

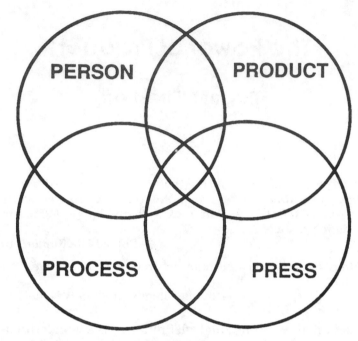

Figure 11.1. The 4 Ps

the creative person, creative process, creative product, and the creative press (environment). A major portion of this chapter will focus on the work conducted in the creative product group and will provide some suggestions on how the results of these discussions can be adapted to research currently underway on the creative product.

When investigating the creative product, it is important to understand that the creative product, the artifact, the outcome of a creative endeavor, does not occur in a vacuum. Researchers artificially isolate the creative product to study it. We are well aware that people create products. People work with processes and they work in environments that can either be supportive or nonsupportive of their creative endeavors. The results of their work—the products—are introduced to environments (press) and subsequently change those environments. As the focus of this chapter is on the creative product, it is important to understand that it is from this particular perspective that the multifaceted concept of creativity will be examined.

The study of the creative product is essential. According to O'Quin (1990), we cannot study creativity directly because it is a highly abstract concept and a complex human phenomenon. One of the ways to study an abstract concept is to make it more concrete. By studying creative products or the outcomes of individual or group creative behavior, we can begin to concretize the concept of creativity and learn more about it.

DEFINING CREATIVE PRODUCTS

The creative product is not a static entity. It cannot be defined by a single dimension but must be examined and evaluated from multiple dimensions. When we attempt to define creative products they must be defined in terms of their relationship with the other three aspects of creativity (person, process, and press).

Creative products are not limited to tangible products. The definition of a creative product can be broadened to include the outcome of a creative process activity. Therefore, creative products can also be intangible outcomes. These might include a positive change in lifestyle, better ways to deal with work-related stress, a behavior change as a result of involvement in team problem solving, or the development of a more effective accounting process. However, the consensus of the product group was that the creative product does need to be produced. It cannot remain in the realm of an idea in order to be considered a creative product. The product must also be useful, even if it is useful only to the person who has created it.

O'Quin and Besemer (1989) have conducted extensive research on evaluating the "creativeness" of tangible products. They have asked groups of people to evaluate a variety of products. These products range from T-shirts to bottle openers. They have found that there are a number of common characteristics of creative products. These common characteristics exist regardless if the product is from the arts or the sciences, whether it is mass produced or homemade, whether it is a "one of a kind" or from a limited edition. Their work has resulted in the development of a scale that allows one to determine if a product is indeed "creative." Named the Creative Product Semantic Scale (CPSS), it consists of three independent dimensions. The product evaluation dimensions are: (a) novelty, (b) resolution, and (c) elaboration and synthesis.

Novelty focuses on the originality that the product exhibits. For a product to be creative it must exhibit some aspect of originality. Resolution measures the degree to which a product meets the practical needs of a problem situation. Resolution determines how well the product solves the problem. Elaboration and synthesis considers aspects of style. This dimension measures how developed or refined the product appears.

It is important to realize that to define creative products, we cannot rely exclusively on pencil-and paper-tests. It is also important to develop other ways of evaluating outcomes such as experts, consensual validation, critical acclaim versus commercial success, and a consideration of the political implications of product evaluation.

Experts in a particular domain might be consulted to determine if a product is creative. Their focus would be to evaluate products in their domain only. Amabile (1983) used a consensual validation technique to evaluate verbal and artistic creative products. According to Amabile, the consensual validation technique relies on the assumption "that experts in a domain do share creativity criteria to a reasonable degree" (p. 38). Firestien, Isaksen, and McCowan (1992) used domain experts to evaluate the quality of ideas generated in creative problem-solving sessions.

Renzulli (1990 personal communication) emphasized the difference between critical acclaim and commercial success. This difference occurs when we contrast the evaluation of a creative product by people with domain-relevant skills and the commercial success of that product. The product may be highly rated by the experts but it might not be commercially successful. The critics might rave about the movie, but the public might not put their money down at the box office.

According to Buijs (1990, personal communication), creative products can also be evaluated in terms of their commercial success. For a creative product to be successful in the marketplace it must be important and relevant to an individual or group. It's creative if it sells. Consumers, with some domain-relevant knowledge (i.e., they know what they want in an automobile, a house, or a laundry detergent) make decisions and therefore evaluate the product by their purchases. With this perspective in mind then, a creative product is better to a greater or lesser degree than the previous product.

In reality, the creative product is not evaluated in isolation. Its evaluation is influenced by people with various personality characteristics, living in a variety of social situations and working in environments that are influenced by politics. Various prejudices, particularly in organizations, can significantly influence the way in which a product is evaluated. If a particular decision maker or decision-making group in an organization believes that a product will take too much time or money to develop, take resources away from "pet" projects, or is inconsistent with the current political agenda, then it is likely that the product will be evaluated negatively and its commercialization will be delayed or prohibited (Basadur, 1990, personal communication).

Because of the political nature of the evaluation process there are several types of motivation behind the evaluation of creative products. This motivation can be both positive and negative. Some motivations are designed to kill the product while others are designed to improve it. There is a need then in evaluating products to be more objective and less prejudicial or personality-based in product evaluation (Besemer, 1990, personal communication).

HOW MIGHT WE IDEALLY EVALUATE CREATIVE PRODUCTS?

The evaluation of creative products is crucial. However, the purpose of evaluation should not be to stop the process of development but to build, refine, synthesize, and enhance the product. Good product evaluation should be designed to develop future learning and should be seen as a stepping stone to better products. It should not be seen as a go or no-go decision. The evaluation process is a significant part of the creative process in the development of more effective and innovative products.

Evaluation of creative products should not be reduced to a single number. Creative products are much more robust and hence the evaluation must occur on a number of levels; not with a single factor, or a single total effective criterion score. According to Renzulli and Reis (this volume), feedback for evaluating a creative product does not necessarily have to be quantitative. Feedback can be more formative or diagnostic, so that from this information the product can be improved.

It is crucial that the product be evaluated honestly. Unfortunately, even an excellent instrument may have difficulty overcoming the personalities, politics, and prejudices in the evaluation of creative products. The instruments currently available to evaluate products are important but they should not drive the entire process of evaluation. The honesty of the evaluator(s) should drive evaluation.

If we look to objectify the process of evaluation it is important to consider that the purpose of being objective is to be neither falsely critical or falsely flattering. We might look to standardize the evaluation procedures for creative products across domains. In doing so, it is important that we also standardize the raters. In other words, these raters would need to know explicitly what to look for and be highly trained. This standardization process might create a problem, however, because creativity by its very nature breaks the commonly held standards in its creation of new concepts. Renzulli (1990, personal communication) suggested a dual-focused evaluation procedure. Instruments that measure the technical aspect of the product should be very precise. Instruments that measure the creative aspects of the product should be more open to surplus interpretation.

As mentioned earlier the Creative Product Semantic Scale (CPSS; Besemer & O'Quin, this volume) was designed to evaluate products across domains. It is also designed to provide formative feedback. In addition to the CPSS, various creative problem-solving process techniques are available that evaluate creative process outcomes across domains and are formative in nature.

Firestien (1989) proposed using a Pluses, Potentials, and Concerns format for evaluating outcomes. Evaluators are instructed to list at least three things that are good about a particular outcome—the pluses. After the pluses have been determined, the potentials in the outcome are then examined. Potentials are speculations or possible future gains that might result if the idea were implemented. Finally, the concerns about the idea are considered. However, when concerns are listed, they are phrased in the form of a problem statement. By wording concerns in this form, a developmental focus is provided to improve the product and invite further speculation and formative development. If the concern about an idea is that it will cost a great deal of money to develop, then the evaluator is asked to rephrase this concern to, "How to reduce the cost?" or "How to raise the necessary capital?"

Renzulli (1990, personal communication) proposed another way that creative products might be evaluated. Creative products might be examined from a local versus a global perspective. A local perspective might focus on a personal or small-group evaluation. In this way, a product might be evaluated for an individual, a family, or a community. If it works for you or your family, then it is creative. A global perspective would call for a larger view of the product. This perspective would move out of the local or personal view into the world. In this way, societies and nations might be involved in the evaluation of the product. From a global perspective, an additional criteria for a creative product is that it can stand the test of time. Societies can look at the products created by their ancestors and still recognize their value.

It was the consensus of the product group that evaluation of creative products should be formative, developmental, and future-oriented. The product is going to exist in the future. If successful product evaluation is to occur, it must take a future focus into account.

HOW MIGHT WE NURTURE CREATIVITY FROM THE PERSPECTIVE OF THE CREATIVE PRODUCT?

It is important to reiterate that to nurture creativity from a product perspective, evaluation needs to be a constructive process and not just destructive criticism. Evaluation should be considered a learning experience and conducted in a supportive manner and context. According to Besemer (1990, personal communication), this type of evaluation leads to further growth and development of the idea rather than a stopping of the person or group who generated the idea and discouragement of the creative process.

Purpose of Creativity Training

It was the consensus of the product group that the major reason to conduct any sort of training designed to nurture creativity would be to help people create more effective outcomes. Those outcomes could be to save money, to make money, to help people work more efficiently as a team, to create new products, to raise the quality of already existing products, or to raise the quality of individuals' lives. According to Basadur (1990, personal communication) before conducting any sort of creativity training it is important to consider the outcomes of that training. It is essential to ask: "What is the product that you want as a result of the creativity training?"

If we are looking to nurture creativity, it is essential to emphasize productivity. It is important to not just "do" creativity for creativity's sake but to "do" creativity to create a product, a change in behavior, or new knowledge. Just being creative in itself is infatuation with a process. Although a great deal of creativity training does help individuals increase their self-actualization capabilities, this is not the total purpose. This behavior is a positive by-product of involvement in creative activities. According to Renzulli (1990, personal communication), the reason why creative people do what they do is for impact on an audience. They want to make a change in society. This audience impact can mean receiving applause from a performance or getting more people to buy their product.

As a result of participating in creativity training programs, participants should have created tangible or intangible products. Firestien and McCowan (1988) found that groups trained in creative problem solving produced different intangible outcomes than groups not trained in creative problem solving. In this study the intangible outcomes were changes in small-group communication behaviors. Subjects were videotaped as they generated ideas for solving a real case problem. Results of the videotape analysis found that groups trained in creative problem solving participated more, criticized ideas less, supported ideas more, and exhibited more verbal and nonverbal indications of humor than untrained groups. Firestien (1990) also found that groups trained in creative problem solving produced significantly more ideas than untrained groups. In subsequent studies, trained groups also produced significantly more high-quality ideas than untrained groups (Firestien, Isaksen, & McCowan, 1992).

Another way to evaluate the effectiveness of programs designed to nurture creativity is to examine the output of those programs. Have people implemented ideas that they have generated in creativity training programs, either to develop new products, to save money, to make money, or to increase the quality of their lives? Keller-Mathers (1990) found that as a result of participating in a 6-day graduate course in creative problem solving, individuals are

> able to apply many of the techniques learned in the course in their personal and professional lives. Furthermore, those techniques were found to be useful to the students up to a year after the course. Students also reported implementing various outcomes from challenges worked on in the course. (Keller-Mathers, 1990, p. 2)

A Process for Nurturing the Development of Creative Products

For many years the misinterpretation has been that creativity is divergent production only. Many creativity training programs have focused on developing divergent production abilities while neglecting convergent production. Firestien and Treffinger (1983) supported this assertion when they stated:

> While great pains have been taken in the field of creative problem solving to develop a multitude of techniques for divergence, little attention has been given to the converging phase of creative problem solving. Convergence is a critical component of creativity. Without convergence, no action can take place, no decisions can be made. (p. 32)

Firestien and Treffinger (1983) listed eight benefits resulting from the effective use of convergent decision making. Those benefits are to reinforce the creative process, keep the process on track, focus on idea "builds," guide idea improvement, set rhythm and pace, provide transition, insure manageable evaluation, and protect ownership.

The final result of convergence in the creative process is a creative product, which is the artifact of diverging and converging activities. Effective creative processes must have the appropriate convergent technology to harness valuable divergence.

A very effective creative process is one developed in Parnes, Noller, and Biondi (1977) and refined by Isaksen and Treffinger (1985). This Creative Problem-Solving process (CPS) emphasizes a balance between divergent and convergent thinking. These two thinking processes are integrated into a 6-stage creative problem-solving model. The 6 stages of the model consist of the following:

1. Mess Finding: searching for and then isolating a general problem or opportunity area on which to work
2. Data Finding: generating and then selecting the most important data regarding the mess situation
3. Problem Finding: generating and then selecting a statement that captures the "essence" of the situation
4. Idea Finding: generating and then selecting the best available idea(s) for solving the problem
5. Solution Finding: using criteria to screen, select and support ideas selected in the convergent phase of idea finding
6. Acceptance Finding: overcoming the weaknesses in idea(s) and then generating ways to implement the refined solution; developing a plan of action

It is crucial to recognize that the convergent thinking used in this process is founded on the concept of "affirmative judgment."

The purpose of affirmative judgment is to screen, select, and support options instead of looking only at the weakness of the idea. Isaksen and Treffinger (1985) described affirmative judgment as looking for strengths or positive aspects of ideas. What intriguing new thoughts are suggested by some of your unusual ideas? What's good about some of the ideas? This approach supports the view of the product group that the evaluation of outcomes should be conducted in a supportive manner.

In further work, Isaksen (1992) classified the six stages into three components. The first three stages—Mess Finding, Data Finding, and Problem Finding—form the first component called Understanding the Problem. The fourth stage, Idea Finding, is subsumed into the component Generating Ideas, and the final two stages—Solution Finding and Acceptance Finding—make up the third component, Planning for Action. This six-stage, three-component model is shown in Figure 11.2.

As indicated in the figure above, the "largest" component in this process is Understanding the Problem. It was the consensus of the product group that to be creatively productive it is important to be personally invested in the process. The individuals must own the problem or challenge if they are to devote the necessary energy to work through the creative process and create a valuable outcome. It is in this first component of the CPS process that individuals or groups establish that ownership (Isaksen & Treffinger, 1985). Firestien and Treffinger (1983) reinforced this point when they stated:

> In a creative problem solving session, we try to insure that some action will result. There is very little satisfaction in a session unless participants leave with a sense of excitement about ideas and ways to use them. This excitement and commitment probably won't occur unless there is a real sense of ownership. (p. 35)

Isaksen and Treffinger (1985) provided three guidelines designed to help individuals check ownership and insure productive use of their problem-solving energies. For an individual or group to have ownership in a situation it is essential that they have: (a) influence or explicit decision-making responsibility; (b) interest and a willingness to submit the challenge to systematic problem-solving effort; and (3) imagination, which is a desire to create something new, meaningful, and novel.

In addition to owning the particular problem situation, it is essential to investigate thoroughly all the possible problem ap-

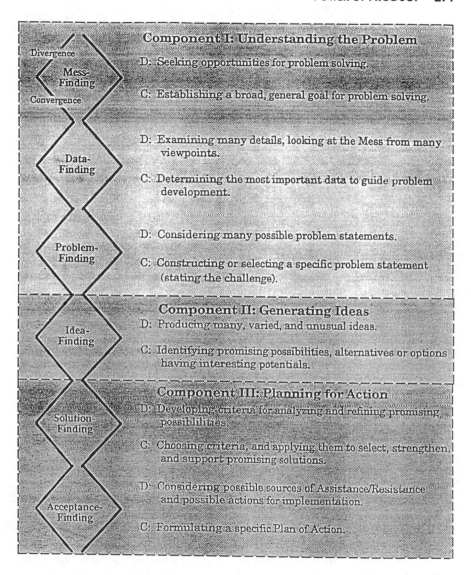

Component I: Understanding the Problem

Divergence

Mess-Finding

Convergence

D: Seeking opportunities for problem solving.

C: Establishing a broad, general goal for problem solving.

Data-Finding

D: Examining many details, looking at the Mess from many viewpoints.

C: Determining the most important data to guide problem development.

Problem-Finding

D: Considering many possible problem statements.

C: Constructing or selecting a specific problem statement (stating the challenge).

Component II: Generating Ideas

Idea-Finding

D: Producing many, varied, and unusual ideas.

C: Identifying promising possibilities, alternatives or options having interesting potentials.

Component III: Planning for Action

Solution-Finding

D: Developing criteria for analyzing and refining promising possiblilities.

C: Choosing criteria, and applying them to select, strengthen, and support promising solutions.

Acceptance-Finding

D: Considering possible sources of Assistance/Resistance and possible actions for implementation.

C: Formulating a specific Plan of Action.

© The Creative Problem Solving Group–Buffalo, 1992. Adapted from S. G. Isaksen & D. J. Treffinger (1985). *Creative problem solving: The basic course.* Buffalo NY: Bearly Limited. Reprinted by permission.

Figure 11.2. Creative Problem Solving: Three Main Components and Six Specific Stages

proaches and then carefully select the problem statement that expresses the "real" problem. The ideas that are then generated for solving that problem will provide maximum return for the problem-solving efforts.

When an individual or group owns the problem situation, the motivation is present for learning and applying the CPS process. According to O'Quin (1990, personal communication) we can teach someone to read but it is unlikely that individuals will expand their reading capabilities if they are not interested in the material they are reading. The same is true for creative problem solving. We can teach creativity techniques outside of a context or domain and people will learn those techniques. However, if the person is interested and has a personal investment in the problem, there is a higher probability that they see a relevance in the creativity techniques and will apply those methods. Once again, one does not do the creative process just to do creativity, one does the CPS process to solve problems. The process must be domain and context related.

The product group agreed that ownership, or the motivation to solve the problem, and skills in creative problem solving are essential for the development of creative products. However, domain-specific knowledge and skills must also be present. If you are to be creative in chemistry, engineering, music, or literature you must have knowledge of those domains. This view is supported by Amabile's (1983) three components required for creative performance: domain-relevant skills, creativity-relevant skills, and task motivation.

Nurturing Creativity in an Organizational Setting

The development of creative products does not occur in isolation. Most creative products are developed in groups or organizations. The product group developed several recommendations for nurturing creativity in organizations.

At an organizational level, it is important that managers, teachers, and leaders learn CPS methods and techniques so they can establish an environment that nurtures creativity. These individuals have domain-relevant knowledge and skills, but it is important that they also have creativity skills to be able to maximize their creative productivity and the creative productivity of their subordinates, students, and constituents.

Managers, teachers, and leaders need to realize the benefit of giving freedom to their employees and students to develop ideas. More emphasis should be placed on affirmative evaluation and considerably less emphasis on punitive evaluation. If employees and students are given the freedom to develop their own ideas, and these ideas are evaluated in a constructive, supportive manner, more effective products will be produced. These can be more effective commercial products or higher quality student projects.

Reward systems in organizations must change to reward people who are good nurturers or facilitators of creativity. The managers and teachers that nurture creativity in their work group or classes hould be rewarded for their ability to use and apply CPS methodologies to assist their employees and students in using their domain-relevant knowledge for the creation of new concepts and products.

Finally, for creativity practitioners to work effectively in organizational or managerial situations in which the outcome might not be a tangible product it is important to establish the criteria for success early on in a creativity intervention with the client(s) who contracted the training.

WHAT ARE THE VALUES AND STANDARDS THAT WE NEED TO CONSIDER IN THE FIELD OF CREATIVITY FROM THE PERSPECTIVE OF THE CREATIVE PRODUCT?

One of the charges that was given to the product group from the co-chairs of the 1990 International Creativity and Research and Networking Conference was to develop some recommendations for the values and standards that should guide the emerging discipline of creativity.

A number of the researchers in the product group were also creative problem-solving practitioners (i.e., facilitators in organizations or educators in creativity). In addition to conducting creativity research, they facilitate creative problem-solving groups. It was the consensus of the product group that the expertise in the field of creativity lies in process skills. Therefore, creativity professionals can help people across disciplines without the necessary domain-relevant knowledge. Our domain is the creative process. A creative problem-solving practitioner can help a chemist, an engineer, and a salesperson equally well because the process methods and techniques that are utilized in CPS can cross domains. As such, one of the values that emerged was that professionals in the field of creativity have process skills and knowledge that are neutral in nature.

As a result of this process orientation, it was the consensus of the product group that to be able to assist people in coming up with new ideas and to move those ideas forward into workable concepts it is crucial to teach converging methods and techniques as well as teaching divergent thinking techniques. Practitioners who teach divergent approaches to creativity without teaching the complementary convergent approaches are doing a disservice to the field. It was a strongly held belief that to teach divergence without teaching convergence is unethical.

Another value that emerged in the deliberations of the product group was that when teaching a creative problem-solving process, we must be careful not to impose our values on the people who are receiving the training. It would be inappropriate for creativity practitioners to expect participants in their training programs to be nicer people now that they know how to use their creativity. The creative process is neutral. However, the use of that process and the resulting outcomes do have value-laden implications. It is important then that creativity practitioners be open but not imposing about their values and be open to accept the legitimacy of the values of others.

The field of creativity is an emerging discipline. As a result of its emergent nature, there are going to be a number of questions that researchers and practitioners might not be able to answer. One of the values of the creativity field is to be open to new knowledge. We acknowledge that we know a great deal about the field of creativity but much more still needs to be known. As a result, it is crucial that we continue to develop questions and relentlessly search for answers to those questions to further our knowledge of creativity. Therefore a value of the field of creativity is that we value uncertainty. According to Besemer (1990, personal communication), this valuing of uncertainty leads us to continue to ask research-related questions which propel the field forward.

The product group strongly supported using validated and reliable instruments as opposed to ad-hoc, seat of the pants, one-time, invalidated measures to evaluate creative products. If the field is to move forward, the emphasis should be on refining and validating instruments already in use as opposed to creating a plethora of new, ad-hoc creative product evaluation measures. In addition to using validated and reliable instruments to evaluate creative products, it is also important to impose scientific rigor in our approach to research and use evaluation techniques that are psychometrically sound.

Even though a great deal of research in the field of creativity focuses on a creative process, it is a value of this field to be productive (Besemer, 1990, personal communication). For a creative process to be effective, a product or an outcome must result.

In a field that is as dynamic and as emergent as creativity, it would be easy to confuse the field by using a great deal of technical jargon. The product group found it important that we value simplicity in terms and parsimony in designs.

Finally, as a result of our discussions, it is important to understand that the field of creativity is not valueless. Upon examination there are a great number of values operating in the field. The development of a set of values is the mark of an emergent discipline.

SHIFTS IN BELIEF AND KEY LEARNINGS OF THE PRODUCT GROUP

There were a number of key learnings and some shifts in thinking that occurred as a result of the product group's deliberations. One of the major shifts in thinking was that the concept of the creative product is much richer than originally thought. It was the feeling of the product group that we underestimated the power of product in the field of creativity. We have focused the majority of our work on trying to understand creative personality characteristics and creative process methodologies. In fact, the main reason for studying creativity is to bring about more effective creative products or outcomes. In this way, we were reminded of MacKinnon's quotation that began this chapter.

Intangible products precede tangible products. If we reverse the commonly held view of the creative process, which focuses on the means to develop the product, and instead focus on the completed product first, the vision of the completed product becomes a compelling creative driver. This vision actually pulls the creative process forward toward its completion. Fritz (1984) supported this view when he advocated focusing on the final outcome of the creative process instead of focusing on the means to accomplish it. According to Fritz, "Vision is the crystallization of what you want to create. Vision takes your generalized desire and shapes it into a clear and definable result. . . . In shaping a vision the result you want to create is what is important" (1984, p. 74).

The members of the product group enjoyed working together and were pleased with the outcome. As we analyzed our interactions, we realized that everyone in the product group was, to varying degrees, trained in CPS. As a result of this training, members felt comfortable with the group process of diverging and converging. By applying the principles of deferred judgment and affirmative judgment and by using trained facilitators to reinforce this process, the members produced valuable outcomes.

Finally, the product group reinforced the interactive nature of the 4 Ps of creativity. A creative person uses a creative process to develop a product that exists in an environment (press). In the process of creating this product the person is changed, and as the product is introduced into the environment, it changes as well. The product that completes this cycle is a stepping stone to the next product. This entire interactive process is cyclical. The product is only a way station in the entire process of change. It is a "snapshot" of the creative person, process, and environment interacting.

REFERENCES

Amabile, T. (1983). *The social psychology of creativity.* New York: Springer-Verlag.

Besemer, S.P. (1984, March/April). How do you know it's creative? *G/C/T,* 30–35.

Firestien, R.L. (1990). Effects of creative problem solving training on communication behaviors in small groups. *Small Group Research,* 21(4), 507- 521.

Firestien, R.L. (1989). *Why didn't I think of that? A personal and professional guide to better ideas and decision making.* Buffalo, NY: United/DOK.

Firestien, R.L., Isaksen, S.G., & McCowan, R.J. (1992). *Effects of creative problem solving training on quality of ideas generated in small groups* Manuscript submitted for publication.

Firestien, R.L., & McCowan R.J. (1988). Creative problem solving and communication behaviors in small groups. *Creativity Research Journal, 1,* 106–114.

Firestien, R.L., & Treffinger, D.J. (1983). Ownership and converging: Essential ingredients of creative problem solving. *Journal of Creative Behavior, 17*(1), 32–38.

Fritz, R. (1984). *The path of least resistance.* Salem, MA: Stillpoint Publishing.

Isaksen, S.G. (1992). *Current approaches and applications of creative problem solving: A focus on facilitation.* Buffalo, NY: Creative Problem Solving Group.

Isaksen, S.G. (Ed.). (1987). *Frontiers of creativity research: Beyond the basics.* Buffalo, NY: Bearly Limited.

Isaksen, S.G., & Treffinger, D.J. (1985). *Creative problem solving: The basic course.* Buffalo, NY: Bearly Limited.

Isaksen, S.G., & Treffinger, D.J. (1991). *Unpublished model of CPS Process.* Buffalo, NY: Center for Studies in Creativity Buffalo State College.

Keller-Mathers, S. (1990). *Impact of creative problem solving training on participants' personal and professional lives: A replication and extension.* Unpublished master's project, Buffalo State College, Buffalo, NY.

MacKinnon, D.W. (1978). *In search of human effectiveness.* Buffalo, NY: Bearly Limited.

O'Quin, K., & Besemer, S.P. (1989). The development, reliability of the revised creative product semantic scale. *Creativity Research Journal, 2,* 268–279.

Parnes, S.J., Noller, R.B., & Biondi, A.M. (1977). *Guide to creative action.* New York: Charles Scribner.

Rhodes, M. (1961, April). An analysis of creativity. *Phi Delta Kappan,* pp. 305–310.

12

Impacts and Outcomes of Creativity in Organizational Settings

Min Basadur

Creativity can be developed, increased, and managed by organizations. Increased creativity can improve virtually every kind of organization. Specific results from organizational creativity can be identified, including new products and methods, increased efficiency, greater motivation, job satisfaction, teamwork, focus on customer satisfaction, and more strategic thinking at all levels. Commitment is needed from senior management to do what is necessary to plan and implement increased creativity. The organization must determine the results it intends to achieve through creativity, and understand that success will not come overnight. A long-term commitment must be made in order to develop creative behavior and reap the benefits that will result.

This chapter will discuss the specific outcomes organizations can expect if they induce and nurture creative activity. These outcomes are organized into two categories: *economic* outcomes and *people* outcomes. Many of the outcomes do not fit exactly into either category and bounce back and forth between the two. Economic outcomes are those which provide economic benefits directly to the organization. People outcomes are those which provide changes to the ways that people in an organization think, feel, and do things. People outcomes are split into two kinds: cognitive and affective. Cognitive people outcomes reflect changes in mental and behavioral processes. Affective people outcomes reflect changes in attitudinal and emotional processes. Most of the cognitive and affective people outcomes are valuable end results in themselves. Most of them also lead to economic outcomes.

Economic outcomes include new and improved products and services, increased quantity and quality, lower costs, quicker reactions to unexpected events, reduced turnover and absentee-ism, clearer corporate visions and goals, more appropriate and successful organizational designs, and faster project completion times. Cognitive people outcomes include higher level thinking skills associated with organizational adaptability; improved stra-tegic thinking and customer satisfaction focus throughout the organization; new managerial leadership skills based on coaching, facilitating, and consulting; greater personal and organizational goal congruency; more rational decision making; interlocking goal setting across departments and between hierarchical levels; and interfunctional cooperation. Affective people outcomes include increased job satisfaction, trust, motivation, commitment, in-volvement, group interaction, teamwork, job enrichment, per-sonal development, initiative, confidence, more accurate selection and placement of people, better matching of interests and skills to jobs and career paths, and better performance appraisal proce-dures. Table 12.1 summarizes these expected outcomes of orga-nizational creativity.

How the outcomes can be realized is easier understood by first defining the term *organizational creativity*. Creativity in organi-zational settings can be defined as an ongoing process of problem finding, problem solving, and solution implementation activity. Problem finding means continuously finding new problems to work on. Problems can be current or future changes, trends, challenges, and opportunities, as well as things that are going wrong. Problem finding includes identifying new product or ser-vice opportunities by anticipating new customer needs. It also includes discovering opportunities for improving existing prod-ucts, services, procedures and processes, and for improving the satisfaction and well-being of the organizational members. It also means redefining seemingly unsolvable problems in new ways that permit solutions from new insights. Problem-solving activity means developing new and useful solutions to problems found. Solution implementation activity means making new solutions work successfully for the good of the organization and its mem-bers. Implementation usually leads to more new problem finding activity. New problems are created as the organization's environ-ment reacts to the impact of each new implemented solution. Thus, simply put, creativity in organizations can be conceptual-ized as a process of continuous improvement, a continuous finding and solving of problems and implementing of new solu-tions for the betterment of the organization and its members. Figure 12.1 depicts this circular ongoing process.

Table 12.1.   Specific Outcomes Organizations Can Expect If They Induce And Nurture Creative Activity

---

ECONOMIC OUTCOMES

- Organizational Effectiveness
- Efficiency
  - Quantity
  - Quality
  - Cost
- Adaptability
  - New, Improved Goods & Services
  - New, Improved Methods
- Flexibility
  - Quick Reaction to Unexpected Problems and Opportunities
- Faster Project Completion Times
- Lower Turnover
- Lower Absenteeism
- Enhanced Functional Performance
- Matrix Teams and Adhocracy Successfully Implemented
- Clear Organizational Goals
- Organizational Structures -
  - Designed Appropriately to Situations

PEOPLE OUTCOMES

Cognitive	Affective
<ul><li>New Higher Level Thinking Skills Associated with Adaptability</li><li>Improved Strategic Thinking<ul><li>Marketing Strategy Development</li><li>Product Development</li><li>Top Management Goal Setting</li><li>Interlocking Goal Setting</li><li>Interfunctional Cooperation</li></ul></li><li>More Rational Organizational Decision-making</li><li>New Leadership Skills for Managers at all Levels<ul><li>Coaching, Facilitating and Consulting Skills Replace Directive Approach</li></ul></li><li>Congruency Between Personal and Organizational Goals</li></ul>	<ul><li>Motivation, Commitment and Involvement</li><li>Job Satisfaction</li><li>Teamwork</li><li>Job Enrichment</li><li>Trust</li><li>Confidence and Initiative</li><li>Personal Development<ul><li>More Accurate Hiring and Placement of People</li><li>Better Matching of Interests and Skills to Job and Career</li></ul></li><li>Better Performance Appraisal Procedures</li></ul>

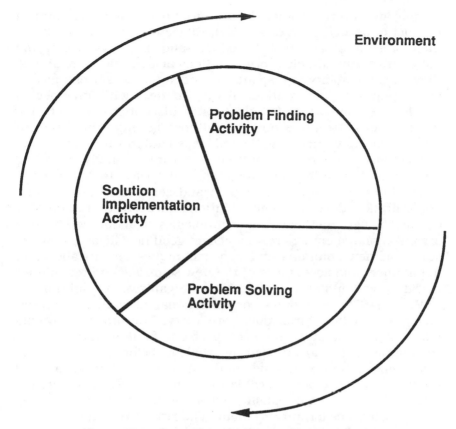

Environment

Problem Finding Activity

Solution Implementation Activty

Problem Solving Activity

Figure 12.1. Creative activity in an organization

THE NECESSITY OF CREATIVITY FOR ORGANIZATIONAL EFFECTIVENESS

Creativity is a necessary requirement for organizational effectiveness (OE). Mott (1972) showed that effective organizations have two major but very different characteristics: efficiency and adaptability. Efficiency means optimizing, stabilizing, and polishing current methods (routines) to get the highest quantity and quality at the lowest cost possible. Adaptability means changing current methods to make new levels of quantity, quality, and cost possible. Both new methods and new products result from adaptability. High efficiency means excellent mastery of routine and high adaptability means high rate of positive change of routine. A routine is a standard method prescribed by which the main work of the organizational unit is carried on. Every organization (including every organizational subunit) turns out some kind of product (a needed good or service). Efficient organizations know their "customer" and their "product" and they master carrying out their routine. Efficient organizations also are flexible, that is, they have the ability to respond to sudden temporary changes or interruptions to the routine. They can deal with unexpected problems and opportunities which cause disruptions and get back to their normal routine quickly, without getting stuck in "red tape." Efficiency, including flexibility, is vital in the short run.

Adaptability refers to continually and intentionally changing routines and to finding new, ongoing, better ways to do business. Adaptable organizations anticipate and seek out problems and opportunities, develop timely solutions ahead of time, and stay abreast of new methods and technologies available externally; organizational members readily accept good new ideas and make sure that new solutions and new techniques get installed and maintained; and acceptance of the new solutions and techniques is widespread and prevalent across all organizational subunits.

Mott's (1972) definition of organizational adaptability is inter-changeable with organizational creativity. The first two components of adaptability represent problem finding and problem solving. These are (a) anticipating problems before they occur and developing timely solutions, and (b) staying abreast of new methods that may be applicable to the technology of the organization, that is, being dissatisfied with the status quo and seeking out opportunities for improvement. The latter two components of adaptability, (c) prompt and (d) prevalent acceptance of new solutions, represent solution implementing. Table 12.2 provides a summary of these parallels. The terms *creativity* and *adaptability* will be used as virtual synonyms for organizational settings for the remainder of this chapter.

In the past, organizations could be effective by concentrating on only efficiency. Efficiency is needed when what needs to be done is well known and how to do it more perfectly is the issue. Said another way, the problems are well defined and getting the best solutions possible is the focus. The product or the method or both are well known; optimizing them is the challenge. Today, adaptability is equally important because of the rapidly accelerating rate of change with which we live (Toffler, 1970). Adaptability is needed when what needs to be done is not clear or is constantly changing. What to do is the issue; identifying the right problems for solving is the focus. The product or method or both are not well

Table 12.2. Organizational Adaptibility and Creativity

Organizational Adaptability	Organizational Creativity
• Anticipating problems before they occur (and developing timely solutions)	Problem Finding
	and
• Staying abreast of new methods that may be applicable to the technology of the organization	Problem Solving
• Prompt acceptance of new solutions	Solution Implementation
• Prevalent acceptance of new solutions	

known. Discovering them is the challenge. Once they are defined, the challenge will evolve later into one of optimization. The most effective organizations are the ones which combine high efficiency with high adaptability. The least effective are low in both. Mediocre organizations unnecessarily compromise, trading off one for the other in a zero-sum fashion as illustrated by the mix line in Figure 12.2.

Many organizations have developed a high efficiency–low adaptability mix because they became comfortable with being surrounded by predictable technology, markets, and other environmental factors. Many companies from the time of the industrial revolution through even as late as the 1970s were able to function this way. As Figure 12.2a shows, a moderate level of organizational effectiveness (represented by the shaded area) is sufficient under these stable conditions.

In the past several years, with rapidly accelerating changes in technology and environment, organizations have become aware of the need to achieve a better combination of adaptability and efficiency. In Figure 12.2b, the shaded area represents the enlarged area of organizational effectiveness available from achieving a high level of both factors.

To increase adaptability, many organizations are trying to find ways to change the way their employees think. They believe them to be overly "efficiency-minded," focusing too much on achieving excellence in performing their routine work assignments daily. This same tough-minded orientation toward optimizing the day-

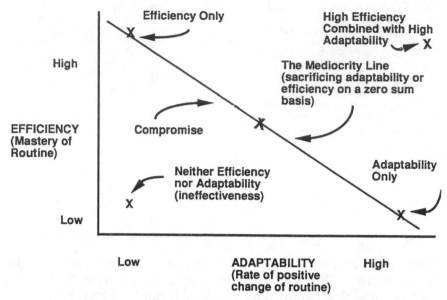

Figure 12.2. The organizational effectiveness grid

to-day routine tends to work against attempts to also be adaptability-minded, to find new opportunities, find new problems (called opportunistic surveillance by Simon, 1960), develop new routines and new products, and solve old persistent problems in new ways. People who are overly efficiency-minded tend to regard adaptability as less important and put in total effort to ensure that their current approaches are as near to perfect as possible (Leavitt, 1975). They fear they must compromise efficiency to gain adaptability, believing the relationship is zero-sum. They worry they will suffer a sharp, immediate drop in efficiency if they attempt to increase adaptability. They assume that people cannot be creative and efficient simultaneously.

ORGANIZATIONAL CREATIVITY AS A PROCESS

Problem finding is a foreign concept to many people in organizations. People tend to wait for others to find problems for them to solve rather than taking the initiative to seek them out. Important problems that cross department lines are often avoided ("That's not our problem"). When confronted with problems and new situations, people tend to evaluate before investigating and re-

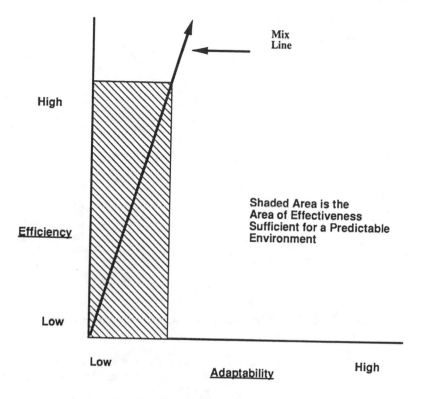

Figure 12.2a. Predictable technology and markets

spond without thinking, precluding inquiry toward a fuller understanding of the situation. Premature assumptions and the inability to understand that the same situation may give rise to
diverse goals and motives for different people leads to an overem-
phasis on problem solutions rather than refreshing, new problem
definitions. Too often people believe that they "already know what
the problem is," assume facts about situations and people based
on preconceived notions and hearsay, and fail to observe and
investigate the obvious. Finding a balance between narrowing a
problem too much (missing the "big picture") and broadening it
too much (not breaking complex problems down into sufficiently
smaller component subproblems) is often difficult.

Even when problems have been found and defined, solving
them creatively and imaginatively is a difficult task for many
people. Individuals frequently believe there are certain ways of
doing things that are unchangeable. When confronted with new
ideas, they are often prematurely critical, which shuts down the

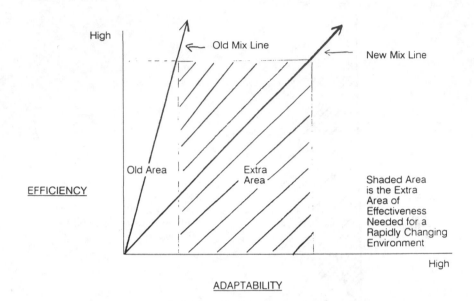

High

← Old Mix Line

New Mix Line ←

Old Area

Extra
Area

Shaded Area
is the Extra
Area of
Effectiveness
Needed for a
Rapidly Changing
Environment

EFFICIENCY

High

ADAPTABILITY

Figure 12.2b. Rapidly changing technology and markets

flow of productive thinking. There is a desire to be perceived as practical and economical above all things, so that judgment comes into play too quickly. Ideas which have some merit but are imperfect are discarded rather than developed. Traditionally taught to be very logical, people often start thinking that every problem has only one right answer. They have difficulty in handling ambiguity, and, tending to believe that things are either right or wrong, are unwilling to take detours to reach goals. Putting too much faith in past experience causes new ideas to be prematurely judged and not tried out. This is unfortunate, because even if the ideas do not work when tried, merely experimenting with them provides further learning and the potential for stumbling upon unexpected outcomes and opportunities. Decisions are directed toward a single goal, whereas many problems involve multiple goals that need simultaneous attention.

Implementing creative solutions to new unprogrammed problems is something most people in organizations are not very good at doing, although they may be good at implementing routine solutions to routine problems. People who are viewed by the organization as proposing too many unusual ideas have great difficulty in getting their ideas accepted and implemented (Kirton,

1987) because others feel uncomfortable and mistrust such activity. It is easier to back off and not to try to implement new solutions even when the solutions are exciting and creative. People are often afraid to implement a creative solution because they fear the solution is not perfect and will be criticized. An overly strong desire to conform to accepted patterns, to not make mistakes, to learn the rules for career success, and the added fear of making a fool of oneself or being ridiculed leads organizational members not to be too inquisitive, nor to express ignorance or ask "Why?" about matters that seem to be accepted or "known" by everyone else. This leads to the "group think" phenomenon in teams (Janis, 1971).

There are many reasons why team work is often uncreative. Group members are unable to communicate clearly in simple terms or to define terms well. They assume that "we all know what we mean." This fuzziness causes time-wasting frustration. Also, group members are unaware that individuals have different styles and methods of thinking and problem solving. Group problem solving is inefficient if people are unable to synchronize these differences. Groups jump into "solving the problem" without first considering how they will go about solving it, then flounder. Unaware of the concept of "process," and focusing only on "content," their meetings tend to be undisciplined discussions where facts, ideas, evaluations, action steps, and new problems are interjected randomly. Interfunctional teams get mired by arguing about territorial issues rather than focusing on the problem at hand. Leaders of meetings do not know how to act as facilitators of the group process. Rather than coaching the group toward innovative action, the leaders steer the group toward their own points of view. Rarely will groups critique their meeting process to examine how their future meetings might be improved. Groups sometimes are satisfied to just "hold" meetings. They are not cohesive and will not stick their necks out to develop bold, innovative solutions.

NEW THINKING SKILLS AND ATTITUDES ASSOCIATED WITH ADAPTABILITY

For all these reasons, and others, inducing the creative process shown in Figure 12.1 is not easy in many organizations. Many people do not think this way. There is a tendency toward a "leave well enough alone" attitude. Serious inadequacies in attitudes, thinking skills, and behaviors needed for organizational creativity can be identified within and among individuals and within and among groups including informal groups, functional work teams, task forces, and matrix teams. These inadequacies are common in organizations and ultimately block creativity within and among whole organizational units such as sections, departments, divisions, and corporations (Basadur, 1994; Elbing, 1978). The inadequacies exist partly because our formal training has often ill prepared us for the creativity needed in today's world of work.

The problems people encounter in business, industry, and other organizations can be placed between two polar opposites (Simon, 1960). One pole is characterized by problems of a more "programmed" nature. Solutions to these problems are based upon applying rules learned during prior experience on the job (what has worked before?) or in school. A knowledge of sequential, linear procedures predesigned to handle similar situations and good judgment and logic are needed for these problems. Solutions are of a "select the right formula" nature. The second pole is characterized by problems of a more "nonprogrammed" nature. Solutions require additional skills such as problem sensing and anticipating, environment scanning, opportunity discovery, fact finding, problem defining, creating and selecting from diverse options, and figuring out how to gain acceptance for and get new ideas implemented successfully. They require the use of imagination as well as sound judgment and logic. These problems often have never been encountered and have no preset rules to guide their handling and are sometimes caused by changing circumstances. Typically less structured and more unpredictable, often the main job in handling these problems is a more strategic one, to discover and define the right *question*. Sensing, anticipating, and defining the problem is often more difficult than solving it.

Traditional formal training primarily addresses the more programmed kind of problems. Individuals tend to learn formulas, problem types, and rules and procedures in high school, university, and in bureaucratic organizations. Business and engineering schools stress this kind of thinking which actually is dysfunctional for the nonprogrammed problems for which higher levels of initiative, imagination, and tolerance of ambiguity are vital. It is difficult for people to do strategic thinking at any level of the organization if all they have been taught and rewarded for is applying set procedures to set problems. For most individuals working in organizations, there is a general tendency for programmcd activities to overshadow nonprogrammed activities. If a person has a series of problems to deal with, those that are more routine and repetitive will tend to be dealt with before those that are unique and require creative thought. This is called Gresham's Law of Planning (Simon, 1977).

Until recent times, many organizations have stressed programmed thinking skills for problem solving to maximize efficiency on routine processes and procedures. Organizational members have been rewarded for learning and applying repetitive business principles and solutions that have proven successful over the years. It is becoming increasingly important, however, for people to be skilled in solving both kinds of problems. The rapid changes in markets, technologies, customers, and environmental demands, and the increasingly global nature of competition are making the skill of finding out what needs to be done very important.

Utilization of the creative process in Figure 12.1 and achievement of the outcomes in Table 12.1 require a change in how the people in organizations think, feel, and behave, both as individuals and as members of groups. Organizations that want to be creative must take deliberate steps to overcome shortcomings such as group think, focusing on content instead of process, and lack of acknowledgment of individual style. Fortunately, research shows that attitudes, behaviors, and thinking skills essential for on the job creative activity can be taught and learned successfully (Basadur, Graen, & Green, 1982). To have them used permanently every day, various organizational, group, and individual factors must be managed. Achieving positive permanent change is a major field of study in industrial and organizational psychology called Organizational Development (OD). Beer (1980) identifies four types of OD interventions: diagnostic, process, individual, and structural.

Diagnostic interventions are problem finding in nature and serve to unfreeze organizational members, that is, get them ready for change. Process interventions and individual interventions provide new attitudes, behaviors, skills, and processes to groups and individuals and cause unfreezing and changing. Structural interventions are often designed to refreeze changes (they make sure new appropriate behaviors solidify rather than fade out). Structural interventions include changing appraisal and reward systems, jobs (e.g., job enrichment), and organizational designs (e.g., moving from functional design to matrix management or adhocracy).

Organizations can expect the specific outcomes outlined in

Table 12.3. Summary of Organizational Intervention Methods (Structured Activities to Induce and Reinforce New Behaviors)

Types			
Diagnostic Interventions	Process Interventions	Structural Interventions	Individual Interventions
Designed to Gather Data and Create a Setting for Feedback and Diagnosis for Improvement.	Designed to Impact Organizational Processes and Behaviors. Members Examine and Improve Behaviors and Relationships	New Organization Structures and Designs to Cope with Changes in People and Environment.	Designed to Change People to Increase Their Effectiveness.
Examples			
1. Survey Feedback 2. Open Systems Planning 3. Problem Definition Mapping 4. Confrontation Meetings	1. Meeting Process Skills Development 2. Team Building 3. Intergroup Meetings 4. Conflict Management	1. Matrix Designs 2. Job Redesign 3. Reward Systems 4. Performance Management and Performance Appraisal Systems 5. Control and Accounting Systems	1. Counseling and Coaching 2. Training and Development 3. Replacement Termination Practices 4. Recruitment and Selection Practices 5. Career Planning 6. Life Planning

Table 12.1 if they systematically tailor and manage an OD process anchored by training in creative thinking for unfreezing and changing. Additional interventions must be integrated for refreezing. One important outcome is an organization full of people equipped with new, higher level, creative thinking skills which are critical to organizational adaptability. Mastery of the new adaptability skills can help a company accelerate corporate problem finding, problem solving and innovation. Accelerating problem finding means more problem anticipation, problem identification, and new project initiation. It also means people tackling problems which are difficult to classify as belonging to one specific department or another. Usually people let such problems fall between the cracks ("It's not *our* job"). Accelerated problem finding also includes improved fact finding, more creative and more accurate problem defining, and increased *catalyzing*. Catalyzing means influencing others to participate in finding and solving problems

that affect the business. It also means generating optimism and pragmatism about finding ways around roadblocks and installing new ideas. Inducing creativity develops people into superior problem solvers, communicators, and team players. A person with high adaptability thinking skills does the following seven things:

1. **Keeps an open mind; separates divergent thinking from convergent thinking.** This means he or she:
   - avoids making premature negative judgments (both when working alone and with others).
   - tends not to jump prematurely to a conclusion as to what the "real problem" is.
   - visibly values and welcomes other points of view as opportunities to strengthen a solution, rather than as a threat to one's ego.
   - displays a low tendency to prematurely criticize a fledgling idea.
   - is visibly open-minded to new ideas and approaches.
   - often pauses deliberately to try an unusual or creative approach to solve a problem instead of automatically relying on an old approach.
   - reacts positively to new ideas.

2. **Thinks divergently.** This means he or she:
   - thinks up many novel options and ideas.
   - searches out many facts and different points of view.
   - defines problems in multiple and novel ways to get a variety of angles on them.
   - creates unusual, thought-provoking ideas.
   - extends effort deliberately to get more options and ideas when it seems that all the options and ideas have already been exhausted.

3. **Thinks convergently.** This means he or she:
   - open-mindedly develops and uses unbiased criteria for selecting from among options, rather than letting preconceptions or hidden motives sway the decision.
   - makes wise choices from among problem definition options in terms of "broadness" vs. "narrowness" of focus.
   - does not wait for the "perfect" answer; instead takes reasonable risks within time limits.
   - pins down implementation plans clearly, simply, and specifically.

- follows up on implementation; does whatever it takes to insure successful installation of the chosen solution.

4. **Differentiates between defining and solving problems.** This means he or she:
   - patiently finds specific, relevant facts before attempting to define the problem.
   - turns premature, negative evaluations of ideas by others into positive challenges and keeps the creative process flowing; changes negative "We can't because . . . " statements into positive "How might we?" statements.
   - questions assumptions for degree of validity.
   - skillfully clarifies and breaks problems down into smaller, more specific subproblems or opens them up into broader, less limiting objectives as needed.

5. **Places higher priority on the process of good, long-term decision making than on getting a short-term result.** This means he or she:
   - will sacrifice optimizing a short-term outcome if a suboptimal approach or even making a mistake will provide an important learning which will be reapplied many times over the long run.
   - realizes that some problems require a long time to solve and does not expect immediate results.

6. **Places overall organizational objectives first when defining problems or getting solutions.** This means he or she:
   - is not concerned over another function getting credit or more resources as a result of a team solution that was clearly the best one for the organization as a whole.
   - shares information and ideas freely with other functions hoping to advance the organizations' overall business.
   - does not go into meetings determined to block any ideas involving change to his or her own function or department.
   - gets teams to develop problem definitions and solutions which transcend individual and functional considerations.

7. **Values and exhibits attitudes associated with effective problem solving.** This means he or she:
   - is willing to tackle problems and infuses an optimistic "can-do" atmosphere around him or her.

- shares bad news as quickly as good news to aid problem solving.
- shows leadership in pinpointing problems and opportunities for improvement throughout the organization.
- convinces others to join up and form teams to meet new challenges.

FOSTERING CREATIVITY TO INCREASE PEOPLE AND ECONOMIC OUTCOMES

Major corporations are slowly but surely becoming aware of the need for widespread competence in higher level thinking skills and are beginning the complex job of learning how to induce and integrate them into day-to-day organizational life. These new thinking skills help increase the organization's adaptability, that is, to intentionally change its routines to find new, ongoing, better ways to do its business. Adaptable organizations anticipate problems and develop timely solutions. They stay abreast of new methods and technologies externally that are applicable to the activities inside the organization. Their employees accept good new ideas promptly and make sure that new methods get installed and institutionalized. Acceptance is prevalent across all the organizational subunits. Adaptability means making deliberate improvements on an ongoing basis.

The concepts of efficiency and adaptability provide a basis for modeling the mechanism by which creativity provides people and economic outcomes which lead to both long- and short-term effectiveness. Research shows that creativity skills can be taught. Organizational members can learn how to be more skilled at problem finding, problem solving, and solution implementing through training. The application of these new skills can be induced in the work setting if appropriate additional organizational interventions are made. Each organization needs to create its own unique combination of interventions (see Table 12.3). Structural interventions work particularly well to refreeze new creativity skills learned. For example, setting up an infrastructure of formal creative problem-solving teams with clear, measurable goals which are important to the organization's strategy works well. It works even better if the performance appraisal process is changed to include rewarding application of the skills learned. Setting up an employee suggestion system infrastructure with rewards tied to usage of the creative skills learned also works well.

The top employee suggestion systems in the world, many found in Japan, are set up exactly this way.

Providing the right training and creating the right infrastructure to obtain continuous problem finding, problem solving, and solution implementation activity (see Figure 12.1) leads to several outcomes. First, it leads directly to new and improved products and methods for doing work which are economic outcomes associated with adaptability. Second, it leads to increased motivation and job satisfaction. These are people outcomes which serve as intermediate steps leading to economic outcomes associated with efficiency. Motivated people work harder at all aspects of their jobs. Not only do they put even more effort into creating new methods, goods, and services, they also put more effort into their routine work. They produce a higher quantity and quality of current goods and services at lower cost. Costs are further decreased because people satisfied with their jobs causes a decrease in absenteeism and less turnover. Third, group interaction and teamwork are increased. People find themselves interested in problems identified by their colleagues and begin working together. The solutions they develop provide economic benefits in turn. Importantly then, people outcomes such as motivation, job satisfaction, and group interaction are the *key* outcomes because they serve as the vital intermediate step in achieving economic benefits. Figure 12.3 models how the variables discussed above relate to one another and how an organization can achieve increased long- and short-term effectiveness by deliberately fostering increased creativity.

CREATIVITY AS A MEANS FOR MOTIVATION

Creativity as a means for motivation is an important idea. In industrial and organizational psychology, the *need* theories (Campbell & Pritchard, 1976) comprise one major category of motivation research. Two important motivational need sets identified in this category are the need for competence (White, 1959) as well as for curiosity, activity, and exploration (Berlyne, 1967). These two needs and related motives provide the most direct explanation of creativity as a means for motivation. People show a desire to master their environment and such mastery is intrinsically pleasurable and independent of outside rewards. This need for competence is increased when people are faced with new challenging situations, and it dissipates after repeated mastery of the task. Intrinsic mo-

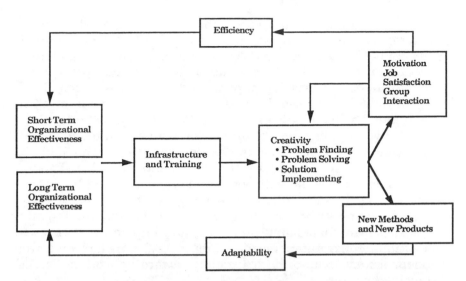

Figure 12.3. Fostering creativity to increase motivation, job satisfaction, teamwork, and organizational effectiveness

tivation is also consistent with early animal research and later studies on humans showing that curiosity, activity, and exploration are enjoyed by organisms for their own sake. People develop negative attitudes toward repetitive tasks and experience fatigue and boredom. Berlyne suggests that people want to take action to maintain appropriate levels of stimulation through new activity. The implication is similar to Herzberg, Mausner, and Snyderman's (1959) research suggesting that challenging jobs are motivating in themselves. Herzberg et al. propose that the way to motivate most people is by redesigning and enriching their jobs so that the work itself provides the opportunity for personal growth, challenge, stimulation, learning, and recognition. Herzberg et al.'s research on job satisfaction suggested a dual factor theory: Satisfaction and motivation can be achieved only by factors intrinsic to the work itself, such as challenge and opportunity for growth and achievement. Extrinsic factors can only remove dissatisfaction about hygiene conditions such as adequacy of salary, security, and working conditions. A comprehensive review of intrinsic motivation is provided in Deci and Ryan (1985).

Other motivation theories in the management literature are consistent with the model in Figure 12.3. The need for achievement as a primary driving force for motivating organizational members has been convincingly advanced by McClelland (1951, 1961). High need for achievement is characterized by a strong desire to assume personal responsibility for finding solutions to problems, a tendency to set moderately difficult achievement goals and take calculated risks, a strong desire for concrete feedback on task performance, and a single-minded preoccupation with task and task accomplishment. Routine or unchallenging work does not usually activate the achievement motive; nonroutine, challenging work usually does. Enriching an employee's job by providing opportunities for variety, autonomy, and responsibility enhances the motivation of people who have a sufficient need for achievement. McClelland has also demonstrated that the need for achievement can be increased by stimulating people to set challenging work goals for themselves. By giving employees the encouragement and opportunity to find and solve their own challenging problems, and implement their own solutions, the process modeled in Figure 12.3 taps into both the need for achievement and intrinsically rewarding work as forces for motivation.

Problem-finding activity is the key to another theory of motivation called the goal setting theory. Locke and Latham (1990) have shown that when people are given a chance to choose their own goals (the problem-anticipating and problem-sensing aspect of problem finding), and the more specifically they state those goals (the problem-definition aspect of problem finding), the more motivated they become to achieve those goals. A goal is defined in terms of a challenge which the individual has consciously decided to pursue. Psychocybernetics research (Maltz, 1969) identifies a "hidden mechanism" within people which automatically propels them toward achieving a goal successfully once a clear, specific vision of that goal (problem) has been pictured (defined) in the mind.

According to Maslow's theory of motivation (1954), offering people at work the opportunity to satisfy their higher level needs for self-esteem and for self-actualization through work accomplishment is the best way to motivate them. Maslow discourages attempts to motivate people through lower level, economic-based needs such as security and salary. Esteem needs represent an individual's need for self-respect, the respect of others, and a stable, positive self-evaluation. An individual's need to self-actualize includes the need to realize one's potential and one's uniqueness. Encouraging organizational members to use their creativity to seek out work related challenges of their own (problem finding) and achieve them successfully (problem solving and solution implementation) helps satisfy both needs.

The vast majority of North American business and industry is still organized and managed on the simplistic, so-called "scientific management" concept made popular by Frederick Taylor (1967), which states that people at work are motivated by one dominant factor—money. This is the concept of "economic man." In spite of much research to the contrary showing that most people at work are multimotivated (money does play a role but in a complex way), most managers ignore it and continue to manage by simplistic, economic formulae. Fortunately, using creativity as a formula for motivation can be almost as simple as using money. There are many straightforward ways to design an infrastructure and provide training which will induce creativity for motivation and ignite the process modeled in Figure 12.3. The next section elaborates on this idea.

Experience proves that there is no real reason why increases in efficiency and adaptability cannot occur simultaneously. A good example is the Japanese manufacturing experience of the past 30 years. Japanese products were of such poor quality in the 1960s that they were the subject of derision around the world. The phrase "Made in Japan" aroused visions of cheap, poorly made junk. These same Japanese products are now world-renowned for their high quality. This change is no accident. Japanese companies made gradual, deliberate, major changes to their management practices. In manufacturing, they began to develop systems of quality circles (QCC), statistical process controls (SPC), and employee suggestion systems (ESS) to get employees involved in identifying and solving problems of quality. They set goals of zero defects and made continuous progress toward such goals. By recognizing a major problem and beginning to deliberately change their routine, they increased their adaptability. By increasing their adaptability, they improved efficiency. They not only improved the quality of goods produced, but they also reduced costs. They developed a new manufacturing paradigm called "do it right the first time" and taught workers to take the responsibility for quality themselves. Although this appears to slow down production time, it actually speeds things up and reduces costs, since fewer quality inspectors are required and customer complaint investigations and service calls are minimized. Therefore, installing the new routine went hand in hand with higher efficiency.

PEOPLE OUTCOMES

Some of the creativity outcomes in Table 12.1 are directly economically oriented and others are not. Importantly, as Figure 12.3

indicates, the secret to obtaining the economic outcomes lies in obtaining the noneconomic, people outcomes first. The rest of this chapter will attempt to identify these key people outcomes first then later describe the economic outcomes. The Japanese Employee Suggestion System (ESS) infrastructure and training is one specific example of how the model in Figure 12.3 can be readily implemented. Fully described in Basadur (1990), this example will be used to identify several outcomes achievable by creativity in any organization. The practical success and theoretical consistency of the Japanese employee suggestion system infrastructure and training demonstrates that important, people-oriented, organizational outcomes such as teamwork, motivation, commitment, employee involvement, and job satisfaction can be achieved through creativity. Such people outcomes can, in turn, be associated with direct economic outcomes such as new and improved products, methods, and greater efficiency.

When the top managers of these leading companies were asked what the primary objective of their employee suggestion system was, none of them mentioned new products or new methods. Furthermore, none of them mentioned lower costs or higher profits. In fact, none of them mentioned any direct economic outcomes. All of them emphatically said that motivated people was the primary objective; most added some combination of job satisfaction, group interaction, and commitment. They all said that they have found when people are given the opportunity to engage in creative activity—to find their own problems, solve them, and implement their own solutions—they become very motivated. When their solutions are accepted and recognized, they want to participate even more in such creative activity (see Figure 12.3). More important, they are motivated to work harder on doing their routine work better as well. They are eager to turn out more quality and more quantity at lower cost, that is, to increase organizational efficiency. When asked how they had learned to concentrate on motivation first, and let economic outcomes fall into place afterwards, the Japanese managers replied, "Why, in your North American textbooks on management."

It is not uncommon for each employee in top Japanese companies to devise and implement as many as 100 new suggestions per year. Employees are trained from the first day on the job that research and development (R&D) is *everybody's* business. For example, in one company of 9,000 employees, 660,000 employee suggestions were implemented in one year. Of these, 6,000 were new products or product improvements. The remainder were new methods (e.g., simplifying jobs, accelerating procedures and work flow). Creative activity is deliberately induced on the job in these companies. The first day hired, employees are trained that problems (discontents) are "golden eggs." One should be "constructively discontented" with one's job and with the company products and seek out ways to improve them. Employees are encouraged to publicly post problems that they sense and anticipate in their work. They are then encouraged to interact with their coworkers to solve such problems and demonstrate that their solutions are implementable. When all three phases are completed (problem *found*, problem *solved*, solution *implemented*), a *suggestion* can be submitted and automatically accepted. Monetary awards are provided for each such implemented suggestion and shared by the participating members. Larger awards are given for suggestions of greater scope, but the vast majority of the suggestions get small rewards. The real rewards, as far as the employees are concerned, are intrinsic to the creative activity itself.

This entire systematic approach of using ESS to induce creativity to foster motivation as an intermediate step to achieving short- and long-term organizational effectiveness follows the model in Figure 12.3. In contrast to this intrinsically based approach, participation in most North American employee suggestion systems is rewarded extrinsically, and there is no intermediate step. Usually, a few employees suggest a few big ideas that save the company large sums of money and win major cash awards for themselves. The top Japanese employee suggestion systems emphasize large numbers of small ideas with everyone participating. While small monetary awards are given for every implementable suggestion and larger awards are given for ideas of greater scope, the vast majority of suggestions win only small awards. The more important rewards are the feelings of accomplishment, recognition, and growth, not the money. The motivation induced is recognized as the indispensable intermediate step to efficiency and adaptability.

The model in Figure 12.3 serves to point out that there *are* deliberate means that organizations can develop to induce creative activity on the job. The Japanese employee suggestion system is merely one way to do so. Its practical success and theoretical soundness demonstrates that outcomes such as teamwork, motivation, commitment, employee involvement, and job satisfaction can be achieved through creativity. These people outcomes in turn help achieve direct economic outcomes including new and improved products and methods, as well as greater efficiency in current products and methods.

Strategic Thinking

Japanese managers in these successful companies are trained to help their employees to think more strategically as they find, solve, and implement problems and solutions. Both managers' and employees' performance appraisals are tied to their suggestion performance, that is, to their creativity. Company goals are clearly articulated and specific objectives and subgoals are communicated downward to guide individuals and teams. Thus, their selection of problems is in alignment with strategic corporate needs. While Quality Circle group activity (QCC) is carefully managed to be a concentrated attack on major theme problems identified by upper management, it also provides a regular forum for spontaneous discussion of many other off-theme problems. In this way, quality circles serve as a deliberate, structural reservoir for new problem finding to fuel the employee suggestion system program. They are part of the infrastructure used to induce creativity on the job as an everyday routine.

Focus on the Customer

Another aspect of strategic thinking is focusing one's efforts on customer satisfaction. Understanding that pleasing one's customers is the central purpose of any organization or job is a creative skill. A simple example of deliberately inducing the creative process to increase customer focus is the practice of some top Japanese companies of starting newly hired research and development (R & D) scientists and engineers in the sales department, then gradually pulling them back into the R & D department over a 2-year period. They serve intermediate stints in other departments along the way including manufacturing and quality control. The purpose is to start new hires interacting with customers. Developing a sensitivity to customer's needs and wants is seen as the most fundamental principle for everyone in the company, and especially for those people whose primary job is to develop new products and services to sell. Sales is as close to the customer as one can get, and new R & D people begin their careers at the problem *finding* stage—learning the customer's problems and needs. These problems and needs then serve as opportunities for new and improved products and services as solutions.

Throughout any organization, the more that creative problem finding skills are honed and used, the greater the focus the employees place on satisfying their customers. Everyone working in an organization has customers. Some of these customers are external to the organization; other customers are internal. External customers include those purchasing and consuming the goods and services outputted. For example, the external customers of a consumer packaged goods company include supermarkets who purchase the goods and shoppers who consume them. Internal customers include members and departments or groups who need goods or services from other departments or groups in order to do their jobs. The shipping department would be a customer of the production department. Employees of successful organizations continually try to anticipate and identify their customers' problems even before their customers are aware of them so they can have solutions ready ahead of time. They lead their customers into valuable changes and do not wait to be asked.

Job Enrichment

Proactive creative activity induced by training and the ESS and QCC infrastructures leads to a continuous flow of new methods and new products and provides organizational adaptability. Not only are new problems deliberately anticipated and solved, but acceptance of the new solutions by employees is assured because they have high ownership of the solutions. They are finding and solving their own problems and implementing the changes themselves. In effect, they are redesigning their *own* jobs, which is consistent with a well-documented axiom of social psychology: People do not resist change; they do resist being changed (Coch & French, 1948). Many North American companies have tried to redesign employee jobs along the idea of making the work itself more intrinsically rewarding, but have gotten inconsistent results. This is likely because in most cases employees have not been asked to participate in the redesign. Often management decides the new design and imposes it on the employee. The Japanese approach to employee suggestion systems goes one step further— it lets employees be creative and make changes to their own jobs through their suggestions. They enrich their *own* jobs by being creative. Perhaps this is the missing link for North American companies who have tried elaborate approaches to job redesign and job enrichment and come up dry.

Trust and Clarity of Goals

Two additional outcomes to be expected by organizations which achieve a high level of creativity are trust and clarity of goals. Mott's (1972) comparative study found that in adaptable, creative organizations, a rational trust relationship exists. This means that members lower in the hierarchy perceive the leaders above them as fair, reasonable, and understanding of their needs, problems, and points of view. They also perceive them as "practicing what they preach." That is, they follow their own rules. They model, coach, and nurture creative leadership behaviors. As Table 12.4 indicates, a second condition that exists in adaptable organizations is clear objectives, goals, rules, policies, and guidelines which help guide employees to pick good goals to achieve and good problems to solve.

In times of uncertainty and change, setting and communicating clear goals and visions of the future is an especially difficult task. The more ambiguous the circumstances, however, the more vital the task, because as top management goals are set, they guide department goal setting.

Deciding what goals to pursue and how to interlock and align with other departments' goals and with the external environment, is an important activity in every organizational unit. These same skills in problem seeking and identification are vital in goal-setting performance. Units must continually ask, "Are we working on the

Table 12.4. Organizational Characteristics And Adaptability

Rational - Trust Relationship

- Extent to Which Intermediate Leaders Are Perceived as Following Their Own Rules
- Extent to Which Intermediate Leaders are Perceived as Understanding Workers' Needs, Problems, and Points of View
- Extent to Which Top Management is Perceived as Fair Reasonable

Clarity of Goals

- Clarity of Objectives Toward Which to Work
- Clarity of Rules, Policies, and Guidelines

right things or just working?" Marketing and product develop-ment planning activities require strong problem finding and cre-ativity skills. Decisions are future oriented and the data are ambiguous. Goal setting and planning cannot be done adequately by simply extrapolating past data. Many organizations are set up bureaucratically and are interfunctional barriers to creative thinking on complex strategic issues and projects requiring coor-dination. Communication is done by agonizingly slow memo writing. Teamwork is required for today's fast-changing environ-ments, but matrix teams and other new organizational designs such as team-based adhocracy are hampered by noncreative attitudes, behaviors, and procedures. The traditional, noncrea-tive, linear approach of making sequential decisions as one depart-ment "hands off" its part of the project to the next is a very slow and inefficient process. It is further slowed by territorial boundary issues and position taking by departments protecting themselves from being blamed for mistakes or not reaching internal, func-tional goals. Situations are overanalyzed for fear of making an overly risky decision. This has been called "paralysis by analy-sis."

New Creative Leadership Skills for Managers

To be successful in our new age of global competition and accel-erating change, managers must learn how to lead creatively. Creative leadership skills include inducing others to initiate problem solving, providing consultation, sharing problems with others to enlist their help, and transferring problem ownership to them. How to get others to take ownership of problems, create, and implement new solutions can be taught and learned. Func-tional leaders must learn to *lead* rather than to administrate, to become facilitators and coaches rather than order givers. Instead of telling them what to do and how to do it, they must learn to ask their subordinates, "How might I use my power and experience to help you achieve your goals?" These skills are the reverse of the old-fashioned individual directive approaches to management which still dominate. The management literature is full of refer-ences calling for the new skills, but few offer any remedies. Inducing organizational creativity is such a remedy (Basadur et al., 1982), however, and one specific outcome is a set of managers and supervisors who possess the new skills.

Improved Interfunctional Teamwork

For organizations to remain strong in today's accelerated, complex, and competitive arena requires an interdisciplinary approach. It is vital to get the knowledge and views of all functions represented and synthesized to manage the business. In interfunctional teamwork, good problem definition performance—determining the right *questions*— is the key. The subsequent solutions and actions appear obvious once the right questions have been determined. If the focus is put on problem definition first, before solutions are considered, cooperation can almost always be achieved, no matter how diverse the team. If solutions are prematurely introduced, different team members will find fault because they feel their functional positions are threatened. Once a creative problem definition that cuts to the real goal is agreed on, new solutions satisfying everyone can be found in a relaxed, trustful atmosphere. Cooperation is needed when one function's idea may cause another function to have an additional headache, yet the net result is positive for the company as a whole. This is especially important when interfunctional teams work on strategic issues which affect the work of many people, because work gets focused on the most significant company challenges.

Creative leadership skills are necessary to achieve a synergy of what could be called horizontal and vertical performance. This is especially true in companies which value functional excellence. If highly competent functions learn to work creatively together, the synergy results in a leveraging effect. Vertical leadership emphasizes technical excellence in one's field of work. Horizontal leadership emphasizes excellence in team play, creative problem definition, and long-term thinking. It discourages zero-sum thinking which limits solutions to compromises and adversarial bargaining.

The leveraging of functional performance is diagrammed in Figure 12.4.

The vertical axis depicts the degree of vertical performance, which means performance within one's function on functional problems. Such performance is largely individual in nature, meets functional goals, and relies on the functional hierarchy to get things done. The horizontal axis depicts the degree of horizontal performance, which means performance across as many functions as necessary to solve organizational problems. Solutions usually affect more than one function and may require what appear at first to be sacrifices by some functions. Ingenuity often

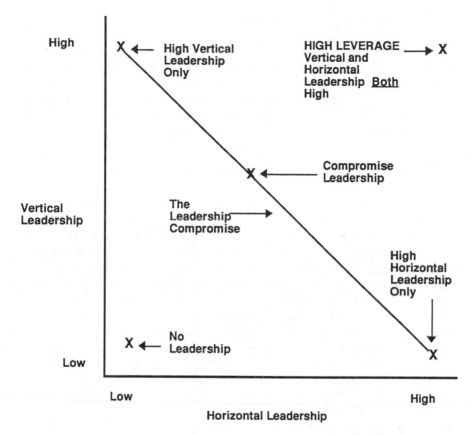

Figure 12.4. Leveraging functional performance

leads to new solutions requiring no sacrifices at all. Horizontal leadership is largely team-oriented in nature. It meets organizational goals and relies on informal networking to get things done rather than on hierarchical approval. It involves influencing people and developing "big picture" understanding. The best leadership is that which combines high skills in both horizontal and vertical leadership. In Figure 12.4, this is the point of high leverage, which contrasts with low leverage points on and below the compromise line.

The creative horizontal leadership skills discussed here have also been used successfully for specific applications as diverse as improving union-management bargaining and supplier-customer working relationships (Basadur, 1988a, 1988b). Unfortunately, horizontal leadership is sadly lacking in many organizations. Matrix teams soon discover that functional and individual priorities dominate over interfunctional team priorities. The reward system often emphasizes individual effort toward functional goals rather than work devoted to overall organizational goals. The few skilled horizontal leaders available often make enemies as they try to cut through functional boundaries. They get discouraged in the long run and often are slow to be promoted in spite of their good work. Effective organizations find ways to develop and reward proficiency in both vertical and horizontal leadership skill.

Increased Initiative, Confidence, and Rationality

The creative process makes participation in problem solving safe and fun. People do not fear advancing fledgling points of view and do not feel they must be constantly on guard. Fostering creativity encourages people to explore new territory, to find new ideas, and to continually bring new energies to problem solving. New breakthroughs are more likely to occur when different points of view are encouraged. People search for new opportunities and new problems, and take a positive attitude that problems can be solved. They value interfunctional problem solving, different points of view, and identifying the right problems to solve. As a result, organizational decision making becomes more rational. The problems selected are more likely to be aligned with company objectives and defined clearly. Company objectives are more likely to be clearly stated and communicated widely in an atmosphere of trust. Fewer problems are likely to be selected and fewer solutions developed that are based on whims or the power and control needs of individuals or groups. Organizational designs can be more fluid and changed more easily as new technologies and environmental needs arise and strategies developed. Focus is put on good organizational decision making toward good goals, not toward maintaining the status quo or other nonrational processes.

Job Satisfaction, Personal Development, and Individual Differences

Job satisfaction is one creativity outcome that is both people and economically oriented. This chapter has demonstrated how creativity can lead directly to job satisfaction, which is an important end product in itself. When job satisfaction is increased, moreover, costs are reduced because there is less turnover and absenteeism. Other outcomes which are both people and economically oriented include better selection, placement, career planning, and personal development for organizational members. For example, if we understand peoples' unique individual thinking and creative problem solving styles better, we can match them with jobs better. Among others, Kirton (1987) and Basadur, Wakabayashi, and Graen (1990) provide instruments to identify how styles of creativity vary. Smart organizations can increase personal satisfaction and development, and synchronize individual differences by using these and other creativity instruments to select, place, and train individuals and to form more effective teams. Managers can give people assignments that match their styles and skills and harmonize individual differences.

The important organizational process of performance appraisal can also be improved by creativity. The process should serve both judgmental and developmental purposes. On the judgmental side, a person's past contribution to the organization needs to be assessed so that rewards can be equitably provided. On the developmental side, his or her strengths and weaknesses need to be identified so they can be built upon and improved. Progressive organizations stress both. Managers who do performance appraisals in this dual, creative manner perform not only the role of judge, but also the role of facilitator and coach. Performance appraisers need to have the creative leadership skill to help the appraisee develop a vision of the future and create opportunities and plans for personal development. Similarly, those being appraised must be creative and open to change. They must be able to view their deficiencies as opportunities for improvement and be willing to implement changes. All these behaviors and attitudes represent creative process skills of problem finding, solving, and implementation.

ECONOMIC OUTCOMES

Turnover and Absenteeism

The link between inducing creativity on the job and increasing job satisfaction and commitment is important not only from the perspective of having happier and more motivated people at work, but in other ways as well. Some of these ways are directly economic. The earlier section dealing with creativity for organizational effectiveness has already shown the direct link to new products and methods. Industrial and organizational psychology research also has found substantial correlations between job satisfaction and commitment and direct economic variables such as lower turnover and lower absenteeism (Locke & Latham, 1990; Organ, 1987). The costs to North American industry of turnover and absenteeism are staggering—billions of dollars annually. Reducing these costs by increasing organizational creativity contributes to higher efficiency in a very concrete, measurable way.

Faster Moving Projects

Creative leadership causes projects to be completed more quickly. Projects move faster, including new ideas for patentable products, cost improvement, meeting test market and national expansion deadlines, and generating new marketing ideas and brand strategies. Thinking is synchronized and the work of different departments is done simultaneously, not sequentially. When project teams operate with the new adaptability skills outlined earlier in this chapter, they get more out of problem solving than is possible with traditional methods. Team members share information they might normally hide, because they feel they are now among allies. The tendency of group members to see the same problem from differing viewpoints increases each person's individual understanding and grasp of the situation. Unwarranted assumptions are more likely to be questioned and, as a result, more imaginative and risky ideas flow forth. Individuals are more willing to share problems with others in order to get help and spark new ideas rather than submerge them.

Improved Functional Performance

The work performed within every corporate function can be improved by increased creative skill. Not only can everyday functional work be done better with the informal use of creative thinking skills on one's job and in teams, but so can special work on major, targeted problems in formal creative application sessions. Application opportunities range widely. Product development department opportunities for creative problem solving range from creating small enhancements to existing products to give the marketing and sales departments new advertising ammunition, to inventing totally new products for new customer needs. Marketing problems range from new idea generation for brand promotion and new brand names to complex strategy formulation. Personnel problems may range from "how to make the company reward system more effective" to "what to do with a 20-year employee who no longer seems to be productive" or "is no longer seen as fitting in with new organizational directions." Engineering problems may range from complex technical challenges such as figuring out how to automate a high-speed manufacturing operation formerly done manually to mapping out a strategy for a staff engineering group to help a manufacturing plant improve its cost-improvement program. The manufacturing function can apply creative thinking to find ways to increase employee involvement and to make new approaches such as "Just in Time" and "Statistical Process Controls" become successful realities rather than philosophical concepts. The purchasing department can use creativity to find ways to reduce the cost of raw materials and to harness the thinking power of suppliers. Sharing important marketing and technical problems openly with suppliers and training and leading them in using the new creative thinking skills opens the door for teamwork. Suppliers are able to add new knowledge and imagination from their own unique points of view to company problems. This leads to better solutions for both the supplier and the company and mutually rewarding long-term relationships. The finance and accounting functions can find more helpful ways to present cost, revenue, and profit figures to managers to increase the quality and speed of decision making. Justification of capital investments can be made on a more sound basis than just over-simplified short-term "marginal revenue" versus "marginal cost" payout calculations. Often, major improvements to customer service, employee motivation, and flexibility and speed of operations are turned down because decision makers are unable to deal with the complexity of quantifying the benefits of such obviously important capital investments. Rather than use creativity to tackle the measurement of the benefits, most financial managers prefer to reject the requests. In short, they lack the creative skill and motivation to develop critical long-term improvement justifications.

Increased creativity can accelerate the identification and solution of similar problems and opportunities in every function and department of any organization. Individual work and teamwork are both improved. For most teams, the problem sensing and redefinition process is the most powerful aspect of creativity.

Investing creative effort in fact finding and in problem definition often pays off in saving time by finding superior solutions which can be implemented more quickly.

SUMMARY AND CONCLUSIONS

Creativity is an important tool which organizations can use to increase their effectiveness, competitiveness, and long-term survival. This chapter identifies many specific positive impacts and outcomes that are attainable by organizations willing to take deliberate steps to increase creativity in their day-to-day work. This chapter also shows how increasing creativity in organizational settings can be accomplished. Probably most importantly, this chapter attempts to describe and model the mechanism by which the impacts and outcomes are achieved by creativity.

To understand the impacts and outcomes of creativity in organizational settings requires an understanding of the term "organizational creativity." Organizational creativity can be depicted as a process of continuous improvement with three stages: problem finding, problem solving, and solution implementing. To induce this process in an organization is not an easy task, and new thinking skills need to be taught and learned by all organizational members. Infrastructures must be created to get the new skills into everyday use on the job.

Organizational creativity is necessary for organizational effectiveness. It provides organizational adaptability and contributes to organizational efficiency as well. Both adaptability and efficiency are necessary for organizational effectiveness.

The specific outcomes available from increased creativity in organizations can be divided into two kinds: economic outcomes and people outcomes. Economic outcomes are those which provide economic benefits directly to the organization. People outcomes include cognitive and affective processes which change the ways that people in an organization think, feel, and do things. Although some of the economic outcomes result *directly* from creative activity, the majority are valuable by-products of placing priority on achieving people outcomes first.

People outcomes are split into two kinds: cognitive and affective. Cognitive people outcomes reflect changes in mental and behavioral processes. Affective people outcomes reflect changes in attitudinal and emotional processes. The cognitive and affective people outcomes are valuable end results in themselves and most of them also lead to economic outcomes as well. Creativity leads directly to a continuous supply of new and improved products and methods for the organization. These are direct economic outcomes which represent adaptability. It also leads to intrinsically motivated, committed, and job-satisfied people who enjoy getting involved and teaming up with others. These are affective people outcomes which are valuable in themselves but more importantly, they lead to vital economic outcomes as well. More motivated people work harder to increase the quality and quantity of their work and to reduce cost. This represents efficiency. Increased job satisfaction is correlated with reduced absentecism and turnover, which means lower costs and higher efficiency. Teamwork results in better problem solving.

Cognitive people outcomes of inducing creativity in the organization include people with new higher level thinking skills which in turn lead to positive economic outcomes. People can be taught and learn to take the initiative and have more confidence in finding opportunities to improve and enrich their own jobs and increase their focus on customer satisfaction. They are able to seek out and define unstructured, unprogrammed situations and problems better and create and implement new solutions. Improved strategic thinking and rational decision making at all levels result from these new thinking skills as people put the long-term goals of the organization as a whole ahead of narrow personal or short-term functional interests.

The new thinking skills also extend to the new brand of combined vertical and horizontal leadership required in today's world of matrix design, adhocracy, and interfunctional cooperation. These leadership skills include coaching, facilitating, and consulting rather than directing. Both functional and interfunctional projects get completed faster and with more ingenuity because of these new skills. People react quicker to unexpected problems and opportunities, increasing organizational flexibility and preserving efficiency.

Organizations which induce creativity also have been found to have higher trust levels and more clarity of organizational goals. This permits people to develop greater congruency between personal and organizational goals. A knowledge of creativity also permits an organization to develop its people to higher levels of their capacity. More accurate hiring, selection, performance appraisal procedures, and matching of interests and skills to jobs and careers results from understanding individual differences in creative style.

Improved organizations are eminently possible through creativity, and virtually every kind of organization can benefit. Commitment is needed, however, by senior management to do what it takes to carefully plan, create, and implement an approach to increasing creativity that makes sense uniquely for its organization. This means both a prior identification of the precise results expected and a trust that this effort will succeed, but not overnight. It also requires structural changes to ensure new creative skills will be solidified and nurtured. Creative behavior must become mainstreamed and institutionalized over the long term in order to make the outcomes identified in this chapter permanent realities.

REFERENCES

Basadur, M.S. (1994). Managing the creative process in organizations. In M.J. Runco (Ed.), *Problem finding, problem solving, and creativity*. Norwood, NJ: Ablex.

Basadur, M.S. (1990). *The Japanese model: Fostering problem finding and creativity to increase motivation, job satisfaction and teamwork* (McMaster University Faculty of Business Research and Working Paper Series, No. 347). Hamilton, Ontario, Canada: McMaster University.

Basadur, M.S. (1988a). *Improving union-management bargaining using a special process of applied creative thinking* (McMaster University Faculty of Business Research and Working Paper Series, No. 300). Hamilton, Ontario, Canada: McMaster University.

Basadur, M.S. (1988b). *The new creative thinking skills today's purchasing professionals must have to be successful* (McMaster University Faculty of Business Research and Working Paper Series, No. 303). Hamilton, Ontario, Canada: McMaster University.

Basadur, M.S., Graen, G.B., & Green, S.G. (1982). Training in creative problem solving: Effects on ideation and problem finding in an applied research organization. *Organizational Behavior and Human Performance, 30*, 41–70.

Basadur, M.S., Graen, G.B., & Wakabayashi, M. (1990). Identifying individual differences in creative problem solving style. *Journal of Creative Behavior, 24*(2), 111–131.

Basadur, M.S., Wakabayashi, M., & Graen, G.B. (1990). Attitudes towards divergent thinking before and after training: Focusing upon the effect of individual problem solving styles. *Creativity Research Journal, 3*(1).

Beer, M. (1980). *Organization change and development: A systems view*. Santa Monica, CA: Goodyear.

Berlyne, D.E. (1967). Arousal and reinforcement. In D. Levine (Ed.), *Nebraska symposium on motivation.* Lincoln, NE: University of Nebraska Press.

Campbell, J.P., & Pritchard, R.D. (1976). Theories of motivation. In M.D. Dunnette (Ed.), *The handbook of industrial and organizational psychology.* Chicago, IL: Rand McNally.

Coch, L., & French, J.R.P., Jr. (1948). Overcoming resistance to change. *Human Relations, 1,* 512–532.

Deci, E.L., & Ryan, R.M. (1985). *Intrinsic motivation and self-determination in human behavior.* New York: Plenum Press.

Elbing, A. (1978). *Behavioral decisions in organizations.* Glenview, IL: Scott, Foresman.

Herzberg, F., Mausner, B., & Snyderman, B. (1959). *The motivation to work* (2nd ed.). New York: Wiley.

Janis, I.L. (1971, November). Group think. *Psychology Today.*

Kirton, M. J. (1987). *KAI Manual.* Hertsford, UK: Hatfield Occupational Research Centre.

Locke, E.A., & Latham, G.P. (1990, July). Work motivation and satisfaction: Light at the end of the tunnel. *Psychological Science, 1*(4), 240–246.

Maltz, M. (1969). *Psycho-cybernetics.* New York: Pocket Books.

Maslow, A.H. (1954). *Motivation and personality.* New York: Harper and Row.

McClelland, D.C. (1951). *Personality.* New York: Dryden Press.

McClelland, D.C. (1961). *The achieving society.* Princeton, NJ: Van Nostrand.

Mott, P.E. (1972). *The characteristics of effective organizations.* New York: Harper and Row.

Organ, D.W. (1987). *Organizational citizenship behavior: The good soldier syndrome.* Lexington, MA: Lexington.

Simon, H.A. (1977). *The new science of management decisions.* Englewood Cliffs, NJ: Prentice-Hall.

Taylor, F.W. (1967). *Principles of scientific management.* New York: W.W. Norton.

Toffler, A. (1970). *Future shock.* New York: Random House.

White, R.W. (1959). Motivation reconsidered: The concept of competence. *Psychological Review, 66*(5), 297–333.

13

Predicting Outcomes of Giftedness Through Intrinsically Motivated Behavior in Adolescence

Roberta M. Milgram

High school reunions are surprising events. The slim become fat, the hairy become bald, and the least likely to succeed are distinguished and prosperous. People from whom we expected important achievements do not fulfill the promise of youth, while others, from whom we expected very little, achieve impressive personal and professional attainments. Many years before their triumphant appearance at the high school reunion, many of these talented people experienced considerable difficulty in identifying and developing their special abilities. They would have benefited greatly from understanding and support from teachers and age peers, but rarely received it. A question that many of these people might, but probably would not ask their teachers and classmates might be, "Where were you when I needed you?" Stories of talented individuals who, despite great adversity, succeed in actualizing their potential abilities can be misleading. We might draw the erroneous conclusion that most able individuals overcome difficulty and fulfill their potential abilities. Many people fail to realize their talents because they did not receive the help and encouragement that they required.

How can we explain the failure to recognize in children and youth the abilities that later emerge as remarkable life accomplishment in adults? One reason for the failure is the difference between what we call remarkable accomplishments in children versus adults. In terms of a stringent standard, it is rare for a child to demonstrate remarkable achievement in a specific area such as music or mathematics. Accordingly, in children, attaining outstanding grades in a wide variety of school subjects is the generally accepted standard for noteworthy accomplishment. High scholastic achievement in children is assumed to be an early indication of remarkable attainments to come.

Neither the practical experience of educators nor research findings support the assumption that school grades are valid predictors of extraordinary adult achievement, especially when the task requirements of the domain differ from those required in formal school settings. Experienced educators are disturbed by the "high school reunion syndrome" described above. Many children identified as gifted on the basis of their school performance and given special educational programs designed to nurture their gifts do not attain notable life achievements, whereas some children who were not identified as gifted and were not given special academic opportunities make major contributions to society.

By the same token, research findings lend little support to the assumption of the validity of the conventionally accepted psychometric measures of giftedness in children. The predictive validity of IQ scores or achievement test scores with reference to gifted behavior in adults is modest at best. Even in the realm of academic achievement where the predictor and criterion are the same, the situation is not much better. Achievement test scores from childhood are only modest predictors of adult academic achievement.

Children with high grade point averages who are considered gifted in elementary and secondary school are indeed admitted to prestigious universities where they continue to earn high grades. Similarly, children identified as gifted generally achieve at a fairly high level in their academic and professional lives as adults (Terman & Oden, 1947, 1959) to the extent that the task requirements of their jobs as adults are formal and academic. Nevertheless, only a few of the 2,000 subjects in the classic Terman study (Terman & Oden, 1947, 1959) achieved a high level of accomplishment that could be called eminence. There is also little evidence that children identified as gifted on the basis of IQ or achievement test scores invariably reach the *highest* occupational levels, achieve *outstanding* vocational success, or provide professional and community leadership (McClelland, 1973; Tannenbaum, 1983; Terman & Oden, 1959; Wallach & Wing, 1969).

One major reason for the low predictive validity of intelligence test scores and school grades with reference to real-world accomplishments is the predictor-criterion difference discussed above. Eminence in adults is very different from conventional academic and professional success. It is extraordinary performance reflecting creative thinking in a specific life domain. Eminence is defined as *great* distinction or superiority in achievement, position, rank, or character. It implies towering above others. It is often preceded by highly focused interest, ability, and activity in a specific sphere of life over a period of many years. The accomplishments of gifted children reflect, for the most part, their general or domain-specific convergent intellectual abilities. By contrast, the attainments of gifted adults reflect domain-specific divergent thinking, an ability not generally reflected in conventional academic accomplishments.

In summary, what is recognized as remarkable achievement in children and in adults is very different. Accordingly, it should come as no surprise that the two phenomena are so frequently unrelated. We can better identify and provide for the needs of children with high potential for becoming gifted adults by:

1.   Expanding our view of giftedness in children from a unidimensional to a multidimensional formulation.
2.   Improving the procedures utilized in the identification of gifted children, especially at the early screening stage.
3.   Providing differentiated curriculum and individualized instruction for gifted children.

Your initial reaction to these three comments may be, "She is beating a dead horse!" You may think that a broad definition of giftedness, the use of identification batteries rather than merely a single intelligence test, and the concepts of differentiation of curriculum and individualization of instruction are widely accepted policies and practice in gifted education. Indeed, in many parts of the United States a broad definition and an expanded process of identification are legal requirements (Tannenbaum, 1983).

Nevertheless, the horse that I am beating is very much alive. Numerous investigators recommend that we should initially "throw a wide net" (Renzulli, 1977; Tannenbaum, 1983) in order to give as many children as possible a chance to be identified as gifted. In many good school systems, the wide net has mandated the administration of a group intelligence test to large numbers of children. These test scores are subsequently used along with teacher recommendations as an initial screening device. In later stages of the identification process, smaller numbers of children receive increasingly larger numbers of tests and interviews. In the end, identification is determined by the individual profile of strengths of each child that has accumulated. This procedure sounds admirable, but it is flawed in several ways: (a) highly gifted children whose abilities are not reflected in intelligence test scores or who do not meet the conventional standard of giftedness that many teachers apply in making their recommendations are systematically eliminated at the first stage; and (b) the relative weight given indices of giftedness other than intelligence is frequently so low that one could claim that their inclusion is merely a "cosmetic" device without genuine consequences (Jenkins-Friedman, 1982).

If the conventional predictors of giftedness—IQ and school grades—are not valid predictors of professional eminence and social leadership, we should consider alternative predictors. I suggest that unconventional predictors like original or creative thinking and creative leisure activities are better predictors of significant adult accomplishments.

The above statements require supporting data. In the first section of this chapter, a 4 x 4 model of giftedness is presented in which four distinct categories of abilities, two conventional and two unconventional, are postulated as predictors of gifted adult behavior. Comparison of the differential predictions for adult attainments that stem from the 4 x 4 model provide the theoretical basis for predicting that the unconventional abilities are more valid predictors of remarkable life accomplishments than the conventional. The second section reports on an 18-year follow-up study comparing the predictive validity of conventional versus unconventional predictors.

THE 4 X 4 MODEL OF GIFTEDNESS

For many years the field of giftedness was dominated by a unidimensional, IQ-oriented view of giftedness (Terman, 1925; Terman & Oden, 1947, 1959). Over the years numerous researchers and practitioners have called for redefining giftedness in terms of our growing understanding that giftedness is dimensional. In the 1950s the definition of giftedness was expanded by Guilford (1956) to include creativity, and we began to speak of the gifted and talented. Marland (1972) added leadership ability and abilities in the performing and visual arts. This definition was adopted by the United States Office of Education and widely accepted in the field of gifted education.

On the basis of the expanded view of giftedness, I developed a 4 x 4 model of the structure of giftedness. In this model, giftedness is classified in terms of (a) four categories, two having to do with aspects of intelligence (general intellectual ability and specific intellectual ability), and two with aspects of original thinking (general original/creative thinking and specific creative talent); (b) four ability levels (profoundly gifted, moderately gifted, mildly gifted, and nongifted), hence the name 4 x 4; and (c) three learning environments, embedded in a circle of individual differences.

The 4 x 4 model is described in detail elsewhere (Milgram, 1989, 1990, 1991). The first category, *general intellectual ability* or *overall general intelligence*, refers to the ability to think abstractly and to solve problems logically and systematically. This ability is most frequently reported in terms of IQ scores. The second category, *specific intellectual ability*, refers to a clear and distinct intellectual ability in a given area, such as mathematics,

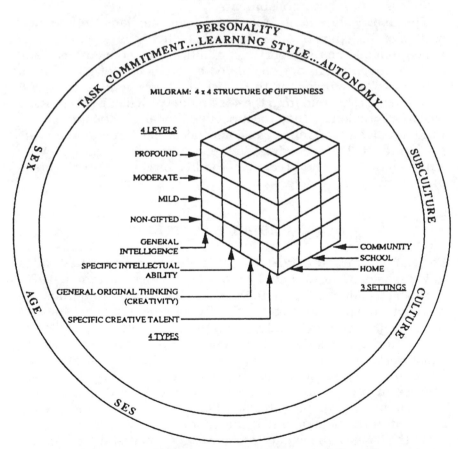

Figure 13.1. Milgram's 4 x 4 structure of giftedness

foreign languages, music, or science, and is reported in terms of school grades and achievement test scores. Specific intellectual abilities reflect competent but not necessarily original performance. The third category is *general original/creative thinking*. Creative thinkers generate solutions to problems that are unusual and of high quality. The solutions may take the form of an idea, a performance, or an actual product. Original-thinking people perceive and define problems differently. They pay attention to cues in the environment that others ignore, and store and retrieve information differently as well. This ability, referred to by Barron and Harrington (1981) as "raw creative ability," is measured by tests of divergent thinking. The fourth category, *specific creative ability*, refers to a clear and distinct domain-specific creative ability in which raw or general original thinking ability is applied to a specific domain such as science, music, business, or politics. At the highest level, this combination results in what is frequently referred to as excellence or creative talent in a specific field of endeavor. The realization of specific creative ability often requires time to incubate and develop as a result of life experience. It is, therefore, more fully manifested in adults. *One way to identify specific creative talent in children before these abilities become fully realized in one's vocation is by examining leisure-time, out-of-school activities.*

An important dimension of the 4 x 4 model is the postulation of four levels of abilities ranging from nongifted to profoundly gifted. In the education of retarded children it has been widely recognized that in order to provide appropriate special education it is essential to evaluate the level of functioning and to determine as exactly as possible the educational achievement that one might reasonably expect from the child. Giftedness, by contrast, is considered a yes or no situation. The categories gifted and nongifted are assumed to represent two distinct levels of functioning in individuals. Some attention has been paid to profound giftedness, a rare and extreme phenomenon (e.g., Albert, 1991; Albert & Runco, 1986, 1987; Bloom, 1985; Feldman, 1986) but the educational needs of gifted children at mild and moderate levels have rarely been treated separately. This is particularly unfortunate since for practical purposes, most of the children identified as gifted are in the mild and moderate ability range. The needs of the two groups are different from each other. Moreover, their needs are probably even more different from those of highly gifted learners than they are from those of the nongifted.

The two general categories cited in the 4 x 4 model—general

intelligence and overall original thinking—have been the subject
of many theoretical papers, and have received considerable empirical support (Wallach, 1970, 1971; Wallach & Kogan, 1965). By
contrast, the two remaining categories—specific intellectual and
specific creative talent—have received little theoretical attention
and still less empirical investigation.

In a recent study (Milgram, 1989) I examined the relationship
between specific intellectual ability and specific creative ability in
mathematics. For ease of presentation, I will refer to the two
abilities as mathematics achievement and mathematics excellence, respectively. The subjects were 97 children in grades seven
to nine. The measure of mathematics achievement was school
grades in the subject. The measure of mathematics excellence was
the child's self-report of creative out-of-school activity in mathematics as reported on items included in the Tel Aviv Activities
Inventory (1990). Examples of such items are deriving original
solutions to mathematical problems and developing original explanations for mathematical problems. The relationship of each
ability to both general intelligence and general original thinking
ability was also investigated. The measure of intelligence was the
Cattell Comprehensive Ability Battery (1975) and the measure of
original thinking an instrument tapping divergent thinking, the
Tel Aviv Creativity Test (Milgram & Milgram, 1976) based upon
the earlier work of Wallach and Kogan (1965).

Mathematics achievement and excellence were found to be
unrelated. As hypothesized, mathematics achievement was moderately related to intelligence ($r = .26, p < .01$) and unrelated to
general original thinking ability. Mathematics excellence, by contrast, was related to overall original thinking ($r = .23, p < .01$) but
not to intelligence.

The relationship between specific intellectual ability and specific creative ability in the same field has been a topic of contro-
versy, particularly in mathematics (Tirosh, 1989). Ridge and
Renzulli (1981) believe that overall intelligence in children is a
necessary, but not sufficient, precondition for the emergence of
remarkable mathematical performance in adults. Other researchers insist that overall intelligence is not a necessary precondition for mathematical giftedness (Heid, 1983; Krutetskii, 1969,
1976). According to these theorists, some people are high in
intelligence and excel in mathematics, others are not. There is,
however, no necessary connection between the two. These findings support the formulation that mathematical academic
achievement in formal academic settings and mathematical ex-

cellence are two distinct cognitive abilities and demonstrate that each is related to the corresponding general ability.

The various relationships among the four abilities probably pertain to other domains, such as science (Yager, 1989) and foreign language (Shrum, 1989). Understanding the distinction between achievement and excellence in each specific domain helps explain why successful and promising pupils do not invariably become eminent adults and suggest ways in which we may help some of these pupils to achieve eminence.

CREATIVE THINKING

Introspective reports of creative people led to the conceptualization of the creative process as problem solving with ideational fluency as an essential component (Mednick, 1962). Many investigators developed measures of original problem-solving based upon ideational fluency (Wallach, 1970) and made strenuous efforts to distinguish ideational fluency from intelligence. Although it is important to establish this point, the preoccupation of researchers with the intelligence-creativity distinction was somewhat unfortunate. It is more important to demonstrate what original thinking *is* and especially what it is good for. Accordingly, the next step in our research was to compare the concurrent validity of creative thinking and of intelligence with reference to real-world creative behavior.

It is difficult to reach agreement about whether a given behavior is creative or not and if a given behavior is creative, to what degree. Accordingly, it is probably more useful to substitute the term *original thinking* for *creative thinking*. An original idea, solution, or product is one that is statistically infrequent. It is not as difficult to get agreement on degree of originality. Unfortunately it is not enough to produce an idea or product that is original. In order to qualify as creative, a solution must be both original and of high quality. On the basis of this approach, I developed the following definition of creativity: Creativity is a process of original problem solving by means of which original (i.e., unusual and high quality) products are generated.

Taken together, the findings that have accumulated over the years provide considerable empirical support for the construct validity of theoretical formulations of original thinking based upon ideational fluency. General original/creative thinking and overall intelligence are empirically distinguishable (Wallach, 1970,

1971). There is a relationship between quantity and quality of ideational output, with high ideational production a precondition for quality responding (Milgram, Milgram, Rosenbloom, & Rabkin, 1978), and there is an order effect with popular responses (more conventional/stereotyped ideas) emitted earlier in the response sequence and more original ideas later (Milgram & Rabkin, 1980).

Some evidence for the concurrent validity of ideational fluency-based measures has accumulated. Ideational fluency, the ability to generate many ideas, predicted the ability to generate many original solutions to laboratory problems in children of school age at all levels and in young adults (Milgram, 1983; Milgram & Arad, 1981).

Data have also accumulated from our work and that of others demonstrating ideational fluency to be related to concurrent nonacademic talented accomplishment (Milgram & Milgram, 1976; Wallach & Wing, 1969; Wing & Wallach, 1971). In an extensive review of the literature, Barron and Harrington (1981) cited 70 studies in which a positive relationship obtained between measures of ideational fluency and nontest real-world indices of creative behavior. The validity of ideational fluency measures of creative thinking is still an open question, however, since Wallach (1985) summarized results of a number of concurrent studies indicating that general original/creative thinking is not related to any significant degree with specific real-world creative perfor-mance. The long-term predictive validity of ideational fluency-based measures of creativity has been rarely investigated.

Creative thinking is a less conventional predictor of adult accomplishment than intelligence or school grades. Nevertheless, the evidence for the construct validity of ideational fluency-based measures of original thinking is considerable. By contrast, the evidence of concurrent predictive validity of these measures is contradictory and inconclusive. The long-term predictive validity of ideational fluency-based measures of original thinking remains to be investigated. Before considering our findings on original thinking as a predictor of real-world adult creative attainments, let us examine a second, equally unconventional, alternative pre-dictor of adult eminence—creative activity in childhood and ado-lescence.

CREATIVE ACTIVITY

Numerous investigators have stressed the importance of ex-panding our view of giftedness, but have not considered the role of out-of-school activities in the development of talent. Although leisure activities might be viewed by some as an unconventional and unlikely predictor of noteworthy adult achievements, domain-specific creative ability is probably evidenced in children as unusual leisure activities of high quality.

Leisure activities are intrinsically motivated out-of-school hobbies and activities that people engage in for their own enjoyment, by their own choice, and not in order to fulfill school requirements or to earn grades or credits. Out-of-school activities are not necessarily nonintellectual (watching TV). Leisure activities may be highly intellectual projects (computer programming) not related to school. They may be competitive or noncompetitive, and may result in a product or not. Children who spend many hours reading, practicing an instrument, painting, or working in their "laboratories" show not only intellectual abilities, but also task commitment, and other cognitive and personal-social attributes that strongly determine life outcomes. One could argue that leisure activities outside of school are more stable and valid indicators of giftedness than school grades or IQ scores.

Measures of leisure activity generally tap nonacademic talented accomplishments in areas such as science, music, fine arts, social leadership, writing, community service, drama, sports, and dance. In a number of studies, high school and college students reported the quantity and quality of their nonacademic talented accomplishments in a wide variety of these (Holland, 1961; Holland & Austin, 1962; Holland & Nichols, 1964; Milgram & Milgram, 1976; Richards, Holland, & Lutz, 1967; Wallach & Wing, 1969; Wing & Wallach, 1971). The findings indicate that creative accomplishments in high school are associated with continuing creative performance in college. This finding is understandable. The best predictor of one's future interest and activity in a given realm is one's past attainments in that area.

To sum up, the above findings are evidence for the *short-term* predictive validity of measures of creative performance. However, the *long-term* predictive validity of measures of creative performance remains to be investigated.

The topic of out-of-school activities does not appear in recent authoritative sources such as Horowitz and O'Brien (1985), Tannenbaum (1983), or Sternberg and Davidson(1986). Interestingly enough, Terman (1925), the pioneer investigator of giftedness, reported a large number and wide variety of out-of-school activities for the intellectually gifted children who he subsequently followed throughout their lives. He did not, however, examine the efficacy of these leisure activities as predictors of future eminent achievements.

THE 18-YEAR FOLLOW-UP

To the best of my knowledge, no study comparing the two conventional predictors of adult eminence—intelligence test scores and school grades—and the two unconventional predictors—general and specific original thinking—has yet been conducted.

We utilized the data collected 18 years ago from the entire senior class (N = 159) of a Tel-Aviv high school (Milgram & Milgram, 1976). These data included both the two conventional and the two unconventional predictors. We compared the activities inventory protocols gathered 18 years ago from adolescents with their current measures of vocational accomplishments, nonacademic talented accomplishments, and leisure activities. We developed and administered a criterion measure of real-world creative accomplishment in six life areas: academic, vocational, military, community service, family, and leisure activities.

On the basis of the theoretical and empirical background cited above, we expected measures of creative thinking and creative performance gathered in adolescence, but not IQ scores and school grades gathered at the same time, to be related to creative accomplishment in adults in major life areas.

We expected raw original thinking ability, as evidenced in ideational fluency and that thrives in a permissive atmosphere when a person adopts a playful nonjudgmental approach, to be related to adult attainments in leisure and family-oriented activities rather than to accomplishments in the academic, work, community service, or military spheres. By the same token, we expected the quantity and quality of creative performance, as evidenced in self-reports of out-of-school accomplishments that result from an enormous investment of time and effort, to be related to adult accomplishments in the academic, work, community service, or military spheres rather than to leisure and family-oriented attainments.

Intensive efforts were made to locate all subjects included in the original study 18 years ago. We succeeded in finding 67 (men and women) of the original 159 subjects. Each subject was called on the phone in order to enlist cooperation in filling out a questionnaire sent in the mail. The inventory of adult attainments, described above, was mailed to each subject. Follow-up calls were made to assure maximal return of the questionnaires. In view of the fact that the original group of subjects was not a sample but a total population, it is reasonable to generalize from data based upon a random sample representing one-third of that population after a hiatus of 18 years. In addition, we compared the predictor scores of the two groups—those who returned the questionnaires and those who did not—and found no differences between the two groups. This finding provided additional justification for generalizing from the follow-up sample to the total original population.

The predictor measures of intelligence, creative thinking, creative performance, and academic achievement used in the early and in the current research are described in detail elsewhere (Milgram & Milgram, 1976). The criterion measure was the Adult Activities Inventory, a pilot version of the Inventory of Adult Accomplishment (Milgram, 1989c) consisting of 63 items tapping adult attainments in six life areas. The six areas and the number of items in each area (in parentheses) were as follows: academic (6), vocational (11), military (7), community service (10), family (11), and leisure activities (18). This instrument is described in detail in Milgram and Hong (1994) and Hong, Milgram, and Whiston (in press).

Intelligence test scores of our subjects during their senior year in high school did not predict high-level accomplishment in any of the six life areas. High school grades predicted continued academic achievement ($r = .28$, $p < .05$). By contrast, leisure activities reported in the senior year in high school were related to significant accomplishments in work ($r = .26$, $p < .05$) and family ($r = .37$, $p > .01$). Creative thinking in high school was related to impressive accomplishment in leisure activities ($r = .31$, $p < .01$), but not to attainment in any of the other five life areas.

CONCLUSIONS

Comparison of recently collected data with those collected 18 years ago provides evidence for predictive validity of two unconventional indices of creativity cited above—ideational fluency-based creative thinking, and leisure activities—but not for the conventional predictors—IQ scores and school grades. These data support the explanation offered at the beginning of this chapter for the "high school syndrome," that is why some students we expect to succeed in life do not, and the opposite. We fail to recognize potential for extraordinary achievement in children because we look for early signs in the wrong place. If we would look at out-of-school activities, we would be more successful in recognizing abilities destined to develop and result in remarkable life achievements.

The data support the theoretical formulation of four distinct kinds of abilities presented in the 4 x 4 model. In the light of the predictive validity of specific creative abilities as evidenced in out-of-school activities in adolescents, the distinction between specific intelligence and specific creativity may be as important, both theoretically and practically, as the distinction between general intelligence and creativity.

The findings that the unconventional predictors—creative thinking and creative leisure activities—were more related to adult achievements than the conventional predictors suggest that measures of leisure activities be included in selection batteries for special programs for the gifted and be given major weight in selection decisions. These data highlight the serious flaw in the procedures of identification of gifted children that begin with general screening on the basis of IQ scores.

In the analyses conducted so far on the baseline data, talented accomplishments in adolescents were summed to give a single index of out-of-school attainments. It seems reasonable that the focused leisure activities and nonacademic attainments in a limited and distinct domain will be more related to their future accomplishments in that same sphere than general creative activity in a wide variety of areas. We intend to examine the efficacy of overall original thinking ability, and nonacademic talented accomplishments in specific domains in young people as long-term predictors of real-world accomplishments in specific life areas.

In summary, intrinsically motivated domain-specific behavior may be viewed among the early indices of eminence. Accordingly, all children should be given the opportunity to develop their potential abilities by being systematically exposed to many types of activities. Not all children have the opportunity for leisure activities. The current data suggest that schools provide opportunities for intrinsically motivated activities to all children. Children from disadvantaged backgrounds will then have the same opportunities for the development of domain-specific leisure-time activities as those frequently made available to advantaged students.

McClelland (1973) called for testing for competence rather than for intelligence and suggested that the best testing is criterion sampling. One reason why his recommendation has not been implemented in the identification of gifted and talented learners is the lack of appropriate psychometric instruments. Our data suggest that self-reports of out-of-school activities may serve as an instrument for criterion sampling testing in children with reference to gifted behavior in adults.

In addition to the predictor-criterion relationship over a period of 18 years between out-of-school activities in adolescence and remarkable accomplishment in young adults, we found a similar concurrent relationship. At this stage in young adult development, accomplishment in the work area was strongly related to significant leisure time activity ($r = .44$, $p < .001$). In the light of the findings reported by Holland (1961) that creative activity in high school is associated with continued creative performance in college, and the findings of the 18-year follow-up reported above, it is reasonable to conclude that the the talented young adult subjects in our sample will continue to develop in the direction of increasingly significant accomplishments.

REFERENCES

Albert, R.S. (1991). People, processes, and developmental paths to eminence: A developmental-interactional model. In R.M. Milgram (Ed.), *Counseling gifted and talented learners: A guide for teachers, counselors, and parents*. Norwood, NJ: Ablex.

Albert, R.S., & Runco, M.A. (1986). The achievement of eminence: A model based upon a longitudinal study of exceptionally gifted boys and their families. In R.J. Sternberg & J.E. Davidson (Eds.), *Conceptions of giftedness* (pp. 323–357). New York: Cambridge University Press.

Albert, R.S., & Runco, M.A. (1987). The possible personality dispositions of scientists and nonscientists. In D.N. Jackson & J.P. Rushton (Eds.), *Scientific excellence: Origins and assessment*. Beverly Hills, CA: Sage Publications.

Barron, F., & Harrington, D.M. (1981). Creativity, intelligence and personality. *Annual Review of Psychology*, 32, 439–476.

Bloom, B.S. (1985). *Developing talent in young people*. New York: Ballantine Books.

Cattell, R.B. (1975). *Comprehensive Ability Battery (CAB)*. Champaign, IL: Institute for Personality and Ability Testing

Feldman, D.H. (1986). *Nature's gambit: Child prodigies and the development of human potential*. New York: Basic Books.

Guilford, J.P. (1956). The structure of intellect. *Psychological Bulletin*, 53, 267–293.

Heid, M.K. (1983). Characteristics and special needs of the gifted student in mathematics. *Mathematics Teacher, 76,* 221–227.

Holland, J.L. (1961). Creative and academic performance among talented adolescents. *Journal of Educational Psychology, 52,* 136–147.

Holland, J.L., & Austin, A.W. (1962). The prediction of the academic, artistic, scientific, and social achievement of undergraduates of superior scholastic aptitude. *Journal of Educational Psychology, 53,* 132–143.

Holland, J.L., & Nichols, R.C. (1964). Prediction of academic and extra-curricular achievement in college. *Journal of Educational Psychology, 55,* 55–65.

Hong, E., Milgram, R.M., & Whiston, S.C. (Eds.). (in press). Leisure activities in adolescence as a predictor of occupational choice in young adults: A longitudinal study. *Journal of Career Development.*

Horowitz, F.D., & O'Brien, M. (Eds.). (1985). *The gifted and talented: Developmental perspectives.* Washington, DC: American Psychological Association.

Jenkins-Friedman, R. (1982). Myth: Cosmetic uses of multiple selection criteria. *Gifted Child Quarterly, 26,* 24–26.

Krutetskii, V.A. (1969). An investigation of mathematical abilities in school children. In J. Kilpatrick & I. Wirszup (Eds.), *The structure of mathematical abilities: Soviet studies in the psychology of learning and teaching mathematics, 2.* Stanford, CA: School Mathematics Study Group.

Krutetskii, V.A. (1976). *The psychology of mathematical abilities in school children.* Chicago, IL: The University of Chicago Press.

Marland, S.P., Jr. (1972). *Education of the gifted and talented.* Washington, DC: U.S. Government Printing Office.

Mednick, S.A. (1962). The associative basis of the creative process. *Psychological Review, 69,* 220–232.

McClelland, D.C. (1973). Testing for competence rather than for "intelligence." *American Psychologist, 28,* 1–14.

Milgram, R.M. (1990). Creativity: An idea whose time has come and gone? In M. A. Runco & R. S. Albert (Eds.), *Theories of creativity.* Newbury Park, CA: Sage.

Milgram, R.M. (Ed.). (1991). *Counseling gifted and talented children: A guide for teachers, counselors, and parents.* Norwood, NJ: Ablex.

Milgram, R.M. (1990). *Tel Aviv Activities Inventory,* Ramat Aviv, Israel: School of Education, Tel Aviv University.

Milgram, R.M. (1989a, June). *Leisure activities as a predictor of excellence in mathematics.* Paper presented at the 46th Annual Convention of the International Council of Psychologists, Halifax, Nova Scotia, Canada.

Milgram, R.M. (1989b). (Ed.). *Teaching gifted and talented children learners in regular classrooms.* Springfield, IL: Charles C. Thomas.

Milgram, R.M. (1989c). *Inventory of adult accomplishment.* Ramet Aviv, Israel: School of Education, Tel Aviv University.

Milgram, R.M. (1983). A validation of ideational fluency measures of original thinking in children. *Journal of Educational Psychology*, 75, 619–624.

Milgram, R.M., & Arad, R. (1981). Ideational fluency as a predictor of original problem-solving. *Journal of Educational Psychology*, 73, 568–572.

Milgram, R.M., & Hong, E. (1994). Creative thinking and creative performance in adolescents as predictors of creative attainments in adults: A follow-up study after 18 years. In R. Subotnik & K. Arnold (Eds.), *Beyond Terman: Longitudinal studies in contemporary gifted education* (pp. 212–228). Norwood, NJ: Ablex.

Milgram, R.M., & Milgram, N.A. (1976). Creative thinking and creative performance in Israeli children. *Journal of Educational Psychology*, 68, 255–259.

Milgram, R.M., Milgram, A., Rosenbloom, G., & Rabkin, L. (1978). Quantity and quality of creative thinking in children and adolescents. *Child Development*, 49, 385–388.

Milgram, R.M., & Rabkin, L. (1980). A developmental test of Mednick's associative hierarchies of original thinking. *Developmental Psychology*, 16, 157–158.

Renzulli, J.S. (1977). *The enrichment triad model: A guide for developing defensible programs for the gifted and talented*. Mansfield Center, CT: Creative Learning Press.

Renzulli, J.S. (1978). What makes giftedness? Re-examining a definition. *Phi Delta Kappan*, 60, 180–261.

Ridge, H.L., & Renzulli, J.S. (1981). Teaching mathematics to the talented and gifted: An interdisciplinary approach. In V.J. Glennon (Ed.), *The mathematical education of exceptional children and youth* (pp. 191–266). Reston, VA: National Council of Teachers of Mathematics.

Richards, J.M., Jr., Holland, J.L., & Lutz, S.W. (1967). Prediction of student accomplishment in college. *Journal of Educational Psychology*, 58, 343–355.

Shrum, J.L. (1989). Challenging linguistically gifted students in the regular foreign language classroom. In R.M. Milgram (Ed.), *Teaching gifted and talented learners in regular classrooms*. Springfield, IL: Charles C. Thomas.

Sternberg, R.J., & Davidson, J.E. (1986). *Conceptions of giftedness*. New York: Cambridge.

Tannenbaum, A.J. (1983). *Gifted children: Psychological and educational perspectives*. New York: Macmillan.

Terman, L.M. (1925). *Genetic studies of genius: Mental and physical traits of a thousand gifted children*. Stanford, CA: Stanford University Press.

Terman, L.M., & Oden, M.H. (1947). *Genetic studies of genius: Vol. 4. The gifted child grows up: Twenty-five years follow-up of a superior group*. Stanford, CA: Stanford University Press.

Terman, L.M., & Oden, M.H. (1959). *Genetic studies of genius: Vol. 4. The gifted child at mid-life: Thirty-five years follow-up of the superior child*. Stanford, CA: Stanford University Press.

Tirosh, D. (1989). Teaching mathematically gifted children. In R.M. Milgram (Ed.),*Teaching gifted and talented learners in regular classrooms*. Springfield, IL: Charles C. Thomas.

Wallach, M.A. (1985). Creativity testing and giftedness. In F.D. Horowitz & M. O'Brien (Eds.), *The gifted and talented: Developmental perspectives* (pp. 99–123). Washington, DC: American Psychological Association.

Wallach, M.A. (1970). Creativity. In P.H. Mussen (Ed.), *Carmichael's manual of child psychology, 1* (3rd ed., pp.1211–1272).

Wallach, M.A. (1971). *The intelligence/creativity distinction*. Morristown, NJ: General Learning Press.

Wallach, M.A., & Kogan, N. (1965). *Modes of thinking in young children: A study of the creativity-intelligence distinction*. New York: Holt, Rinehart, & Winston.

Wallach, M.A., & Wing, C.W., Jr. (1969). *The talented student: A validation of the creativity-intelligence distinction*. New York: Holt, Rinehart, & Winston.

Wing, C.W., Jr., & Wallach, M.A. (1971). *College admissions and the psychology of talent*. New York: Holt, Rinehart, & Winston.

Yager, R.E. (1989). Teaching science to gifted science students. In R.M. Milgram (Ed.), *Teaching gifted and talented learners in regular classrooms*. Springfield, IL: Charles C. Thomas.

14

Assessing Creative Products: Progress and Potentials*

Susan P. Besemer
Karen O'Quin

Right behind me a woman's voice says, "Well, they certainly are different." . . . The show itself attracts bad adjectives: "abrasive," "aggressive" and "shrill." It's mostly Jody's statues and Carolyn's quilts that are called these things. Zillah's lintscapes are termed "subjective," "introverted" and "flimsy." Compared with the rest of them I get off easy.

—Atwood, 1989, pp. 371, 375

Making things is an active process; it can be exciting and fun. Analyzing things and evaluating them is a reflective process; it can be ponderous and dull. The creative process tickles the psyche in a way that is said by some to be a reason for living, while the process of evaluation sometimes blows the dark cloud of gloom across an idea, dampening the spirit of the maker.

WHY ANALYZE PRODUCTS?

If this is so, why would anyone purposely analyze and evaluate the results of the creative process? Several reasons exist. First, whether we like it or not, we all evaluate what is made. Critics make their livings by attending concerts, eating out, going to the movies, and looking at art exhibits. They must then, of course, share their evaluations of these products with their readers or listeners. Teachers have to decide about those who succeed and those who fail in their assignments, be they first-grade art projects or graduate-level dissertations. Businesses must pick products to

---

*The authors may be reached at the following BITNET addresses: BESEMER@ FREDONIA and OQUINK@SNYBUFVA.

make and promote which they think will be successful. Consumers evaluate products through their choices of what to buy; they complain loudly if they judge that they have bought "a lemon." The evaluation of products takes place constantly and everywhere, but it is usually done in an off-handed, intuitive way. Perhaps that is part of the reason it hurts so much to be the maker of a product idea that is put to death by a casual and cursory evaluation.

Products are the artifacts of the creative process which give, through analysis, insights into the process and the personality of the maker who created them. This is one of the prime reasons for studying creative products. Perhaps by studying the result, we can catch a glimpse of the process itself, observing it as with a mirror, so as not to frighten it away. The insights gleaned from studying products are not simply deduced from looking at a single product and observing, for example, that since this product is simple, the maker or the process must be simple. The insights are much more subtle. Studying many products allows one to generalize to see what is in common among the examples being considered (Barron & Harrington, 1981; Osowski, 1986; Welsh, 1973). Regardless of whether the products are generated in the arts or sciences, using traditional methods or the newest technology, whether they be mass-produced, one-of-a-kind, homemade, commercial, or from limited editions, there are recognizable features in common among highly creative products that allow them to be recognized by even lay persons as "creative."

A second argument for looking analytically at products is simply to articulate the scientific approach to life, which seeks to understand a phenomenon by examining it in detail. Like Mount Everest, products are "there." "Climbing the mountain" by going through a careful process of analysis can be a challenging and interesting process alone.

A third reason for studying the creative product is that some researchers have stated that the best approach to the study of creativity is through product analysis (Besemer & Treffinger, 1981; Briskman, 1980; Ghiselin, 1958). At a conference of creativity researchers held in September 1987, the value of using products to assess the creative personality was discussed (Shallcross & Gawienowski, 1989). The importance of studying the product, advocated by some for more than 30 years, was again stressed as a way to identify creative talent. Again, the problem of identifying criteria for judging the creative value of products was stated. "We cannot," it was asserted, "presume to know who is creative without the evidence of creative work, and work is adjudged creative only by means of consensual appreciation" (p. 79).

A further reason for studying products analytically is suggested in the notion that evaluation can kill ideas. Many agree that there ought to be a type of criterion-based evaluation or descriptive analysis that is formative in nature and does not hurt, but helps the viability of a product idea (Baker & Albaum, 1986; Reynolds & Craddock, 1988; Udell, 1989). Thus, it is possible that such an evaluation might be used to nurture rather than destroy an early idea.

ISSUES INVOLVED IN EFFECTIVELY ASSESSING PRODUCTS

Problems of Definition

Several issues emerge from the literature as challenges in the study of creative products. One of the continuing issues in the study of creativity remains the problem of defining the phenomenon. Likewise, simply defining the term "creative product" and describing situations when the term is appropriately used is a problem.

How important is a product's novelty in determining its creativity? Novelty always seems to be an important feature (Besemer & Treffinger, 1981). Nearly everything written about creative products states the importance of newness. Many authors also insist on other crucial factors in defining creativity in products. MacKinnon (1962) suggested a three-element definition in stressing the importance of novelty, usefulness in accomplishing a goal, and the elaboration of the original insight. Pearlman (1983b) stated that creative things must also be "workable, efficient, and significant in satisfying a goal" (p. 294). He wrote that the "magical" quality that often accompanies highly creative products results from a combination of qualities, including, but not limited to, novelty. Pearlman credited this magic to the synergistic workability of the finished product with its novel features.

Briskman (1980) discussed a similar concept in his analysis of the "mysterious" quality of creativity and cited the importance of the "essential element of unpredictability" or novelty (p. 87). He also emphasized the connection of the product with earlier efforts and its fit with the tradition of earlier work in stating that although novelty is important, "novelty must be put to some good purpose" (p. 95). He stressed, as have other writers, the view of creativity as problem solving, yielding value to society in one way or another.

Hausman (1984, 1985) made a point to relate the importance of novelty to "intelligibility" and value. Making sense, or intelligibility, is fully as important as novelty in this view. Intelligibility places the new product in its tradition and allows comparison with earlier works. This also allows for the extension of the idea into the future, further adding to the value of the element of newness, further extending and modifying the tradition. The combination of newness and intelligibility is seen by Hausman (1985) to relate to style. Hausman emphasized, however, the importance of differentiating the creative process from mere problem solving. Creative products must solve problems, but they must do it in a way that is different. Again, we see the elements of a definition of the creative product as combining novelty with practical values in a synergistic way that produces a magical quality, still connected with its past, but with a special originality.

Even in the down-to-earth world of business, mere novelty does not a creative product make. Gilad (1984), in his discussion of creativity in the marketplace, stated that "a merely bizarre product will not command profits" (p. 157). The number of truly innovative new product ideas has been estimated at being only between 5% and 10% of those introduced each year (Dugas, 1985).

The ways of looking at products discussed above allow for consideration of all kinds of artifacts resulting from the creative process occurring in the diverse fields of the arts and sciences and the pragmatic work of daily business. Attempts to limit discussions to one area or another may appear to simplify the topic, but writers have gone to great length to show that the processes and products are not very different (Briskman, 1980; Tang & Leonard, 1985). In line with these thoughts, the Creative Product Analysis Matrix (CPAM) described by Besemer and Treffinger (1981) pursued an integrative theoretical path. Although the practitioners of the arts and sciences, commerce, and technology sometimes believe that their processes are unique, many similarities exist. Briskman (1980) concluded his paper with the suggestion that in creating their products, both scientists and artists not only transcend traditions, but they also transcend themselves. In a sense, the maker creates the self through the process. This theory is echoed in the psychoanalytic literature where most references to creative products concern the value of creative products as tools in the process of creating the self (Graves, 1984; Lett, 1987; Sanville, 1987).

Good, workable, multivariate definitions of creativity and creative products do exist (Mumford & Gustafson, 1988), allowing an emerging discipline to move forward while the debate about the best definition of creativity proceeds, since "the ultimate concern in studies of creativity is the production of novel, socially valued products" (Mumford & Gustafson, 1988, p. 27). While we may quibble about exactly what creativity is, it is often easier to achieve agreement about what is creative. Moving from "Wow, that's creative!" to being able to articulate just why it is creative has been the subject of our research over nearly a decade. As discussed below, this research has been theoretical, but it has also involved the development and testing of the Creative Product Semantic Scale (CPSS) through validity and reliability studies (O'Quin & Besemer, 1989).

Most of the literature discussed in this chapter, and in all of our empirical studies, deals only with the tangible products such as paintings, chairs, student projects, or keychains. However, it is important to realize that the concept of "product" should be envisioned as being much wider than that. Products can be transitory like dramatic or musical performances, or intangible products like new values or appreciation of students in school, a higher level of motivation for employees, or an improved corporate climate or culture. We believe that the same issues about evaluation apply to all types of products. It seems that the destructive power of careless evaluation may be considerably greater with intangible products than it is with tangible ones.

Product Evaluation as an "Afterthought"

Another very important issue involved in effectively assessing products is the "afterthought" nature of the problem. Analyzing products in a deliberate, objective way is an unfamiliar process to most people, whether they be consumers of commercial products, art critics, or product design team members (Baker & Albaum, 1986; Cooper & Kleinschmidt, 1986; Mosteller, 1981; Opatow, 1985; Reynolds & Craddock, 1988).

Not surprisingly, many studies done in psychology and education to observe the creative process through products are more interested in the personality of the maker or the subtleties of the process than in the characteristics of the product itself. These studies often used the product to "identify" the process (Alter, 1984; Traxler, 1987; Welsh, 1973). Torrance and Presbury (1984) reported that in evaluating the effectiveness of creativity training in nearly 250 studies, although many projects still use standard tests of creative personality to evaluate the training effectiveness, "there is also considerable evidence of the use of more 'real life' creativity indicators, such as the evaluation of creative products" (p. 242). Some studies count the number of products made (Olenchak, 1988) as evidence of the subjects' fluency of ideas. Some evaluate the products using expert judges (Parke & Byrnes, 1984). Some researchers train either expert or lay judges using guidelines decided in advance (Alter, 1984; Jellen & Urban, 1986; Pearlman, 1983a), while others simply rely on the subjective expertise of the judge. Studies that have the goal of developing valid, reliable, judging instruments for products are less common (Baker & Albaum, 1986; Besemer & O'Quin, 1986; O'Quin & Besemer, 1989; Reynolds & Craddock, 1988; Udell, 1989).

In discussing gifted education, Traxler (1987) stated that although surprisingly few programs of gifted education had formal evaluation components, 68.8% of the programs that were evaluated relied on the judgment of creative products. Traxler repeated the theme mentioned above: "In many districts, evaluation seemed to be an afterthought as evidenced by the lack of evaluation design prior to program implementation" (p. 112).

The evidence from the world of commerce also suggests that product evaluation is often a by-product and an afterthought to the more exciting process of thinking up new ideas. Cooper and Kleinschmidt (1986) considered the success factors in bringing new products to the market in an impressive survey examining more than 250 new products in 123 companies. They noted that even when business research in North America, Britain, and Europe suggests logical strategies that can improve product success, businesses frequently omit one or more activities that are known to be beneficial. Prime among these identified as needing improvement were initial screening of new product ideas and the product-development phase. Although initial screening took place in 92.3% of the product histories, it was rated as the weakest link in the process by the subjects of the study—senior managers in the companies whose products were followed. The screening sessions were described:

> Group processes dominated this critical screening decision: the initial "go" decision was a group decision in more than three

quarters of the cases. Screening remains very much an informal decision, that is, no consistently used checklist of criteria or scoring or rating procedures. For example, in less than 2% of the projects, evaluators used a formal checklist questionnaire or scoring model to rate projects. (Cooper & Kleinschmidt, 1986, p. 77)

Product development after the initial screening is another area where managers believed that more time and effort were warranted. In both of these activities in the new product development cycle, it appears that the products could have been strengthened by reference to a conceptual model and a judging instrument that could identify areas of strength and those needing improvement. Cooper and Kleinschmidt ended their article with the recommendation that more focus be placed on initial screening "involving multidisciplinary, multifunctional inputs, and preferably based on a written checklist of criteria" (p. 85).

Baker and Albaum (1986) also discussed the way that new product ideas are screened. The authors stated that "many companies rely on an intuitive approach to screening new products rather than completing a formal analysis" (p. 34). Problems involved in the use of checklists and rating models have made some practitioners reluctant to use them, but using "a model might reduce the incidence of introducing new products that will fail in the marketplace. This will, in effect, significantly reduce the overall cost of new product introductions" (p. 38).

Even brand names are products for the companies that use them to help establish their identities. Opatow (1985) stated that "choosing the name is one part of the product development process where there is often little or no structured analysis" (p. 254). Repeatedly the literature reveals that the products of the creative process are evaluated, early and often, but that objective, methodical analysis is infrequently practiced.

The Issue of Many Unique Environments

There are many worlds in which it is necessary to evaluate products. These include the psychological world and the world of education, both in the arts and sciences, as well as in education for gifted children. The world of business has many environments: new product development, marketing, and advertising, for example. The entire field of advertising terms the result of its efforts "creative product," and spends most of its energies trying to improve the quality and effectiveness of its products in that special world. Even geography and culture create a segmented world view.

Given these varied environments, or multiple worlds, the sense in each that its needs are unique is not surprising. Certainly each is correct in believing that there are unique factors and features in every student, every business decision, each locale, and each organization. The fear that the uniqueness of the local environment will be passed over in an attempt to standardize and objectify evaluation was expressed by Tonemah (1987). In discussing the importance of "style," "originality," "presence," "presentation," and "depth of character," in products made by American Indian children, Tonemah wrote, "Such subjective intangibles may be converted to objective measurement, but will these ways be superficial assessments, such as through rating scales?" (p. 188).

To assure aptness for the unique environments, many have created their own particular judging instruments to assess products. Sometimes these instruments are then published and shared with others in similar worlds. An individual school district can, as did the Detroit Public Schools, make a contribution to the process of product evaluation by publishing in the professional literature the guidelines it uses in developing its product evaluation plan. Parke and Byrnes (1984) described the need for designing an instrument to be used in the Detroit system for assessing students' creative products. The goal was to objectify the process of evaluating student works in art, music, creative writing, and other performance areas. The scales are used by trained professionals in the fields under consideration, and are recommended by their authors for three main purposes: assessing talent for placement in gifted programs, program planning and development, and the evaluation of students and programs after the program is in place. The usefulness of this type of strategy is reinforced by the comments made by Traxler (1987) cited above.

The Student Product Assessment Form (Reis & Renzulli, 1991) verifies the importance of product evaluation to the concept of productive creativity in gifted children. As an important component of the learning experience, students are expected to do something with what they have learned. Stories, reports, models, works of art, computer programs: All of these and more are appropriate results of the students' productivity. It is not enough just to learn a great deal; students must demonstrate their learning through real products, tangible or intangible.

In the world of business, the sense that each group's needs are unique is commonly felt and expressed. Here is the view of a business executive:

> Because business must, to survive, transcend the merely novel, and reach for the creatively useful, the proportionate mix of these two defining qualities of creativity may need to be looked at differently in business contexts than in the arts, the laboratory, or research with creative children. That does not, however, make the business-success version of creativity any less valid. (DeToro, 1987, p. 140)

Another factor that separates the larger world of product analysis into separate entities is the existence of geographic and ethnocentric areas of influence and interaction. Much research on business products, because it is proprietary, is never published. Of that which is reported, access to it is perhaps most widely available through electronic databases located in the United States. However, American sources report primarily American research. One can read occasionally about new product evaluation in the United Kingdom (Mosteller, 1981; Udell, 1989), and be aware that much is going on in Canada, Japan, Scandinavia, Germany, and Holland. Although it is extremely difficult to trace them in the United States through searching computer databases, such efforts as those of the *Specialistisch Innovatie Centrum voor Uitvindingen ID* in Rotterdam deserve wider dissemination. As a global orientation overtakes our more limited view in the next century, perhaps we can learn more from sharing information through a global network of product researchers.

Structured Analytical Techniques

The expression of belief that the enterprise is so unique that it cannot share views with practitioners from "other worlds" is, of course, complicated by the proprietary interests of most firms working to develop new products. There is, however, an opportunity for business decisions to be informed by more analytical techniques to clarify and objectify the evaluation of products. Researchers in business have used several successful analytical techniques for improving products.

A common problem in consumer research is the inability of consumer panels to articulate reasons for their preferences in the products that they are commenting upon. In an interesting study of consumer preference relating to product shape, Berkowitz (1987) gave consumers an opportunity to indicate their preferences for two very similar food products. One was "natural" frozen ears of corn, while the other was identical corn-on-the-cob, trimmed to produce a squared-off shape. Although the untrimmed ears were preferred by consumers, many used the same "stock phrases" to explain their choice, regardless of their preferences. Berkowitz (1987) wrote: "the dominant reason for their prefer-ence—whether for the untrimmed shape or the squared-off shape—was taste" (p. 278).

A beneficial technique used by Sunbeam Appliance Company was described by Page and Rosenbaum (1987). Conjoint analysis allows researchers to better understand consumers when they discuss product attributes by structuring the process and offering prototype choices that allow consumer preferences to be differen-tiated. The process allows for the weighting of values for preferred attributes, improving the likelihood that the designed product has put its efforts in the most important areas for consumers. Page and Rosenbaum (1987) concluded "while he or she cannot articulate these functions, and may not even be aware of them, the overall evaluations of each of the multivariate alternatives in terms of preference for purchase reflects these utility functions" (p. 134).

Another product development and analysis technique using attribute listing is called by its author, Ann Keely, "maxi-niching" (1989). Using this technique, consumers imagine a "perfect" product without regard to anticipating an appropriate target market through segmentation or niche marketing.

Other analytical techniques intended to assist product devel-opers to find opportunities for new products as extensions of existing lines were described by Kane (1987). Spectrum analysis is a semantic differential technique that asks consumers to place brand names on a continuum between two contrasting terms, allowing the company to recognize gaps that may be filled by product line extensions. Unfinished scenarios, a different se-mantic technique, allow consumers to verbalize reasons for product choices more clearly by creating hypothetical situations involving stories about other shoppers.

The Need for a Multipurpose Judging Instrument

As useful as these techniques and evaluative formats are to the businesses and schools that use them, the data collected through such studies are not comparable with those gathered in other circumstances. The sense of urgency to get on with the teaching, learning, making, and creating means that time to develop and validate a more generic judging instrument is often limited.

The Creative Product Semantic Scale (CPSS) was designed and tested (Besemer & O'Quin, 1986, 1987; O'Quin & Besemer, 1989) to fill the need for a useful, reliable, valid judging instrument that could be used in many of the varied environments in which products are created.

THE CREATIVE PRODUCT SEMANTIC SCALE (CPSS)

The need for a valid and "portable" judging instrument is clear. Those scholars interested in testing creativity training theories or in assessing creative personality do not have the time or inclination to reinvent a wheel. They just want to get rolling. This recognition, paired with another important strand of motivation, the desire to follow the integrative theoretical path based on the Creative Product Analysis Matrix (CPAM; Besemer & Treffinger, 1981), has led us to propose, test, refine, retest, and further refine our Creative Product Semantic Scale (CPSS).

A general theoretical framework for understanding creative products, the CPAM was developed to apply to a wide variety of products. It includes three independent dimensions, each of which is further divided into several attributes.

The first dimension considered in the CPAM is novelty, and the three attributes of this dimension are original, surprising, and germinal. The last attribute is related to a product's perceived influence in suggesting other new products. The second dimension is the resolution of the product, which measures the extent to which a product meets the practical needs of the problem situation. Its three attributes are valuable, logical, and useful. The third dimension, elaboration and synthesis, considers the aspects of style or production values. This dimension of the CPAM includes five attributes: organic, elegant, complex, understandable, and well crafted.

Scale Development

The development of the CPSS occurred in several stages. The earliest scale developed by Besemer, based on the CPAM's theoretical framework, used an 110-item adjective checklist (VanGundy,

1984). When this early judging instrument produced confusion over definitions of the terms among subjects, our collaboration began. Our first series of collaborative studies (Besemer & O'Quin, 1987) examined the model's three dimensions using a variant of the adjective check list. Respondents used a 4-point scale, indicating how well each word described the product being rated. Because of measurement problems revealed by this early work, a shorter instrument, the CPSS (Besemer & O'Quin, 1986), was developed from the theoretical matrix.

It employed the semantic differential format based on the work of Osgood, Suci, and Tannenbaum (1957). The original CPSS contained 71 bipolar adjective pairs divided into 11 subscales, each measuring an attribute of the three dimensions of the CPAM. Good to excellent reliabilities were found for most of the subscales, and the validity of the novelty dimension was supported.

This version of the CPSS was still too lengthy to be of practical value, producing fatigue among our subjects. Our subsequent developmental work involved the process of refining the scale by eliminating redundant pairs of adjectives while retaining the scales' reliabilities. We also selected clearer alternatives for ambiguous items in the subscales.

Finally, the Revised CPSS (O'Quin & Besemer, 1989), containing 55 items, was developed. Its 11 subscales were shown to be reliable. The validity of novelty, and to a lesser degree, elaboration and synthesis, was sustained. The usefulness of the instrument is shown in its consistently good to high reliabilities, which range from .54 to .93, with most in the area of .80. The CPSS has been adopted for studies by other researchers (Howe, 1992; Phillips, 1989), and will soon be available on a cost recovery basis to other scholars. Some will share data to establish norms for product groups.

Theory Development

Some aspects of the CPAM have received empirical support from the authors' work. For example, novelty and resolution have consistently remained statistically independent dimensions in several studies that have used different products. The subscales of elaboration and synthesis, however, do not seem to be independent, but have been related mostly to novelty in some research (Besemer & O'Quin, 1986), and to resolution in other studies (O'Quin & Besemer, 1989).

To date, our subjects have used only two dimensions to describe creative products. It may be that the style dimension is inherently confounded with one of the other two dimensions, but it is too early in the research process to determine if that is true. Perhaps the type of product is a critical factor, or the circumstances under which the products are evaluated. In addition, we have not yet examined whether the type of rater is important in product evaluation, although some evidence suggests that rater differences exist (Phillips, 1989). Before we can rule out a third independent dimension, the possibility also exists that the method of measuring elaboration and synthesis needs to be revised.

FUTURE PROSPECTS

Future Research with the CPSS

Several strands of interest lead us into the future. First, we wish to confirm the validity of the resolution dimension of the CPAM. Our work encourages our confidence about the existence of this dimension as independent from others, but in our most recent study (O'Quin & Besemer, 1989), subjects saw no difference in the functionality of the products analyzed. We want to examine products that are seen as equally novel, but some of which are high and some of which are low in resolution.

The most tantalizing area for our research falls within the dimension that we call elaboration and synthesis. This "style" dimension deserves much fuller exploration, such as observing the loading, in factor analysis, of the five subscales of this theoretical dimension. With more evidence, we may change our model for analyzing products. Much of our data demonstrates a moving, shifting style dimension, showing some subscales loading with novelty or resolution, depending upon the type of product being analyzed.

Another interesting area for our research involves further development of the judging form, perhaps creating a short form or a self-scoring form to be used in product development teams.

Using the full-scale CPSS or a short form with groups could be part of a training program designed to teach trainees to attend more carefully and objectively to product attributes. This practice could improve products through the careful and deliberate use of a model, so often recommended, especially in the business literature.

As mentioned earlier, it will be possible to share with and collect data from other researchers to establish norms for product comparisons. Through modern telecommunications, researchers in the United States and in other countries can send files electronically to add their findings to those data already collected. This electronic networking through BITNET, EARN, JANET, NetNorth, and the Internet also allows for modification of the view of the isolated worlds where product analysis is possible only on an intuitive, ad hoc basis. Perhaps a global view can emerge.

Considering the growing interest in academic assessment in American colleges and universities, it may also be possible to use the CPSS more extensively to give formative evaluation for student projects and products. To be able to use the CPSS to train students more adequately to improve their products for course work would be a stimulating and challenging opportunity. This could open the door to using the scale and model not only for screening and winnowing, but also for opening career doors through education and training.

Future of the Field

In addition to our visions for the future of the CPSS, we also want to suggest some fertile areas for the future of the field of creative product analysis. These include more emphasis on measurement issues with increasing methodological sophistication, the increased use of electronic communication, development of a data archive for creative studies, theoretical development of new models, and a narrowing of the gap between the field's conceptual and operational levels of knowledge of creativity.

Measurement and Methodology

We hope to see greater concern for reliability and validity of measurement. Reliability, or consistency of measurement, is an important step in establishing the methodological soundness of any measuring instrument (Nunnally, 1978). Reliability is important in its own right, and because it sets the upper bound on validity.

Validity, or the extent to which an instrument measures what it is supposed to measure, is also a critical component in establishing methodological soundness. However, unlike reliability, which is fairly easy to examine, validity does not lend itself to a simple yes or no answer.

Nonetheless, these issues are crucial to further development of the field. A concern for measurement issues suggests just how important it is to plan the study thoroughly, approaching assessment of the product of creative endeavor early in the research process rather than as an afterthought. As more creativity researchers are trained in research methods, their greater methodological sophistication will allow careful design of studies to attempt to unravel the direction of causation.

More Extensive Use of Electronic Communication

As discussed earlier, it can be difficult and expensive for researchers in different parts of the country and the world to share ideas, data, and theories. As a more global orientation overtakes our somewhat limited views in the next century, perhaps we can learn more from sharing information through a global electronic-mail network. Electronic communication allows researchers to share data for the purposes of further analysis and norm establishment, as well as to share ideas quickly and impulsively. Likewise, cross-cultural research is of value to reveal both similarities and differences among cultures. This will be possible without the waiting for replies in the mail that formal correspondence entails, yet with more permanence and less expense than telephone calls.

Development of a Data Archive

Rosenthal (1991) noted that a chronic pessimistic feeling in the social and behavioral sciences seems to exist: Compared to natural sciences, progress in social science has been slow or nonexistent. Rosenthal pointed out that the cumulation of research results is needed to help social sciences show the orderly progress and development of the older "hard" sciences.

Cumulation of research results in creative studies would be greatly facilitated by the development of a data archive: a collection of original data maintained in a standard format which could be retrieved by researchers worldwide. Such a data archive (e.g., Card & Peterson, 1991) can be a valuable contribution both to emerging disciplines and to established ones. Instituting such a data archive in creative studies would facilitate secondary analyses; as new statistical techniques became available, they could be applied to the data. Such an archive would also facilitate meta-analyses of research results (Rosenthal, 1991). Meta-analysis is a powerful technique for cumulation of research results; it becomes even more powerful if original data are available.

Theoretical Development

In many ways, it seems that evaluation of creative products has been a neglected area within the existing research in creativity. The literature of creativity has traditionally focused on the creative person and the creative process, and much less on the creative product. While personality and process may be the ultimate concern for a study of creativity, it is widely acknowledged that direct measurement of creativity in the person is difficult without a consideration of product (Briskman, 1980; MacKinnon, 1962; Mumford & Gustafson, 1988).

Conceptual and Operational Levels of Knowledge

The whole issue of the operationalization of creativity needs further development. If products are not studied, how can we know that creativity exists? Does not the operational definition of creativity involve the creative product of necessity? There are some advantages to taking this position. First, the creative product is relatively objective, and potentially easier to evaluate than the creative person, even considering that the issue remains of criteria used to evaluate the product. Further, even though a person has been identified as creative by some measurement method, there is no guarantee that a particular product of that person will be evaluated as creative.

The theoretical definition of creativity is vitally important. This discussion illustrates the gap that exists between the conceptual and operational levels of knowledge (e.g., Crano & Brewer, 1986). In our own recent work, we have tended to focus on the operational level, in developing and evaluating the CPSS. We believe that the CPSS is one valuable operational definition of the creativity manifested in products, but of course it is critical for researchers to recognize that their theoretical concepts are never perfectly embodied in any single tool. We look forward to developments in the field where other researchers will develop other instruments, based on sound theoretical footings, and tested with scientific concern for measurement issues.

Nurturing and developing creative productivity without a sound theoretical basis, judging instruments, and the process of judgment can be at best superficial, and at worst, harmful. The importance of an objective assessment of creative productivity cannot be overstated. The harm that can be done to the spirits of both children and adults when their creative work is judged in a cavalier way is a loss that cultures should not and need not sustain. When based on a valid theoretical schema, judgment can be formative, pointing to a direction for growth. It is our hope and belief that efforts to nurture creative growth can be promoted by increasingly sophisticated development in the area of creative product analysis.

REFERENCES

Alter, J.B. (1984). A factor analysis of new and standardized instruments to measure the creative potential and high-energy action preference of performing arts students: A preliminary investigation. *Personality and Individual Differences, 5,* 693–699.

Atwood, M. (1988). *Cat's eye.* New York: Bantam Books.

Baker, K.G., & Albaum, G.S. (1986). Modeling new product screening decisions. *Journal of Product Innovation Management, 3*(1), 32–39.

Barron, F., & Harrington, D.M. (1981). Creativity, intelligence, and personality. In M.R. Rosenzweig & L.W. Porter (Eds.), *Annual Review of Psychology* (pp. 439–476). Palo Alto, CA: Annual Reviews.

Berkowitz, M. (1987). Product shape as a design innovation strategy. *Journal of Product Innovation Management, 4*(4), 274–283.

Besemer, S.P., & O'Quin, K. (1986). Analyzing creative products: Refinement and test of a judging instrument. *Journal of Creative Behavior, 20*(2), 115–126.

Besemer, S.P., & O'Quin, K. (1987). Creative product analysis: Testing a model by developing a judging instrument. In S.G. Isaksen (Ed.), *Frontiers of creativity research: Beyond the basics* (pp. 341–357). Buffalo, NY: Bearly Limited.

Besemer, S.P., & Treffinger, D.J. (1981). Analysis of creative products: Review and synthesis. *Journal of Creative Behavior, 15*(3), 158–178.

Briskman, L. (1980). Creative product and creative process in science and art. *Inquiry, 23*(1), 83–106.

Card, J.J., & Peterson, J.L. (1991). Establishing and operating a social science data archive. In J.E. Sieber (Ed.), *Sharing social science data.* Newbury Park, CA: Sage.

Cooper, R.G., & Kleinschmidt, E.J. (1986). An investigation into the new product process: Steps, deficiencies, and impact. *Journal of Product Innovation Management, 3*(2), 71–85.

Crano, W.D., & Brewer, M.B. (1986). *Principles and methods of social research*. Boston, MA: Allyn & Bacon.

DeToro, I.J. (1987). Quality circles and the techniques of creativity: A case history. *Journal of Creative Behavior, 21*(2), 137–144.

Dugas, C. (1985). Managing new ideas. *Ad Forum, 6*(4), 34–38.

Ghiselin, B. (1958). Ultimate criteria for two levels of creativity. In C.W. Taylor (Ed.), *The Second (1957) University of Utah Research Conference on the Identification of Creative Scientific Talent* (pp. 141–155). Salt Lake City, UT: University of Utah Press.

Gilad, B. (1984). Entrepreneurship: The issue of creativity in the market place. *Journal of Creative Behavior, 18*(3), 151–161.

Graves, P.L. (1984). Life event and art. *International Review of Psycho-Analysis, 11*(1), 355–365.

Hausman, C.R. (1984). *A discourse on novelty and creation*. Albany, NY: SUNY Press.

Hausman, C.R. (1985). Can computers create? *Interchange, 16*(1), 27–37.

Howe, R.P. (1992). Uncovering the creative dimensions of computer-graphic design products. *Creativity Research Journal, 5*, 233–243.

Jellen, H.G., & Urban, K.K. (1986). The TCT-DP (Test for Creative Thinking-Drawing Production): An instrument that can be applied to most age and ability groups. *Creative Child and Adult Quarterly, 11*(3), 138–155.

Kane, C.L. (1987). How to increase the odds for successful brand extension. *Journal of Product Innovation Management, 4*(3), 199–203.

Keely, A. (1989). Maxi-niching the way to a strong brand: Positioning according to systemic dynamics. *Journal of Product Innovation Management, 6*(3), 202–206.

Lett, W.R. (1987). A conundrum: Counseling and creativity. *Australian Psychologist, 22*(1), 29–41.

MacKinnon, D.W. (1962). The nature and nurture of creative talent. *American Psychologist, 17*, 484–495.

Mosteller, F. (1981). Innovation and evaluation. *Science, 211*, 881–886.

Mumford, M.D., & Gustafson, S.B. (1988). Creativity syndrome: Integration, application, and innovation. *Psychological Bulletin, 103*, 27–43.

Nunnally, J.C. (1978). *Psychometric theory*. New York: McGraw-Hill.

Olenchak, F.R. (1988). The schoolwide enrichment model in elementary schools: A study of implementation stages and the effects on educational excellence (Doctoral dissertation, University of Connecticut, 1988). *Dissertation Abstracts International, 49*, 1100.

Opatow, L. (1985). Creating brand names that work. *Journal of Product Innovation Management, 2*(4), 254–258.

O'Quin, K., & Besemer, S.P. (1989). The development, reliability and validity of the Revised Creative Product Semantic Scale. *Creativity Research Journal, 2*, 268–279.

Osgood, C.E., Suci, G.J., & Tannenbaum, P.H. (1957). *The measurement of meaning*. Urbana, IL: University of Illinois Press.

Osowski, J.V. (1986). Metaphor and creativity: A case study of William James (Doctoral dissertation, Rutgers University, 1986). *Dissertation Abstracts International, 47,* 2142.

Page, A.C., & Rosenbaum, H.F. (1987). Redesigning product lines with conjoint analysis: How Sunbeam does it. *Journal of Product Innovation Management, 4*(2), 120–137.

Parke, B.N., & Byrnes, P. (1984). Toward objectifying the measurement of creativity. *Roeper Review, 6,* 216–218.

Pearlman, C. (1983a). Teachers as an informational resource in identifying and rating student creativity. *Education, 103,* 215–222.

Pearlman, C. (1983b). A theoretical model for creativity. *Education, 103,* 294–305.

Phillips, S.S. (1989). *Identification of elaboration strategies used by college students in performing a visual design task.* Unpublished doctoral dissertation, University of Washington.

Reis, S.M., & Renzulli, J.S. (1991). The assessment of creative products in programs for gifted and talented students. *Gifted Child Quarterly, 35*(3), 128–134.

Reynolds, T.J., & Craddock, A.B. (1988). The application of the MECCAS model to the development and assessment of advertising strategy: A case study. *Journal of Advertising Research, 28*(2), 43–54.

Rosenthal, R. (1991). *Meta-analytic procedures for social research.* Newbury Park, CA: Sage.

Sanville, J. (1987). Creativity and the constructing of the self. *Psychoanalytic Review, 74*(4), 263–279.

Shallcross, D.J., & Gawienowski, A.M. (1989). Top experts address issues on creativity gap in higher education. *Journal of Creative Behavior, 23*(2), 75–84.

Tang, P.C., & Leonard, A.R. (1985). Creativity in art and science. *Journal of Aesthetic Education, 19*(3), 5–19.

Tonemah, S. (1987). Assessing American Indian gifted and talented students' abilities. *Journal for the Education of the Gifted, 10*(3), 181–194.

Torrance, E.P., & Presbury, J. (1984). The criteria of success used in 242 recent experimental studies of creativity. *Creative Child and Adult Quarterly, 9*(4), 238–243.

Traxler, M.A. (1987). Gifted education program evaluation: A national review. *Journal for the Education of the Gifted, 10*(2), 107–113.

Udell, G. (1989). Invention evaluation services: A review of the state of the art. *Journal of Product Innovation Management, 6*(3), 157–168.

VanGundy, A.B. (1984). *Managing group creativity: A modular approach to problem-solving.* New York: American Management Association.

Welsh, G.S. (1973). Perspectives in the study of creativity. *Journal of Creative Behavior, 7*(4), 231–246.

Author Index

Subject Index